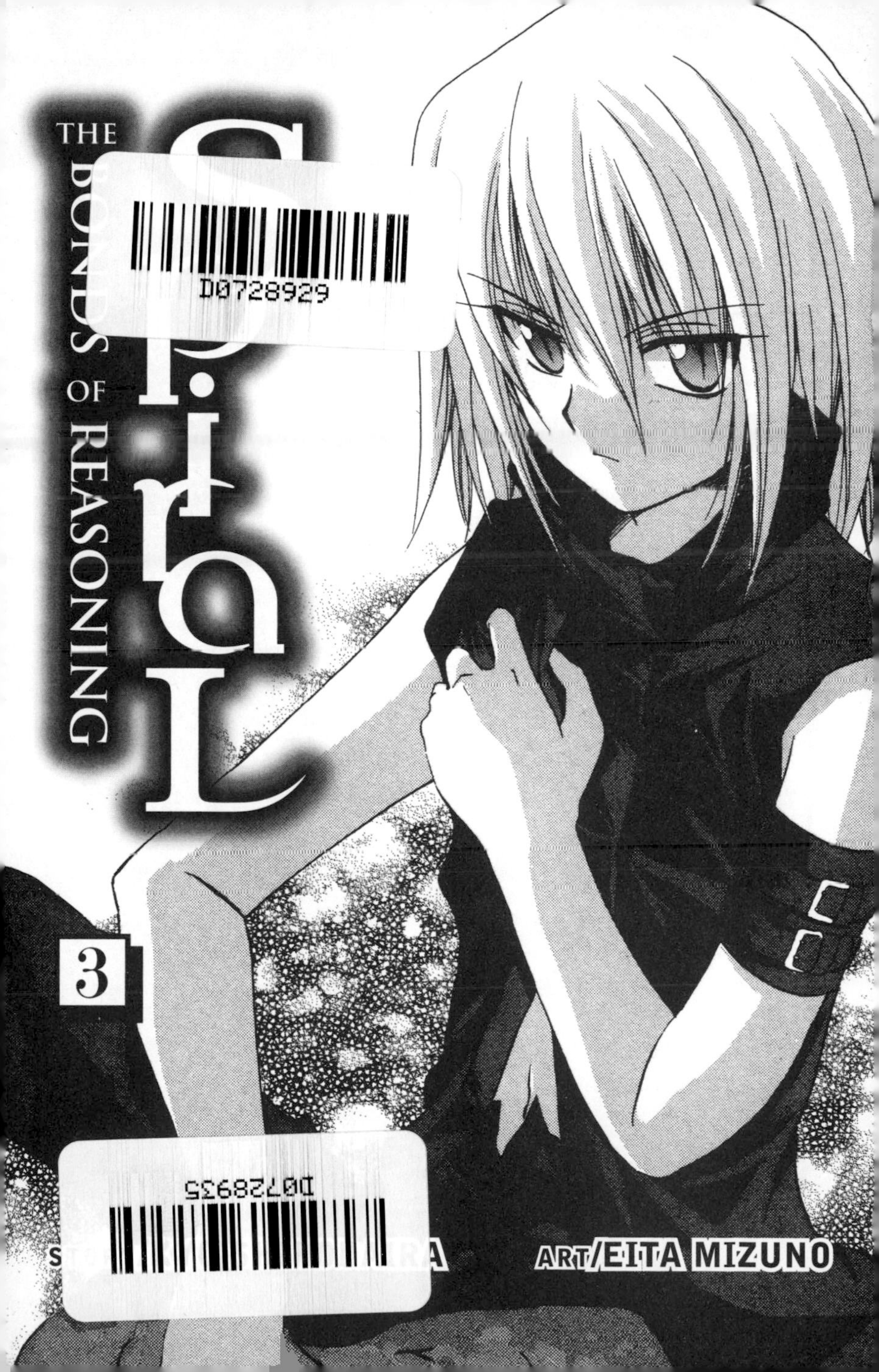
Spiral
THE BONDS OF REASONING
3
ART/EITA MIZUNO

THERE WAS ONCE A
MAN CALLED THE GREAT
DETECTIVE AT POLICE
HEADQUARTERS.

IN OTHER WORDS,
HE IS NO MORE.

HE LEFT BEHIND THE
MYSTERIOUS WORDS "I'M
GOING AFTER THE BLADE
CHILDREN" AND THEN
VANISHED.

EVEN NOW,
NOBODY KNOWS
WHERE HE IS...

The SPIRAL
Of fortune
Is Beginning
To go around

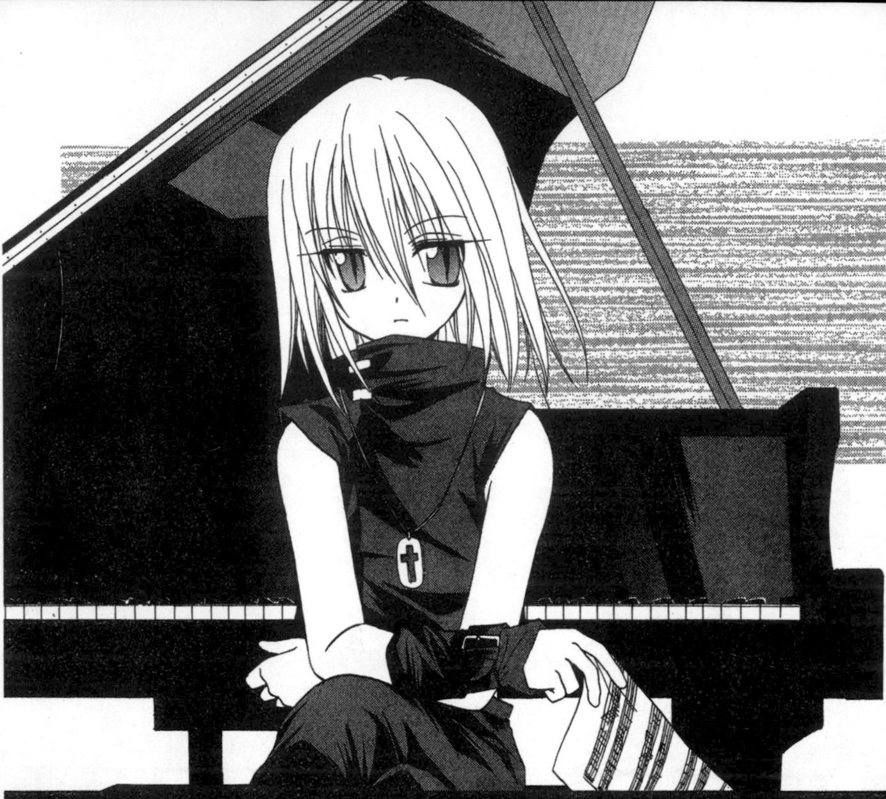

CONTENTS

CHAPTER ELEVEN
A BOY'S STRENGTH

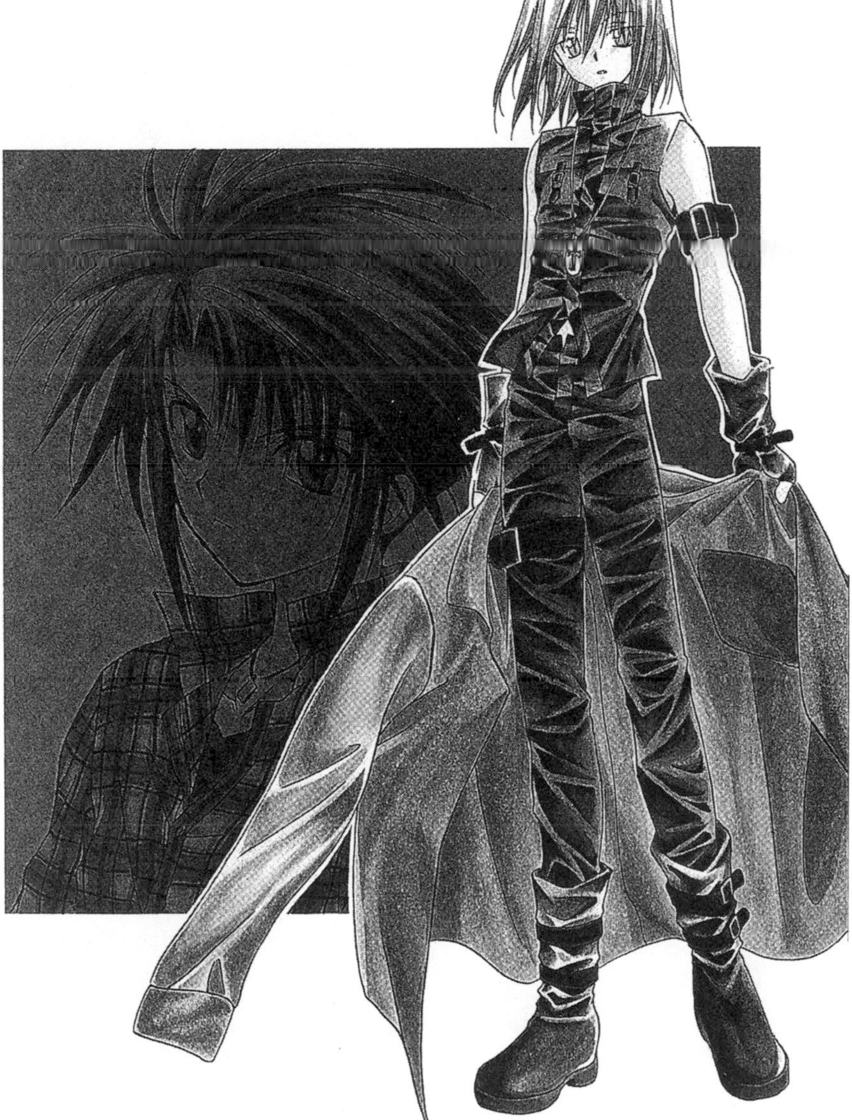

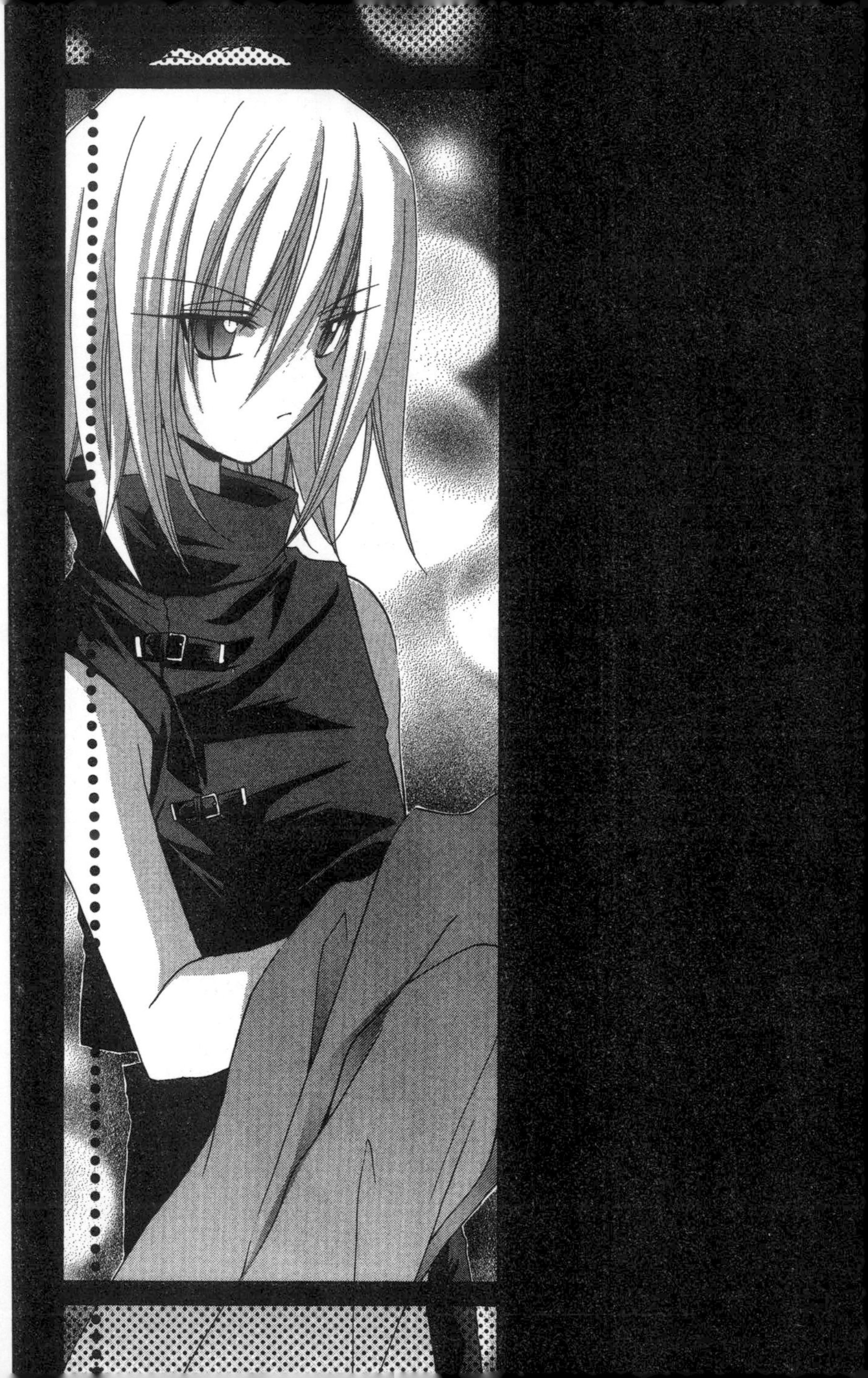

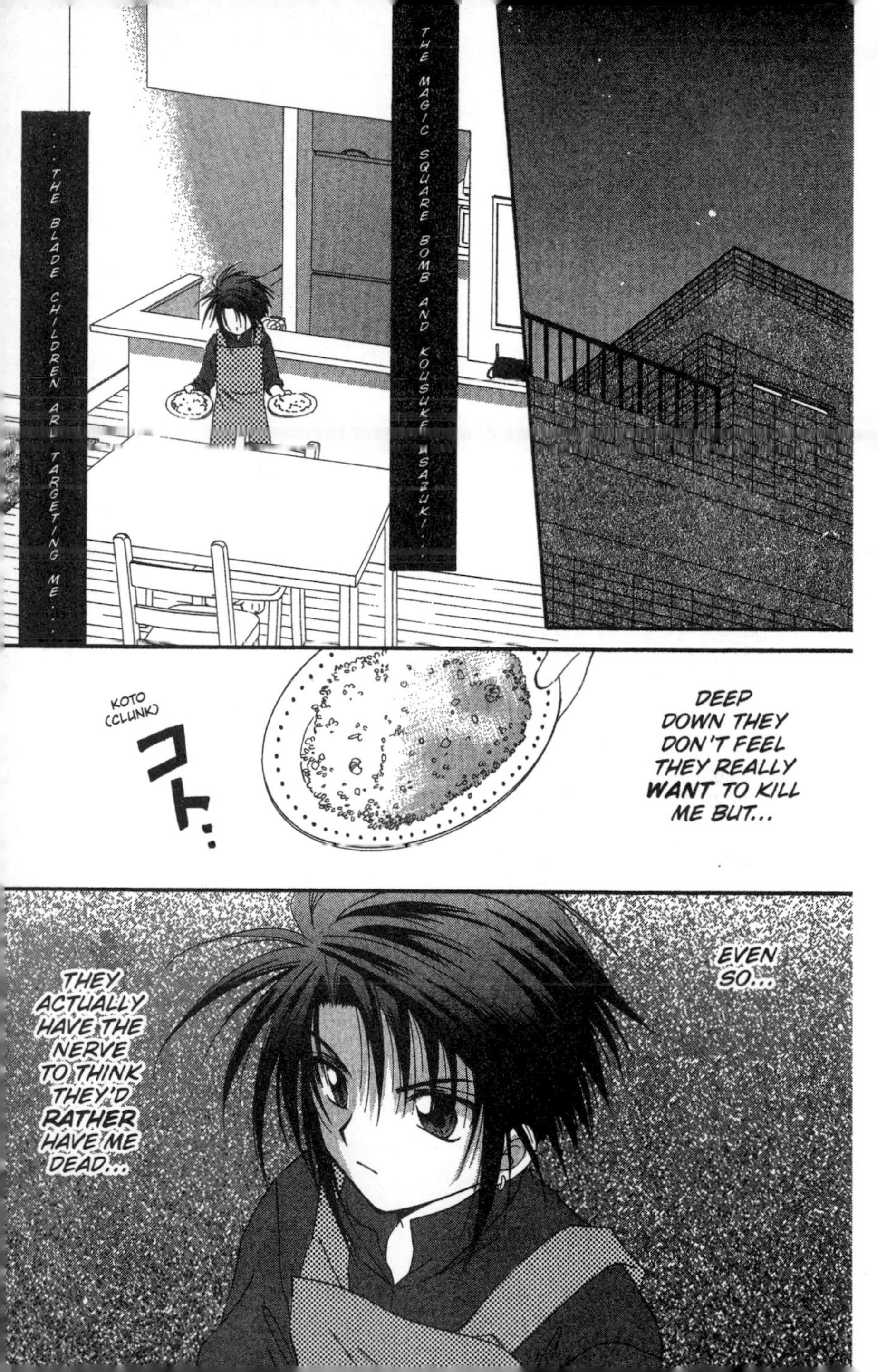
THE MAGIC SQUARE BOMB AND KOUSUKE ASAZUKI...
...THE BLADE CHILDREN ARE TARGETING ME...
DEEP DOWN THEY DON'T FEEL THEY REALLY WANT TO KILL ME BUT...
KOTO (CLUNK)
コト
EVEN SO...
THEY ACTUALLY HAVE THE NERVE TO THINK THEY'D RATHER HAVE ME DEAD...

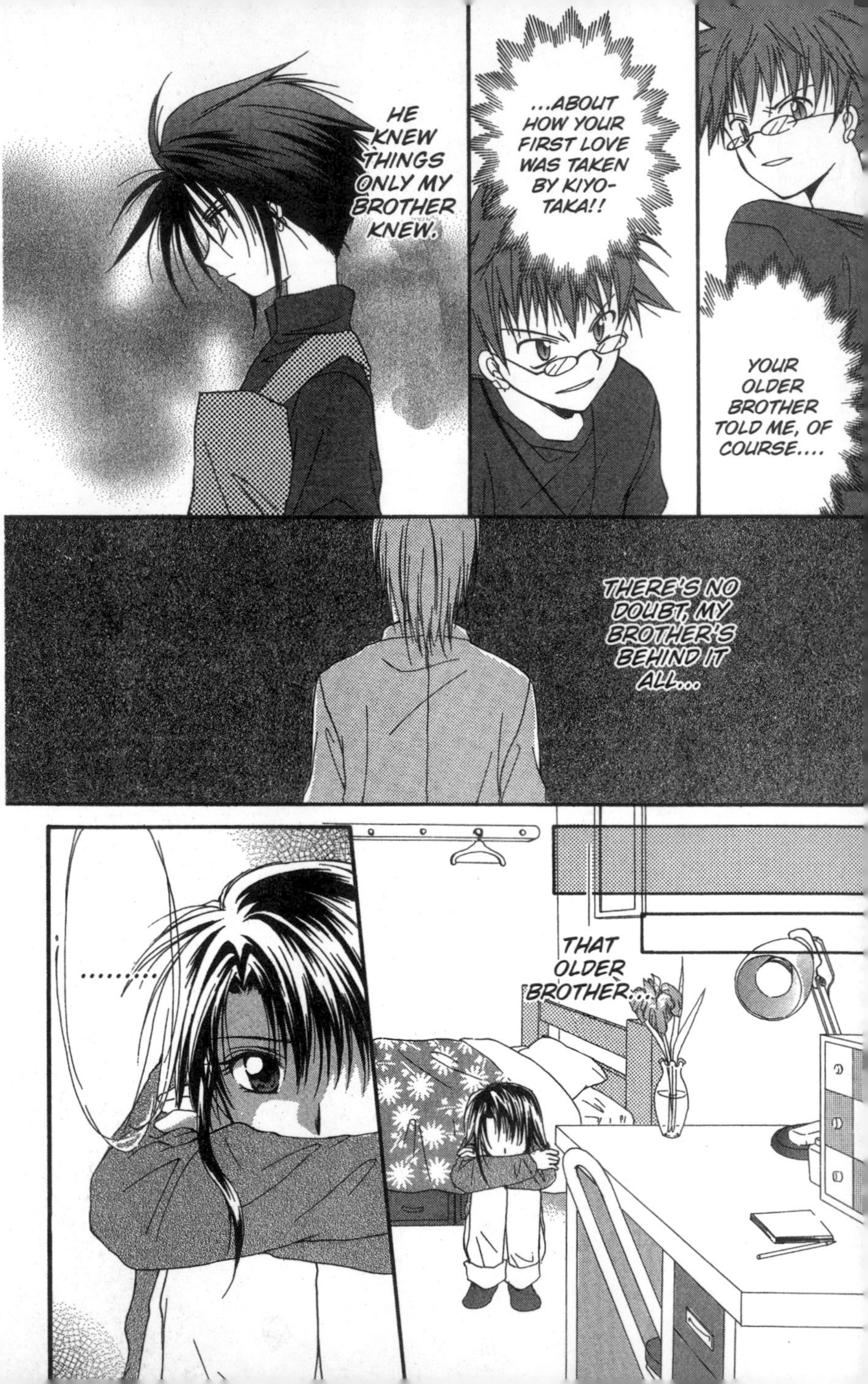
YOUR OLDER BROTHER TOLD ME, OF COURSE....
...ABOUT HOW YOUR FIRST LOVE WAS TAKEN BY KIYO-TAKA!!
HE KNEW THINGS ONLY MY BROTHER KNEW.
THERE'S NO DOUBT, MY BROTHER'S BEHIND IT ALL...
THAT OLDER BROTHER...
....

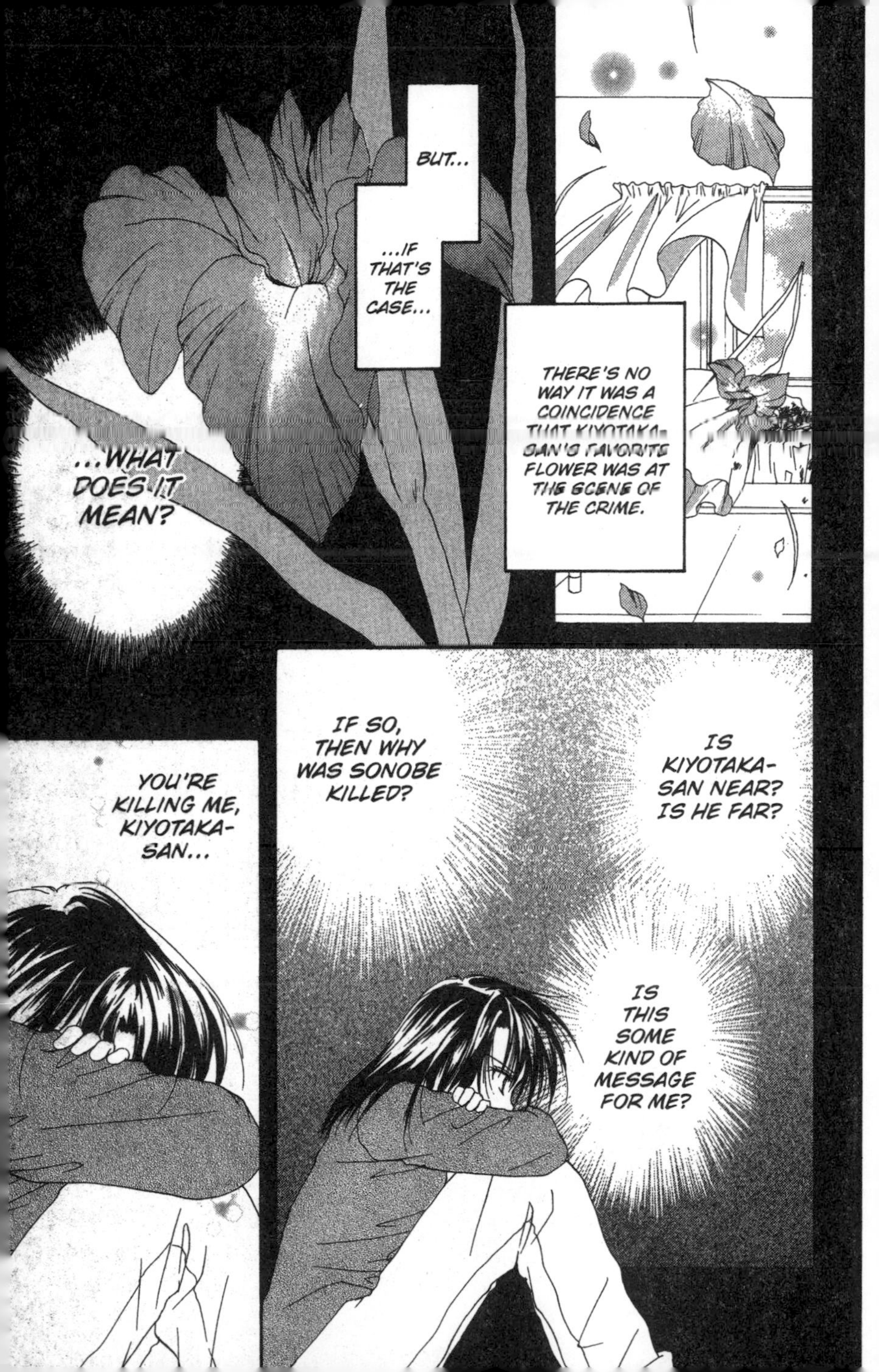
THERE'S NO WAY IT WAS A COINCIDENCE THAT KIYOTAKA-SAN'S FAVORITE FLOWER WAS AT THE SCENE OF THE CRIME.
BUT...
...IF THAT'S THE CASE...
...WHAT DOES IT MEAN?
IS KIYOTAKA-SAN NEAR? IS HE FAR?
IF SO, THEN WHY WAS SONOBE KILLED?
IS THIS SOME KIND OF MESSAGE FOR ME?
YOU'RE KILLING ME, KIYOTAKA-SAN...

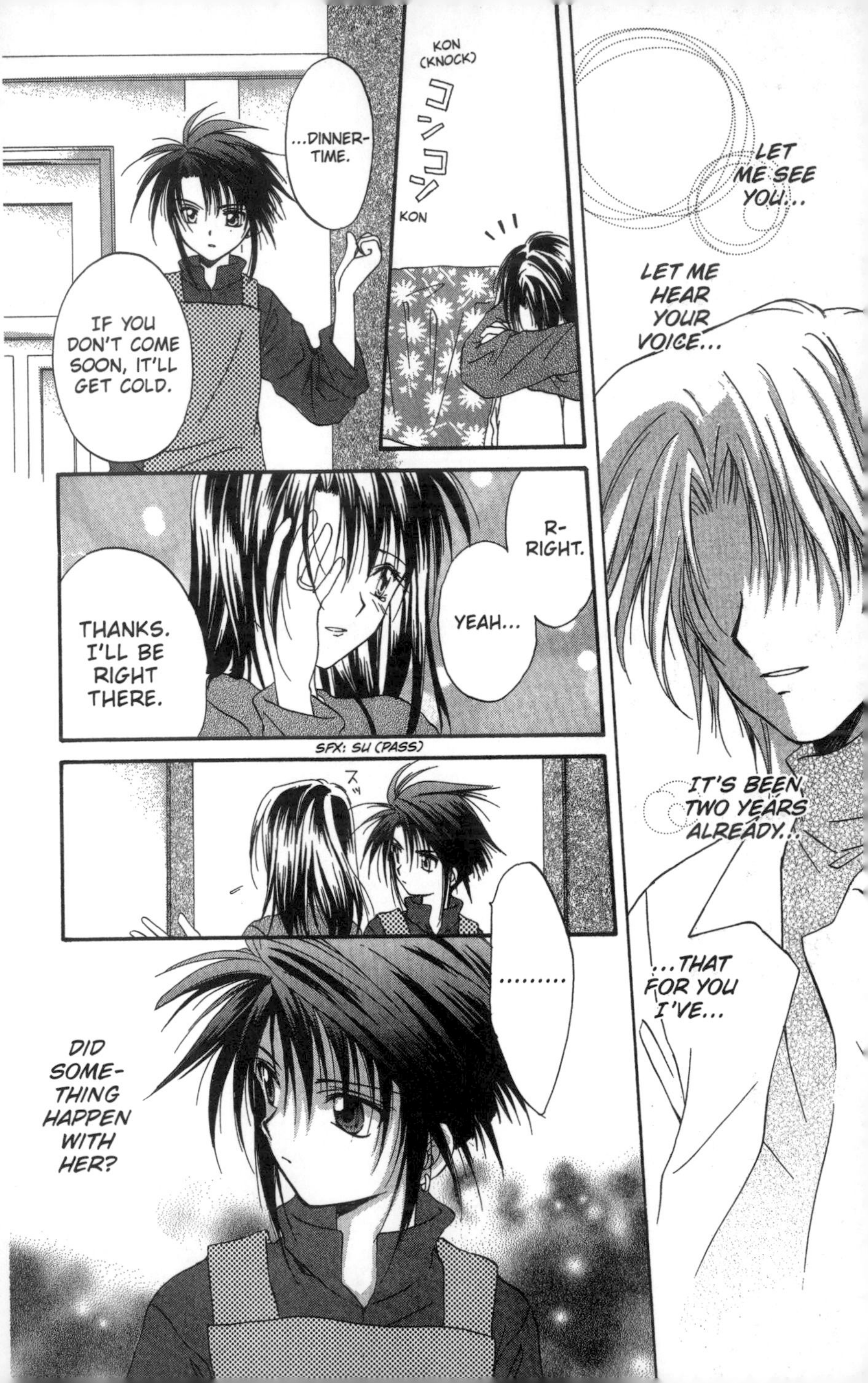
LET ME SEE YOU...
LET ME HEAR YOUR VOICE...
IT'S BEEN TWO YEARS ALREADY...
...THAT FOR YOU I'VE...
KON (KNOCK)
コンコン
KON
...DINNER-TIME.
IF YOU DON'T COME SOON, IT'LL GET COLD.
R-RIGHT.
YEAH...
THANKS. I'LL BE RIGHT THERE.
SFX: SU (PASS)
スッ
....
DID SOMETHING HAPPEN WITH HER?

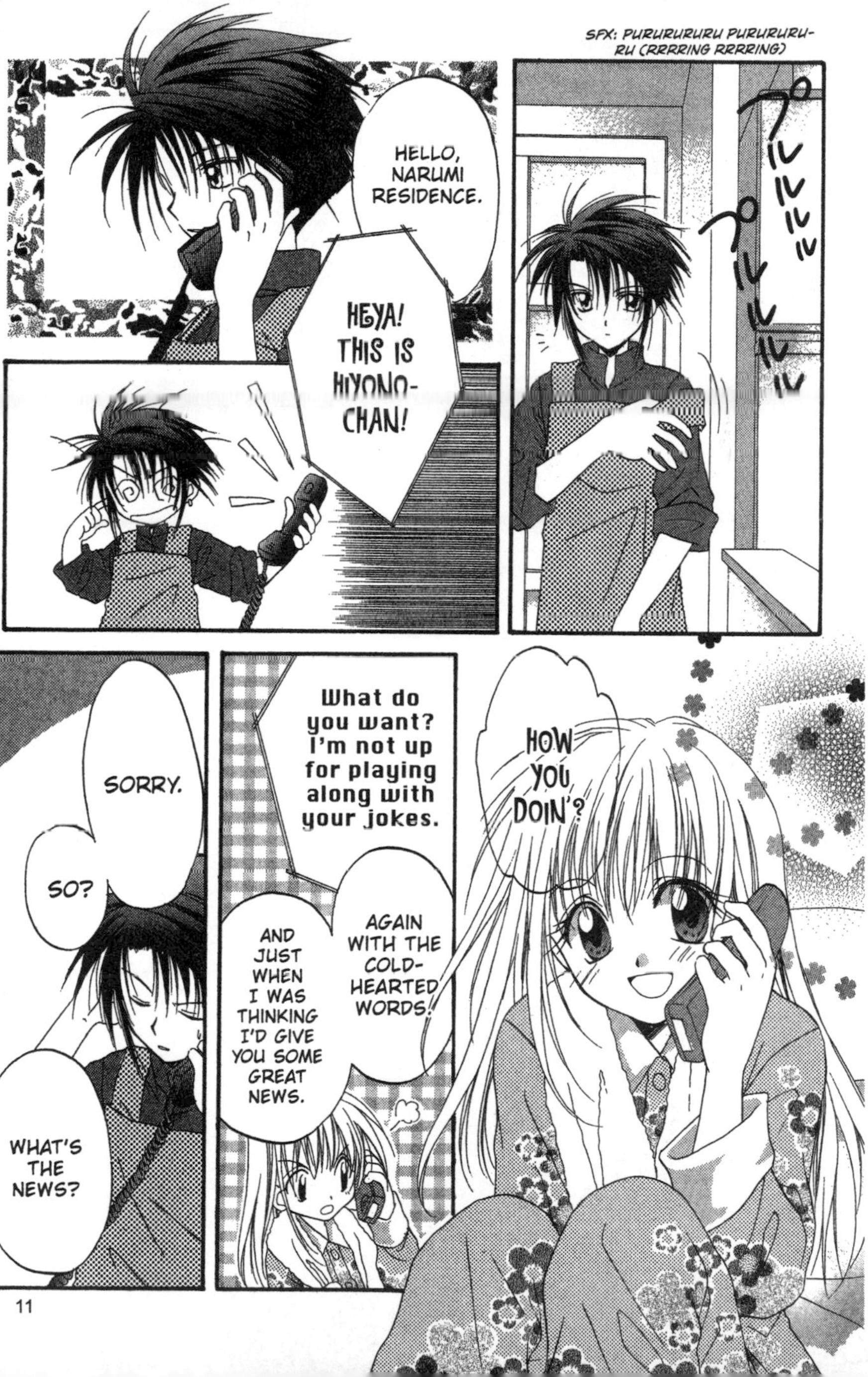
SFX: PURURURURU PURURURURURU (RRRRING RRRRING)
HELLO, NARUMI RESIDENCE.
HEYA! THIS IS HIYONO-CHAN!
HOW YOU DOIN'?
What do you want? I'm not up for playing along with your jokes.
AGAIN WITH THE COLD-HEARTED WORDS!
AND JUST WHEN I WAS THINKING I'D GIVE YOU SOME GREAT NEWS.
SORRY.
SO?
WHAT'S THE NEWS?

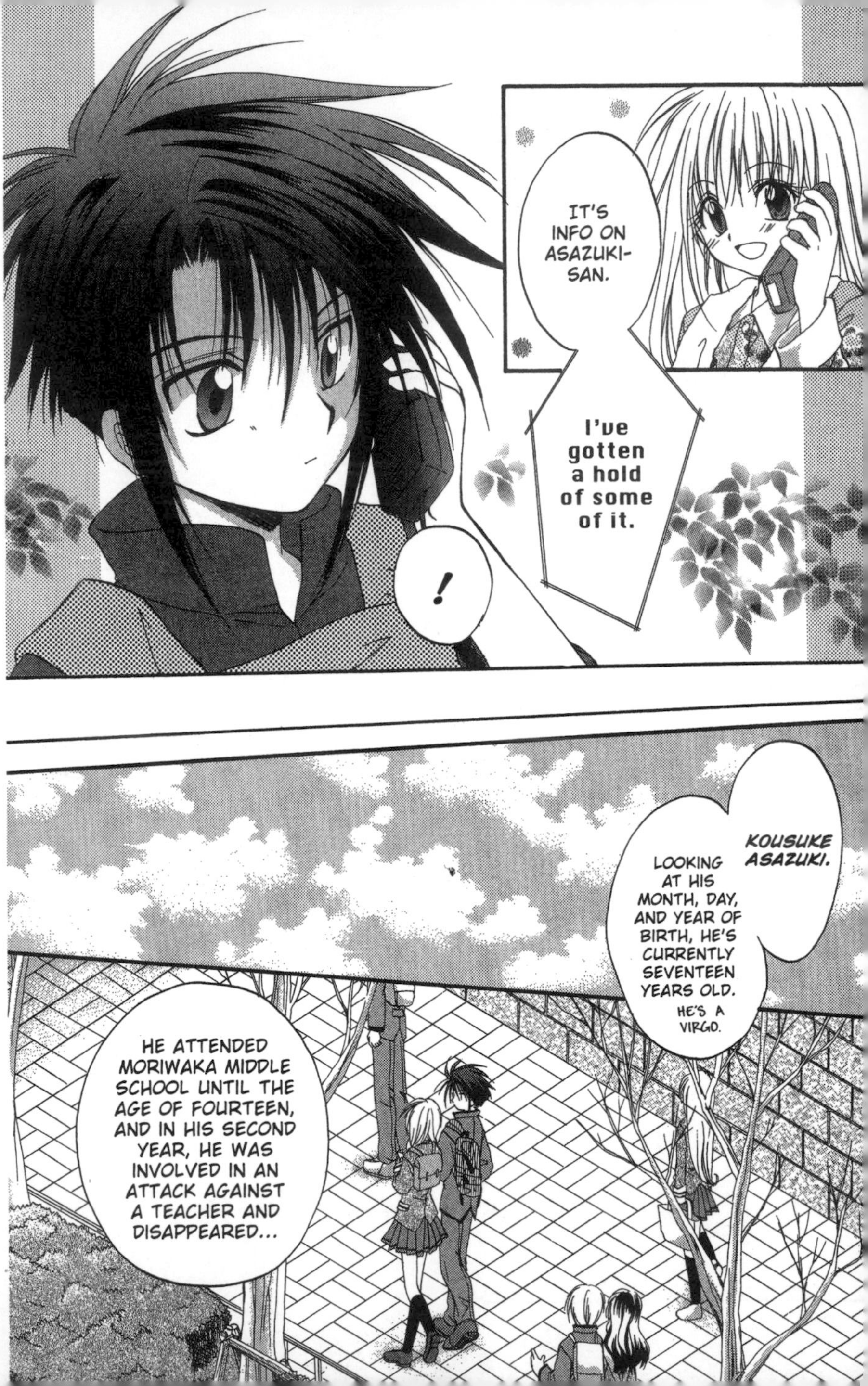
IT'S INFO ON ASAZUKI-SAN.
I've gotten a hold of some of it.
!
KOUSUKE ASAZUKI.
LOOKING AT HIS MONTH, DAY, AND YEAR OF BIRTH, HE'S CURRENTLY SEVENTEEN YEARS OLD.
HE'S A VIRGO.
HE ATTENDED MORIWAKA MIDDLE SCHOOL UNTIL THE AGE OF FOURTEEN, AND IN HIS SECOND YEAR, HE WAS INVOLVED IN AN ATTACK AGAINST A TEACHER AND DISAPPEARED...

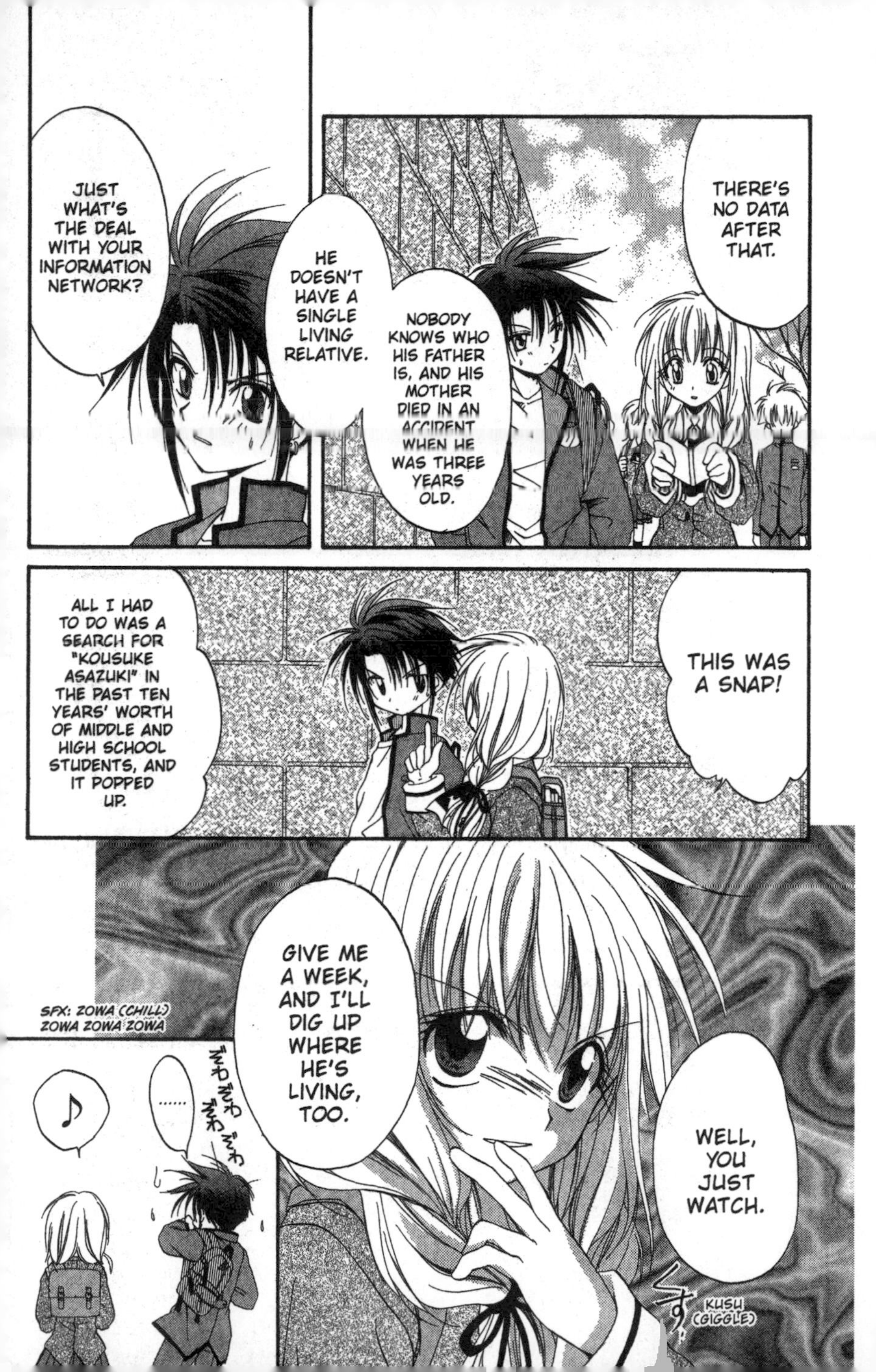
HE DOESN'T HAVE A SINGLE LIVING RELATIVE.
NOBODY KNOWS WHO HIS FATHER IS, AND HIS MOTHER DIED IN AN ACCIDENT WHEN HE WAS THREE YEARS OLD.
THERE'S NO DATA AFTER THAT.
JUST WHAT'S THE DEAL WITH YOUR INFORMATION NETWORK?
THIS WAS A SNAP!
ALL I HAD TO DO WAS A SEARCH FOR "KOUSUKE ASAZUKI" IN THE PAST TEN YEARS' WORTH OF MIDDLE AND HIGH SCHOOL STUDENTS, AND IT POPPED UP.
WELL, YOU JUST WATCH.
GIVE ME A WEEK, AND I'LL DIG UP WHERE HE'S LIVING, TOO.
KUSU (GIGGLE)
SFX: ZOWA (CHILL) ZOWA ZOWA ZOWA
......
♪

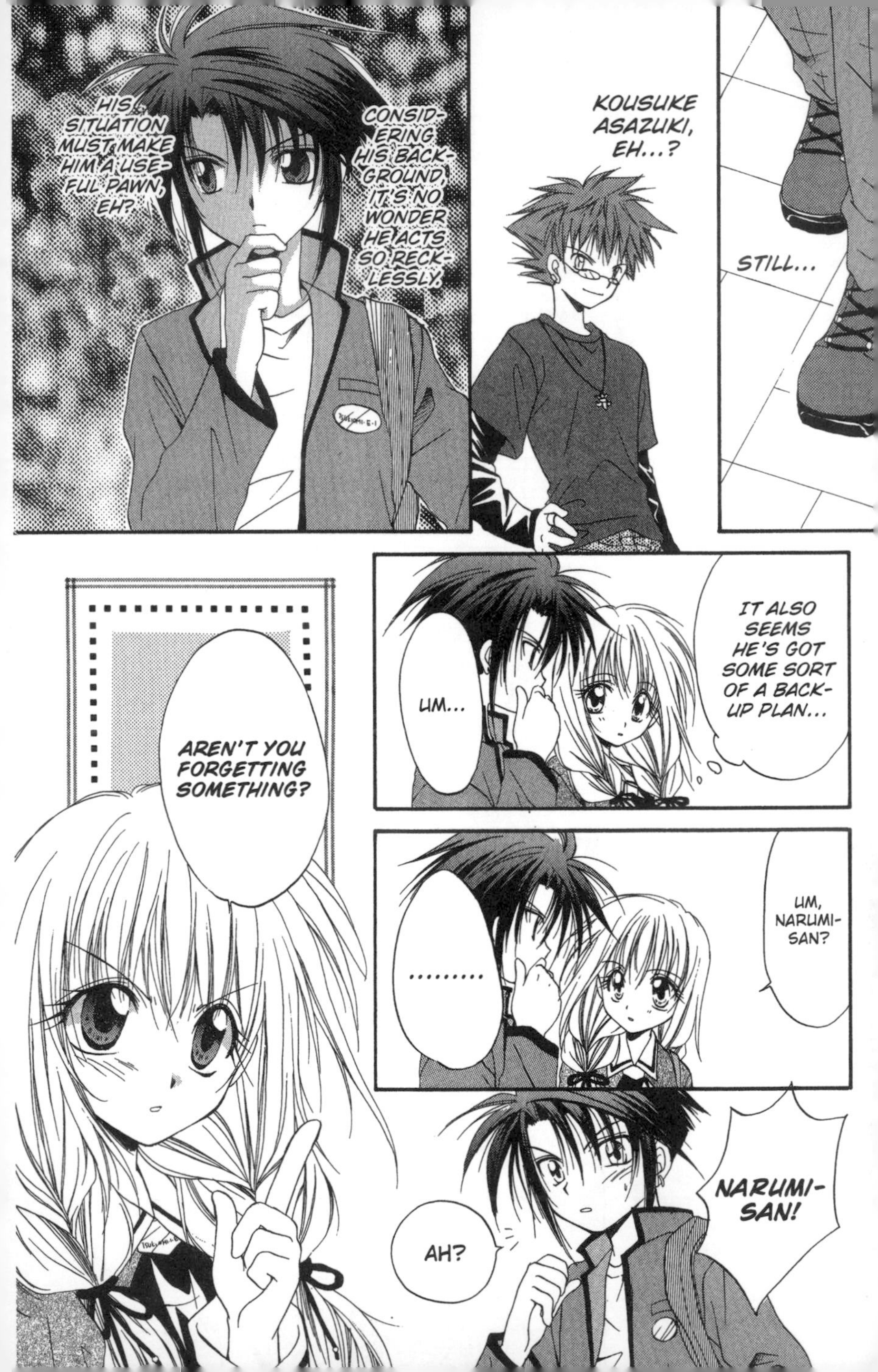
STILL...
KOUSUKE ASAZUKI, EH...?
CONSIDERING HIS BACKGROUND, IT'S NO WONDER HE ACTS SO RECKLESSLY.
HIS SITUATION MUST MAKE HIM A USEFUL PAWN, EH?
IT ALSO SEEMS HE'S GOT SOME SORT OF A BACK-UP PLAN...
UM...
UM, NARUMI-SAN?
....
NARUMI-SAN!
AH?
AREN'T YOU FORGETTING SOMETHING?

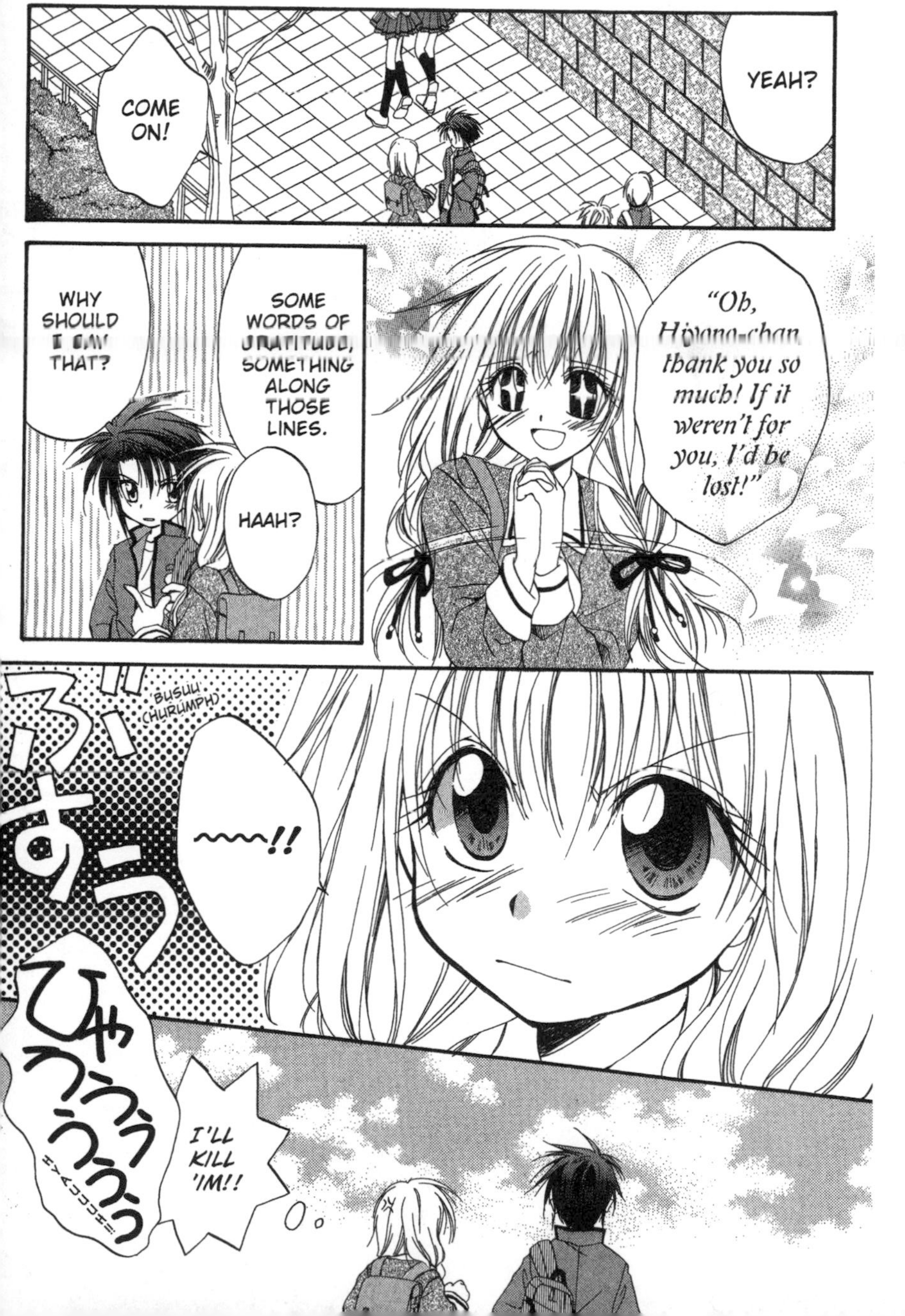
YEAH?
COME ON!
"Oh, Hiyono-chan thank you so much! If it weren't for you, I'd be lost!"
SOME WORDS OF GRATITUDE, SOMETHING ALONG THOSE LINES.
WHY SHOULD I SAY THAT?
HAAH?
BUSUU (HURUMPH)
~~~~!!
I'LL KILL 'IM!!
~~~~

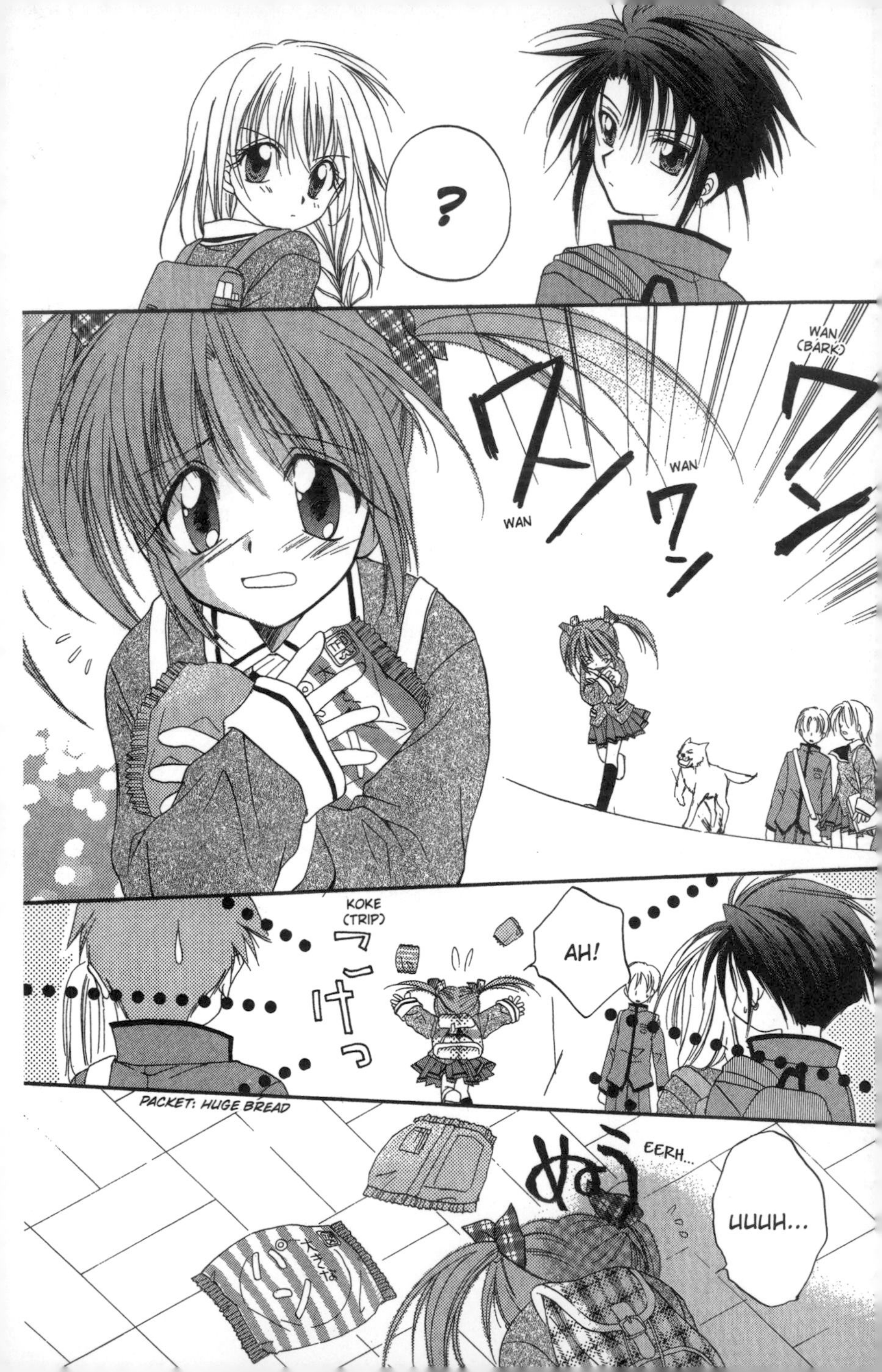
?
WAN
(BARK)
ワン
WAN
ワン
WAN
ワン
AH!
KOKE
(TRIP)
こけっ
PACKET: HUGE BREAD
UUUH...
EERH...
ぬう
大きな
パン

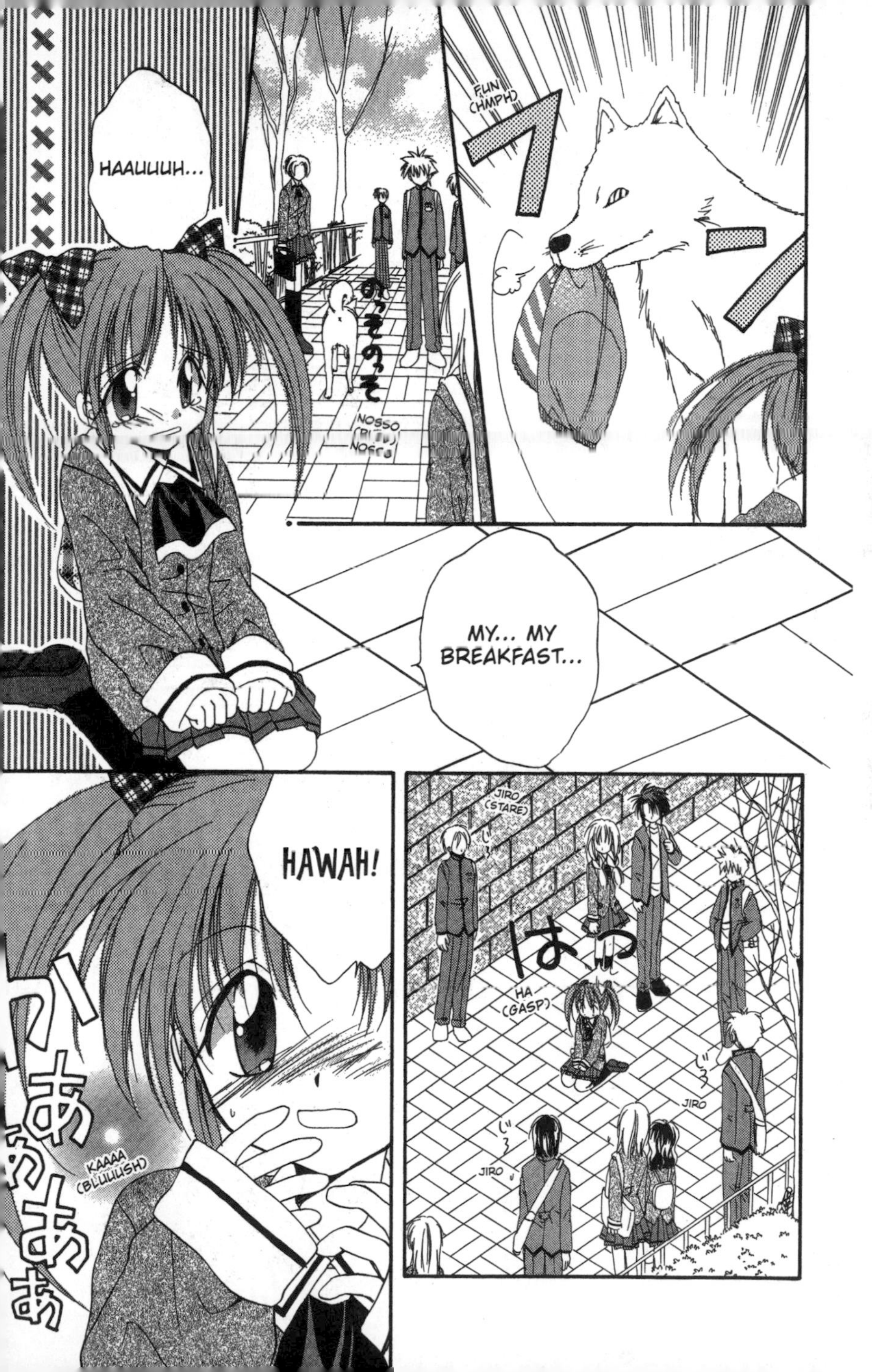

FUN (HMPH)
NOSSO
NOSSO
HAAUUUH...
MY... MY BREAKFAST...
JIRO (STARE)
HA (GASP)
JIRO
JIRO
HAWAH!
KAAAA (BLUUUSH)

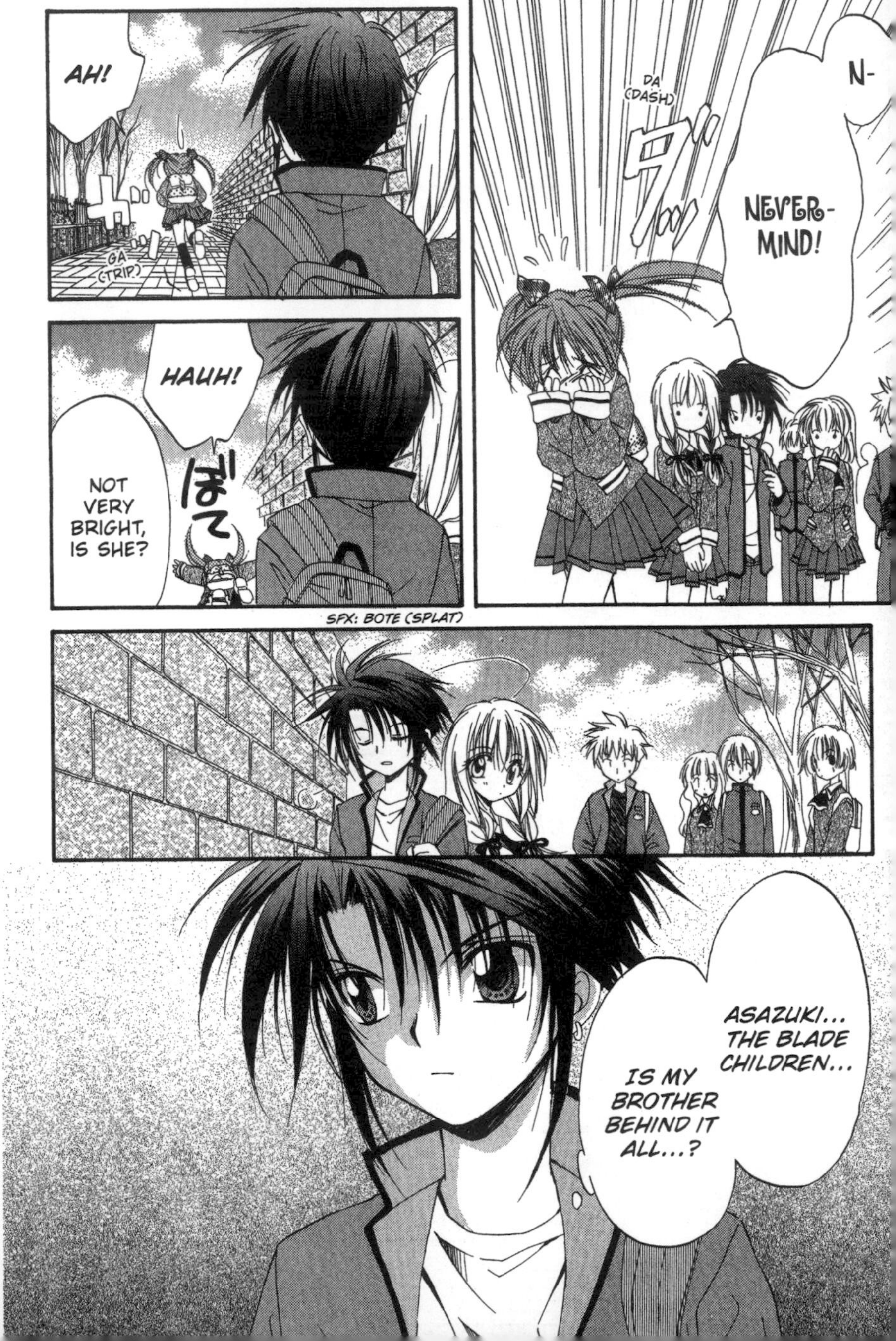
N-
NEVER-MIND!
DA (DASH)
ダッ
AH!
GA (TRIP)
HAUH!
NOT VERY BRIGHT, IS SHE?
ぼて
SFX: BOTE (SPLAT)
ASAZUKI... THE BLADE CHILDREN...
IS MY BROTHER BEHIND IT ALL...?

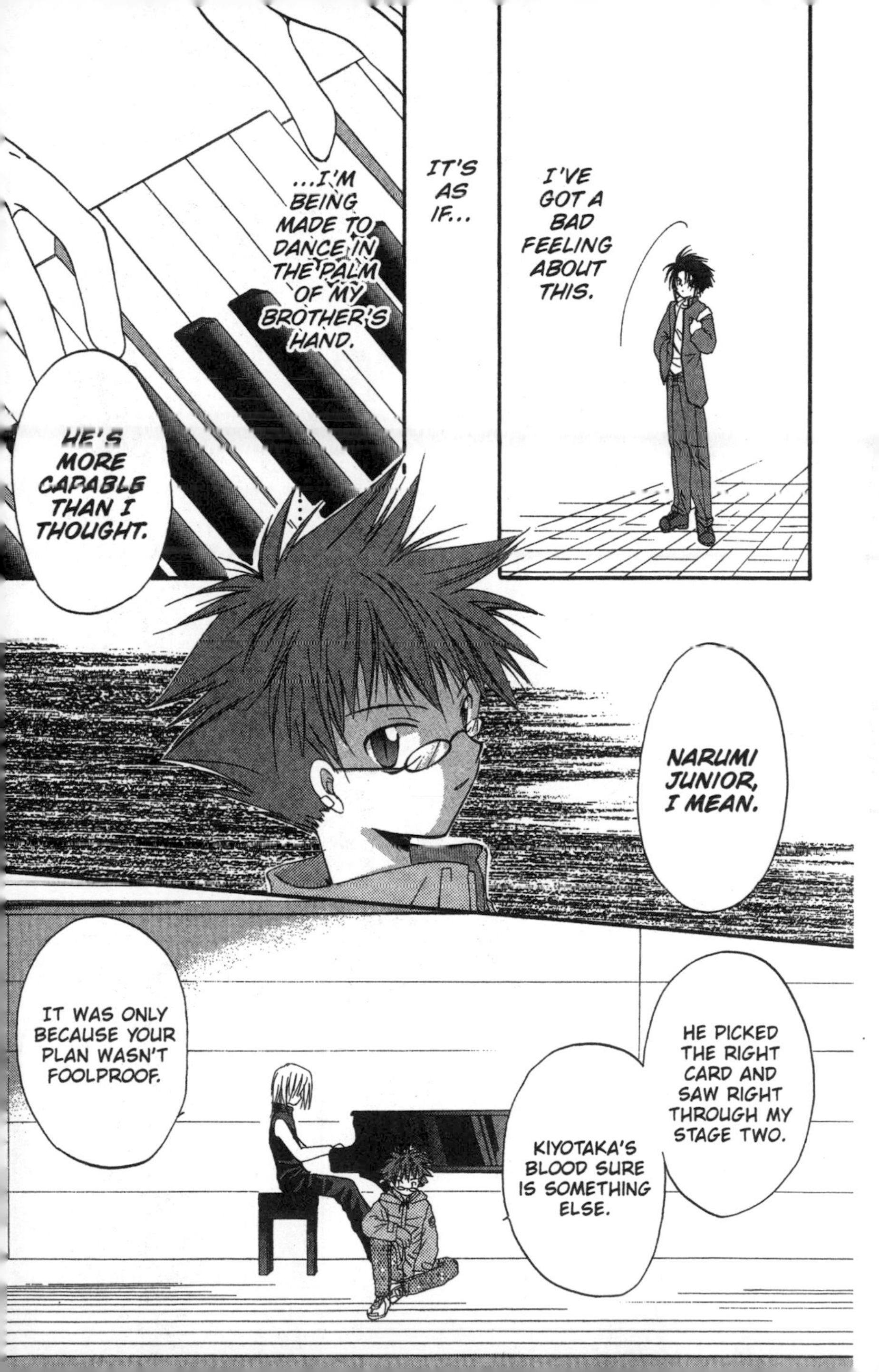
I'VE GOT A BAD FEELING ABOUT THIS.
IT'S AS IF...
...I'M BEING MADE TO DANCE IN THE PALM OF MY BROTHER'S HAND.
HE'S MORE CAPABLE THAN I THOUGHT.
NARUMI JUNIOR, I MEAN.
HE PICKED THE RIGHT CARD AND SAW RIGHT THROUGH MY STAGE TWO.
KIYOTAKA'S BLOOD SURE IS SOMETHING ELSE.
IT WAS ONLY BECAUSE YOUR PLAN WASN'T FOOLPROOF.

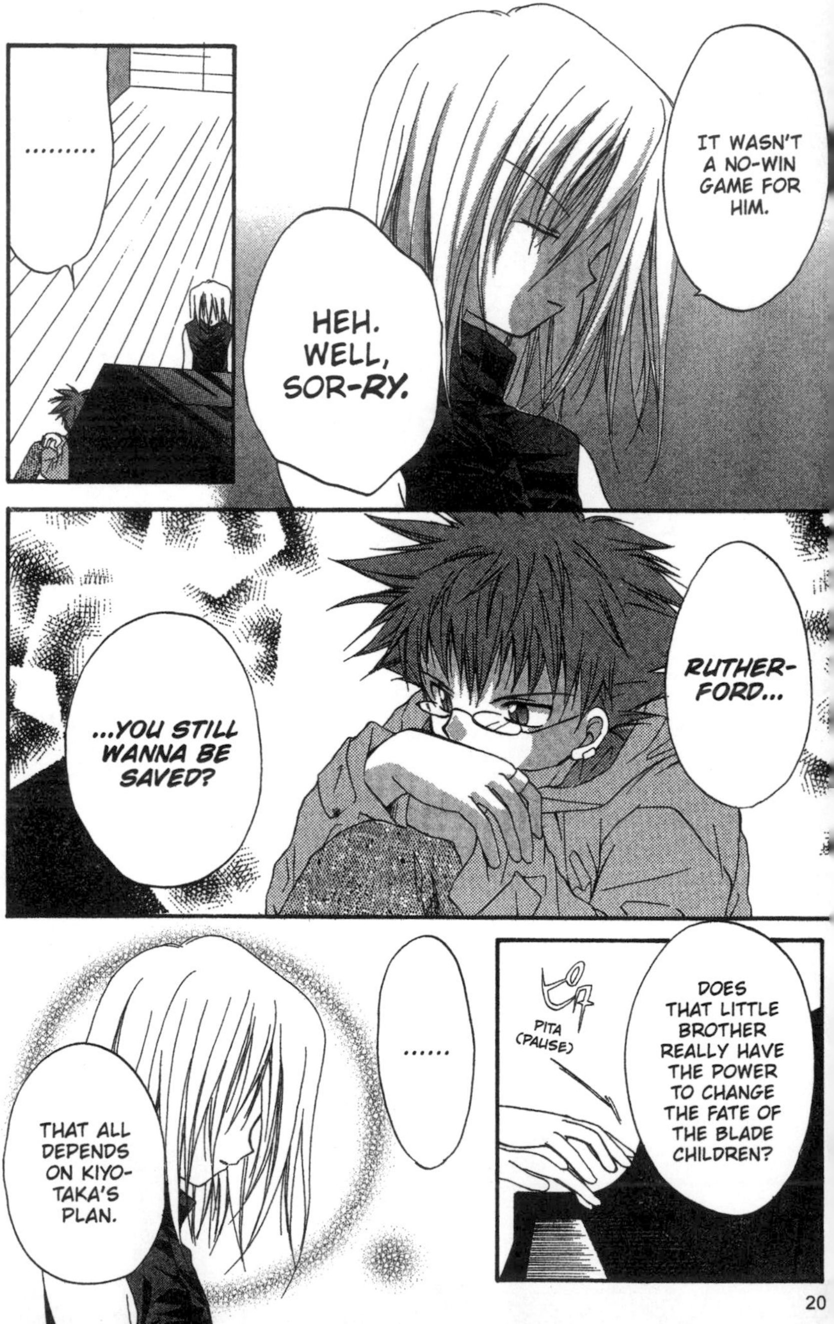
IT WASN'T A NO-WIN GAME FOR HIM.
HEH. WELL, SOR-RY.
....
RUTHER-FORD...
...YOU STILL WANNA BE SAVED?
DOES THAT LITTLE BROTHER REALLY HAVE THE POWER TO CHANGE THE FATE OF THE BLADE CHILDREN?
PITA (PAUSE)
......
THAT ALL DEPENDS ON KIYO-TAKA'S PLAN.

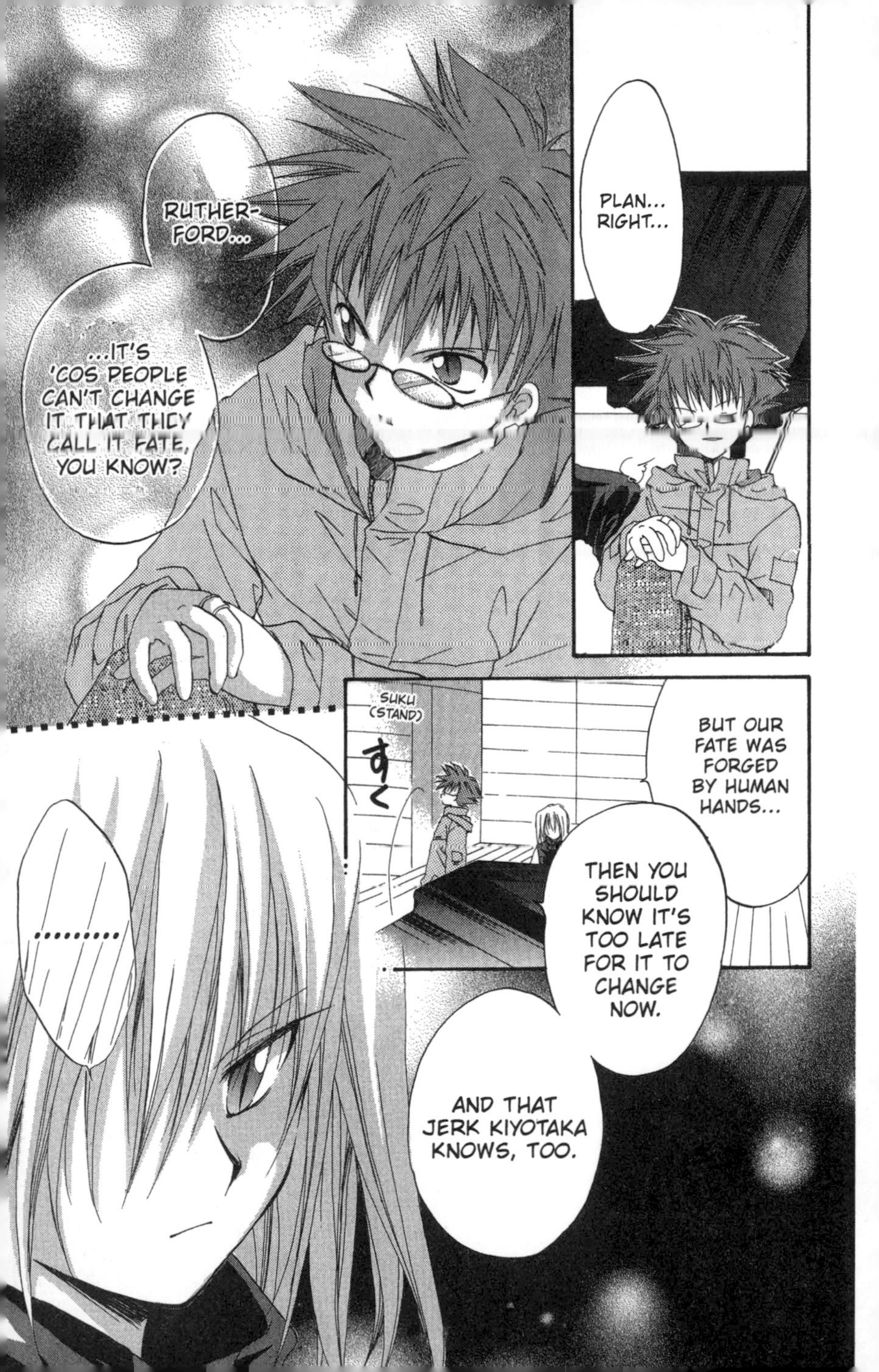
PLAN... RIGHT...
RUTHER-FORD...
...IT'S 'COS PEOPLE CAN'T CHANGE IT THAT THEY CALL IT FATE, YOU KNOW?
SUKU (STAND)
すく
BUT OUR FATE WAS FORGED BY HUMAN HANDS...
THEN YOU SHOULD KNOW IT'S TOO LATE FOR IT TO CHANGE NOW.
AND THAT JERK KIYOTAKA KNOWS, TOO.
....

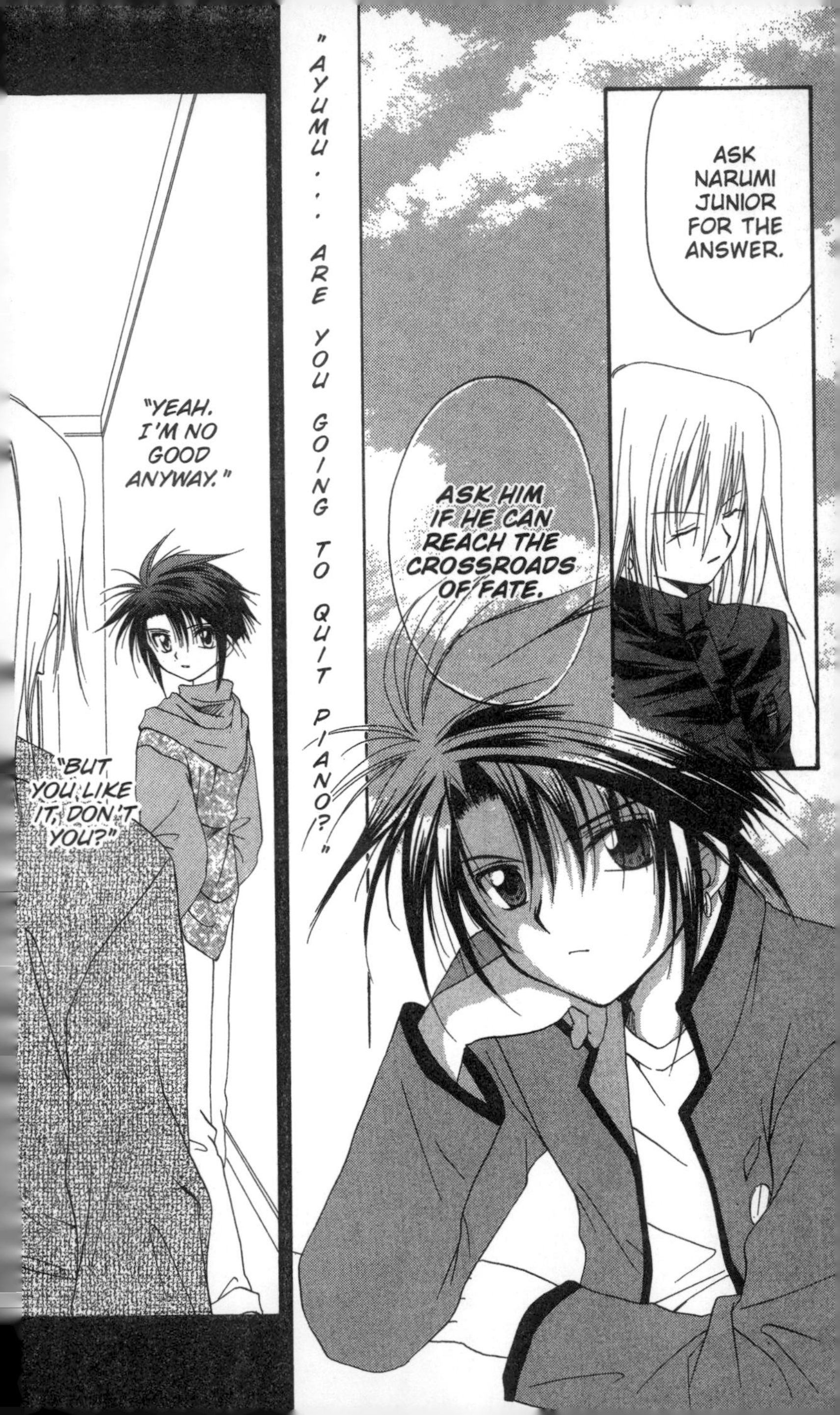
ASK NARUMI JUNIOR FOR THE ANSWER.
ASK HIM IF HE CAN REACH THE CROSSROADS OF FATE.
"AYUMU... ARE YOU GOING TO QUIT PIANO?"
"YEAH. I'M NO GOOD ANYWAY."
"BUT YOU LIKE IT, DON'T YOU?"

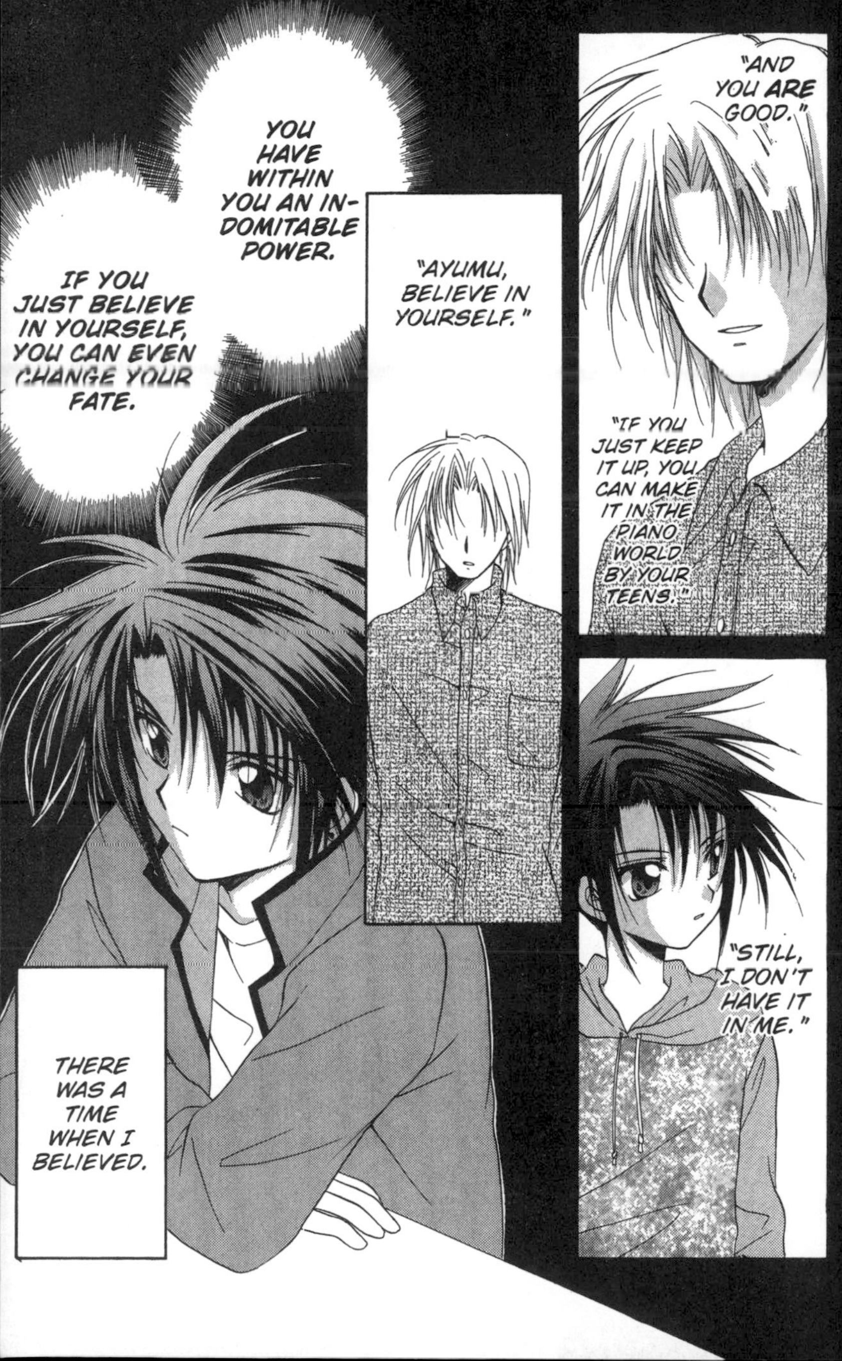
"AND YOU ARE GOOD."
"IF YOU JUST KEEP IT UP, YOU CAN MAKE IT IN THE PIANO WORLD BY YOUR TEENS."
"AYUMU, BELIEVE IN YOURSELF."
YOU HAVE WITHIN YOU AN IN-DOMITABLE POWER.
IF YOU JUST BELIEVE IN YOURSELF, YOU CAN EVEN CHANGE YOUR FATE.
"STILL, I DON'T HAVE IT IN ME."
THERE WAS A TIME WHEN I BELIEVED.

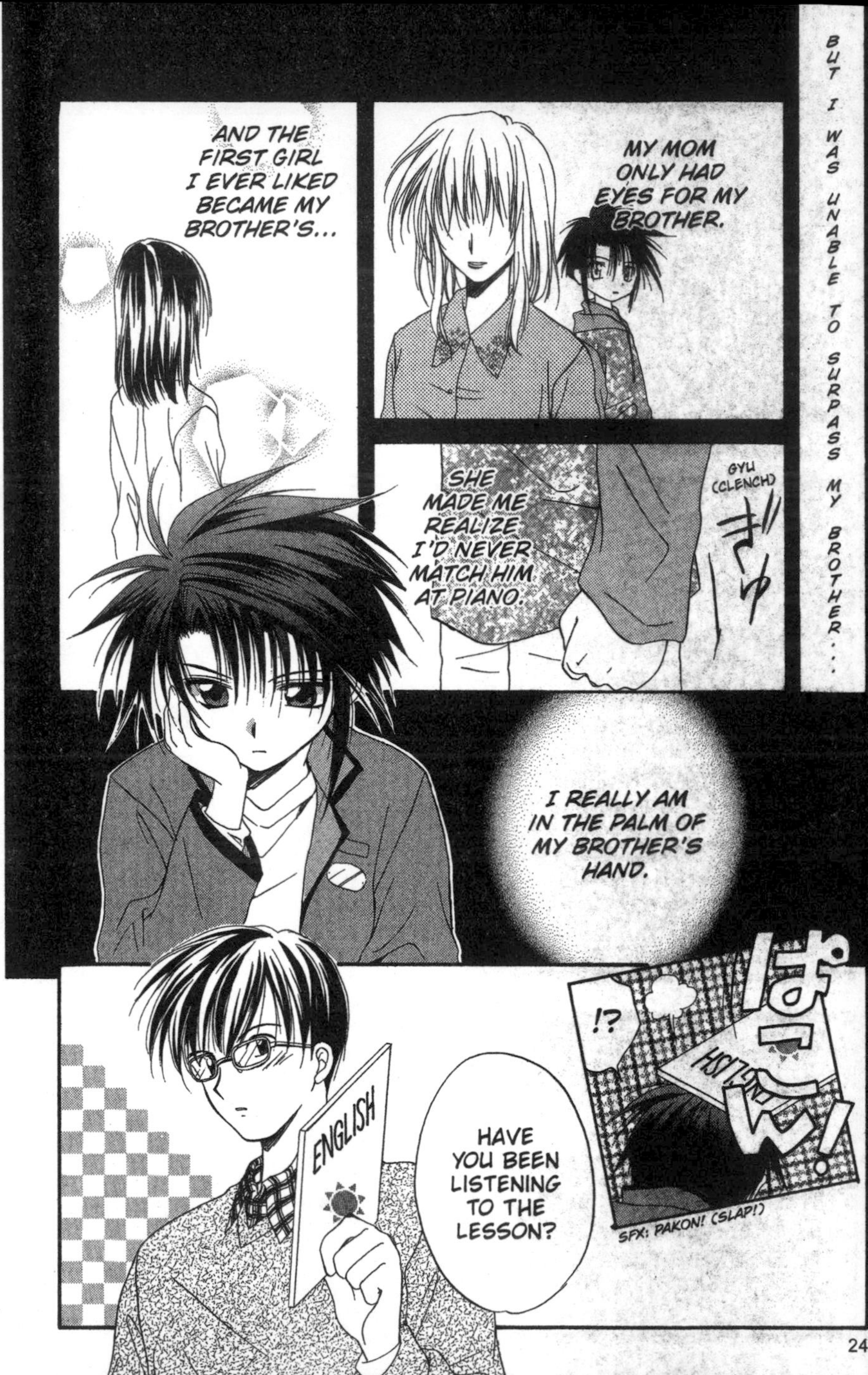
BUT I WAS UNABLE TO SURPASS MY BROTHER...
MY MOM ONLY HAD EYES FOR MY BROTHER.
GYU (CLENCH)
SHE MADE ME REALIZE I'D NEVER MATCH HIM AT PIANO.
AND THE FIRST GIRL I EVER LIKED BECAME MY BROTHER'S...
I REALLY AM IN THE PALM OF MY BROTHER'S HAND.
!?
ENGLISH
SFX: PAKON! (SLAP!)
ENGLISH
HAVE YOU BEEN LISTENING TO THE LESSON?

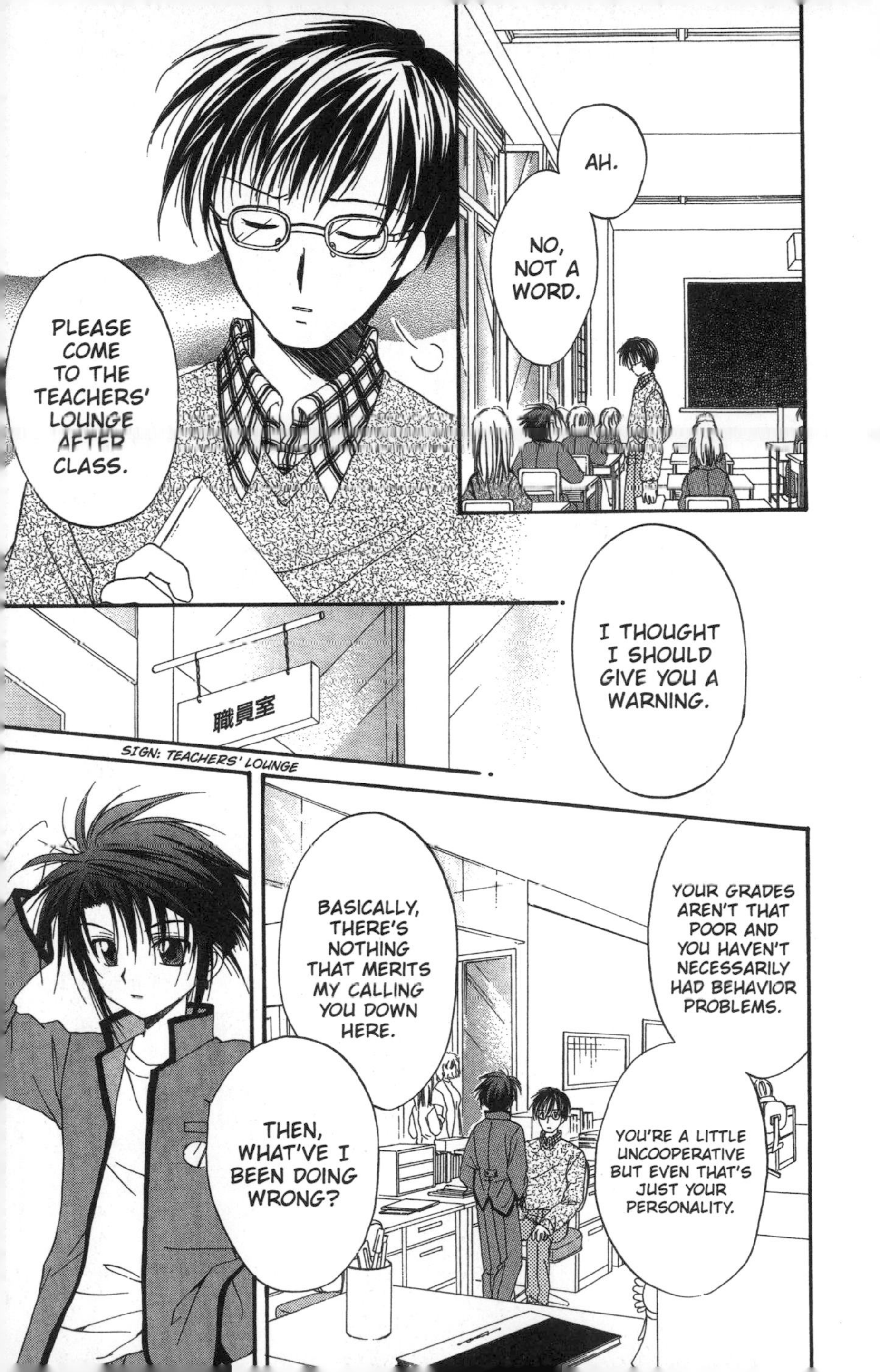
AH.
NO, NOT A WORD.
PLEASE COME TO THE TEACHERS' LOUNGE AFTER CLASS.
I THOUGHT I SHOULD GIVE YOU A WARNING.
職員室
SIGN: TEACHERS' LOUNGE
YOUR GRADES AREN'T THAT POOR AND YOU HAVEN'T NECESSARILY HAD BEHAVIOR PROBLEMS.
BASICALLY, THERE'S NOTHING THAT MERITS MY CALLING YOU DOWN HERE.
THEN, WHAT'VE I BEEN DOING WRONG?
YOU'RE A LITTLE UNCOOPERATIVE BUT EVEN THAT'S JUST YOUR PERSONALITY.

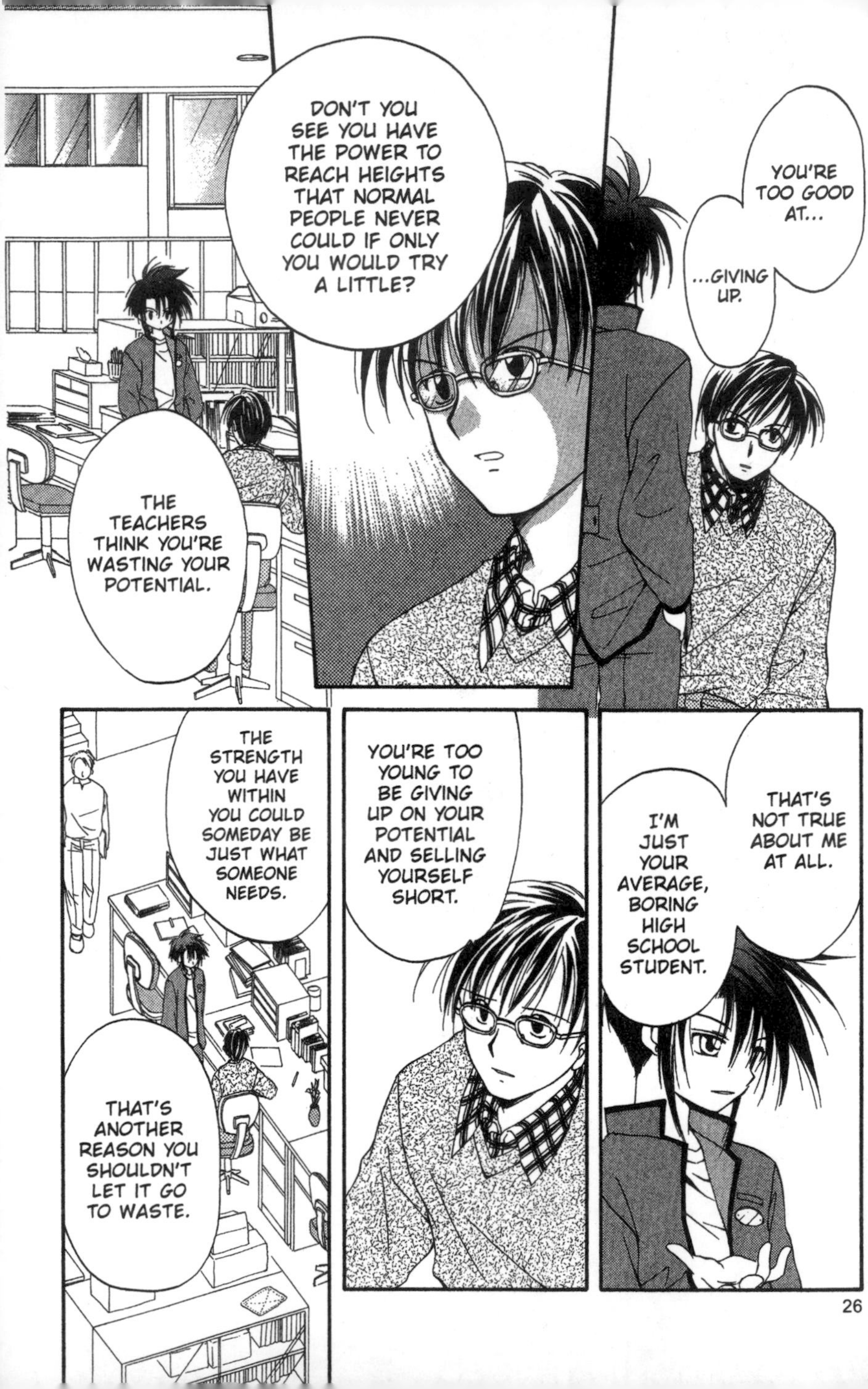
YOU'RE TOO GOOD AT...
...GIVING UP.
DON'T YOU SEE YOU HAVE THE POWER TO REACH HEIGHTS THAT NORMAL PEOPLE NEVER COULD IF ONLY YOU WOULD TRY A LITTLE?
THE TEACHERS THINK YOU'RE WASTING YOUR POTENTIAL.
THAT'S NOT TRUE ABOUT ME AT ALL.
I'M JUST YOUR AVERAGE, BORING HIGH SCHOOL STUDENT.
YOU'RE TOO YOUNG TO BE GIVING UP ON YOUR POTENTIAL AND SELLING YOURSELF SHORT.
THE STRENGTH YOU HAVE WITHIN YOU COULD SOMEDAY BE JUST WHAT SOMEONE NEEDS.
THAT'S ANOTHER REASON YOU SHOULDN'T LET IT GO TO WASTE.

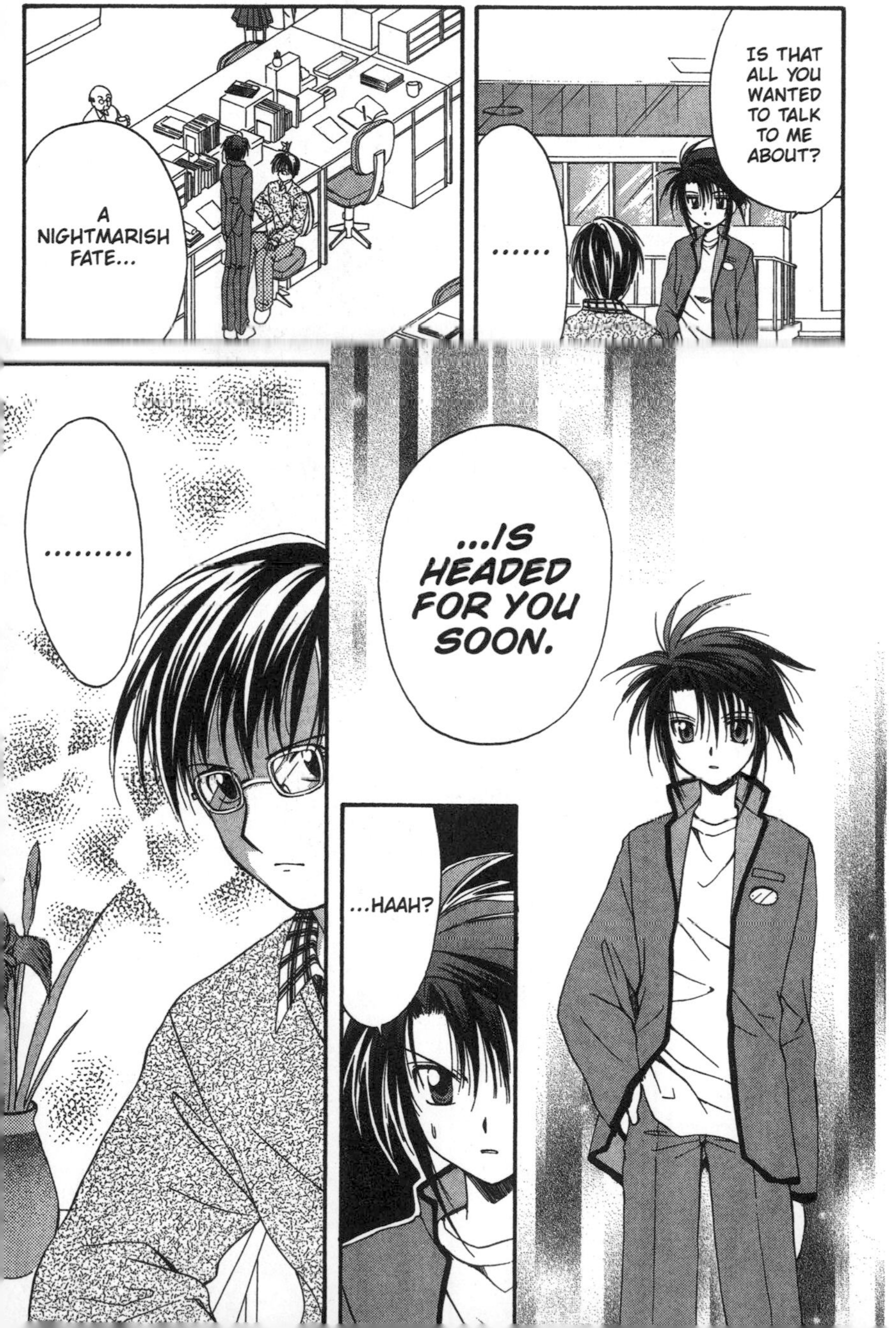
IS THAT ALL YOU WANTED TO TALK TO ME ABOUT?
......
A NIGHTMARISH FATE...
...IS HEADED FOR YOU SOON.
...HAAH?
....

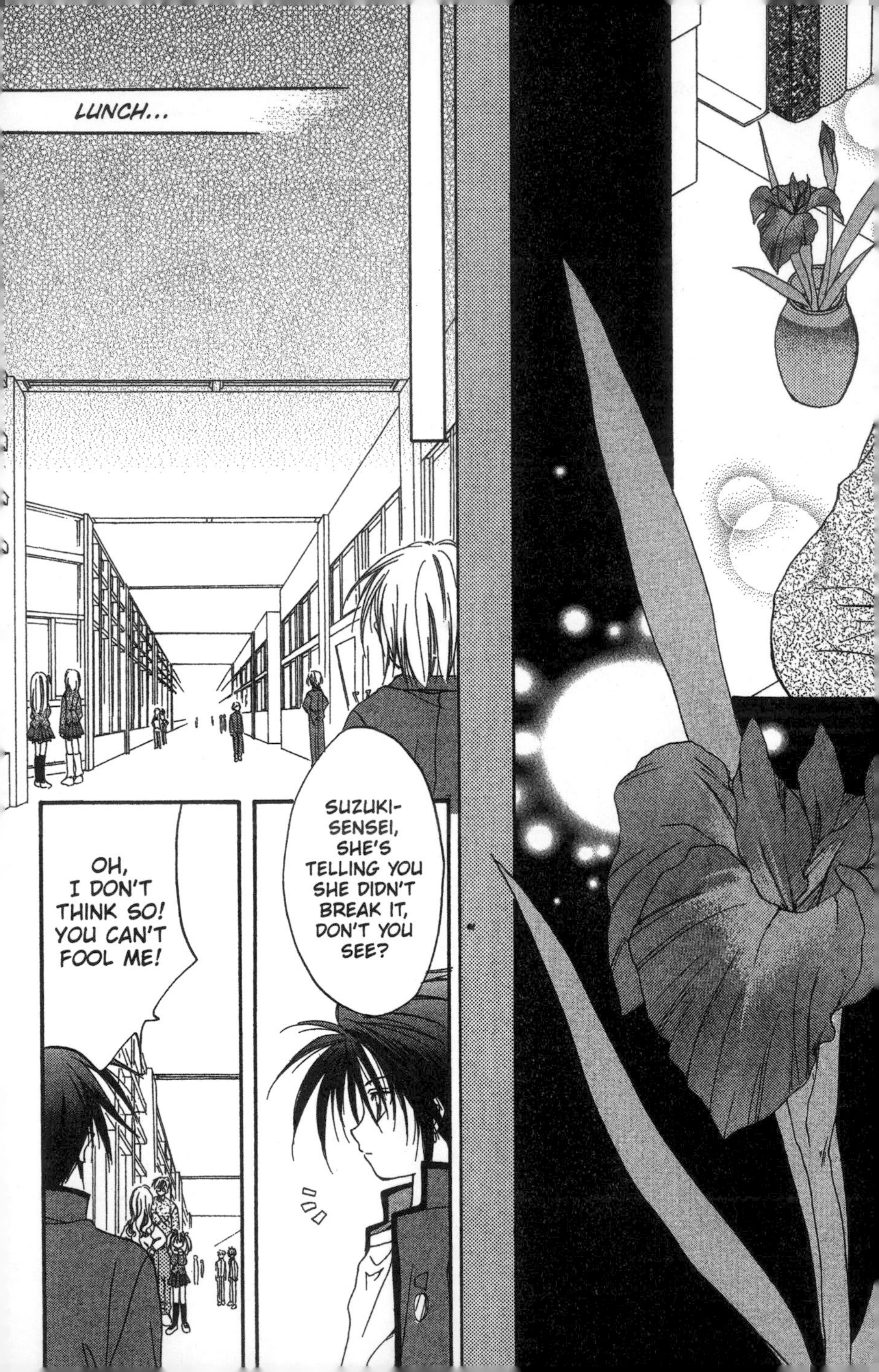
LUNCH...
SUZUKI-SENSEI, SHE'S TELLING YOU SHE DIDN'T BREAK IT, DON'T YOU SEE?
OH, I DON'T THINK SO! YOU CAN'T FOOL ME!

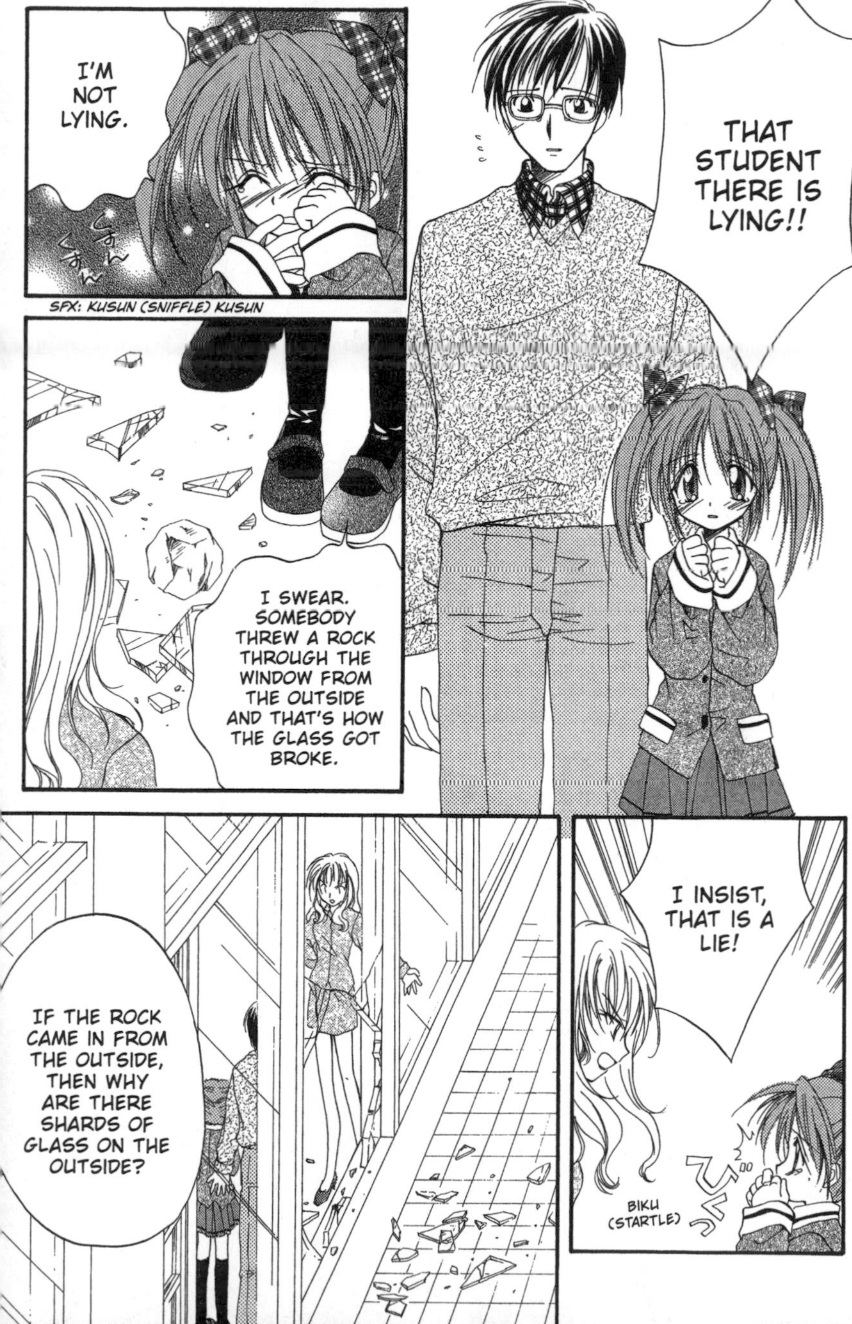
THAT STUDENT THERE IS LYING!!
I'M NOT LYING.
くすん くすん
SFX: KUSUN (SNIFFLE) KUSUN
I SWEAR. SOMEBODY THREW A ROCK THROUGH THE WINDOW FROM THE OUTSIDE AND THAT'S HOW THE GLASS GOT BROKE.
I INSIST, THAT IS A LIE!
BIKU (STARTLE)
IF THE ROCK CAME IN FROM THE OUTSIDE, THEN WHY ARE THERE SHARDS OF GLASS ON THE OUTSIDE?

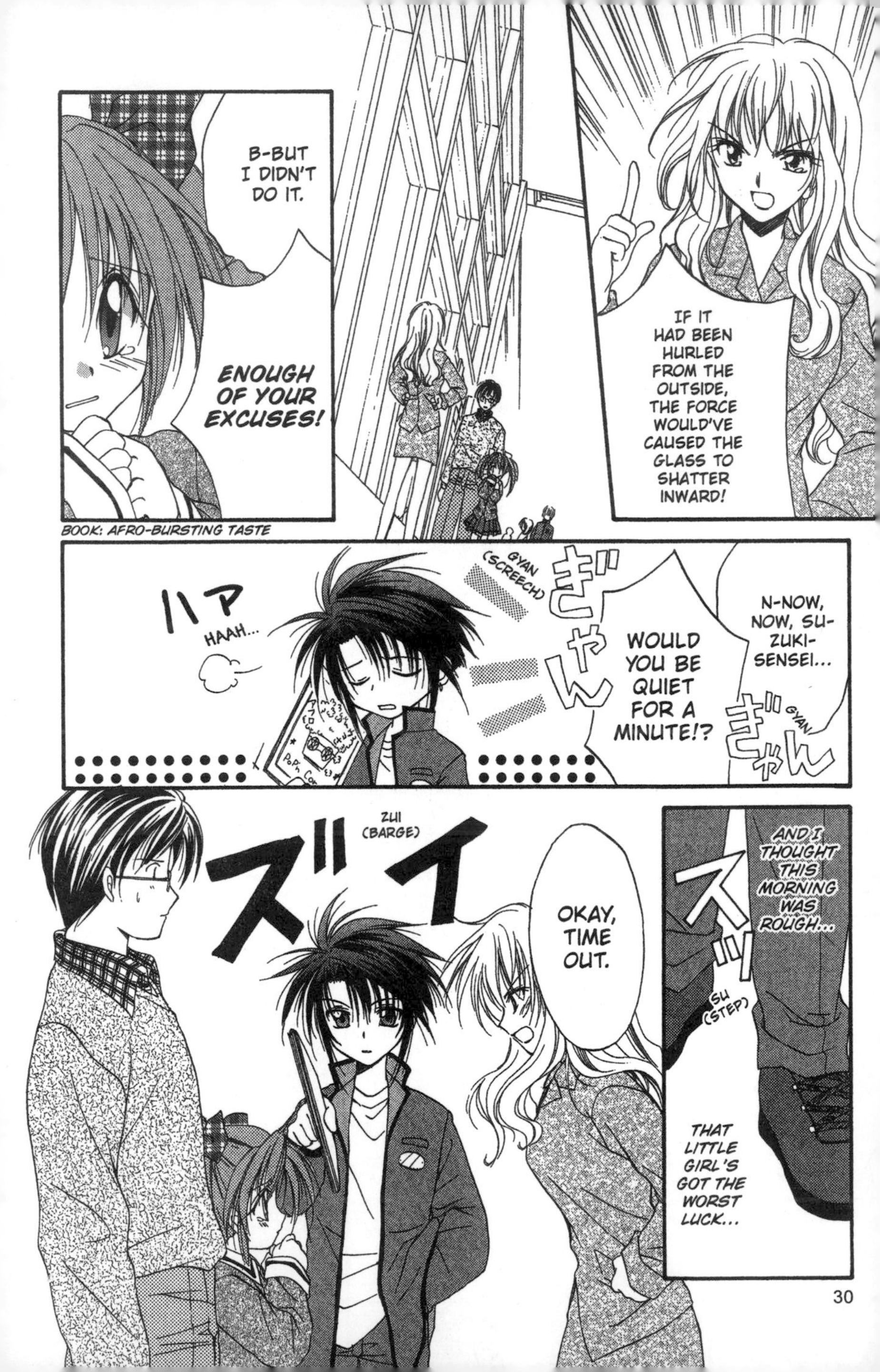

IF IT HAD BEEN HURLED FROM THE OUTSIDE, THE FORCE WOULD'VE CAUSED THE GLASS TO SHATTER INWARD!
B-BUT I DIDN'T DO IT.
ENOUGH OF YOUR EXCUSES!
BOOK: AFRO-BURSTING TASTE
N-NOW, NOW, SU-ZUKI-SENSEI...
ぎゃん
GYAN
WOULD YOU BE QUIET FOR A MINUTE!?
ぎゃん
GYAN (SCREECH)
ハア
HAAH...
AND I THOUGHT THIS MORNING WAS ROUGH...
スッ
SU (STEP)
THAT LITTLE GIRL'S GOT THE WORST LUCK...
OKAY, TIME OUT.
ズイ
ZUI (BARGE)

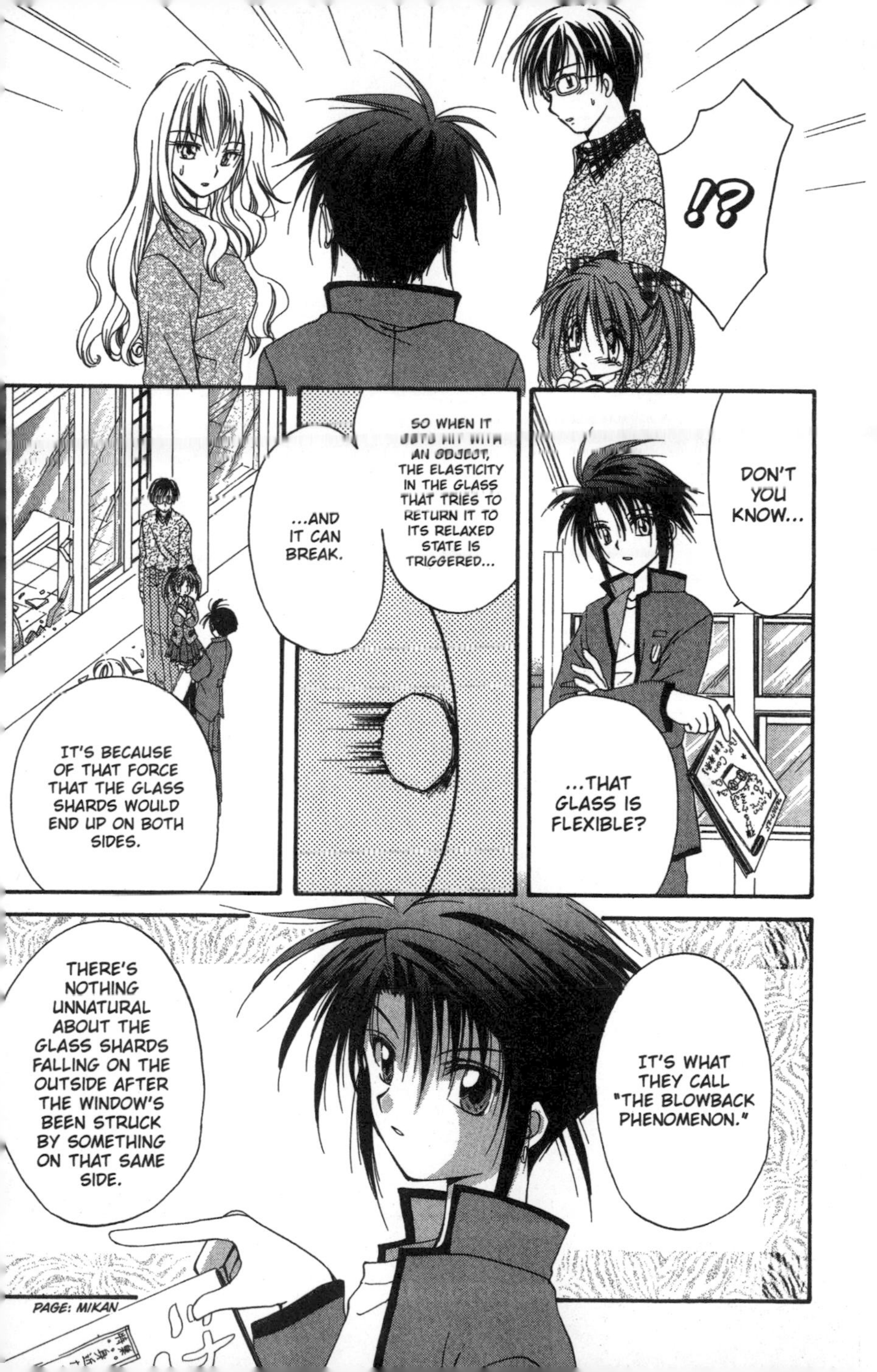
!?
DON'T YOU KNOW...
...THAT GLASS IS FLEXIBLE?
SO WHEN IT GETS HIT WITH AN OBJECT, THE ELASTICITY IN THE GLASS THAT TRIES TO RETURN IT TO ITS RELAXED STATE IS TRIGGERED...
...AND IT CAN BREAK.
IT'S BECAUSE OF THAT FORCE THAT THE GLASS SHARDS WOULD END UP ON BOTH SIDES.
IT'S WHAT THEY CALL "THE BLOWBACK PHENOMENON."
THERE'S NOTHING UNNATURAL ABOUT THE GLASS SHARDS FALLING ON THE OUTSIDE AFTER THE WINDOW'S BEEN STRUCK BY SOMETHING ON THAT SAME SIDE.
PAGE: MIKAN

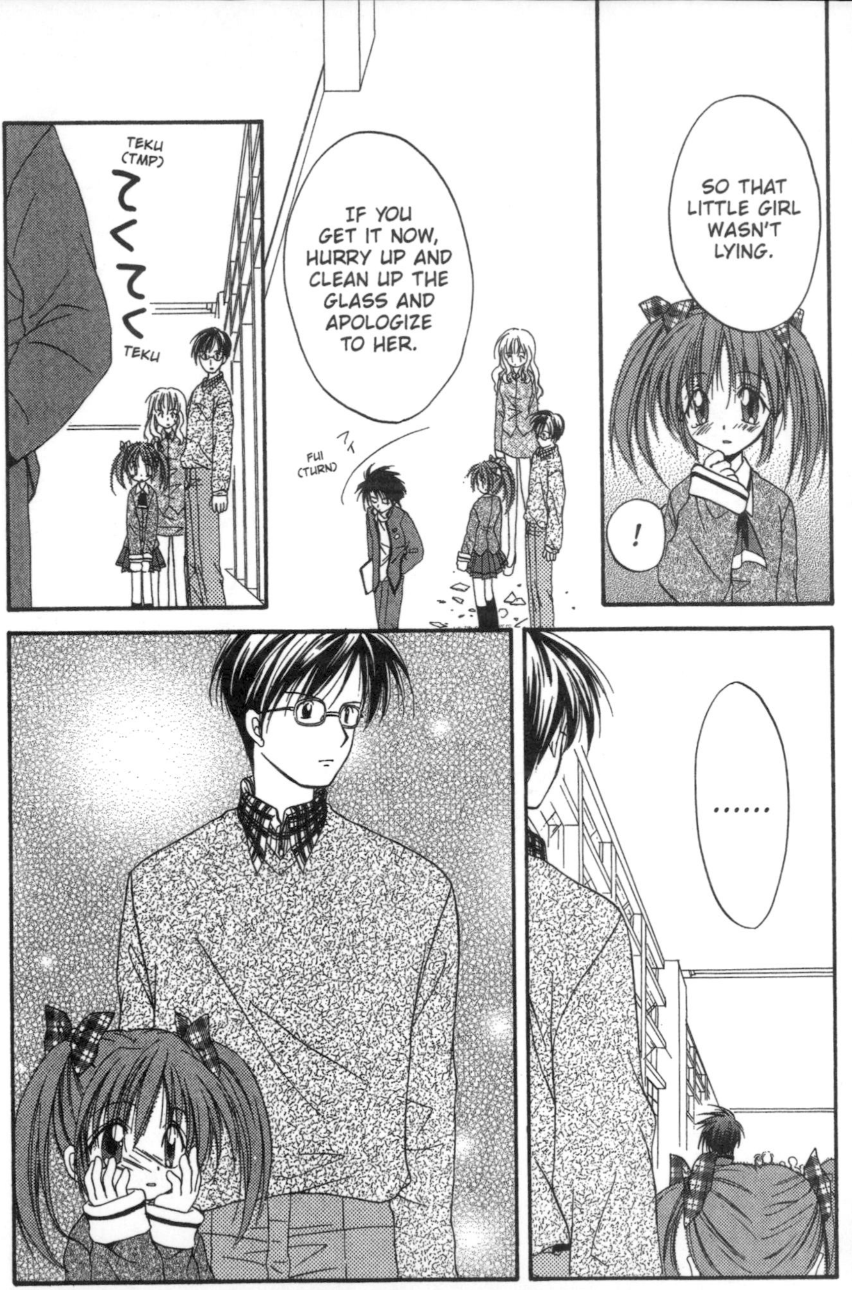
SO THAT LITTLE GIRL WASN'T LYING.
!
IF YOU GET IT NOW, HURRY UP AND CLEAN UP THE GLASS AND APOLOGIZE TO HER.
FUI (TURN)
TEKU (TMP)
てくてく
TEKU
......

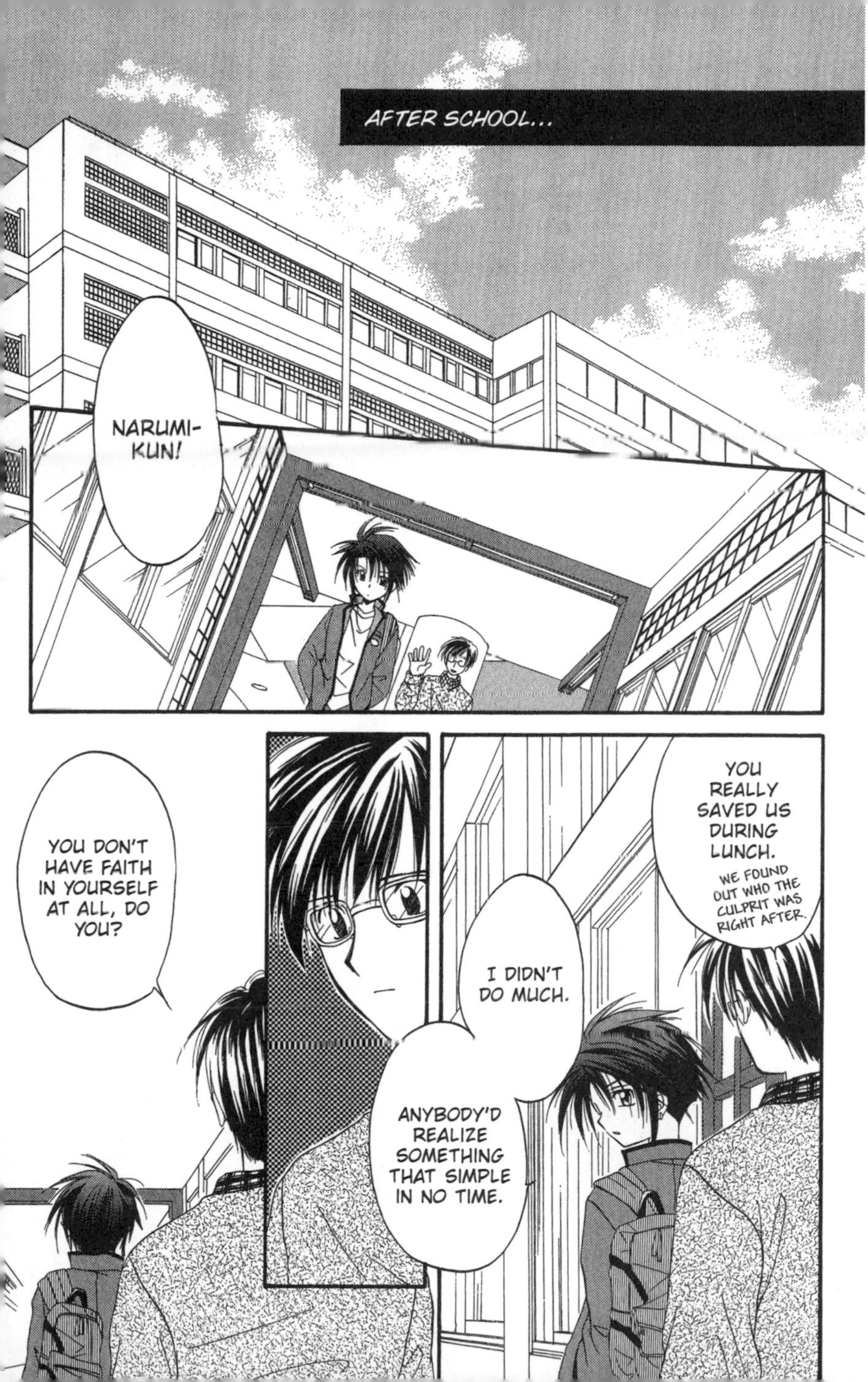
AFTER SCHOOL...
NARUMI-KUN!
YOU REALLY SAVED US DURING LUNCH.
WE FOUND OUT WHO THE CULPRIT WAS RIGHT AFTER.
I DIDN'T DO MUCH.
ANYBODY'D REALIZE SOMETHING THAT SIMPLE IN NO TIME.
YOU DON'T HAVE FAITH IN YOURSELF AT ALL, DO YOU?

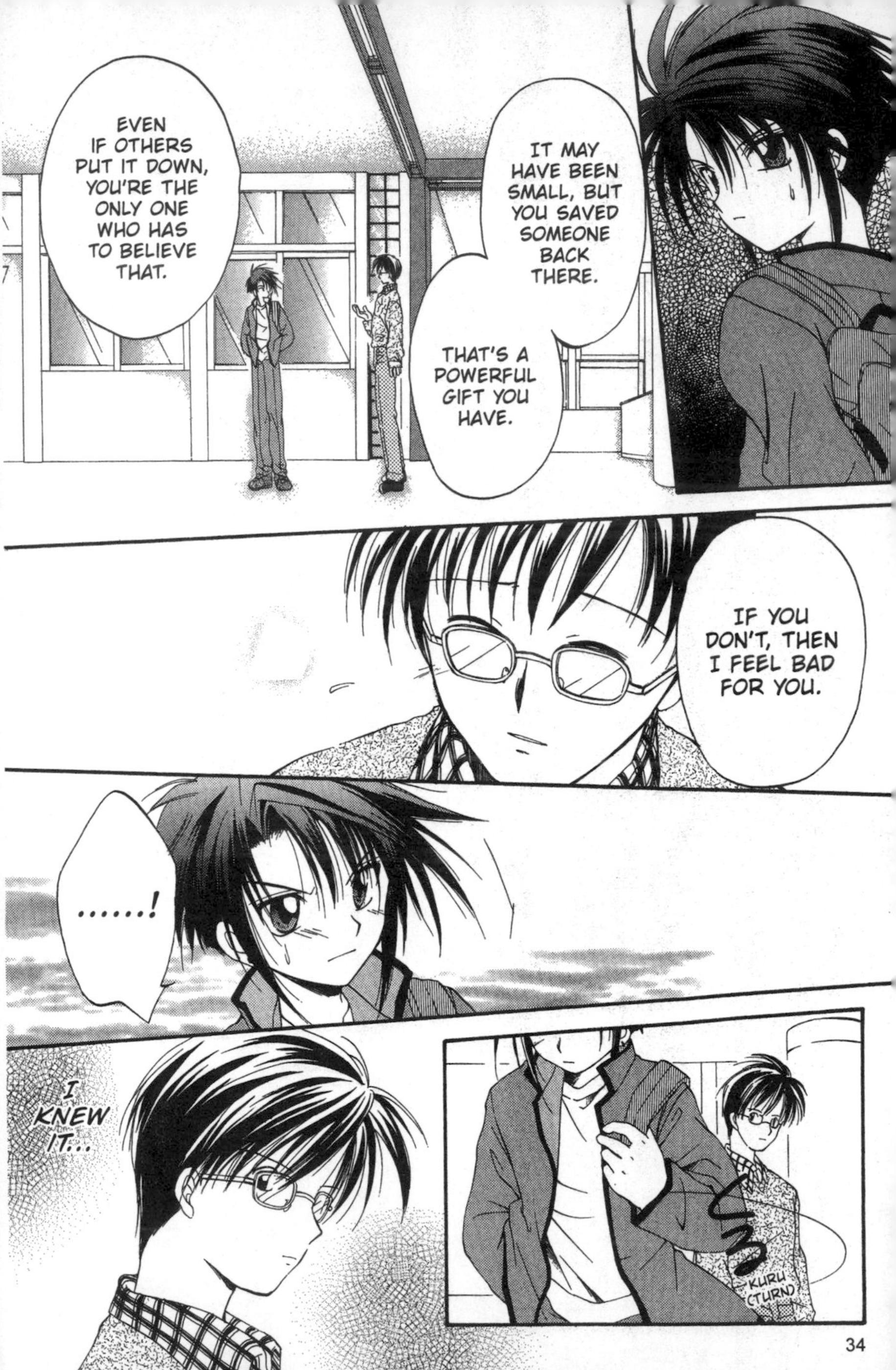
IT MAY HAVE BEEN SMALL, BUT YOU SAVED SOMEONE BACK THERE.
THAT'S A POWERFUL GIFT YOU HAVE.
EVEN IF OTHERS PUT IT DOWN, YOU'RE THE ONLY ONE WHO HAS TO BELIEVE THAT.
IF YOU DON'T, THEN I FEEL BAD FOR YOU.
......!
KURU (TURN)
I KNEW IT...

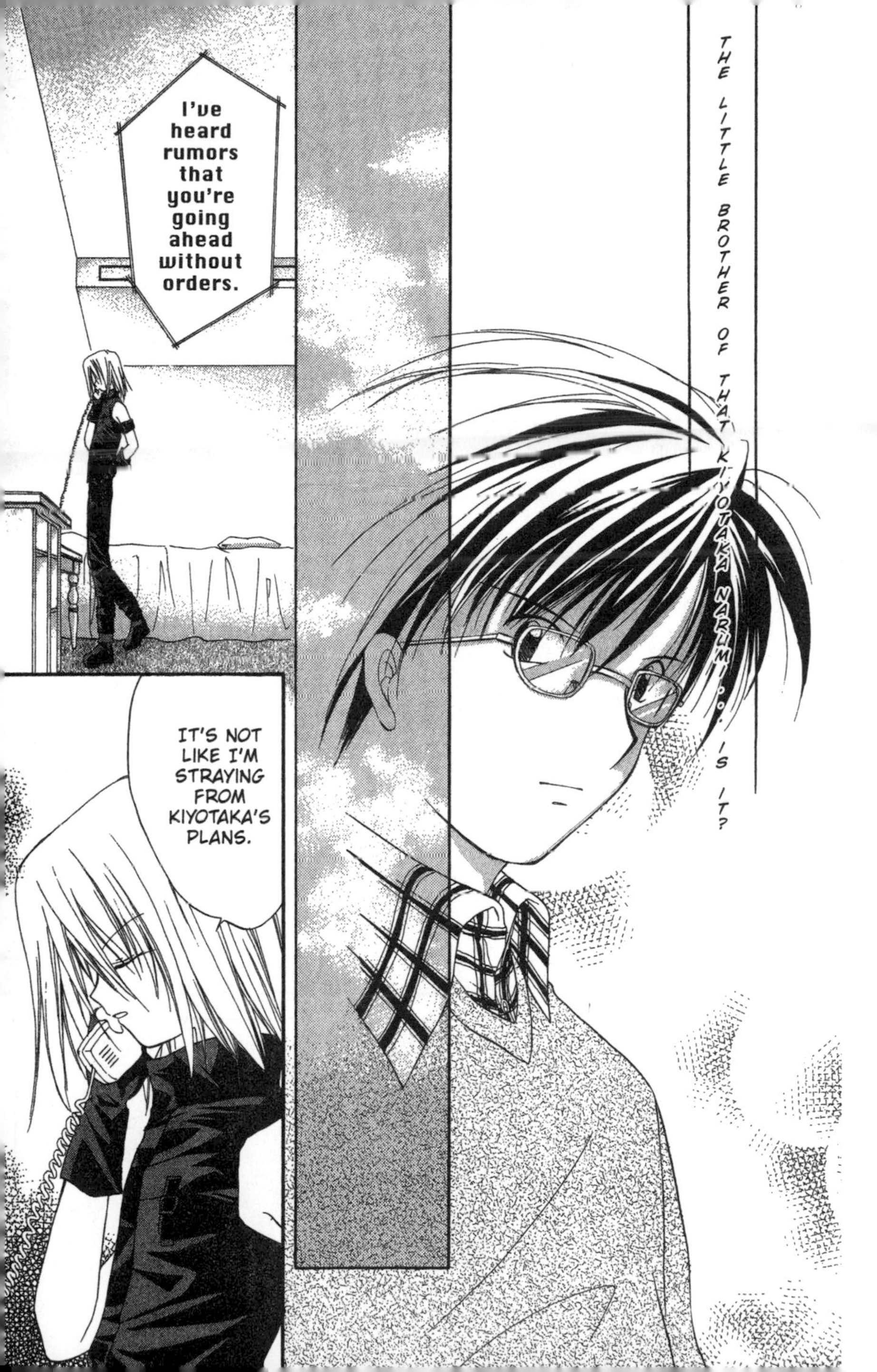
THE LITTLE BROTHER OF THAT KIYOTAKA NARUMI... IS IT?
I've heard rumors that you're going ahead without orders.
IT'S NOT LIKE I'M STRAYING FROM KIYOTAKA'S PLANS.

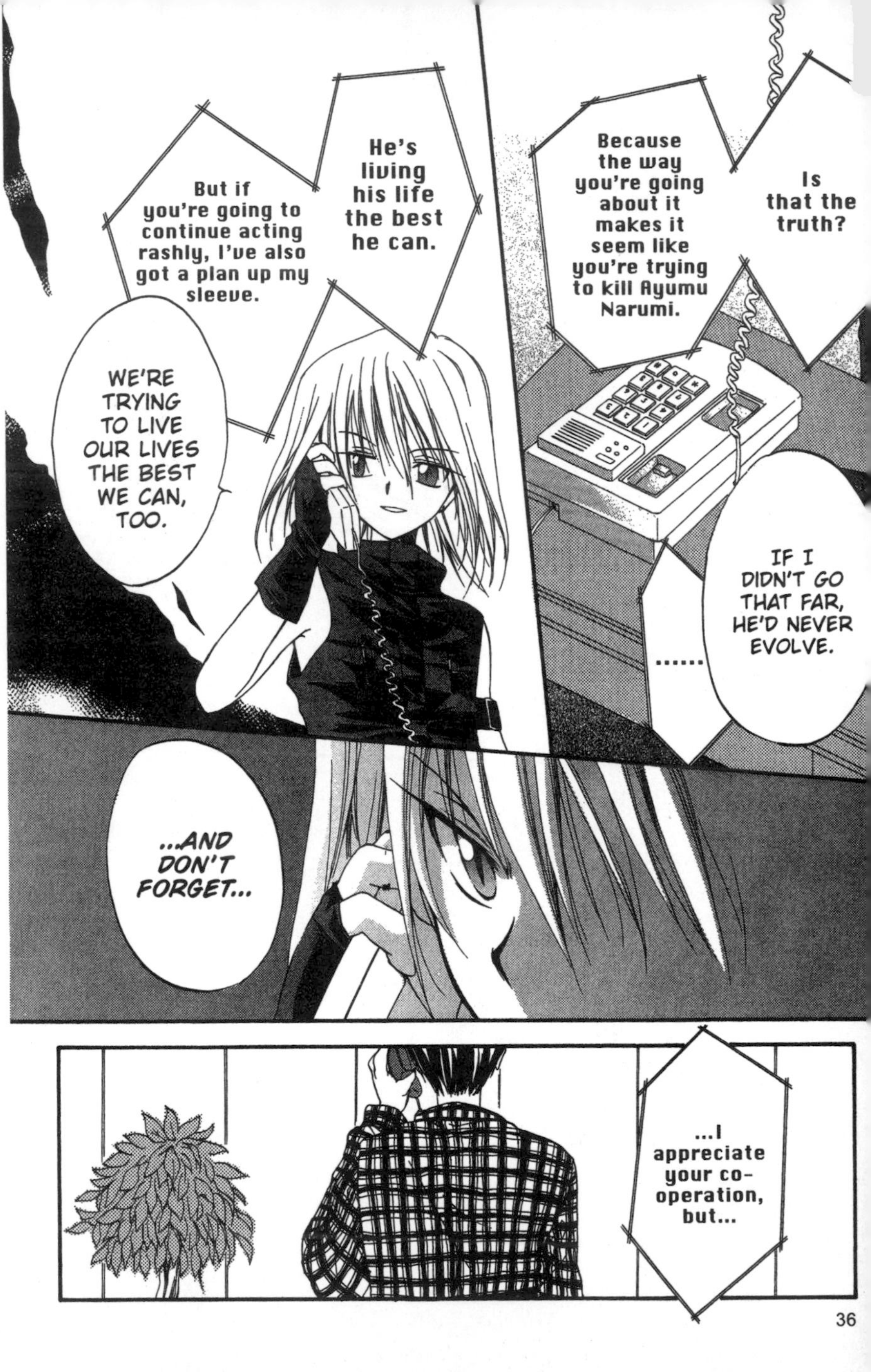

Is that the truth?
Because the way you're going about it makes it seem like you're trying to kill Ayumu Narumi.
......
IF I DIDN'T GO THAT FAR, HE'D NEVER EVOLVE.
He's living his life the best he can.
But if you're going to continue acting rashly, I've also got a plan up my sleeve.
WE'RE TRYING TO LIVE OUR LIVES THE BEST WE CAN, TOO.
...AND DON'T FORGET...
...I appreciate your co-operation, but...

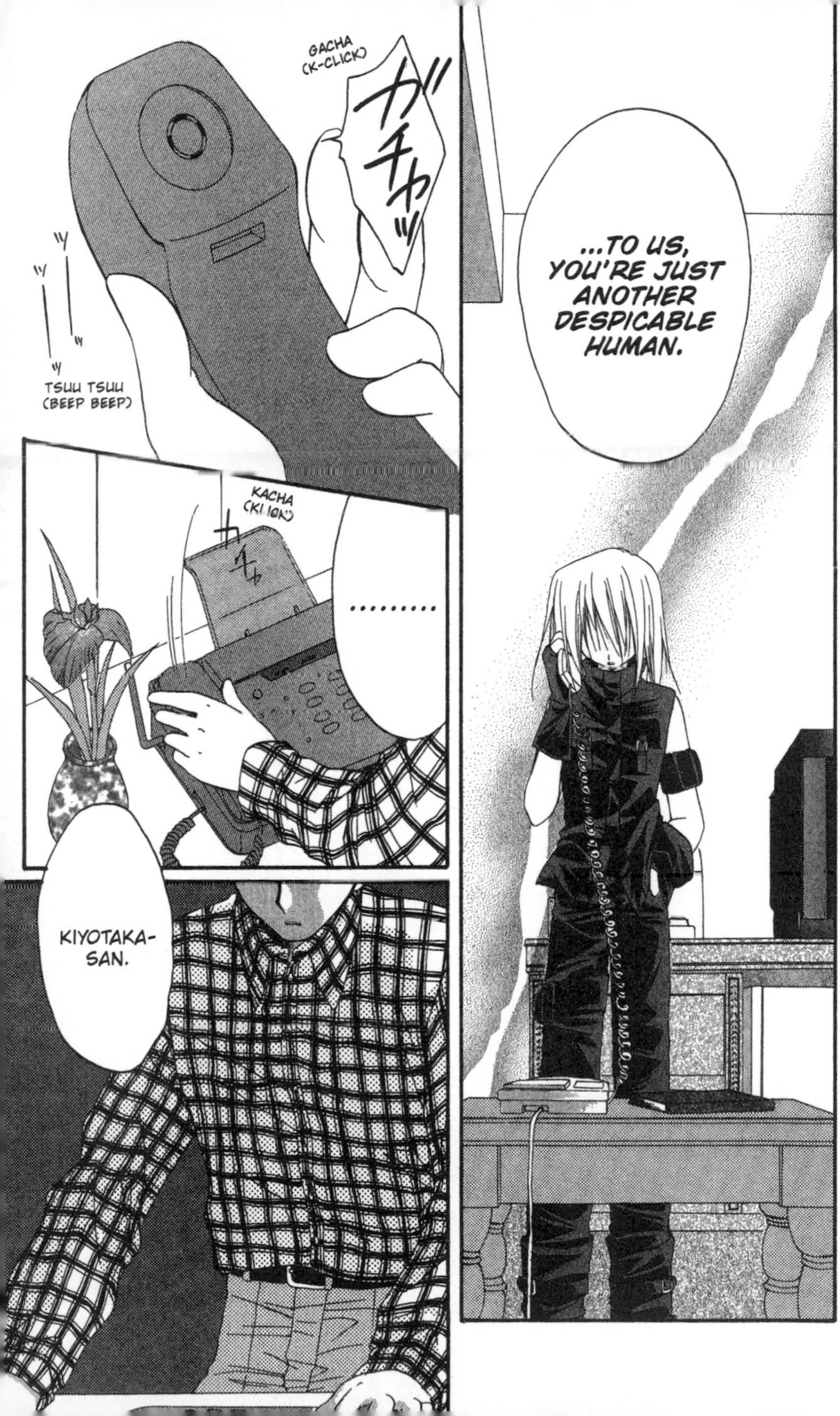
...TO US, YOU'RE JUST ANOTHER DESPICABLE HUMAN.
GACHA (K-CLICK)
TSUU TSUU (BEEP BEEP)
KACHA
....
KIYOTAKA-SAN.

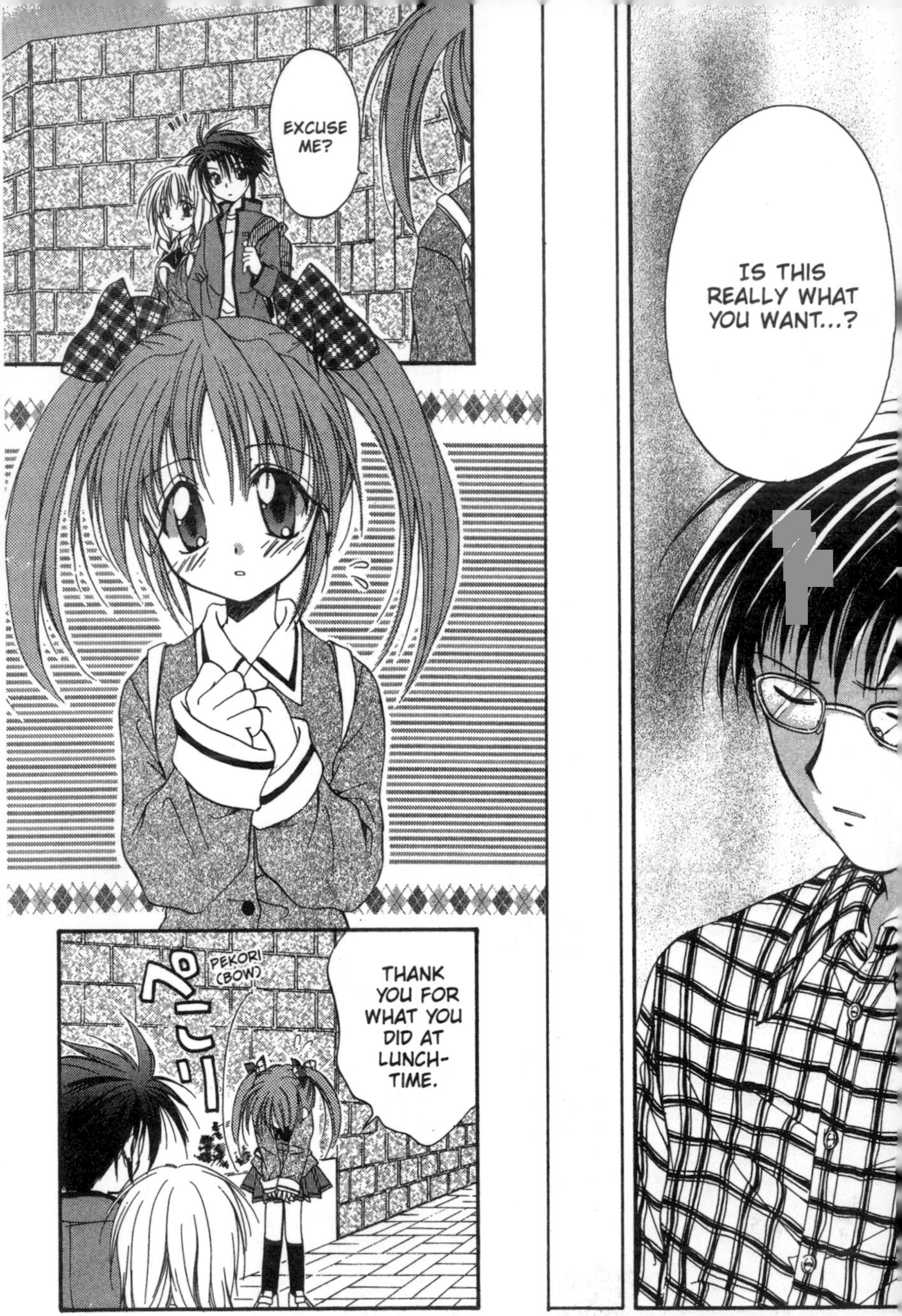
IS THIS REALLY WHAT YOU WANT...?
EXCUSE ME?
THANK YOU FOR WHAT YOU DID AT LUNCH-TIME.
PEKORI (BOW)

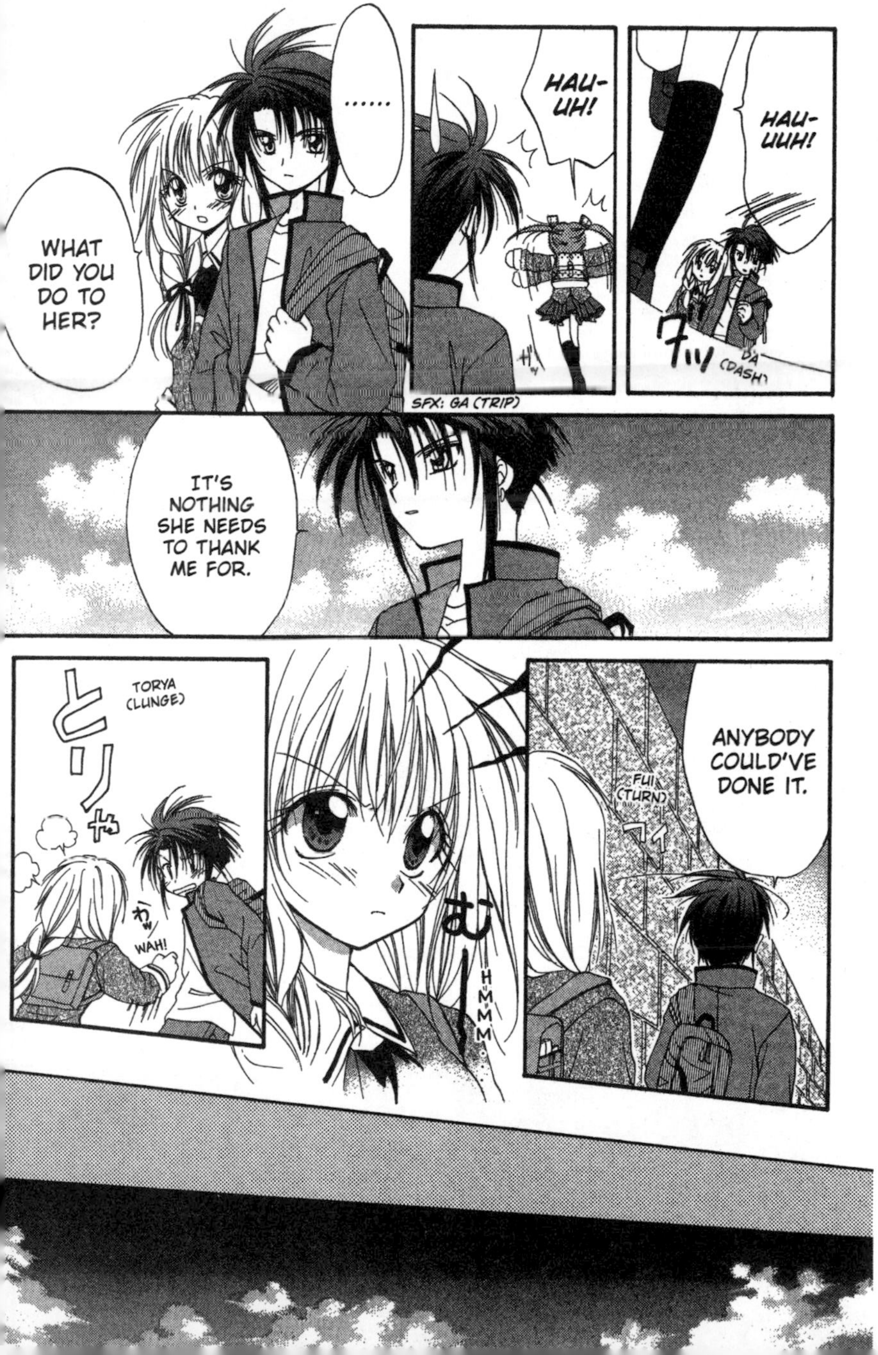

HAU-UUH!
DA (DASH)
HAU-UH!
SFX: GA (TRIP)
......
WHAT DID YOU DO TO HER?
IT'S NOTHING SHE NEEDS TO THANK ME FOR.
ANYBODY COULD'VE DONE IT.
FUI (TURN)
HMMM
TORYA (LUNGE)
WAH!

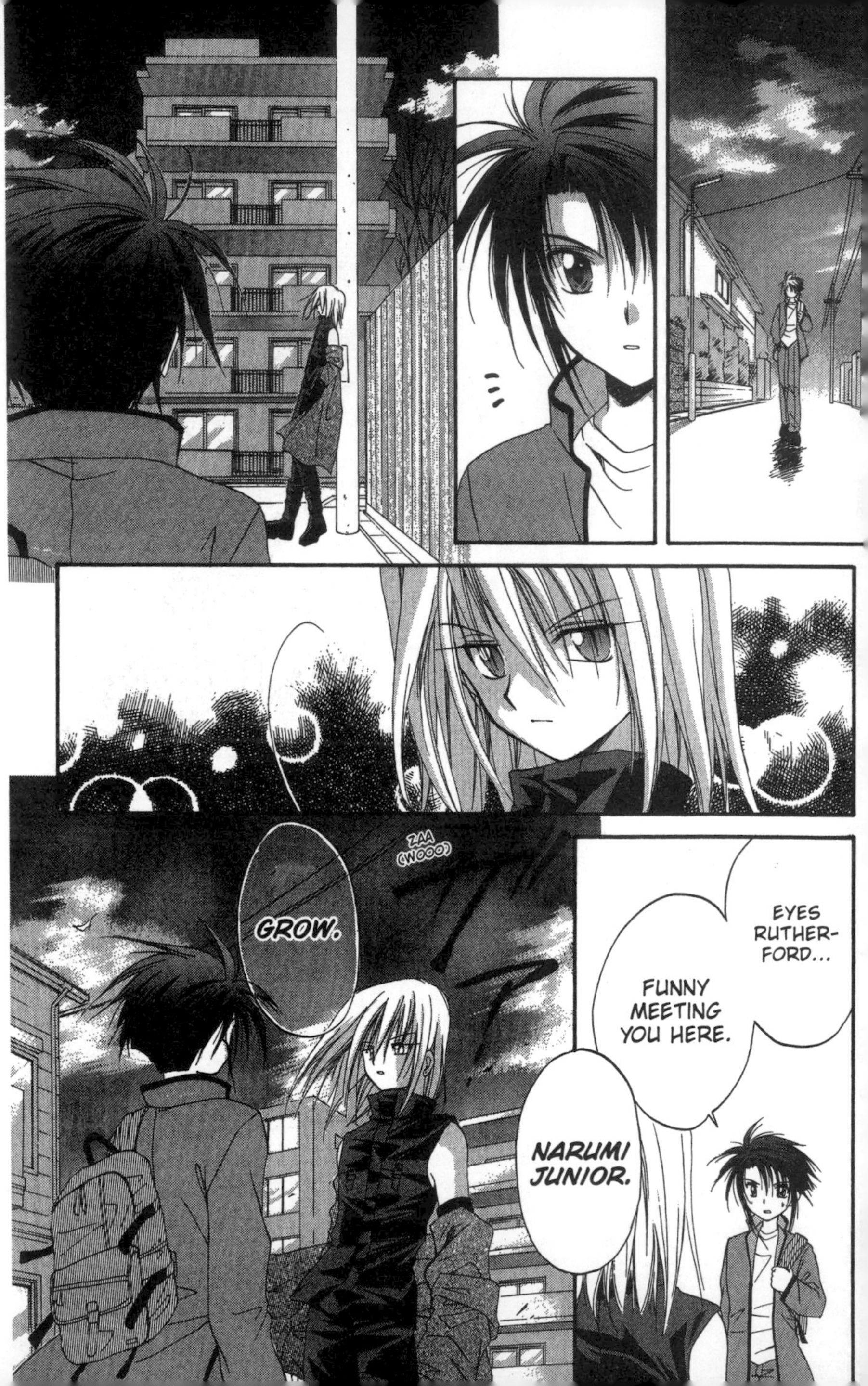
EYES RUTHER-FORD...
FUNNY MEETING YOU HERE.
NARUMI JUNIOR.
ZAA (WOOO)
GROW.

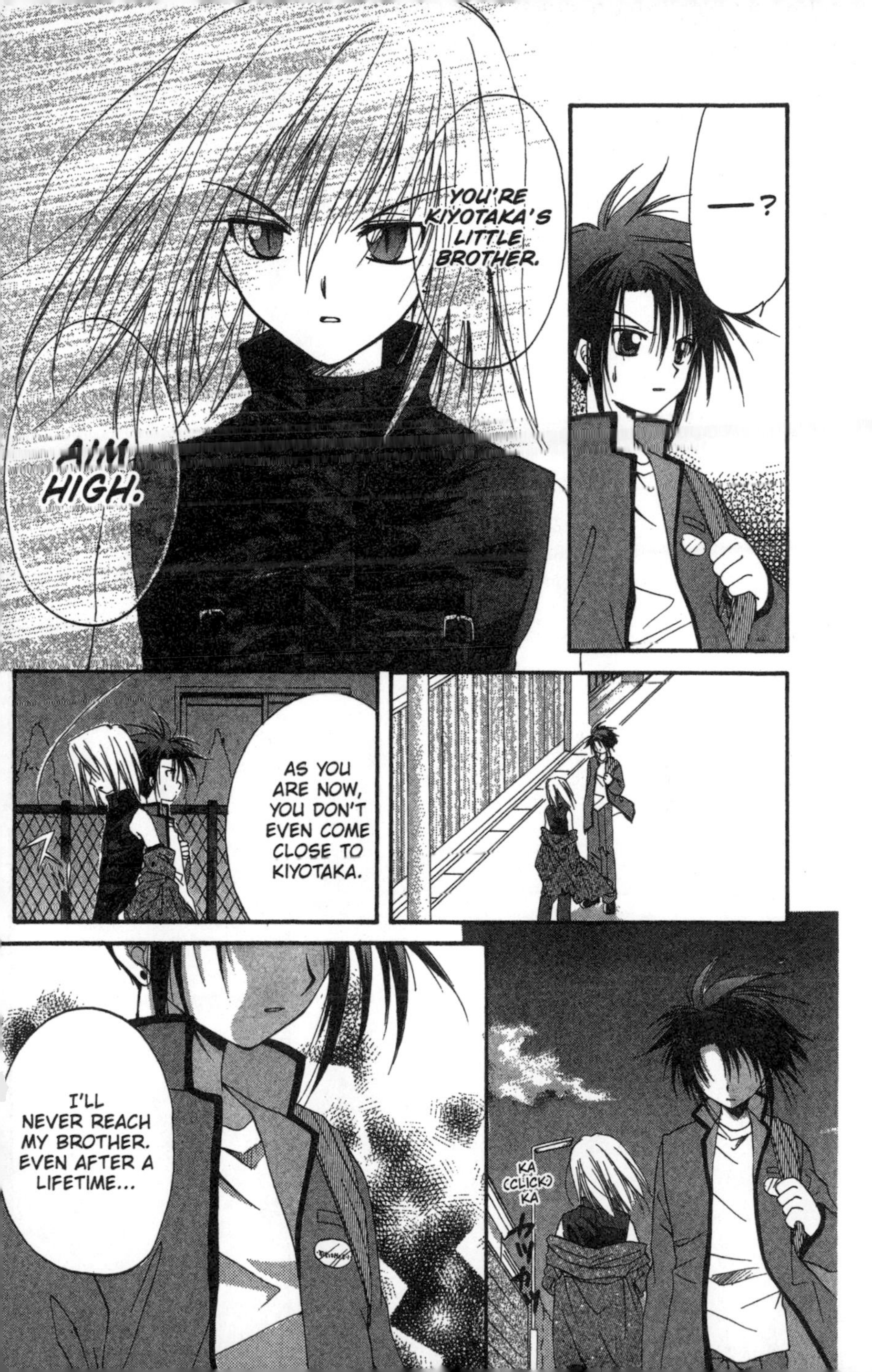
—?
YOU'RE KIYOTAKA'S LITTLE BROTHER.
AIM HIGH.
AS YOU ARE NOW, YOU DON'T EVEN COME CLOSE TO KIYOTAKA.
KA (CLICK) KA
I'LL NEVER REACH MY BROTHER. EVEN AFTER A LIFETIME...

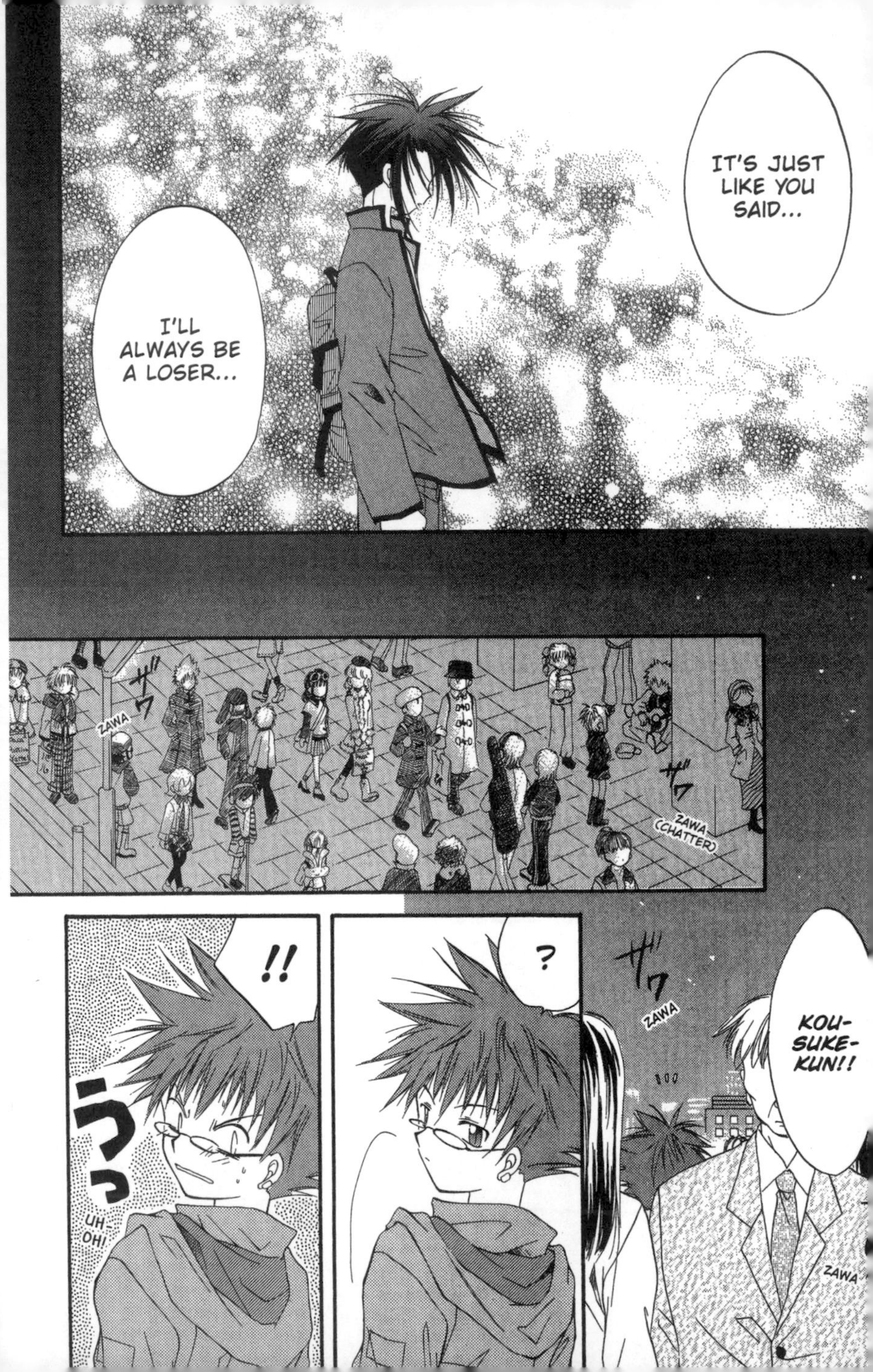
IT'S JUST LIKE YOU SAID...
I'LL ALWAYS BE A LOSER...
ザワ
ZAWA (CHATTER)
ザワ
ZAWA
ザワ
ZAWA
KOU-SUKE-KUN!!
ZAWA
?
!!
うっ
UH-OH!

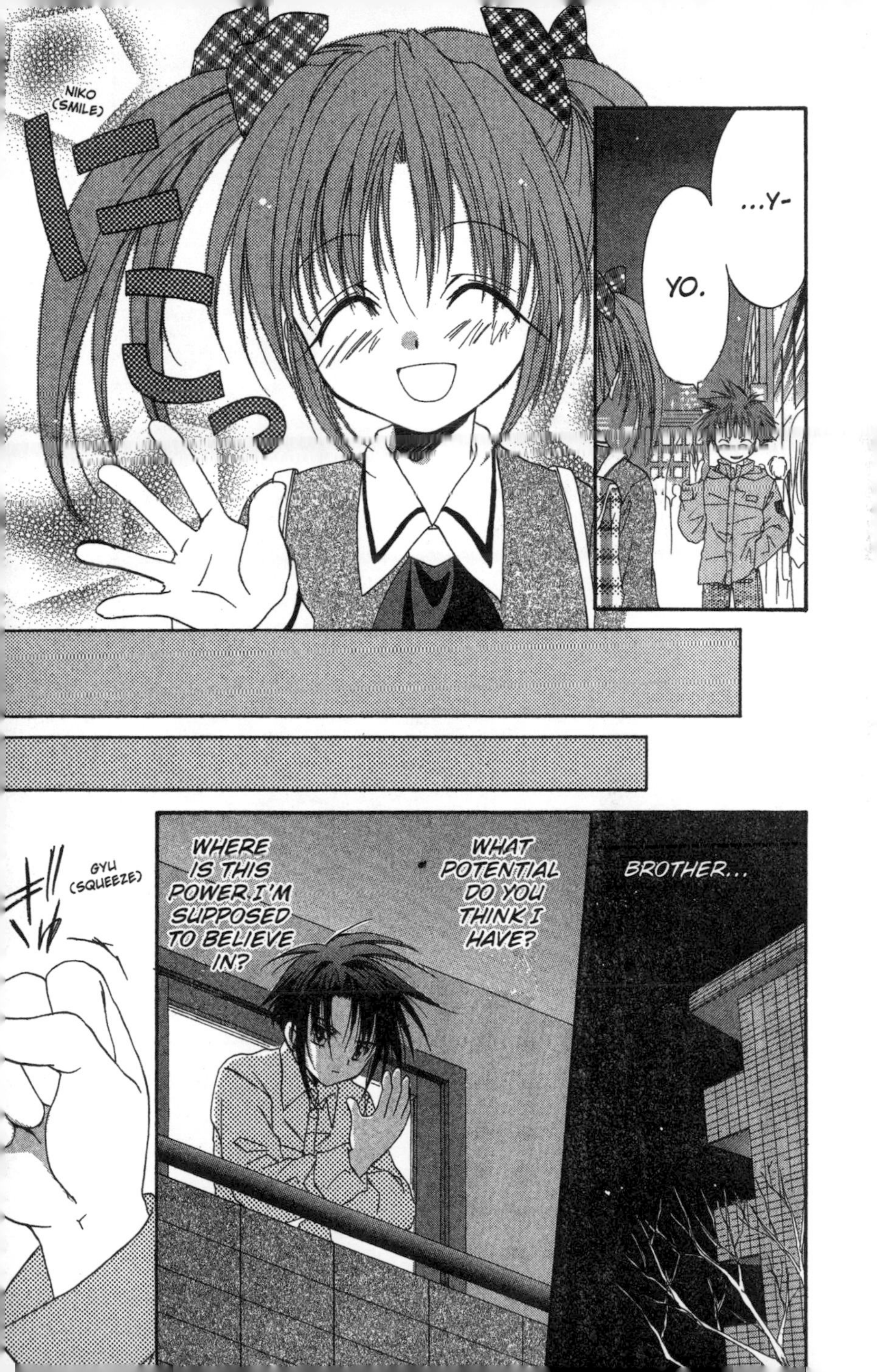
...Y-
YO.
NIKO (SMILE)
BROTHER...
WHAT POTENTIAL DO YOU THINK I HAVE?
WHERE IS THIS POWER I'M SUPPOSED TO BELIEVE IN?
GYU (SQUEEZE)

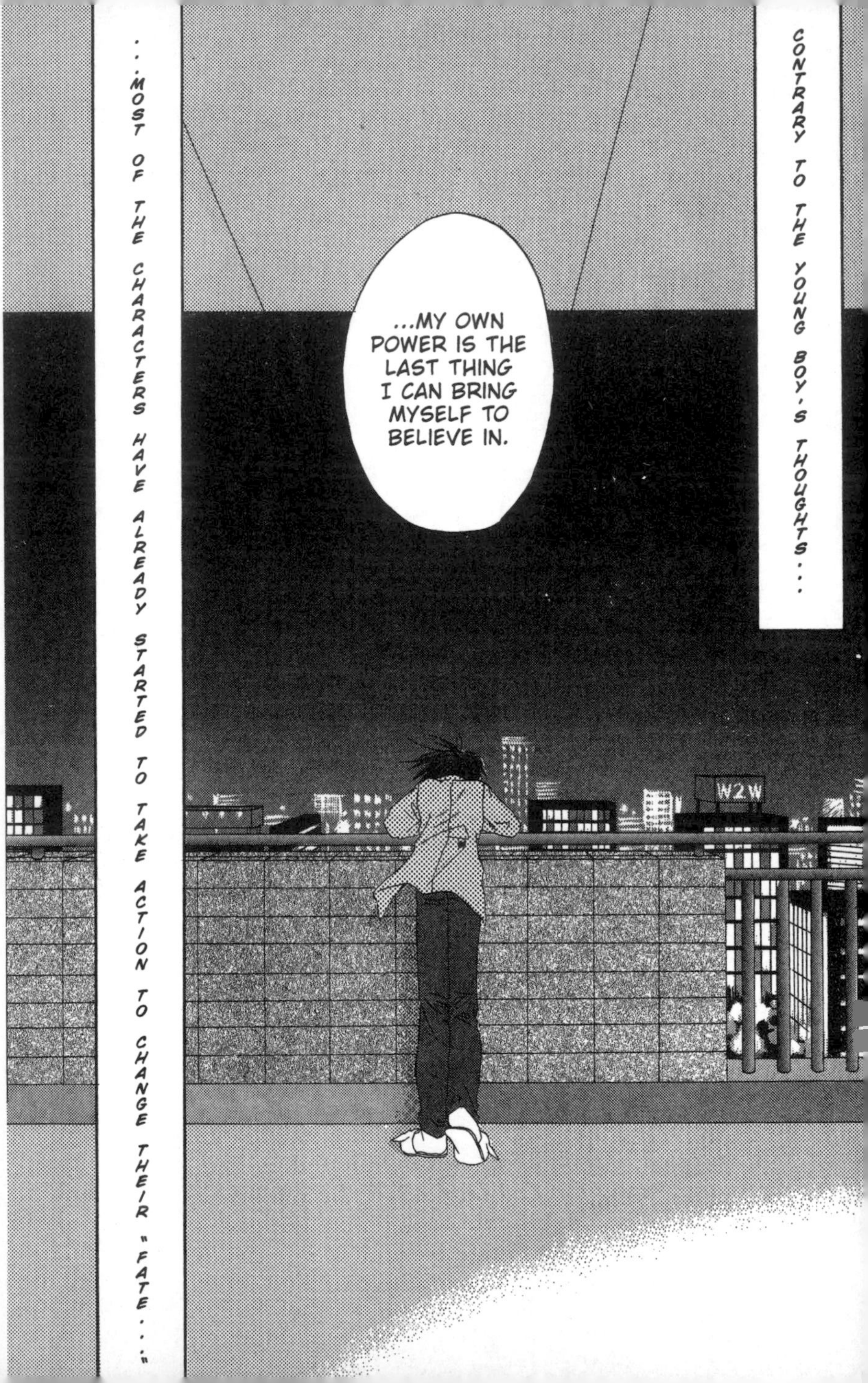
CONTRARY TO THE YOUNG BOY'S THOUGHTS...
...MY OWN POWER IS THE LAST THING I CAN BRING MYSELF TO BELIEVE IN.
...MOST OF THE CHARACTERS HAVE ALREADY STARTED TO TAKE ACTION TO CHANGE THEIR "FATE..."

Spiral

THE BONDS OF REASONING

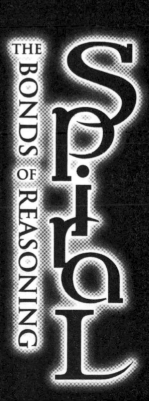

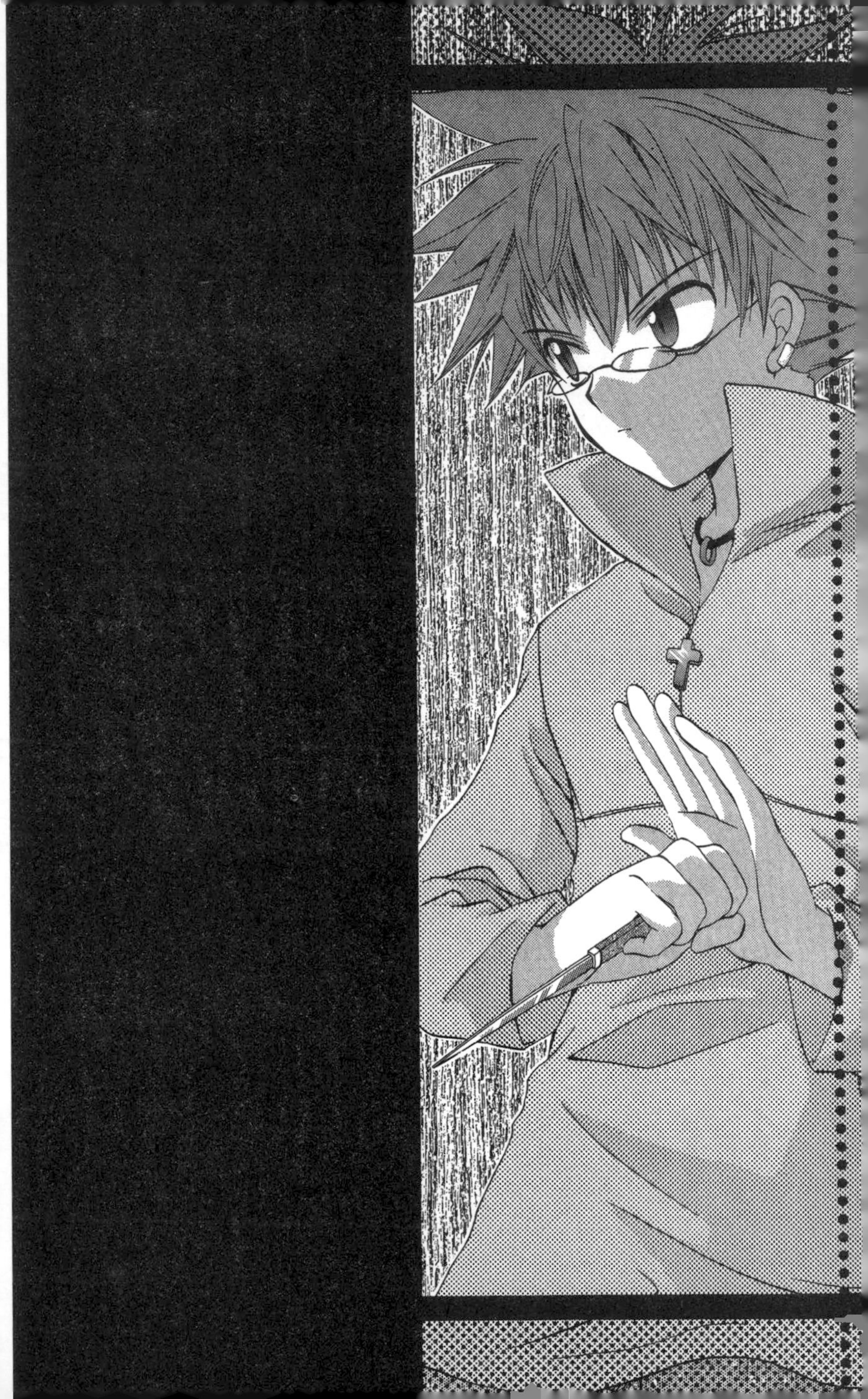

CHAPTER TWELVE
VERSUS RIO

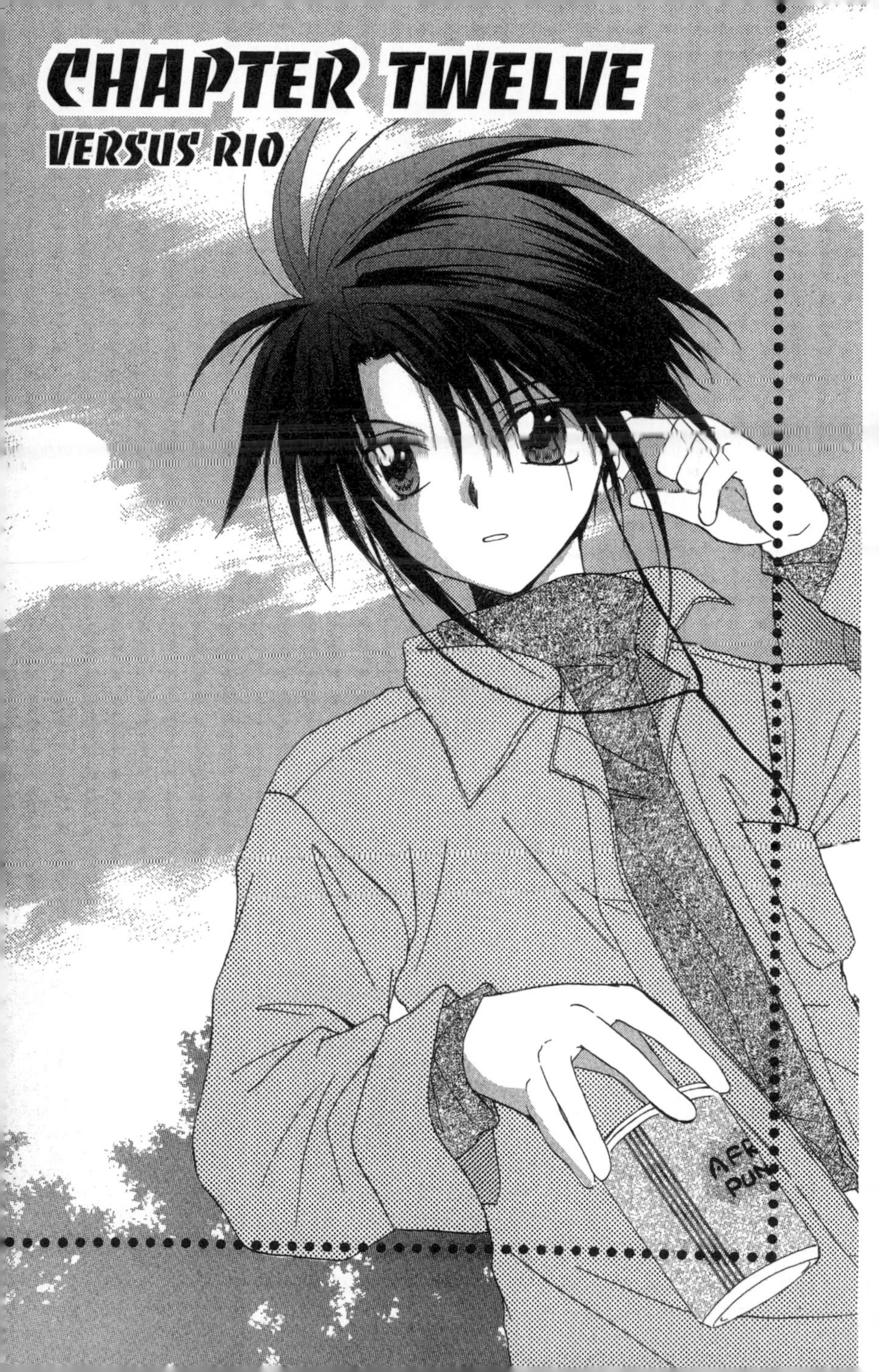
AFR
PUN

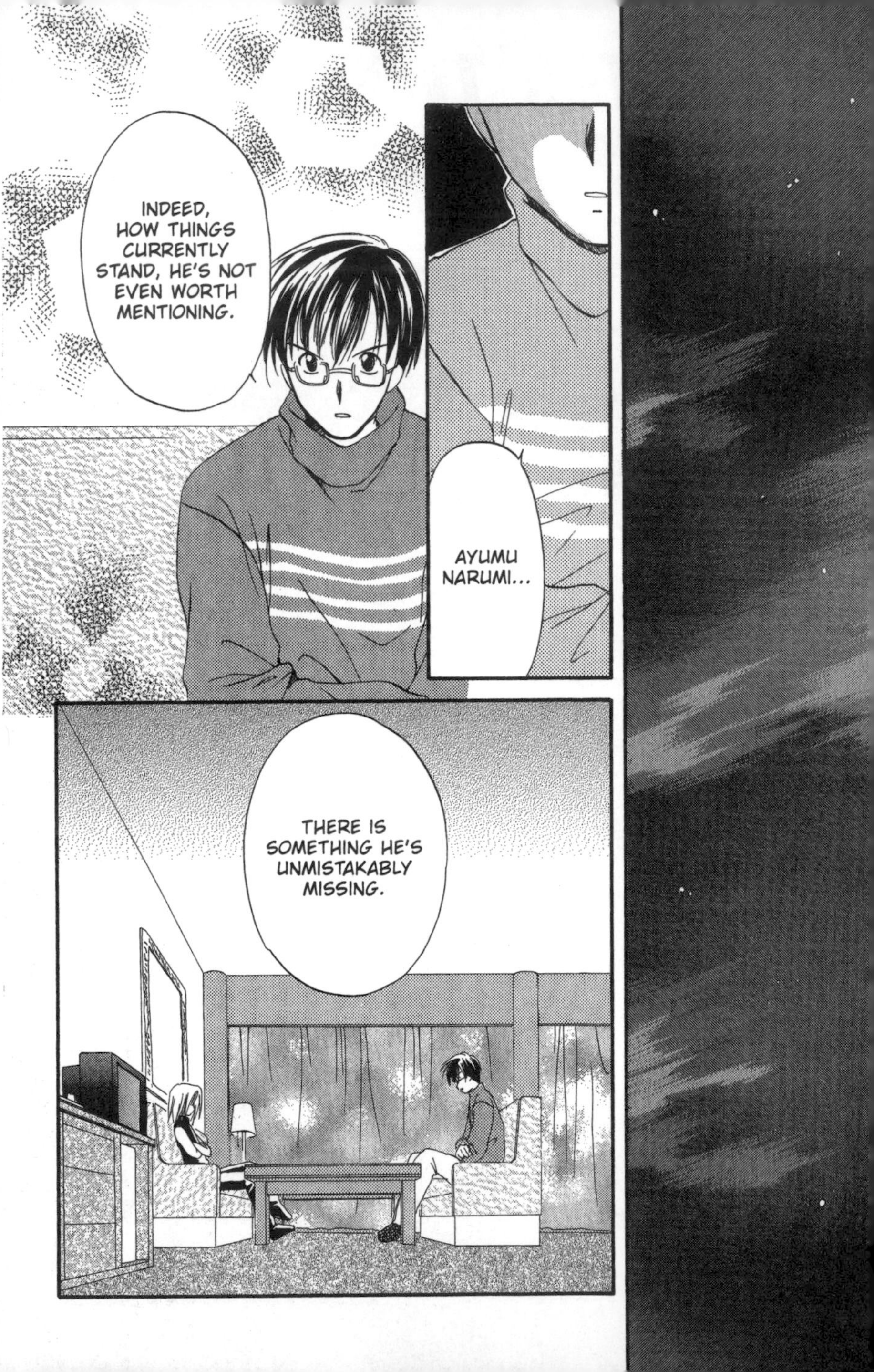
AYUMU NARUMI...
INDEED, HOW THINGS CURRENTLY STAND, HE'S NOT EVEN WORTH MENTIONING.
THERE IS SOMETHING HE'S UNMISTAKABLY MISSING.

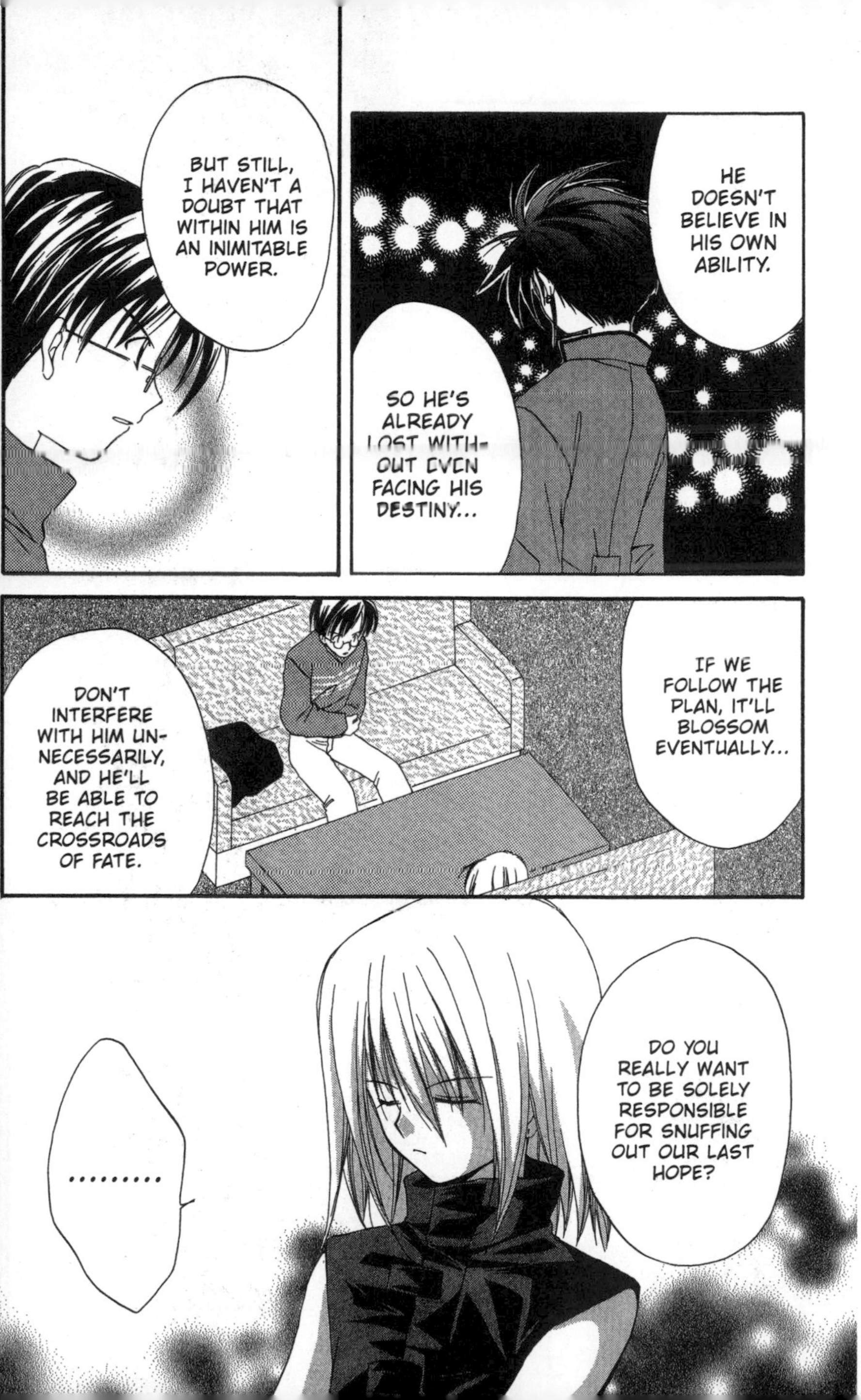
HE DOESN'T BELIEVE IN HIS OWN ABILITY.
SO HE'S ALREADY LOST WITH-OUT EVEN FACING HIS DESTINY...
BUT STILL, I HAVEN'T A DOUBT THAT WITHIN HIM IS AN INIMITABLE POWER.
IF WE FOLLOW THE PLAN, IT'LL BLOSSOM EVENTUALLY...
DON'T INTERFERE WITH HIM UN-NECESSARILY, AND HE'LL BE ABLE TO REACH THE CROSSROADS OF FATE.
DO YOU REALLY WANT TO BE SOLELY RESPONSIBLE FOR SNUFFING OUT OUR LAST HOPE?
....

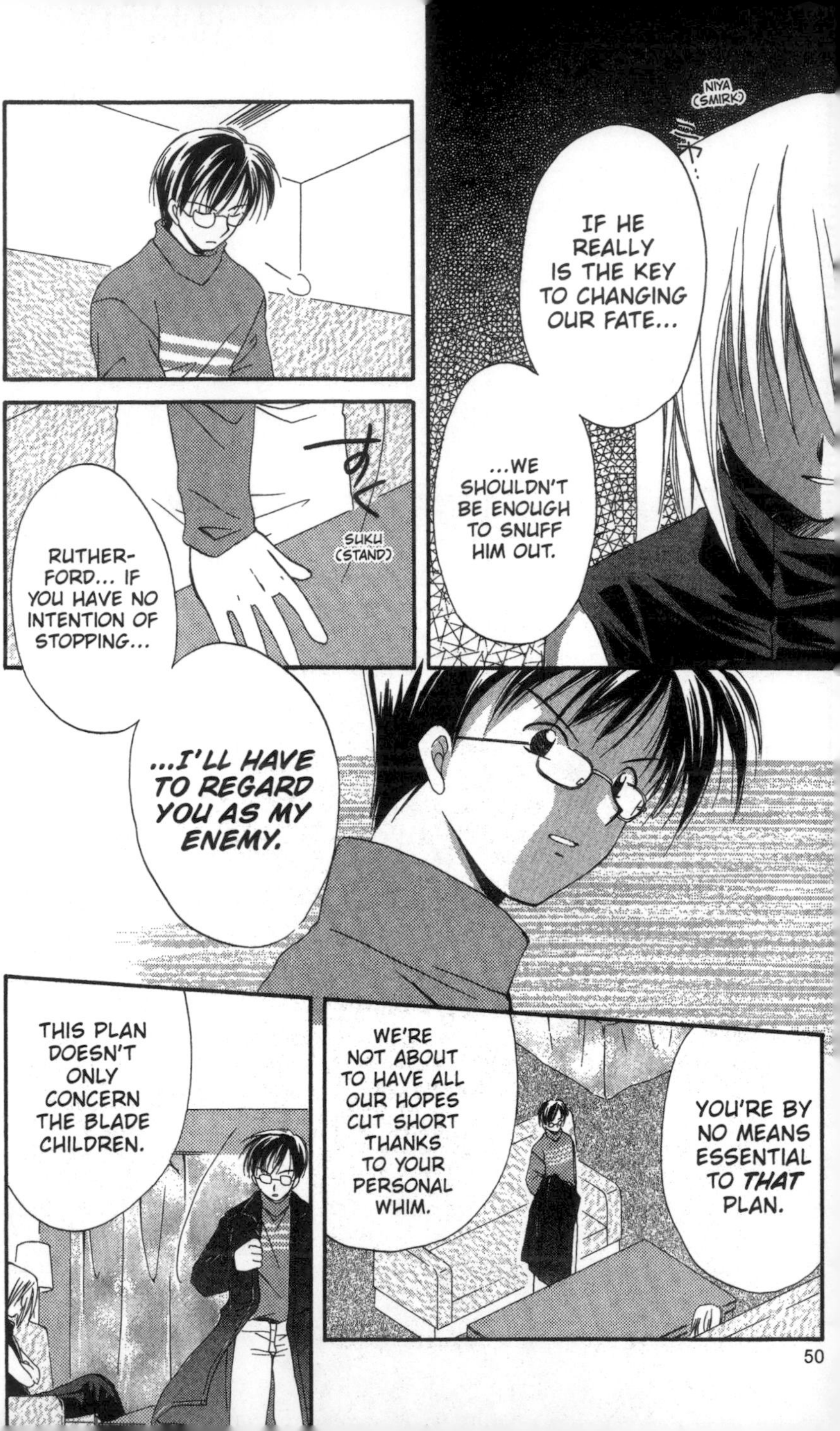
NIYA (SMIRK)
IF HE REALLY IS THE KEY TO CHANGING OUR FATE...
...WE SHOULDN'T BE ENOUGH TO SNUFF HIM OUT.
SUKU (STAND)
RUTHER-FORD... IF YOU HAVE NO INTENTION OF STOPPING...
...I'LL HAVE TO REGARD YOU AS MY ENEMY.
YOU'RE BY NO MEANS ESSENTIAL TO THAT PLAN.
WE'RE NOT ABOUT TO HAVE ALL OUR HOPES CUT SHORT THANKS TO YOUR PERSONAL WHIM.
THIS PLAN DOESN'T ONLY CONCERN THE BLADE CHILDREN.

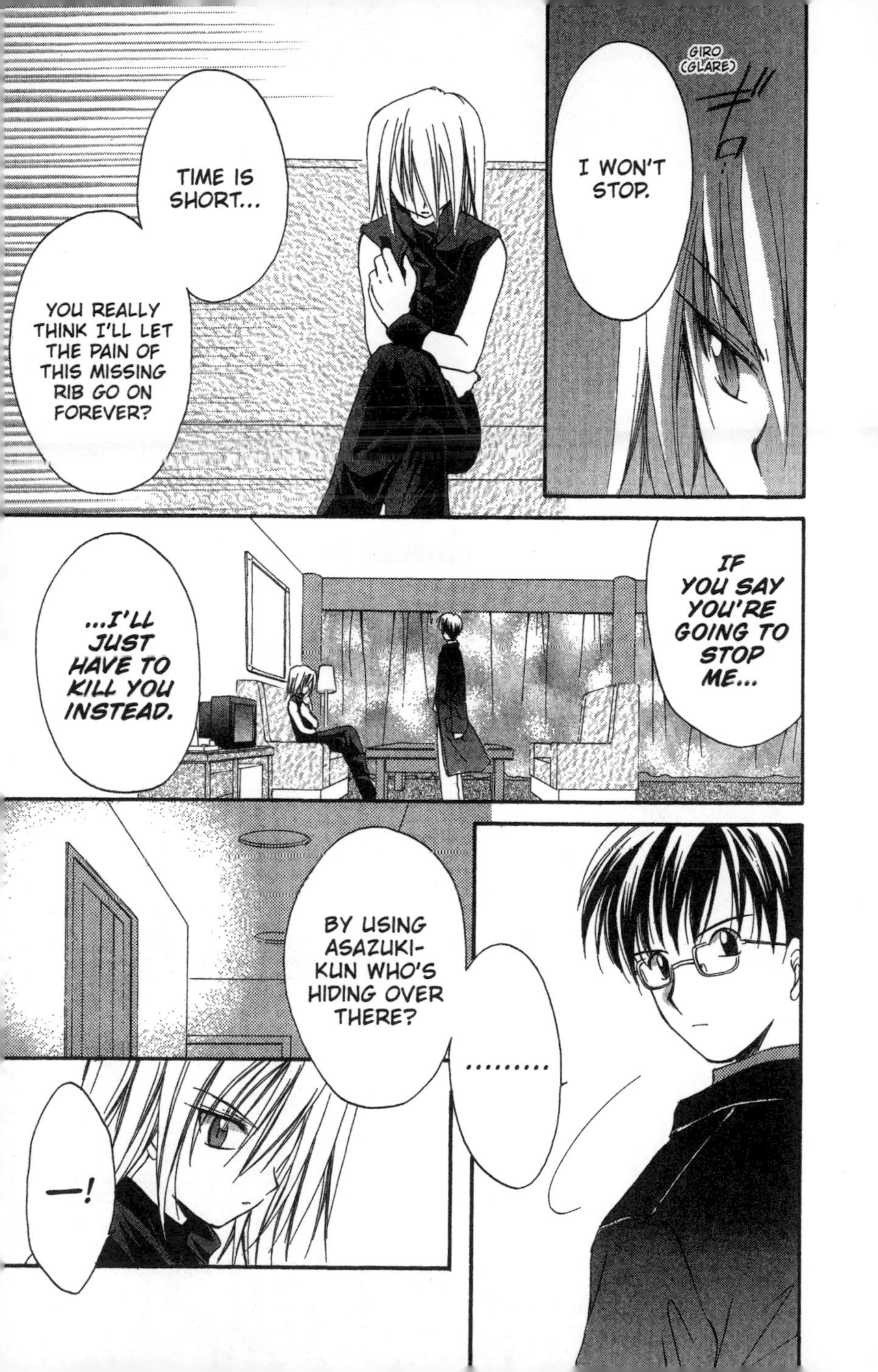

GIRO (GLARE)
I WON'T STOP.
TIME IS SHORT...
YOU REALLY THINK I'LL LET THE PAIN OF THIS MISSING RIB GO ON FOREVER?
IF YOU SAY YOU'RE GOING TO STOP ME...
...I'LL JUST HAVE TO KILL YOU INSTEAD.
BY USING ASAZUKI-KUN WHO'S HIDING OVER THERE?
....
—!

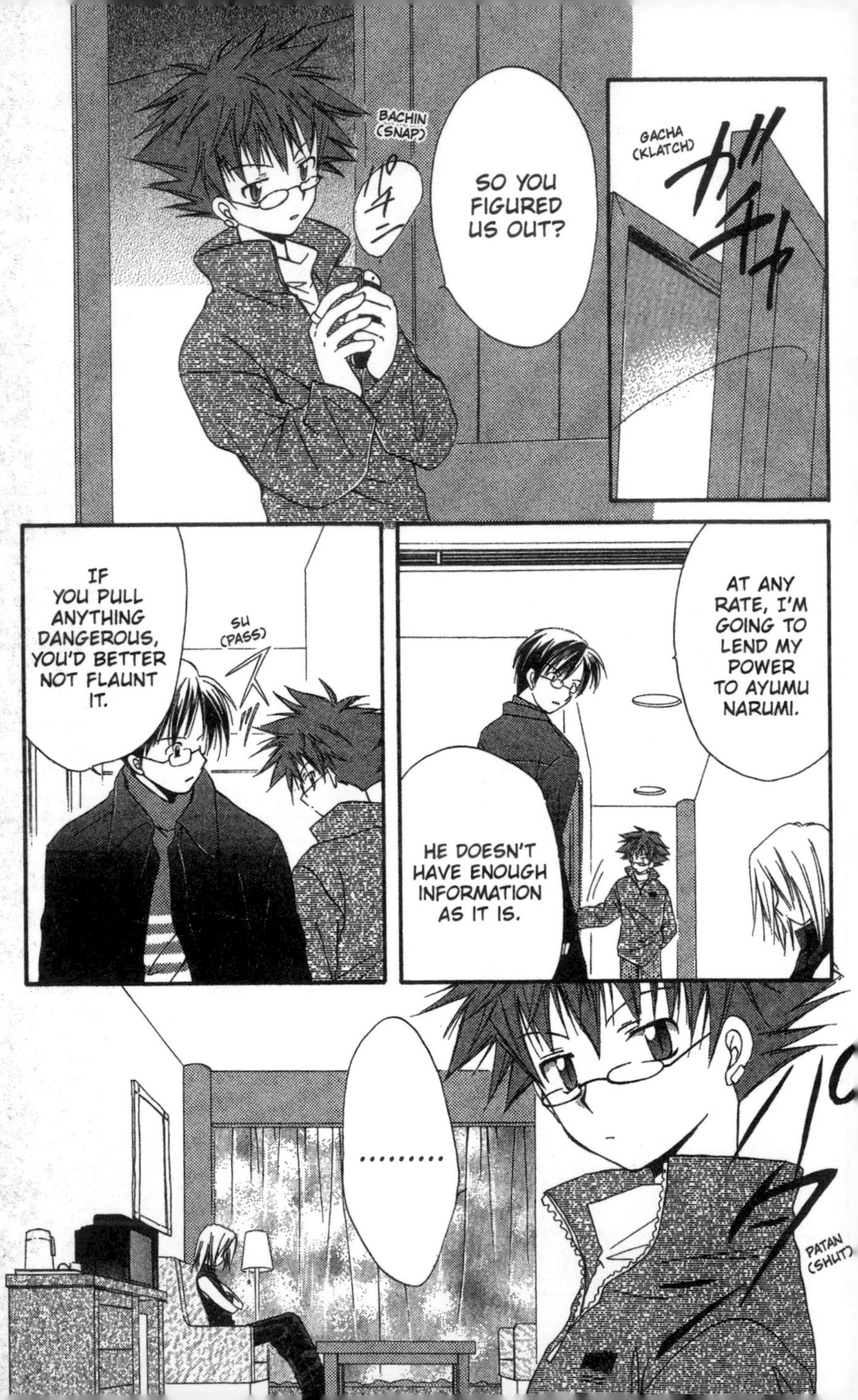
GACHA (KLATCH)
SO YOU FIGURED US OUT?
BACHIN (SNAP)
AT ANY RATE, I'M GOING TO LEND MY POWER TO AYUMU NARUMI.
HE DOESN'T HAVE ENOUGH INFORMATION AS IT IS.
IF YOU PULL ANYTHING DANGEROUS, YOU'D BETTER NOT FLAUNT IT.
SU (PASS)
PATAN (SHUT)
....

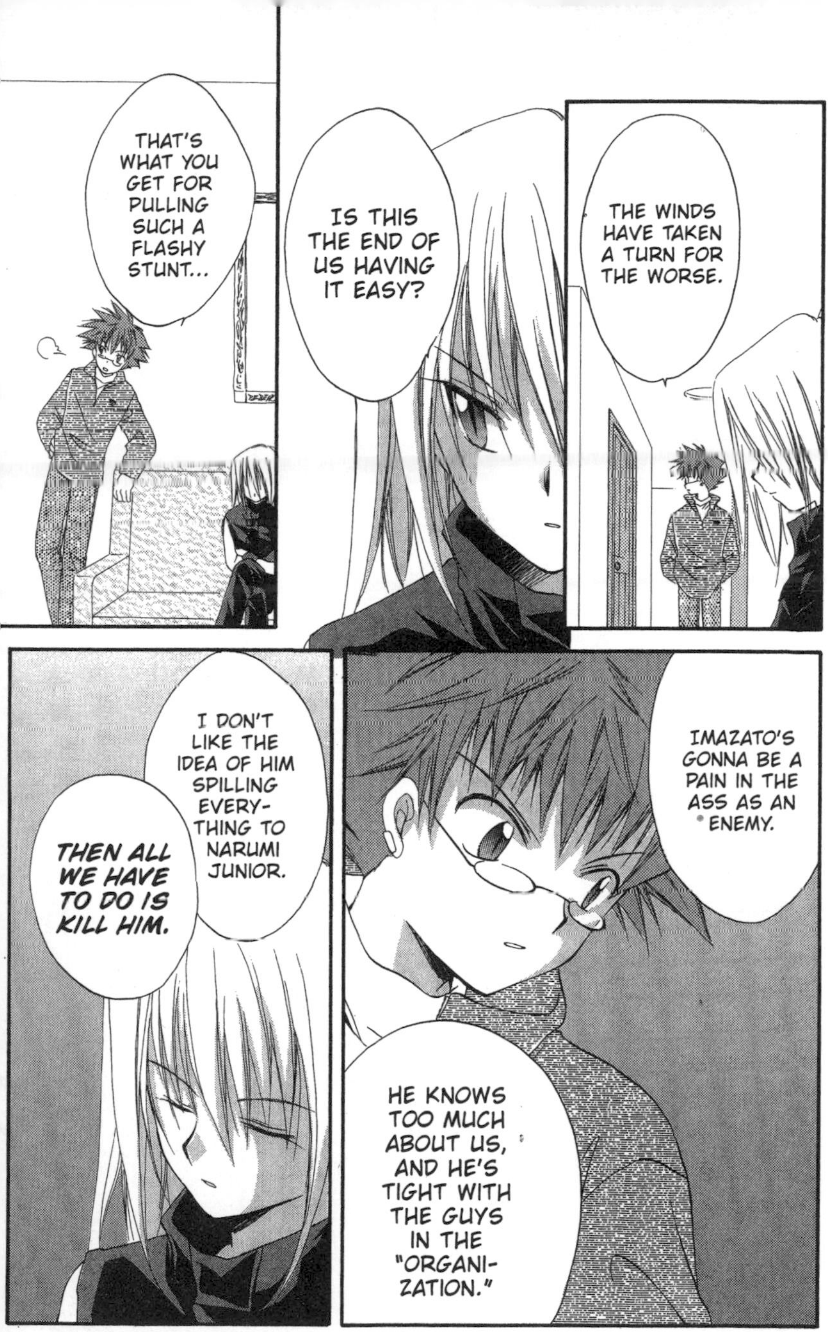
THE WINDS HAVE TAKEN A TURN FOR THE WORSE.
IS THIS THE END OF US HAVING IT EASY?
THAT'S WHAT YOU GET FOR PULLING SUCH A FLASHY STUNT...
IMAZATO'S GONNA BE A PAIN IN THE ASS AS AN ENEMY.
HE KNOWS TOO MUCH ABOUT US, AND HE'S TIGHT WITH THE GUYS IN THE "ORGANI-ZATION."
I DON'T LIKE THE IDEA OF HIM SPILLING EVERY-THING TO NARUMI JUNIOR.
THEN ALL WE HAVE TO DO IS KILL HIM.

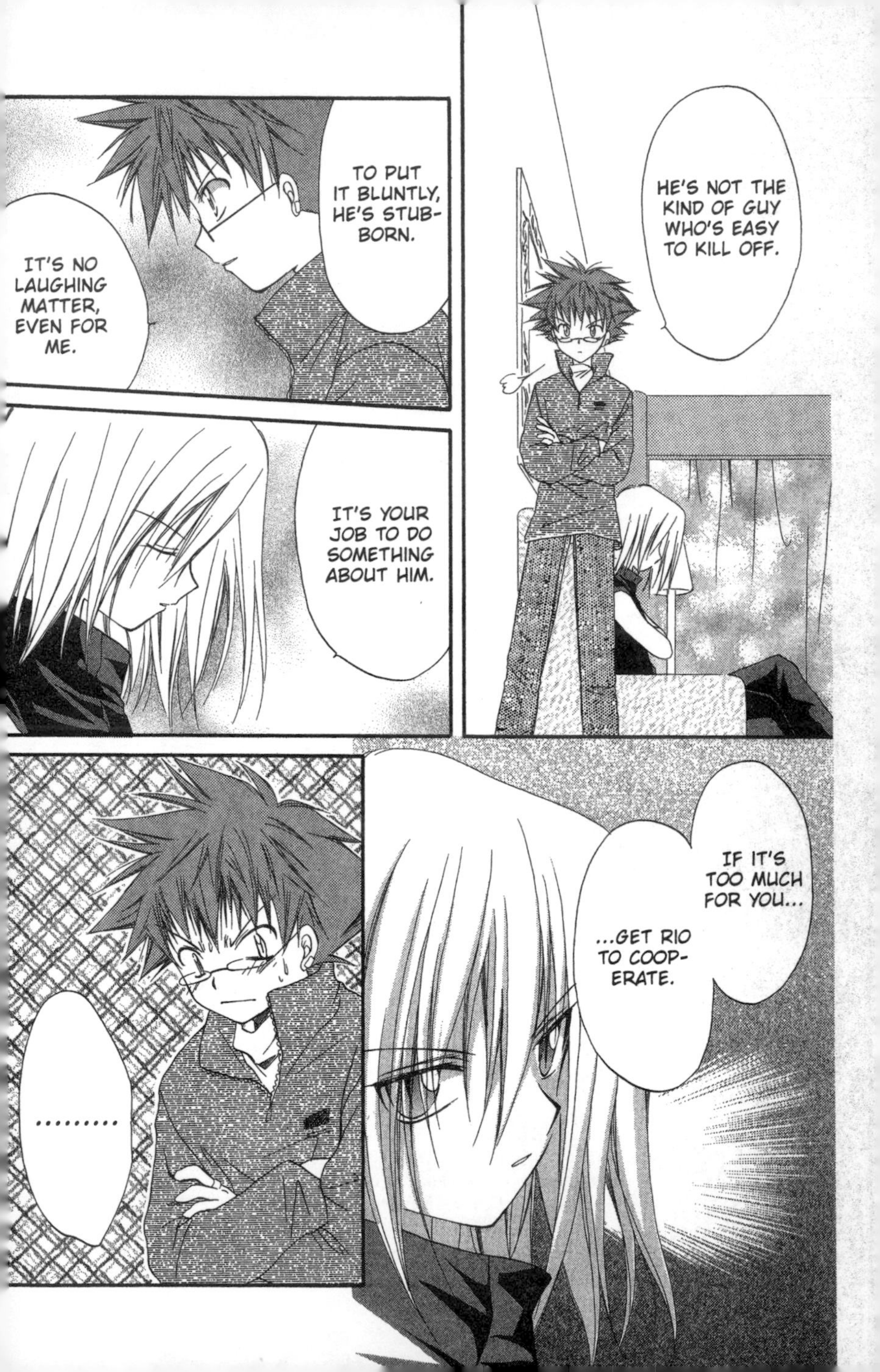
HE'S NOT THE KIND OF GUY WHO'S EASY TO KILL OFF.
TO PUT IT BLUNTLY, HE'S STUB-BORN.
IT'S NO LAUGHING MATTER, EVEN FOR ME.
IT'S YOUR JOB TO DO SOMETHING ABOUT HIM.
IF IT'S TOO MUCH FOR YOU...
...GET RIO TO COOP-ERATE.
....

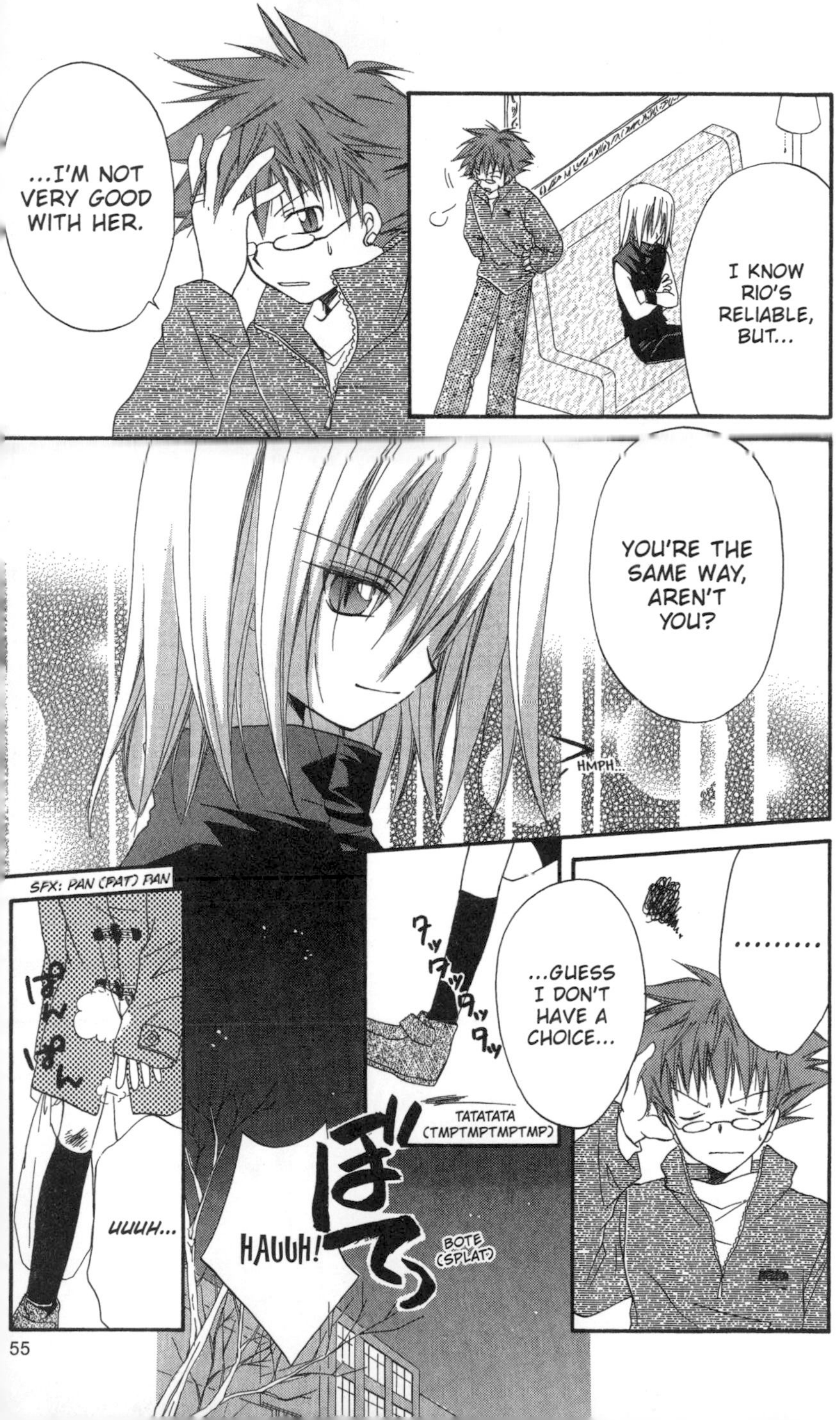
I KNOW RIO'S RELIABLE, BUT...
...I'M NOT VERY GOOD WITH HER.
YOU'RE THE SAME WAY, AREN'T YOU?
HMPH...
....
...GUESS I DON'T HAVE A CHOICE...
TATATATA (TMPTMPTMPTMP)
HAUUH!
BOTE (SPLAT)
SFX: PAN (PAT) PAN
uuuh...

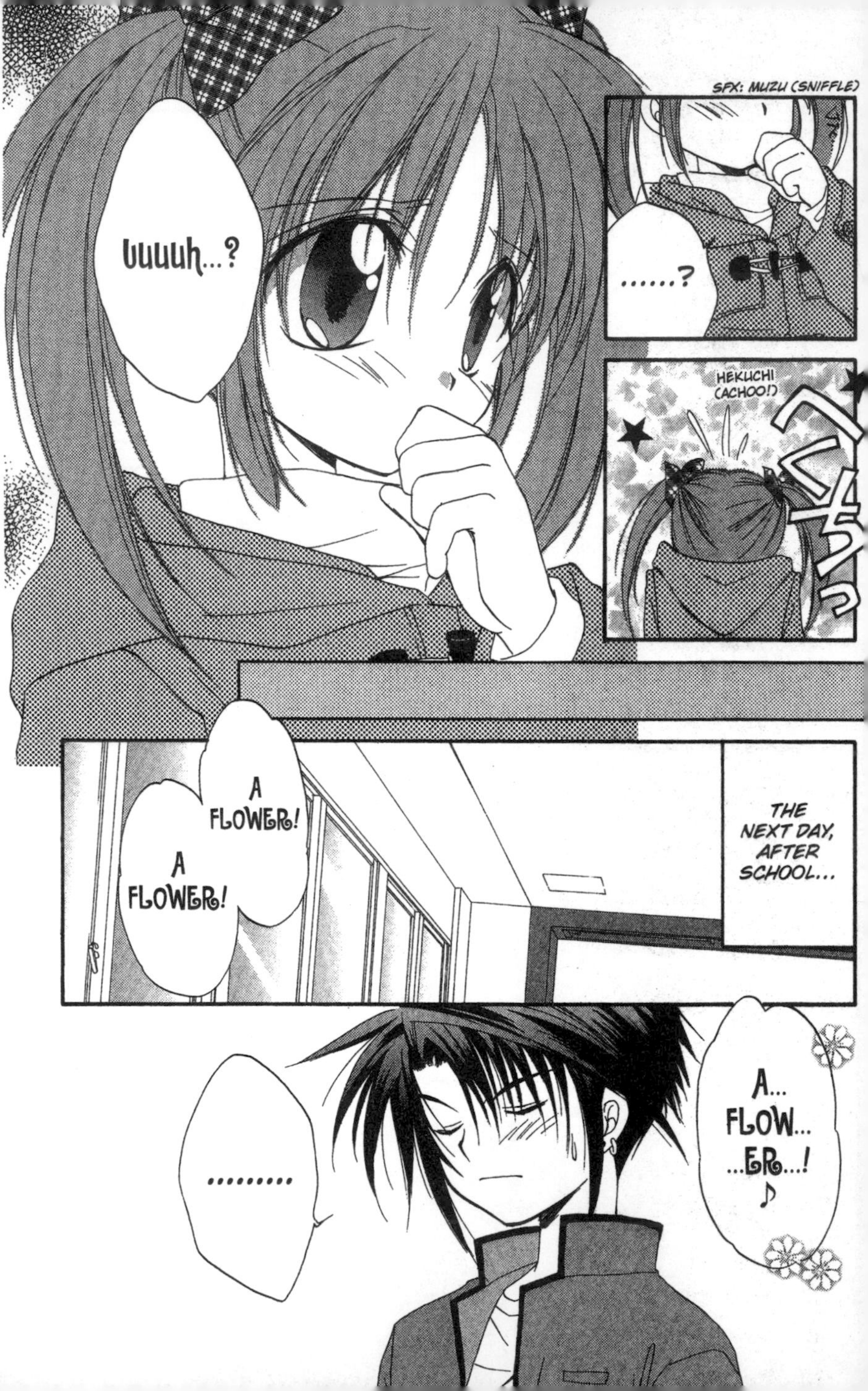

SFX: MUZU (SNIFFLE)
......?
HEKUCHI (ACHOO!)
へくちっ
Uuuuh...?
THE NEXT DAY, AFTER SCHOOL...
A FLOWER!
A FLOWER!
A... FLOW... ...ER...! ♪
....

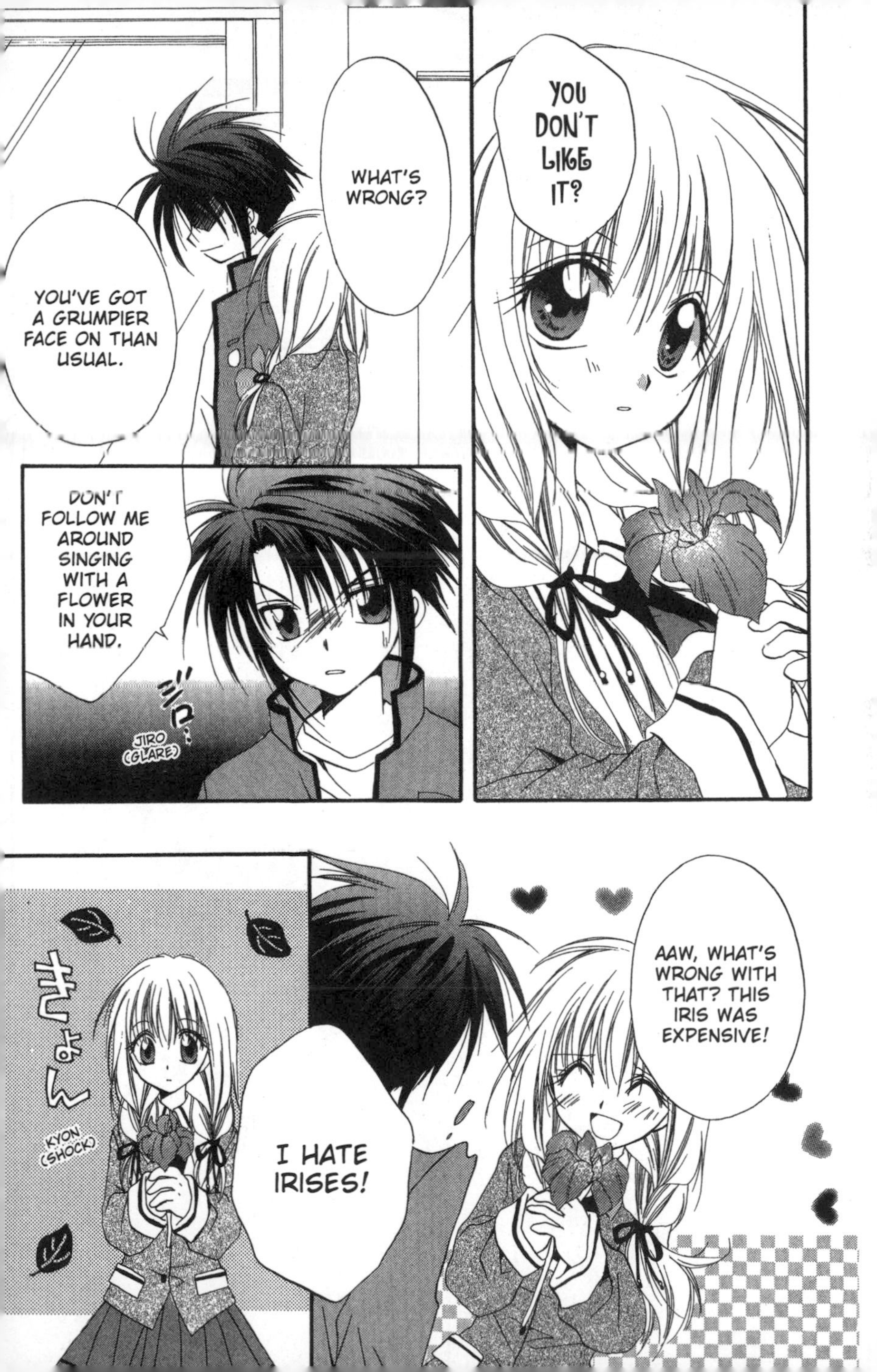
YOU DON'T LIKE IT?
WHAT'S WRONG?
YOU'VE GOT A GRUMPIER FACE ON THAN USUAL.
DON'T FOLLOW ME AROUND SINGING WITH A FLOWER IN YOUR HAND.
ジロ…
JIRO (GLARE)
AAW, WHAT'S WRONG WITH THAT? THIS IRIS WAS EXPENSIVE!
I HATE IRISES!
きょん
KYON (SHOCK)

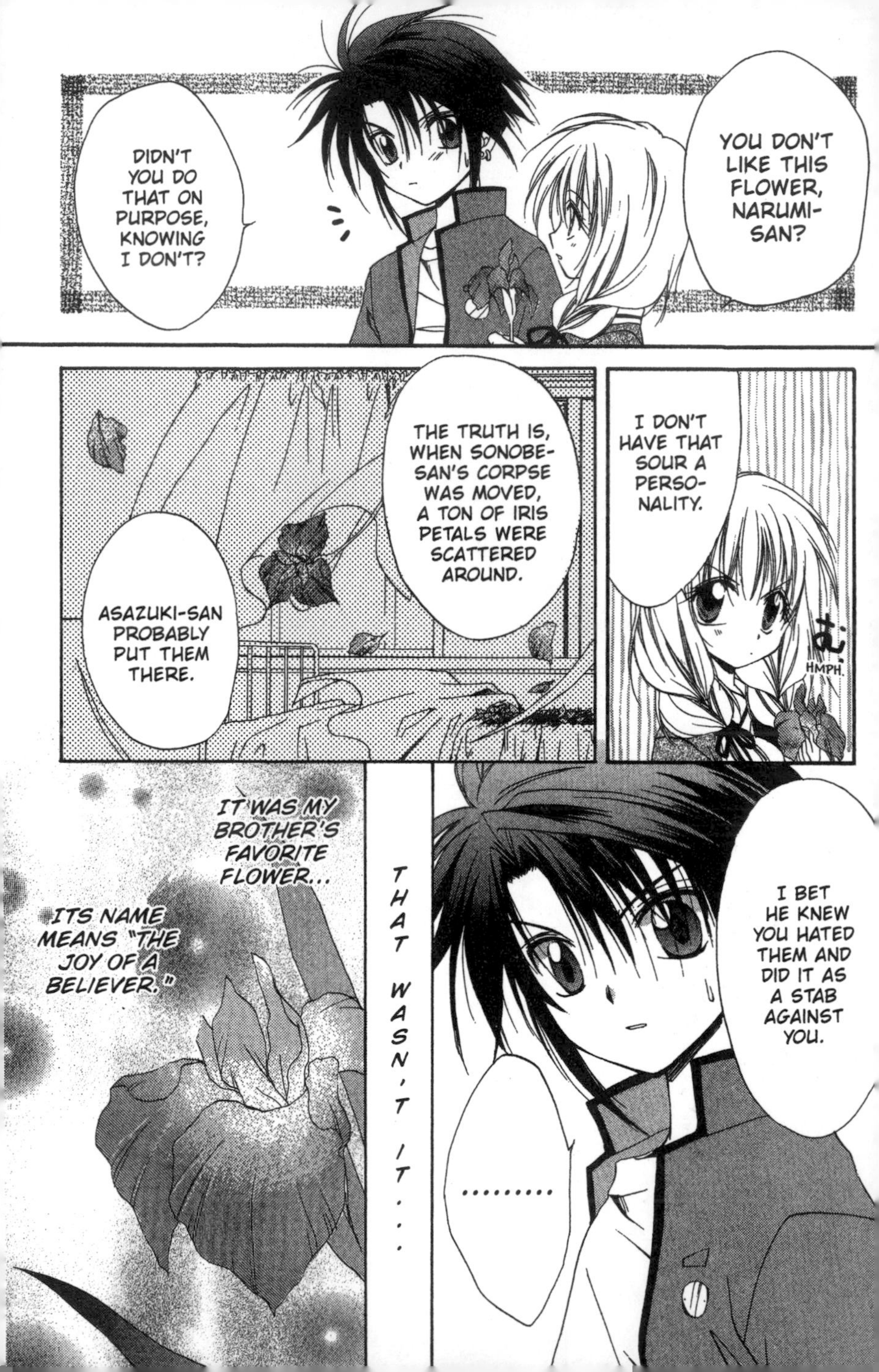
YOU DON'T LIKE THIS FLOWER, NARUMI-SAN?
DIDN'T YOU DO THAT ON PURPOSE, KNOWING I DON'T?
I DON'T HAVE THAT SOUR A PERSONALITY.
HMPH.
THE TRUTH IS, WHEN SONOBE-SAN'S CORPSE WAS MOVED, A TON OF IRIS PETALS WERE SCATTERED AROUND.
ASAZUKI-SAN PROBABLY PUT THEM THERE.
I BET HE KNEW YOU HATED THEM AND DID IT AS A STAB AGAINST YOU.
....
THAT WASN'T IT...
IT WAS MY BROTHER'S FAVORITE FLOWER...
ITS NAME MEANS "THE JOY OF A BELIEVER."

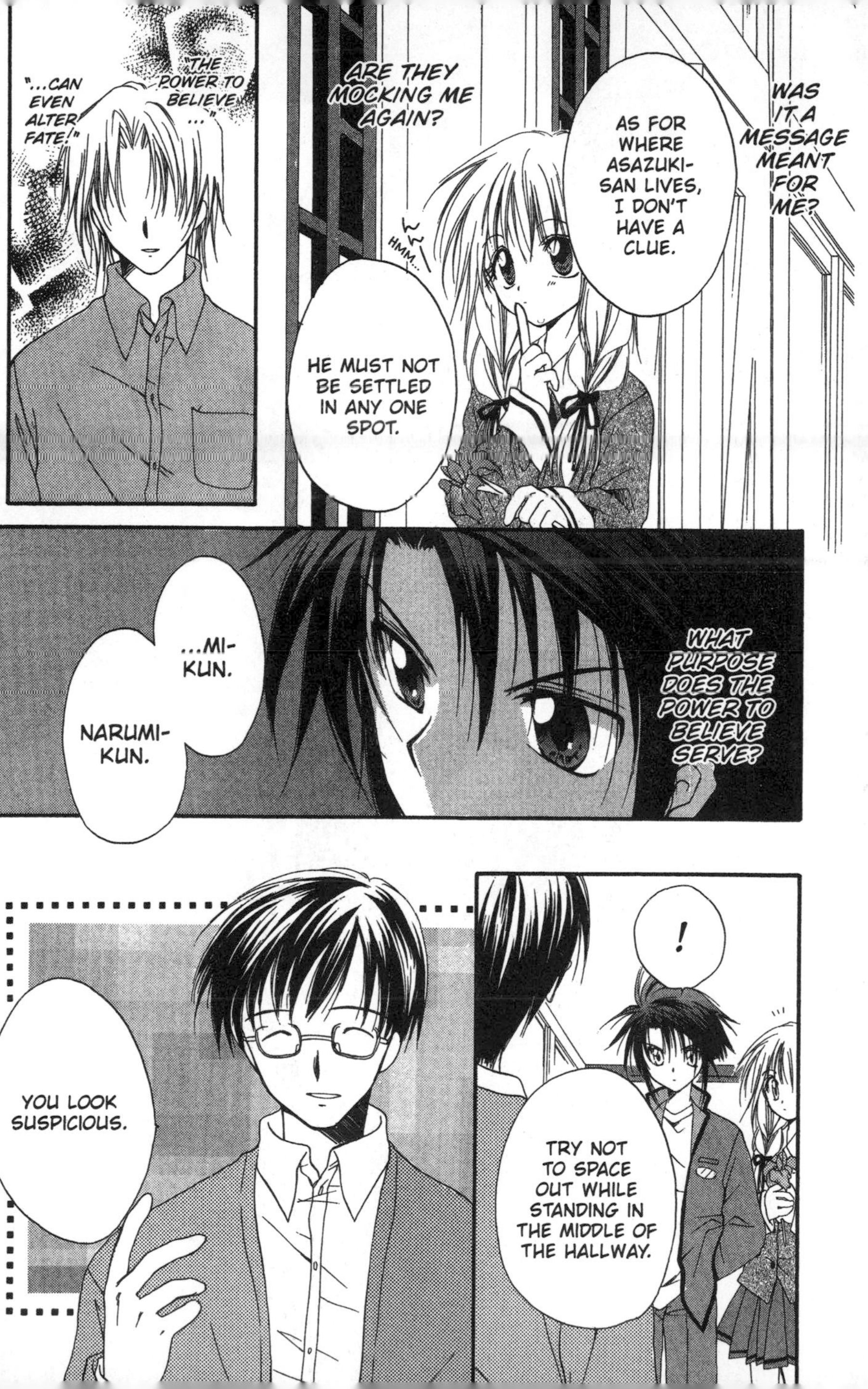
WAS IT A MESSAGE MEANT FOR ME?
AS FOR WHERE ASAZUKI-SAN LIVES, I DON'T HAVE A CLUE.
HMM...
HE MUST NOT BE SETTLED IN ANY ONE SPOT.
ARE THEY MOCKING ME AGAIN?
"THE POWER TO BELIEVE..."
"...CAN EVEN ALTER FATE!"
WHAT PURPOSE DOES THE POWER TO BELIEVE SERVE?
...MI-KUN.
NARUMI-KUN.
!
TRY NOT TO SPACE OUT WHILE STANDING IN THE MIDDLE OF THE HALLWAY.
YOU LOOK SUSPICIOUS.

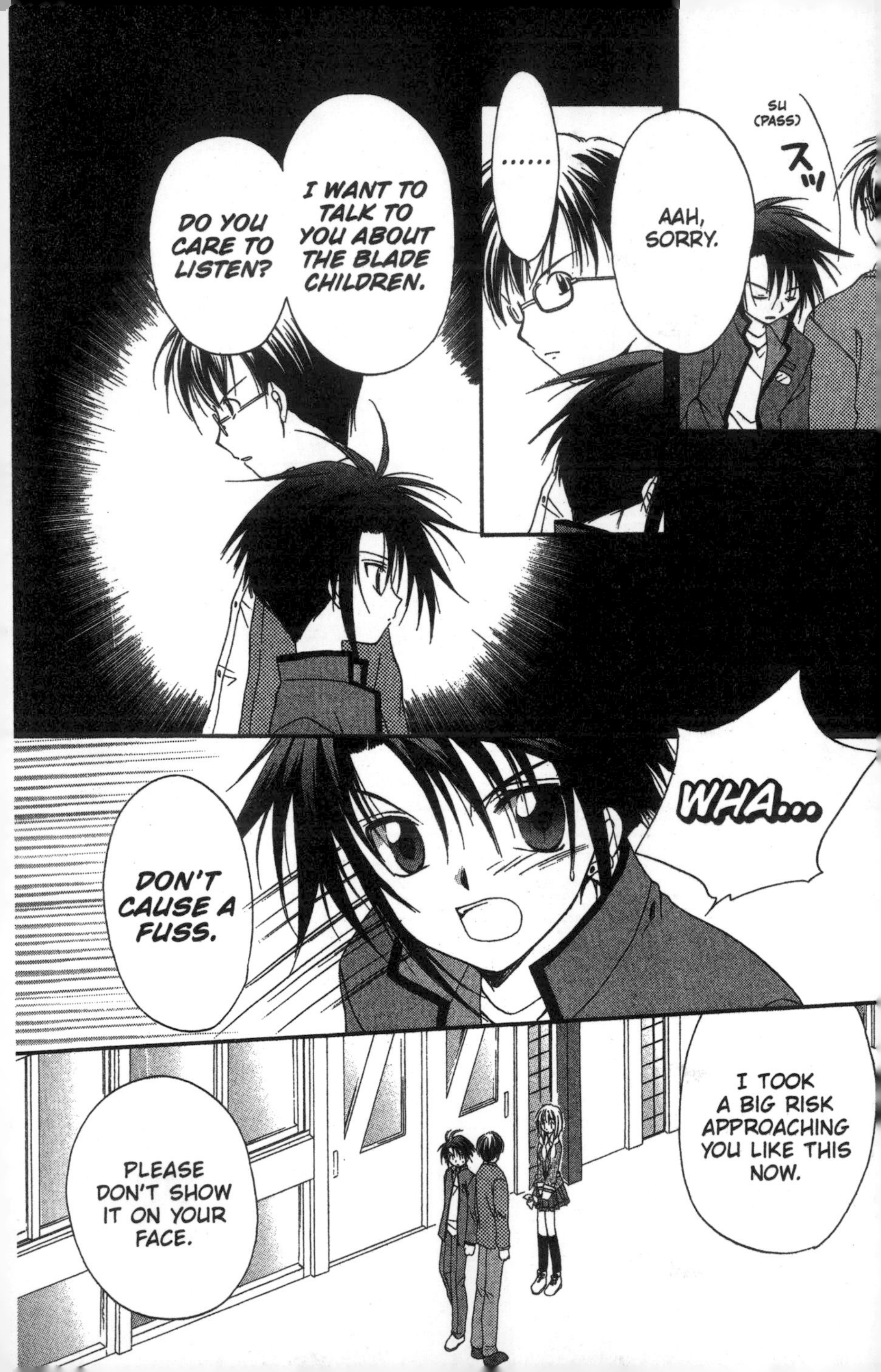
SU (PASS)
スッ
AAH, SORRY.
......
I WANT TO TALK TO YOU ABOUT THE BLADE CHILDREN.
DO YOU CARE TO LISTEN?
WHA...
DON'T CAUSE A FUSS.
I TOOK A BIG RISK APPROACHING YOU LIKE THIS NOW.
PLEASE DON'T SHOW IT ON YOUR FACE.

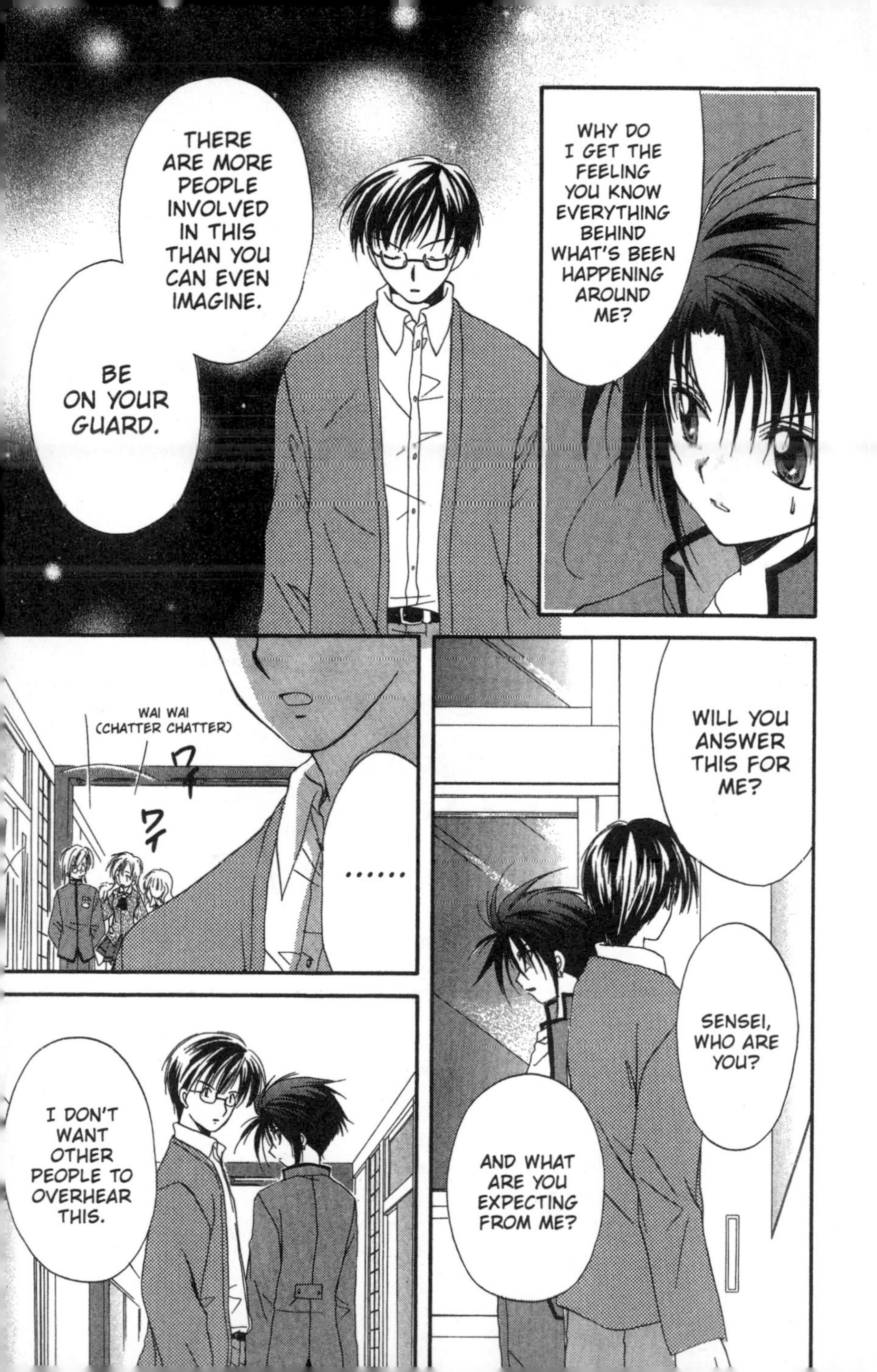
WHY DO I GET THE FEELING YOU KNOW EVERYTHING BEHIND WHAT'S BEEN HAPPENING AROUND ME?
THERE ARE MORE PEOPLE INVOLVED IN THIS THAN YOU CAN EVEN IMAGINE.
BE ON YOUR GUARD.
WILL YOU ANSWER THIS FOR ME?
SENSEI, WHO ARE YOU?
AND WHAT ARE YOU EXPECTING FROM ME?
......
WAI WAI (CHATTER CHATTER)
I DON'T WANT OTHER PEOPLE TO OVERHEAR THIS.

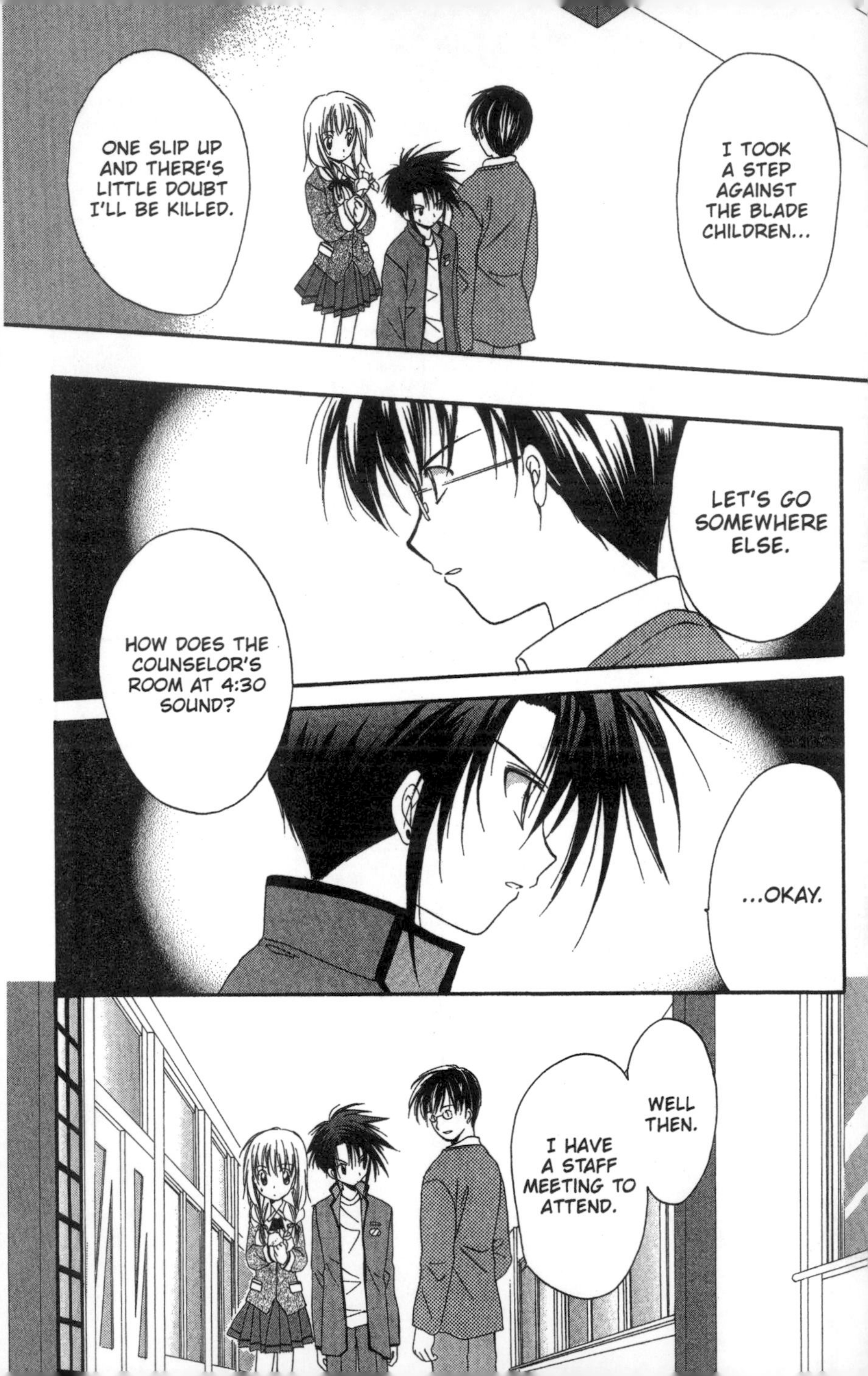
I TOOK A STEP AGAINST THE BLADE CHILDREN...
ONE SLIP UP AND THERE'S LITTLE DOUBT I'LL BE KILLED.
LET'S GO SOMEWHERE ELSE.
HOW DOES THE COUNSELOR'S ROOM AT 4:30 SOUND?
...OKAY.
WELL THEN.
I HAVE A STAFF MEETING TO ATTEND.

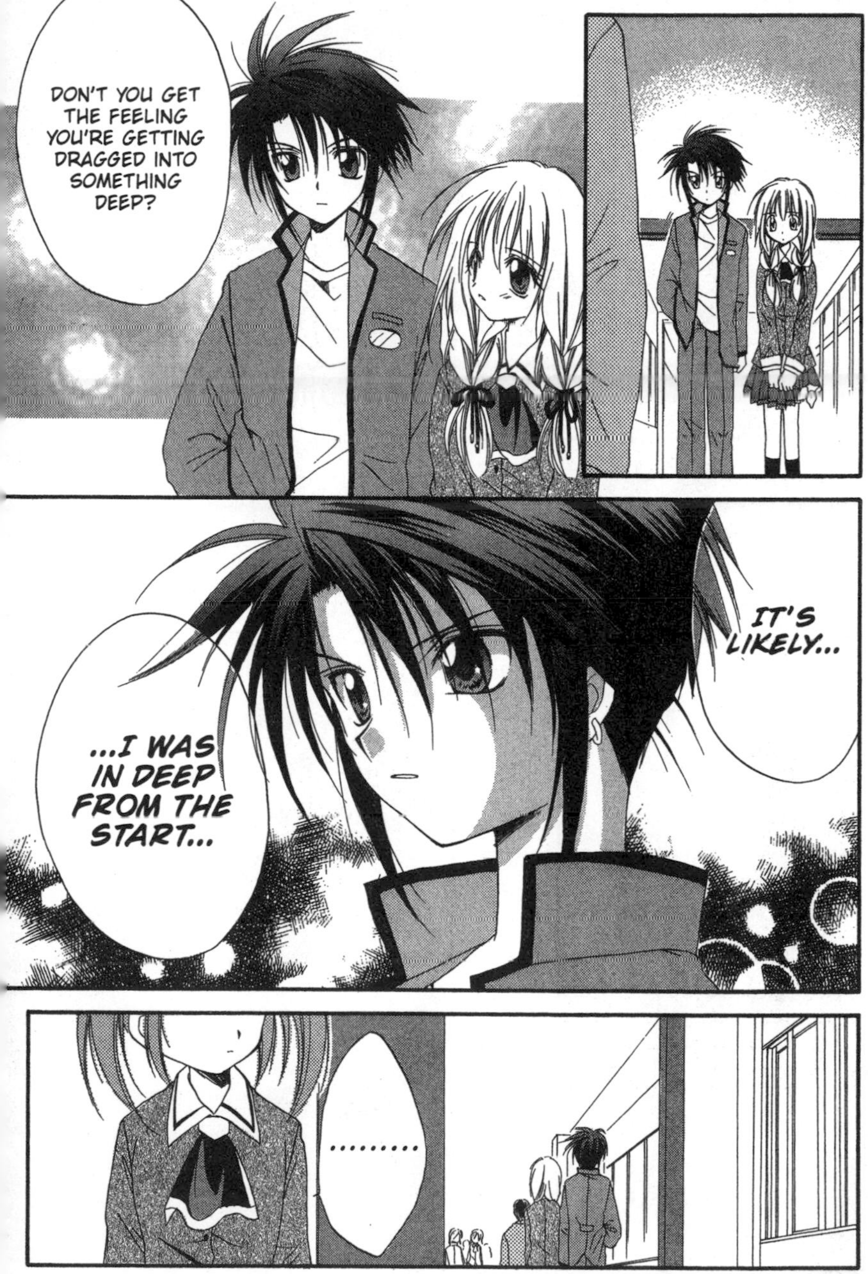
DON'T YOU GET THE FEELING YOU'RE GETTING DRAGGED INTO SOMETHING DEEP?
IT'S LIKELY...
...I WAS IN DEEP FROM THE START...
....

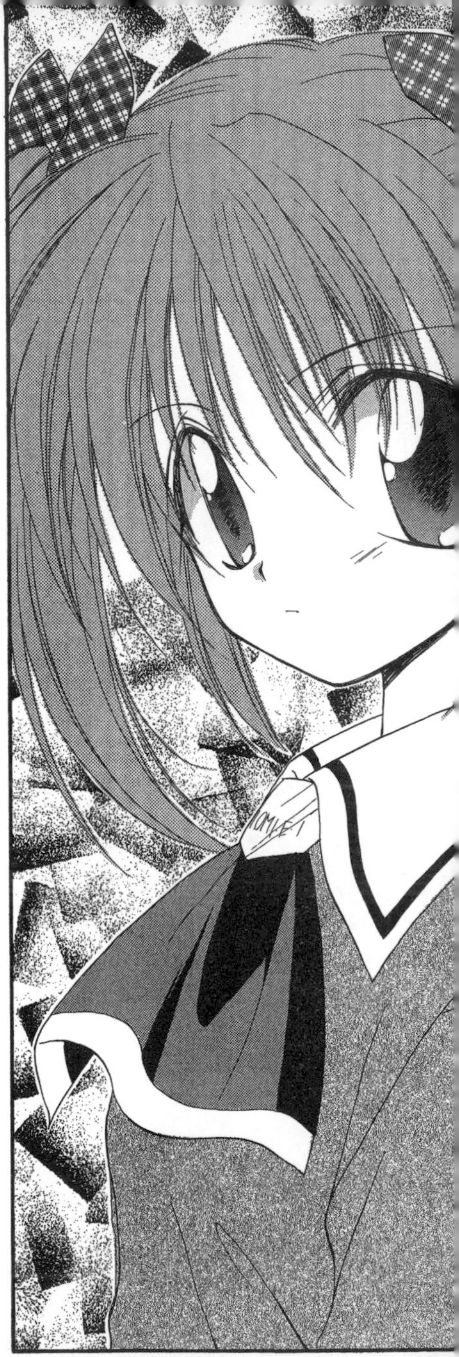

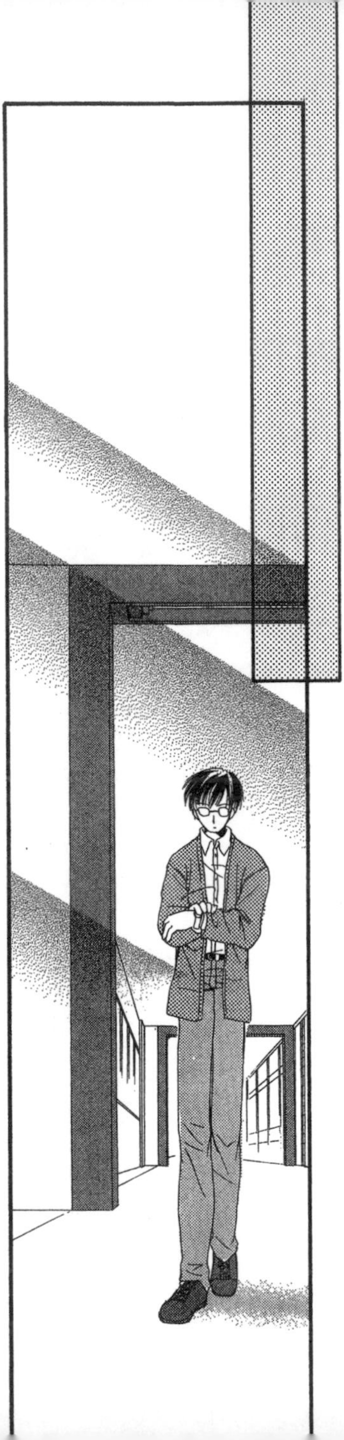

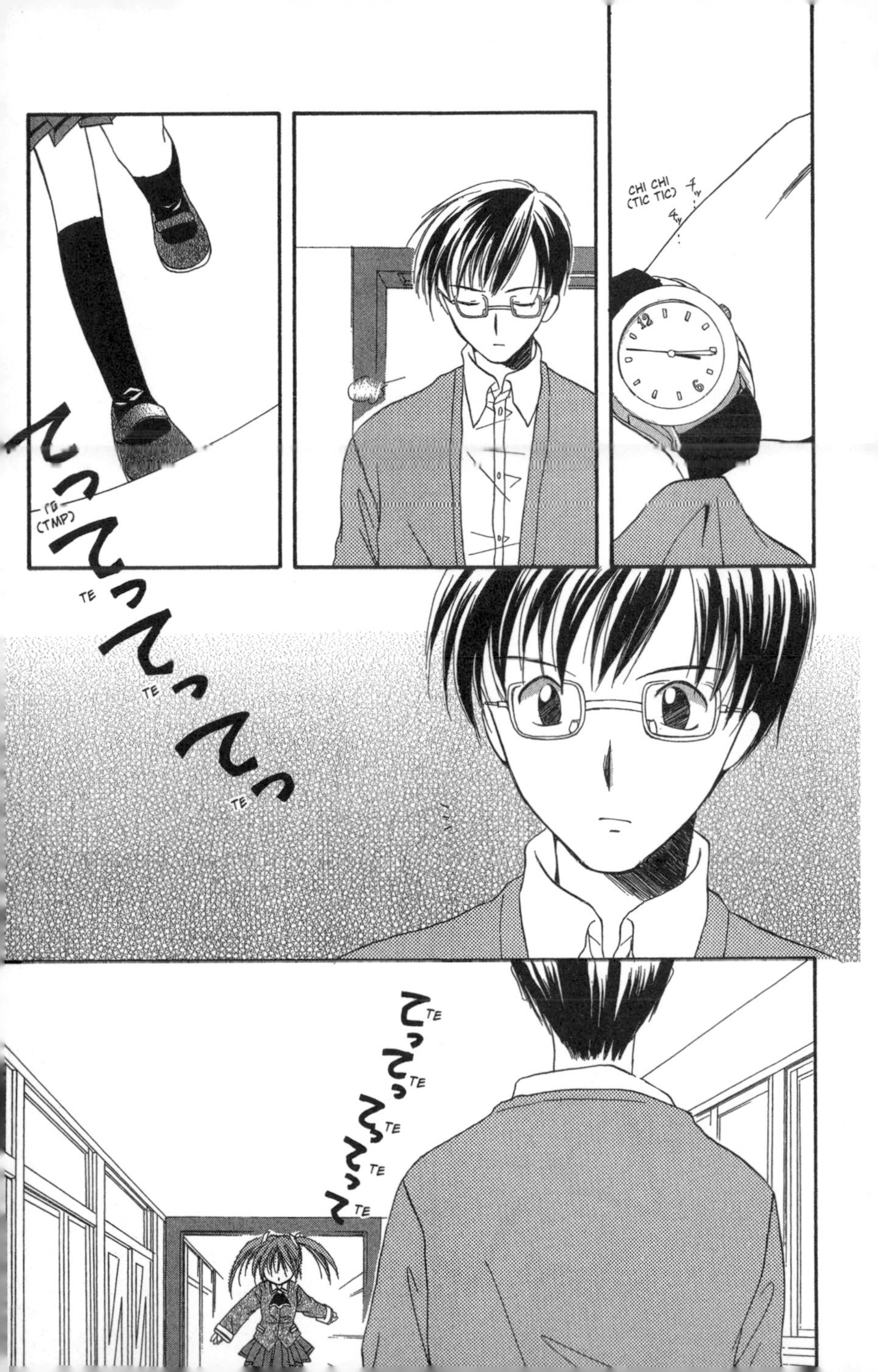

CHI CHI (TIC TIC)
チッ チッ
TE (TMP)
てっ
TE TE TE
てっ てっ てっ
TE TE TE TE TE
てっ てっ てっ てっ てっ

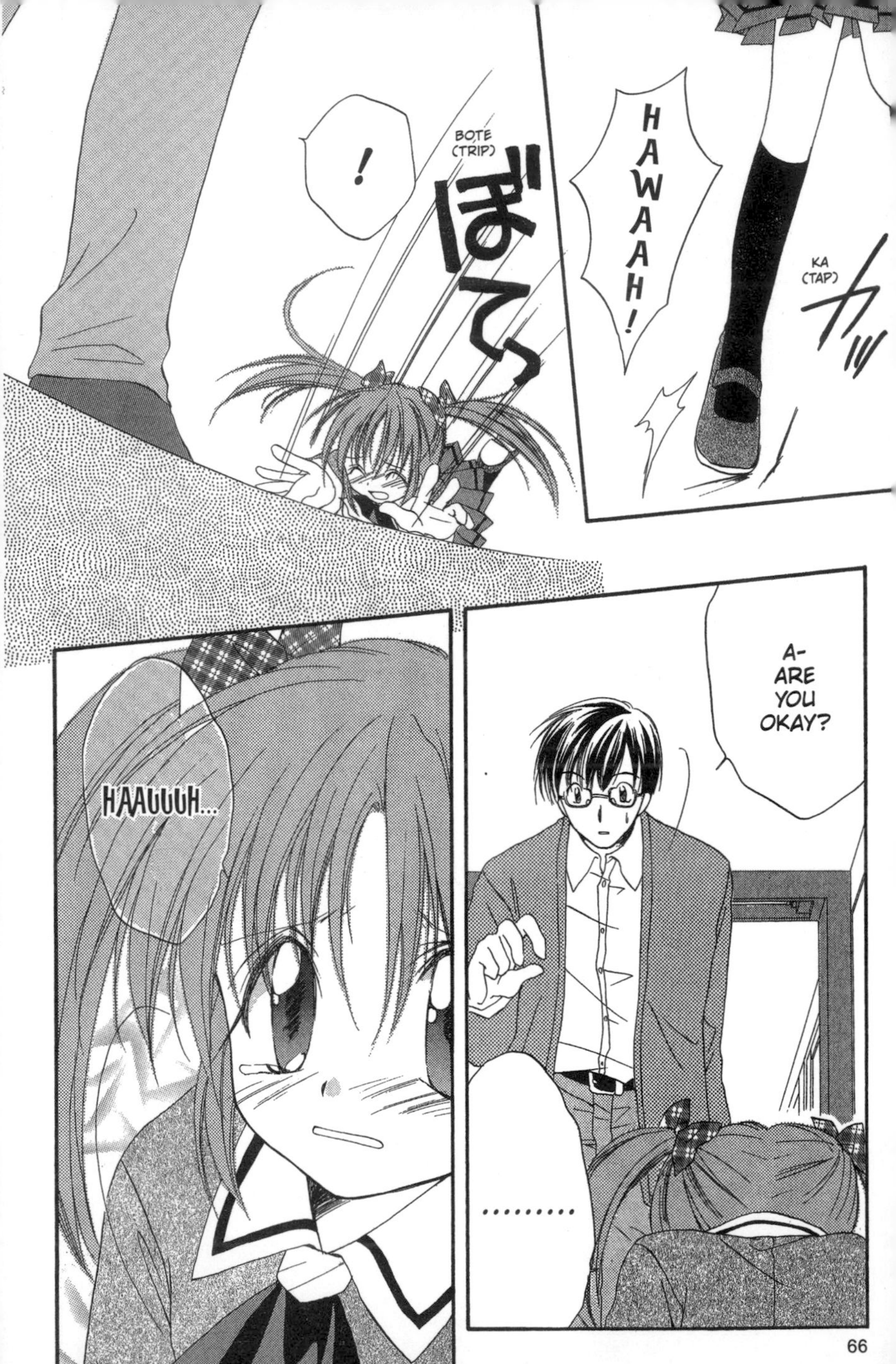
HAWAAAH!
KA (TAP)
カッ
BOTE (TRIP)
ぼてっ
!
A- ARE YOU OKAY?
....
HAAUUUH...

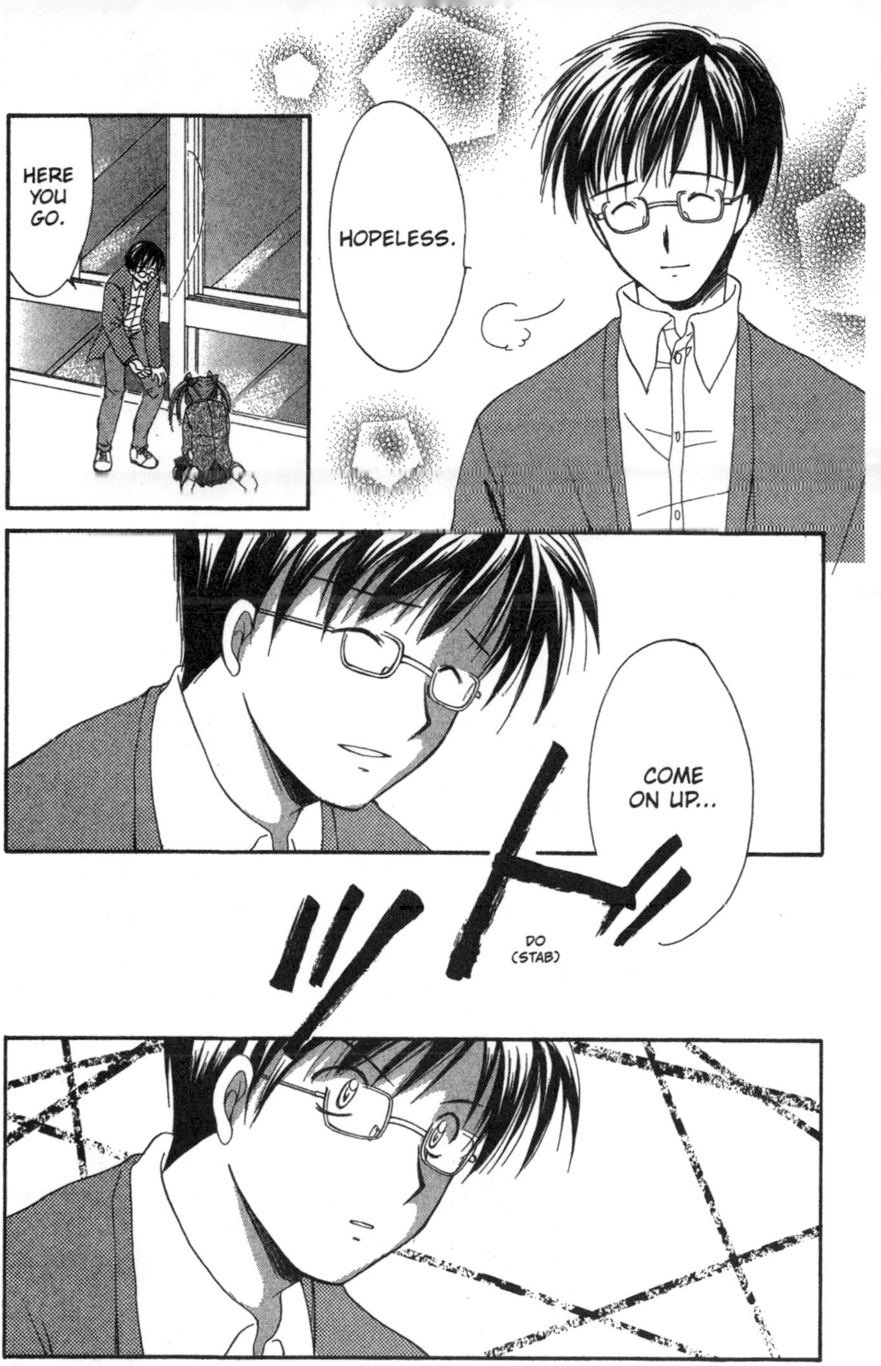
HOPELESS.
HERE YOU GO.
COME ON UP...
DO (STAB)

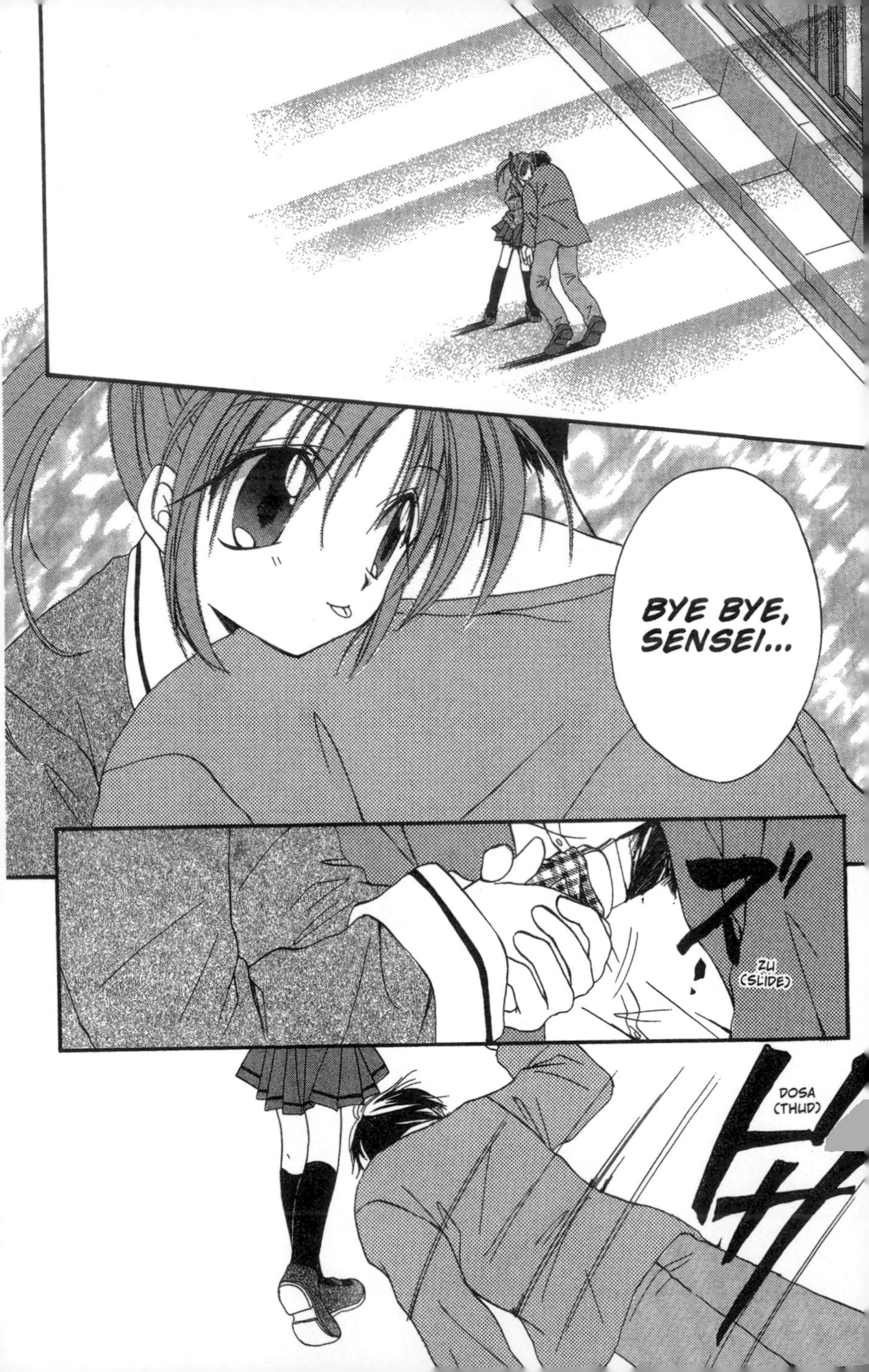
BYE BYE, SENSEI...
ZU
(SLIDE)
DOSA
(THUD)

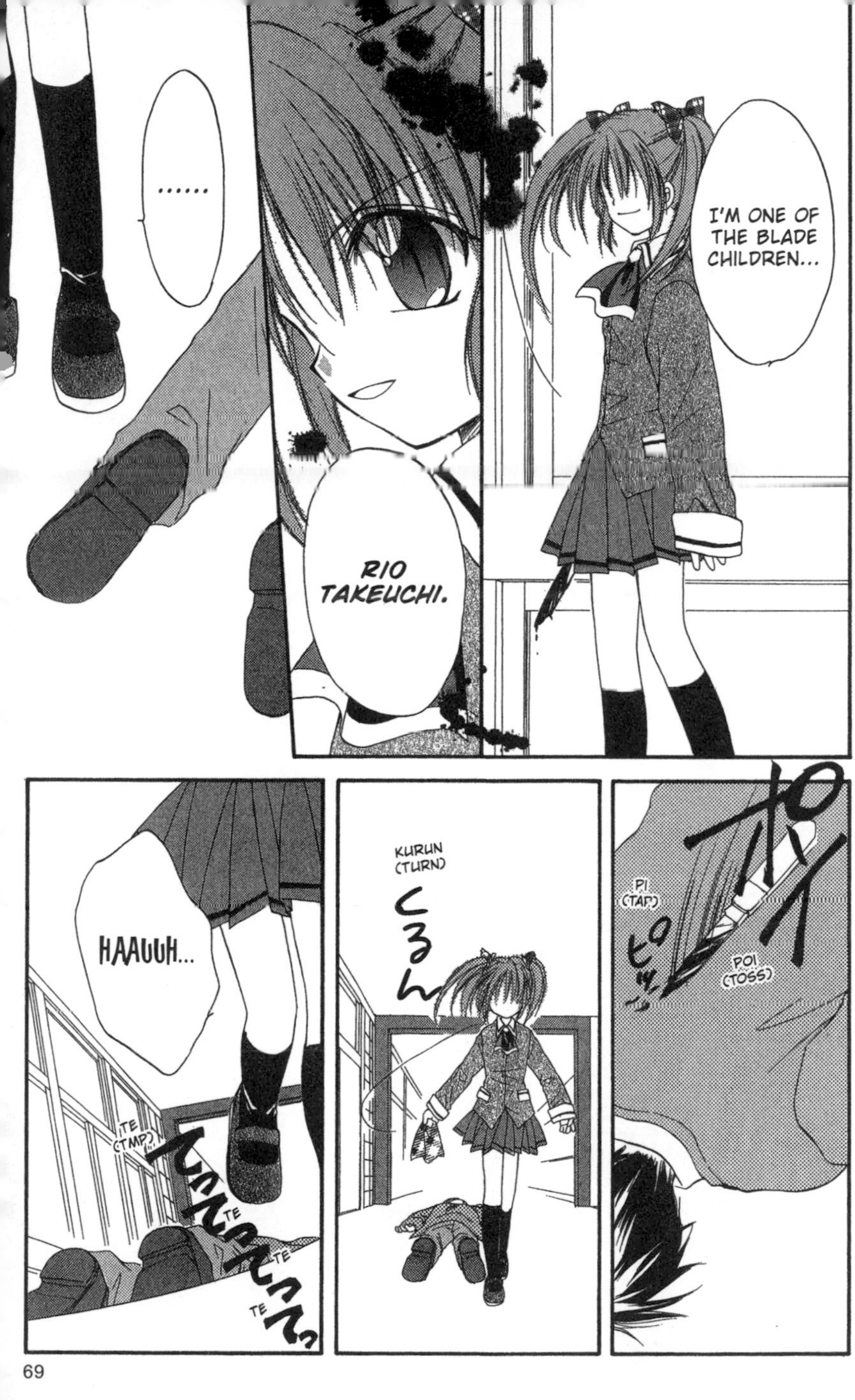
I'M ONE OF THE BLADE CHILDREN...
RIO TAKEUCHI.
......
ポイ
PI (TAP)
ピッ
POI (TOSS)
KURUN (TURN)
くるん
HAAUUH...
TE (TAP)
TE
TE
TE
てててて

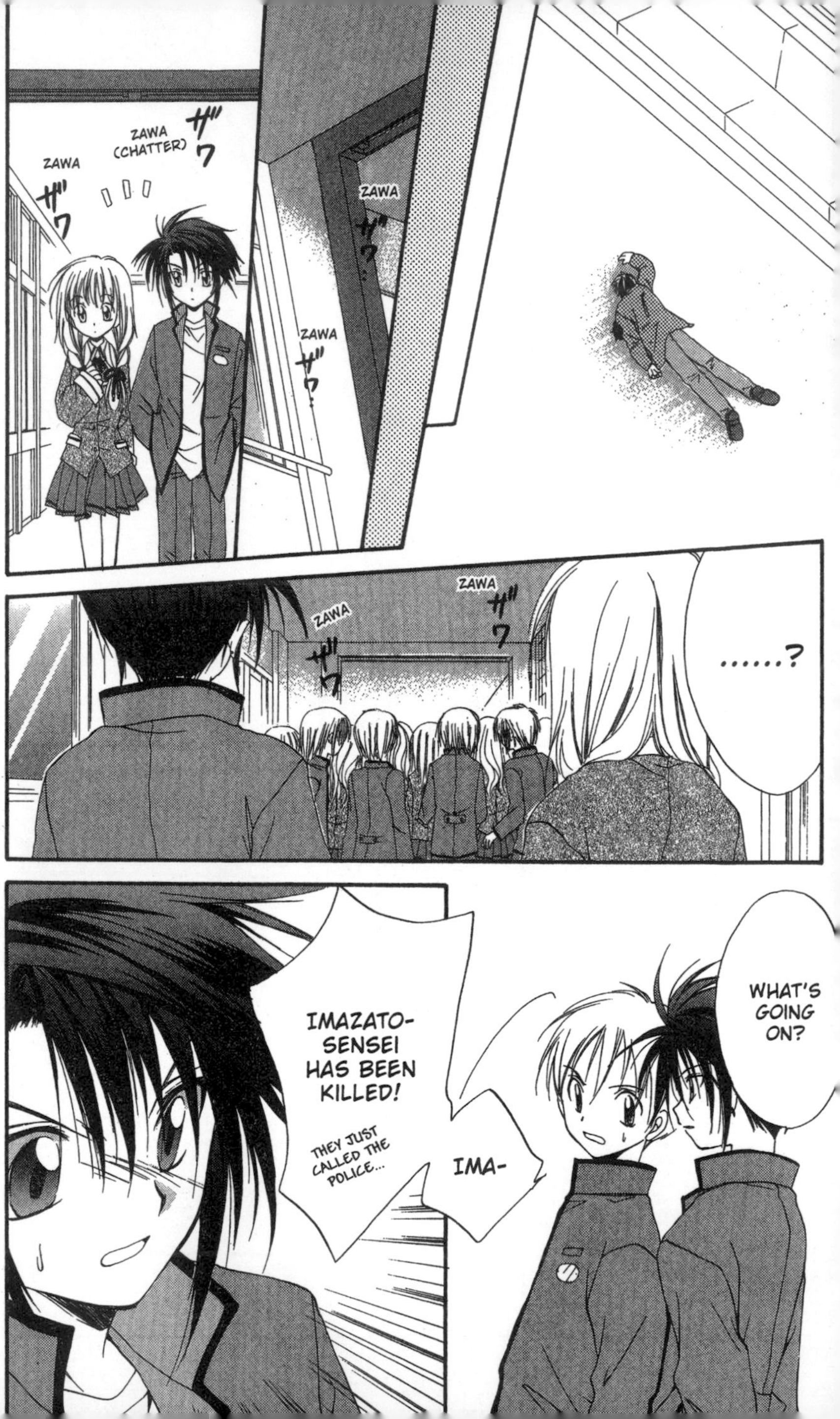
ZAWA
ザワ
ZAWA
ザワ
ZAWA (CHATTER)
ザワ
ZAWA
ザワ
ZAWA
ザワ
ZAWA
ザワ
......?
WHAT'S GOING ON?
IMA-
IMAZATO-SENSEI HAS BEEN KILLED!
THEY JUST CALLED THE POLICE...

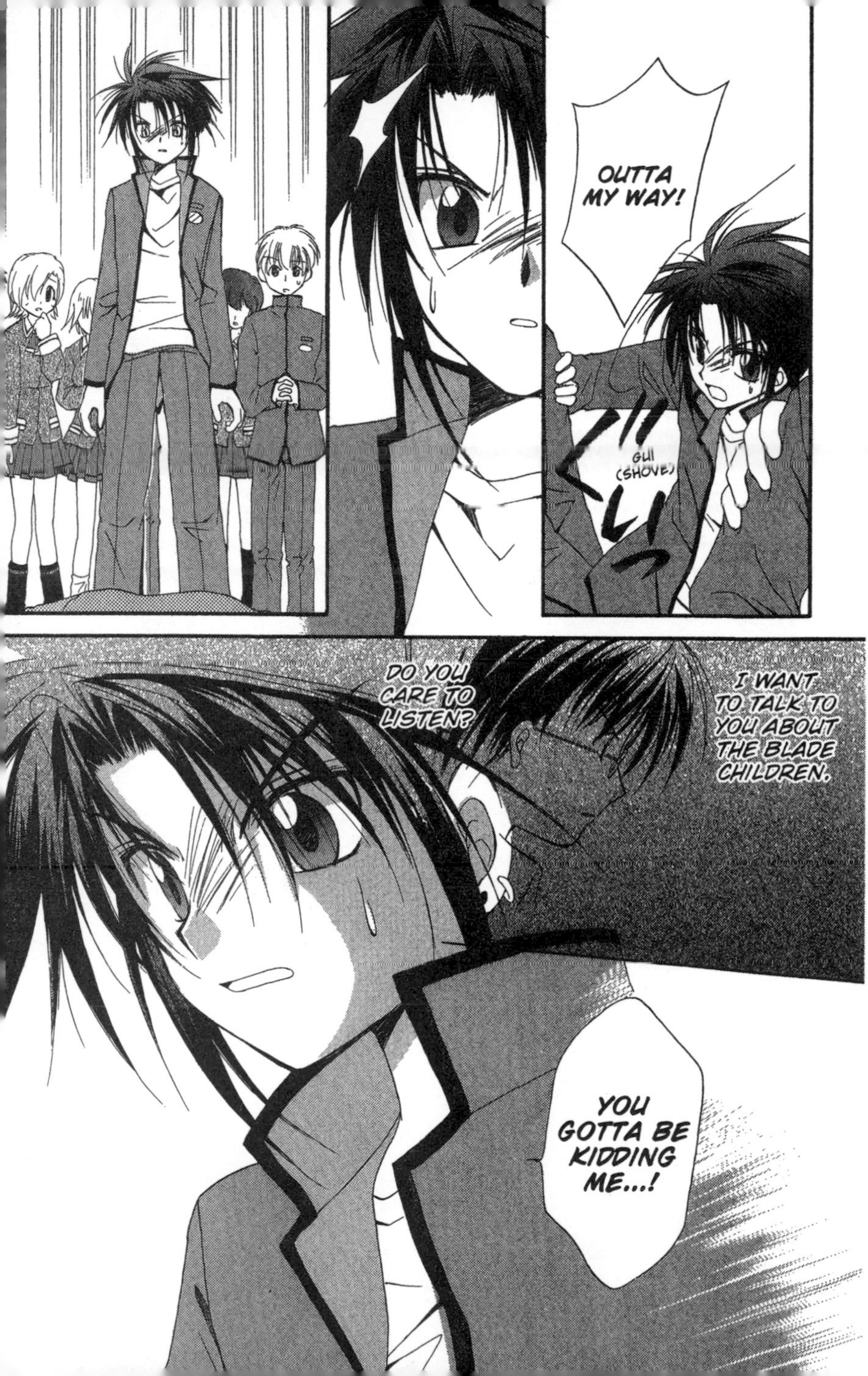
OUTTA MY WAY!
ぐいっ
GUI (SHOVE)
I WANT TO TALK TO YOU ABOUT THE BLADE CHILDREN.
DO YOU CARE TO LISTEN?
YOU GOTTA BE KIDDING ME...!

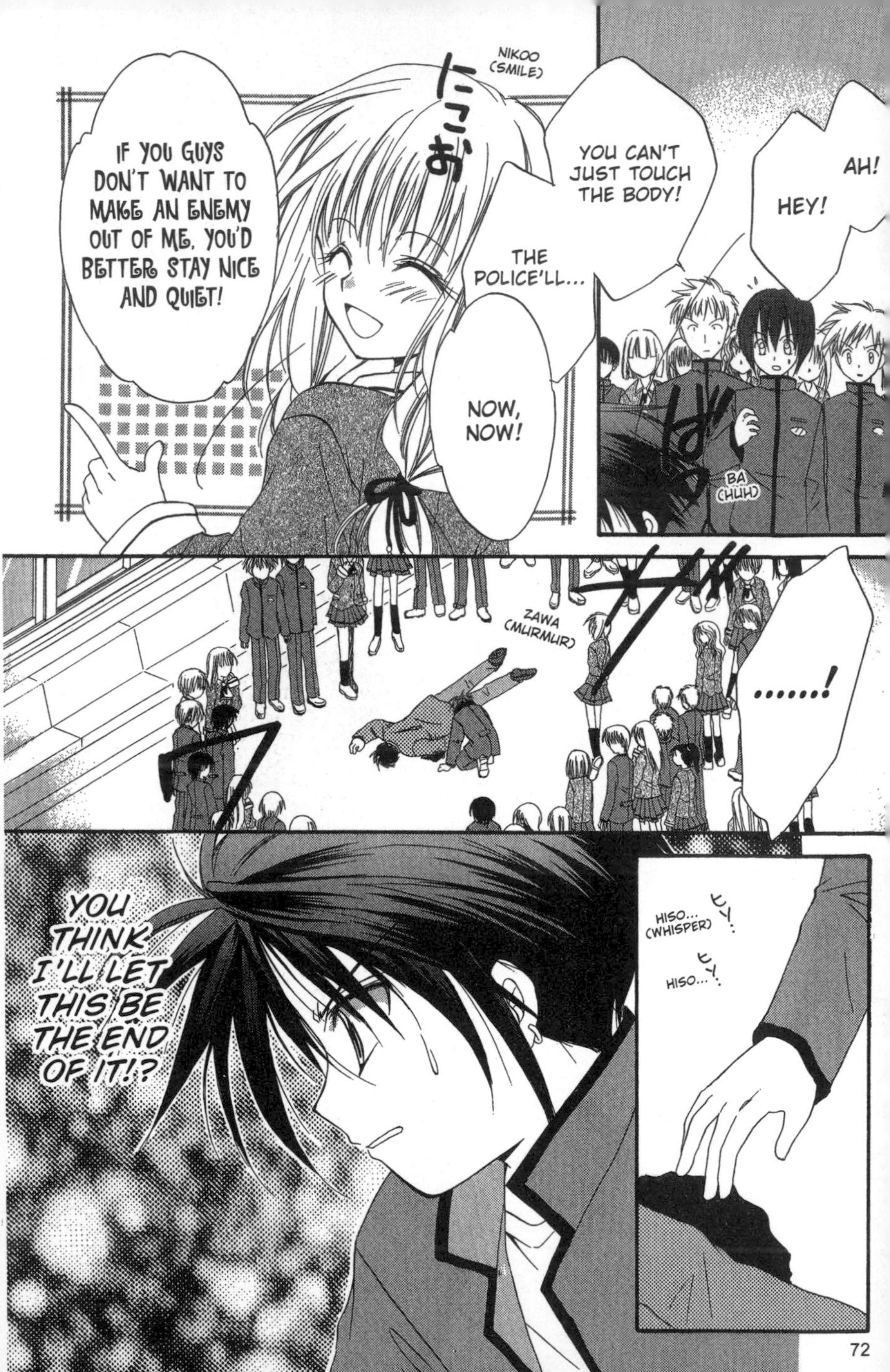
AH!
HEY!
YOU CAN'T JUST TOUCH THE BODY!
THE POLICE'LL...
BA (HUH)
NOW, NOW!
NIKOO (SMILE)
IF YOU GUYS DON'T WANT TO MAKE AN ENEMY OUT OF ME, YOU'D BETTER STAY NICE AND QUIET!
......!
ZAWA (MURMUR)
HISO... (WHISPER)
HISO...
YOU THINK I'LL LET THIS BE THE END OF IT!?

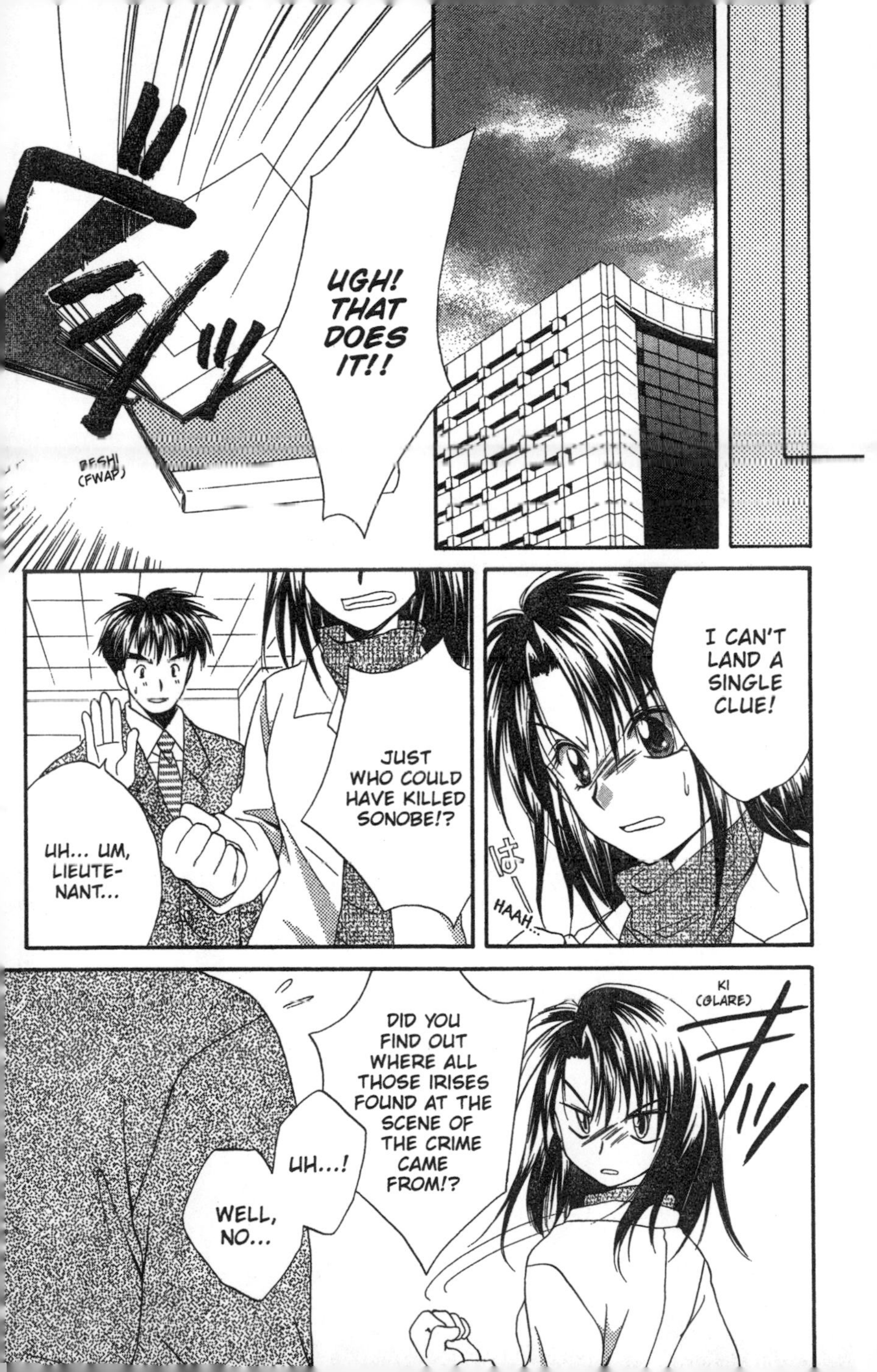
UGH! THAT DOES IT!!
BESHI (FWAP)
I CAN'T LAND A SINGLE CLUE!
HAAH...
JUST WHO COULD HAVE KILLED SONOBE!?
UH... UM, LIEUTE-NANT...
KI (GLARE)
DID YOU FIND OUT WHERE ALL THOSE IRISES FOUND AT THE SCENE OF THE CRIME CAME FROM!?
UH...!
WELL, NO...

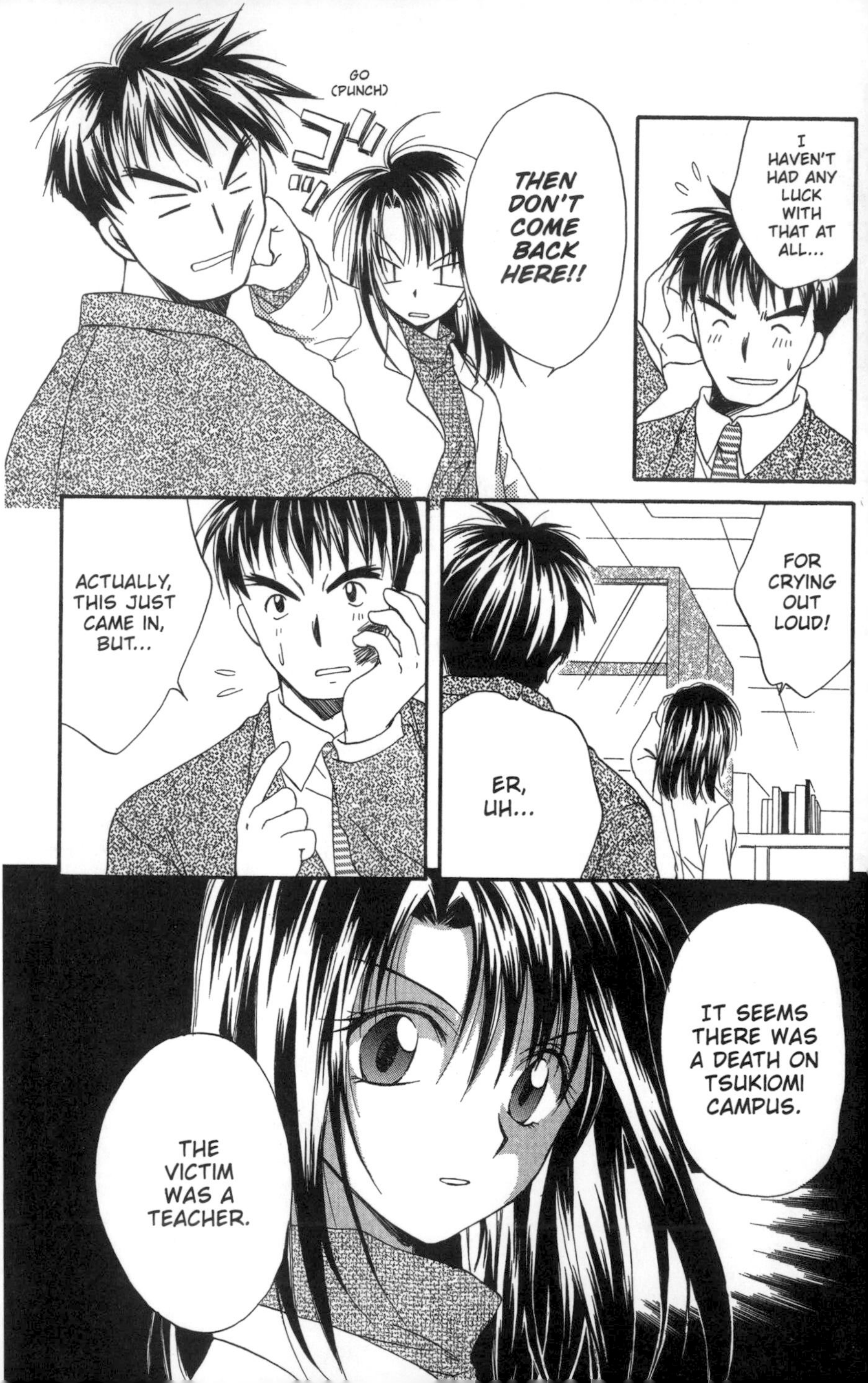
I HAVEN'T HAD ANY LUCK WITH THAT AT ALL...
THEN DON'T COME BACK HERE!!
GO (PUNCH)
FOR CRYING OUT LOUD!
ER, UH...
ACTUALLY, THIS JUST CAME IN, BUT...
IT SEEMS THERE WAS A DEATH ON TSUKIOMI CAMPUS.
THE VICTIM WAS A TEACHER.

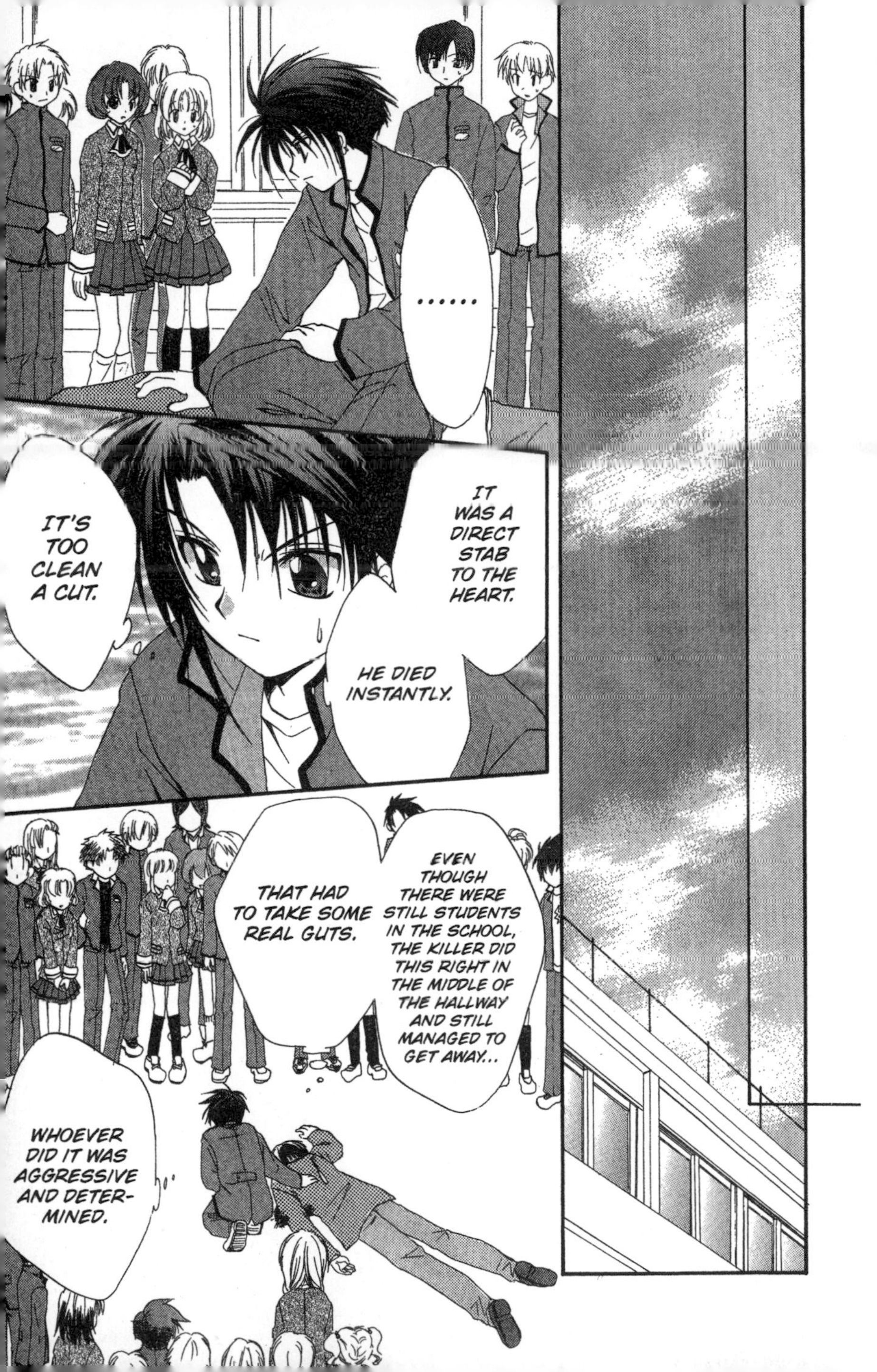
......
IT WAS A DIRECT STAB TO THE HEART.
HE DIED INSTANTLY.
IT'S TOO CLEAN A CUT.
EVEN THOUGH THERE WERE STILL STUDENTS IN THE SCHOOL, THE KILLER DID THIS RIGHT IN THE MIDDLE OF THE HALLWAY AND STILL MANAGED TO GET AWAY...
THAT HAD TO TAKE SOME REAL GUTS.
WHOEVER DID IT WAS AGGRESSIVE AND DETER-MINED.

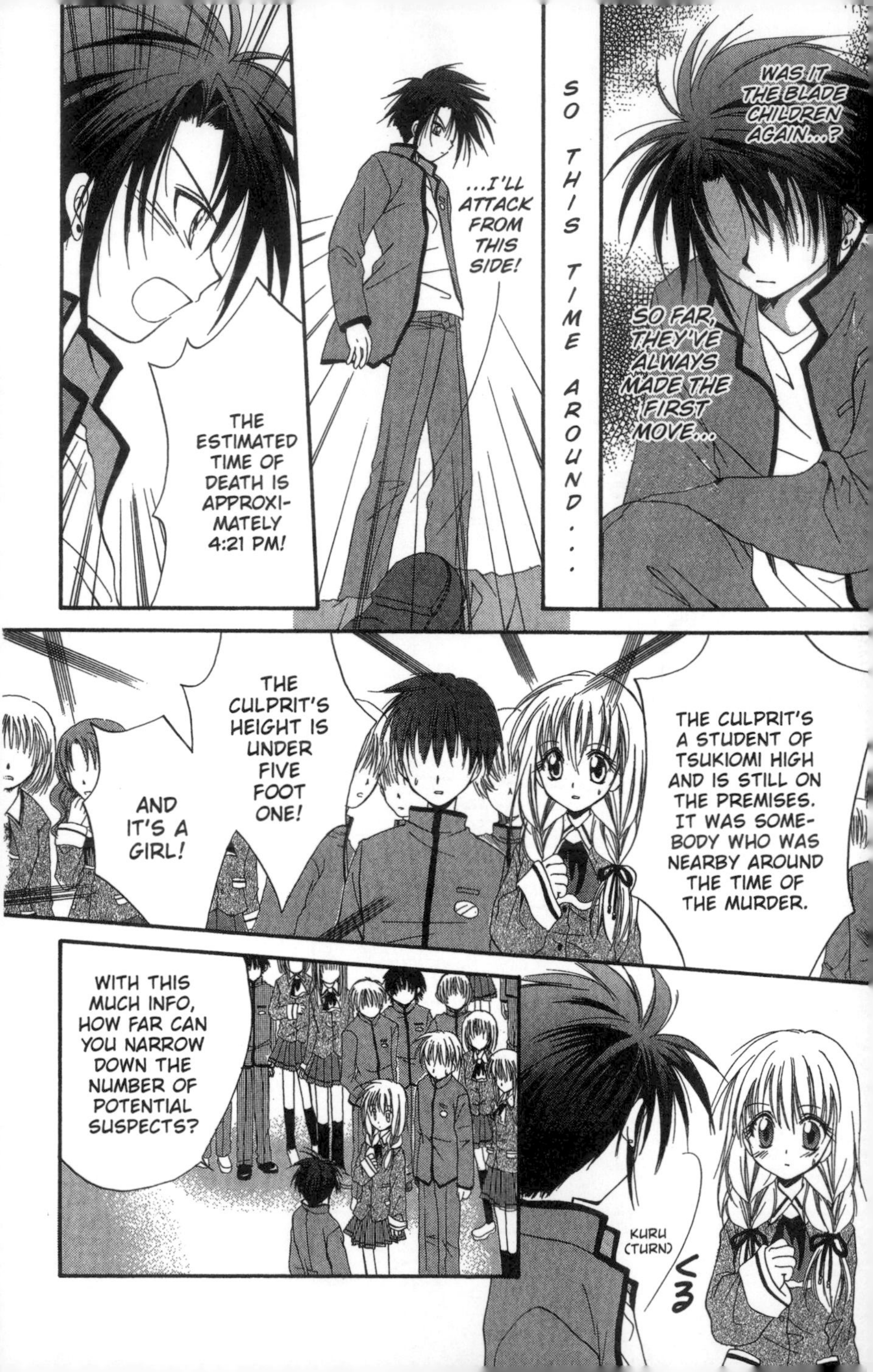
WAS IT THE BLADE CHILDREN AGAIN...?
SO FAR, THEY'VE ALWAYS MADE THE FIRST MOVE...
SO THIS TIME AROUND...
...I'LL ATTACK FROM THIS SIDE!
THE ESTIMATED TIME OF DEATH IS APPROXI-MATELY 4:21 PM!
THE CULPRIT'S A STUDENT OF TSUKIOMI HIGH AND IS STILL ON THE PREMISES. IT WAS SOME-BODY WHO WAS NEARBY AROUND THE TIME OF THE MURDER.
THE CULPRIT'S HEIGHT IS UNDER FIVE FOOT ONE!
AND IT'S A GIRL!
KURU (TURN)
くる
WITH THIS MUCH INFO, HOW FAR CAN YOU NARROW DOWN THE NUMBER OF POTENTIAL SUSPECTS?

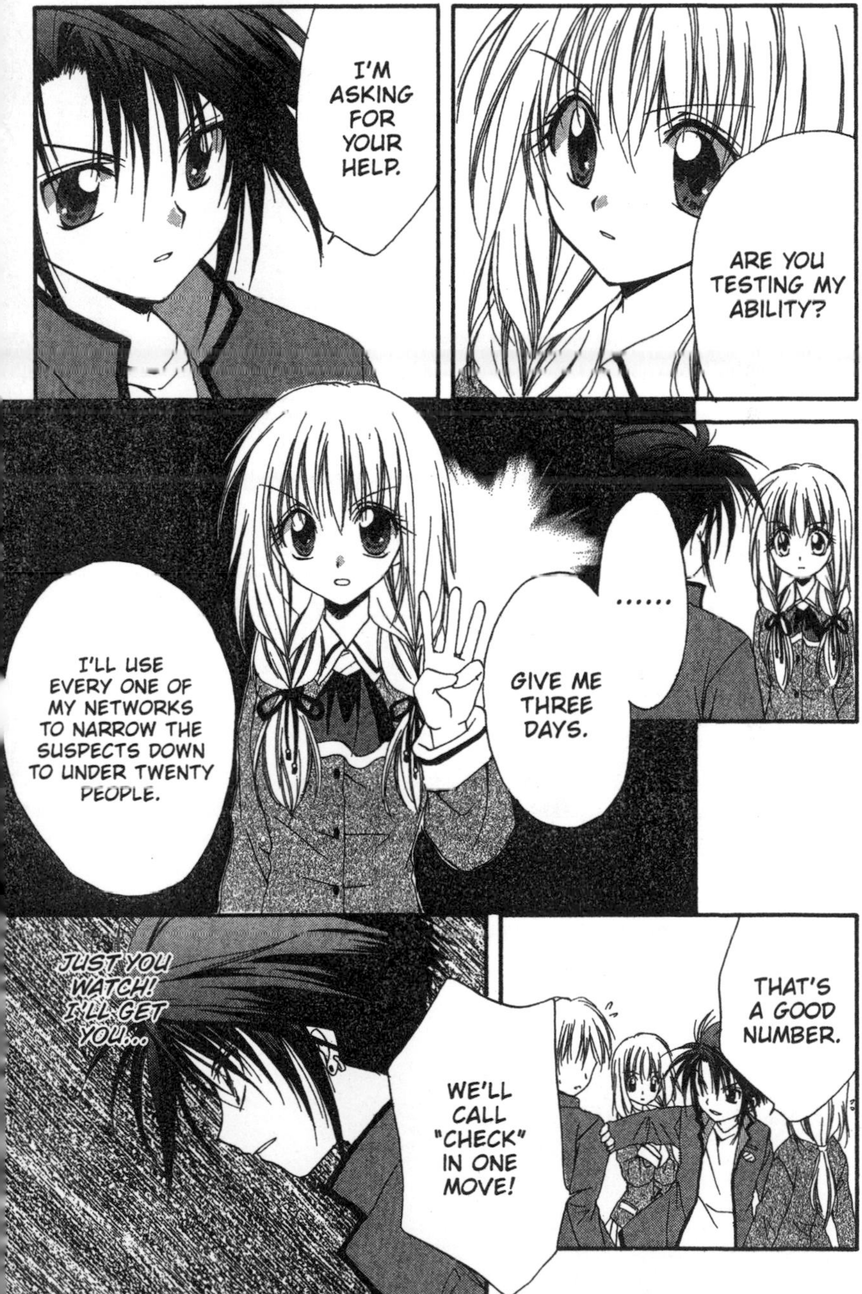
ARE YOU TESTING MY ABILITY?
I'M ASKING FOR YOUR HELP.
......
GIVE ME THREE DAYS.
I'LL USE EVERY ONE OF MY NETWORKS TO NARROW THE SUSPECTS DOWN TO UNDER TWENTY PEOPLE.
THAT'S A GOOD NUMBER.
WE'LL CALL "CHECK" IN ONE MOVE!
JUST YOU WATCH! I'LL GET YOU...

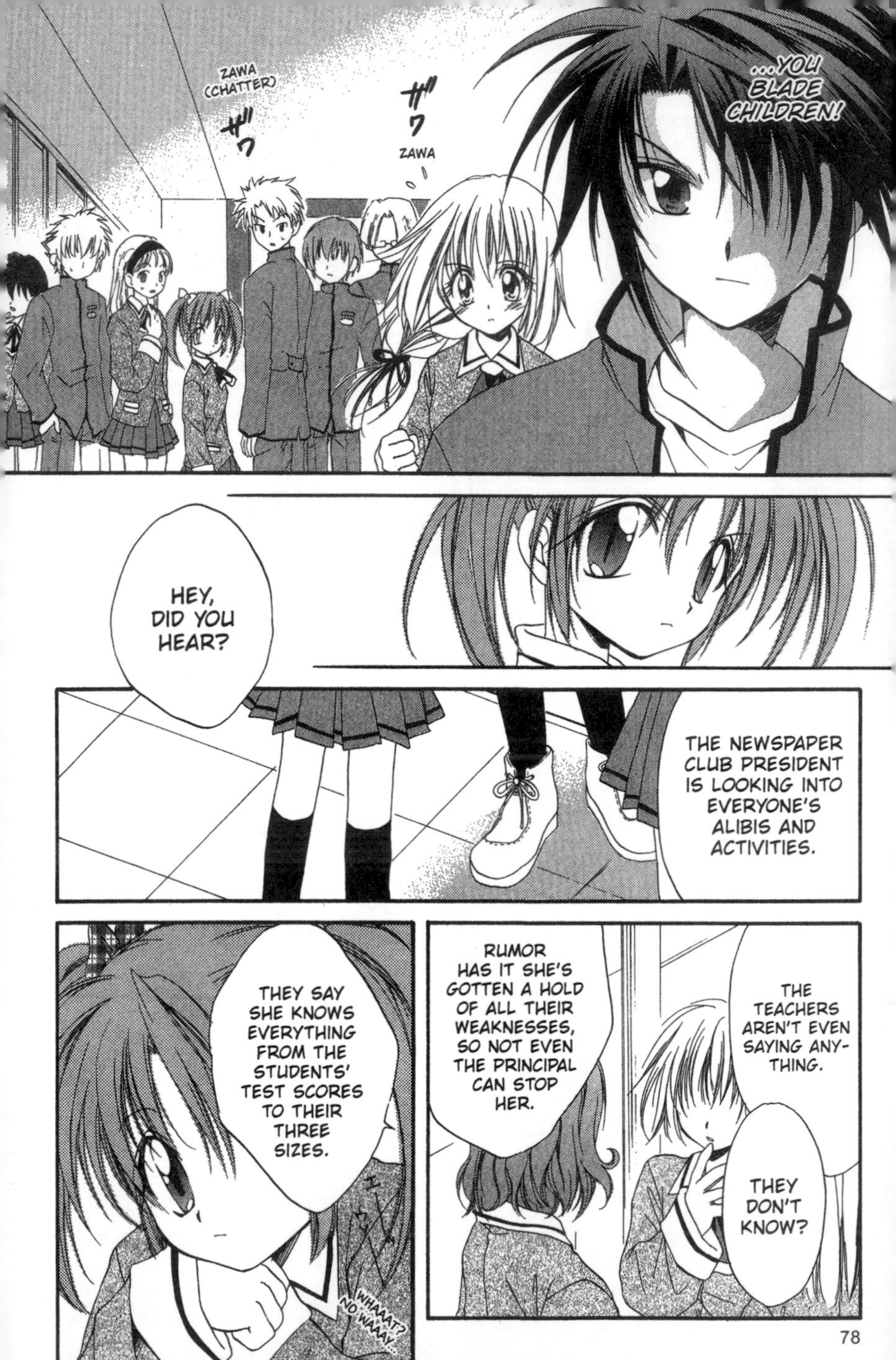
...YOU BLADE CHILDREN!
ザワ
ZAWA
ZAWA (CHATTER)
ザワ
HEY, DID YOU HEAR?
THE NEWSPAPER CLUB PRESIDENT IS LOOKING INTO EVERYONE'S ALIBIS AND ACTIVITIES.
THE TEACHERS AREN'T EVEN SAYING ANY-THING.
RUMOR HAS IT SHE'S GOTTEN A HOLD OF ALL THEIR WEAKNESSES, SO NOT EVEN THE PRINCIPAL CAN STOP HER.
THEY DON'T KNOW?
THEY SAY SHE KNOWS EVERYTHING FROM THE STUDENTS' TEST SCORES TO THEIR THREE SIZES.
WHAAAT? NO WAAAY...

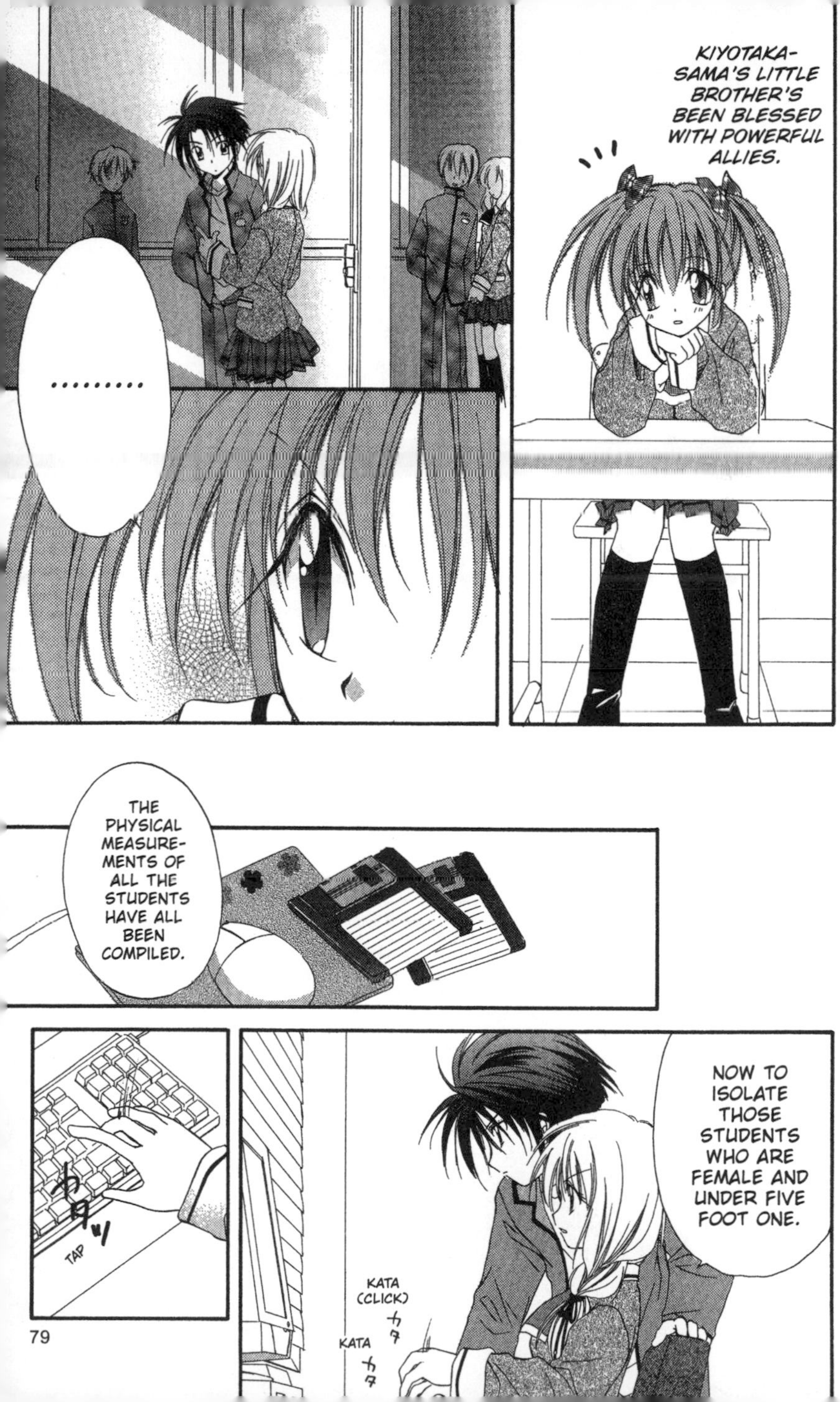
KIYOTAKA-SAMA'S LITTLE BROTHER'S BEEN BLESSED WITH POWERFUL ALLIES.
....
THE PHYSICAL MEASUREMENTS OF ALL THE STUDENTS HAVE ALL BEEN COMPILED.
NOW TO ISOLATE THOSE STUDENTS WHO ARE FEMALE AND UNDER FIVE FOOT ONE.
KATA (CLICK)
KATA
TAP

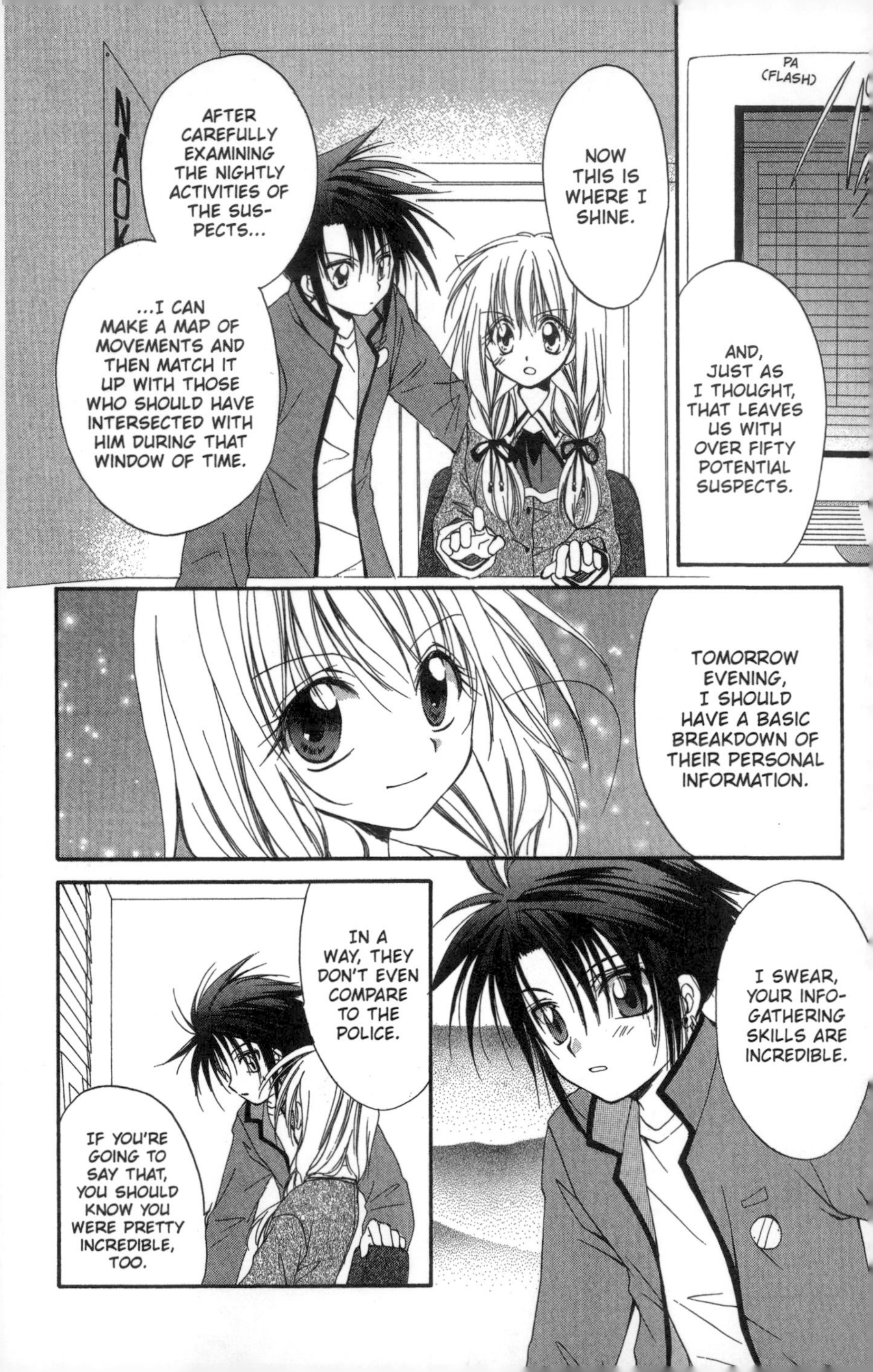
NOW THIS IS WHERE I SHINE.
AFTER CAREFULLY EXAMINING THE NIGHTLY ACTIVITIES OF THE SUS-PECTS...
...I CAN MAKE A MAP OF MOVEMENTS AND THEN MATCH IT UP WITH THOSE WHO SHOULD HAVE INTERSECTED WITH HIM DURING THAT WINDOW OF TIME.
PA (FLASH)
AND, JUST AS I THOUGHT, THAT LEAVES US WITH OVER FIFTY POTENTIAL SUSPECTS.
TOMORROW EVENING, I SHOULD HAVE A BASIC BREAKDOWN OF THEIR PERSONAL INFORMATION.
I SWEAR, YOUR INFO-GATHERING SKILLS ARE INCREDIBLE.
IN A WAY, THEY DON'T EVEN COMPARE TO THE POLICE.
IF YOU'RE GOING TO SAY THAT, YOU SHOULD KNOW YOU WERE PRETTY INCREDIBLE, TOO.

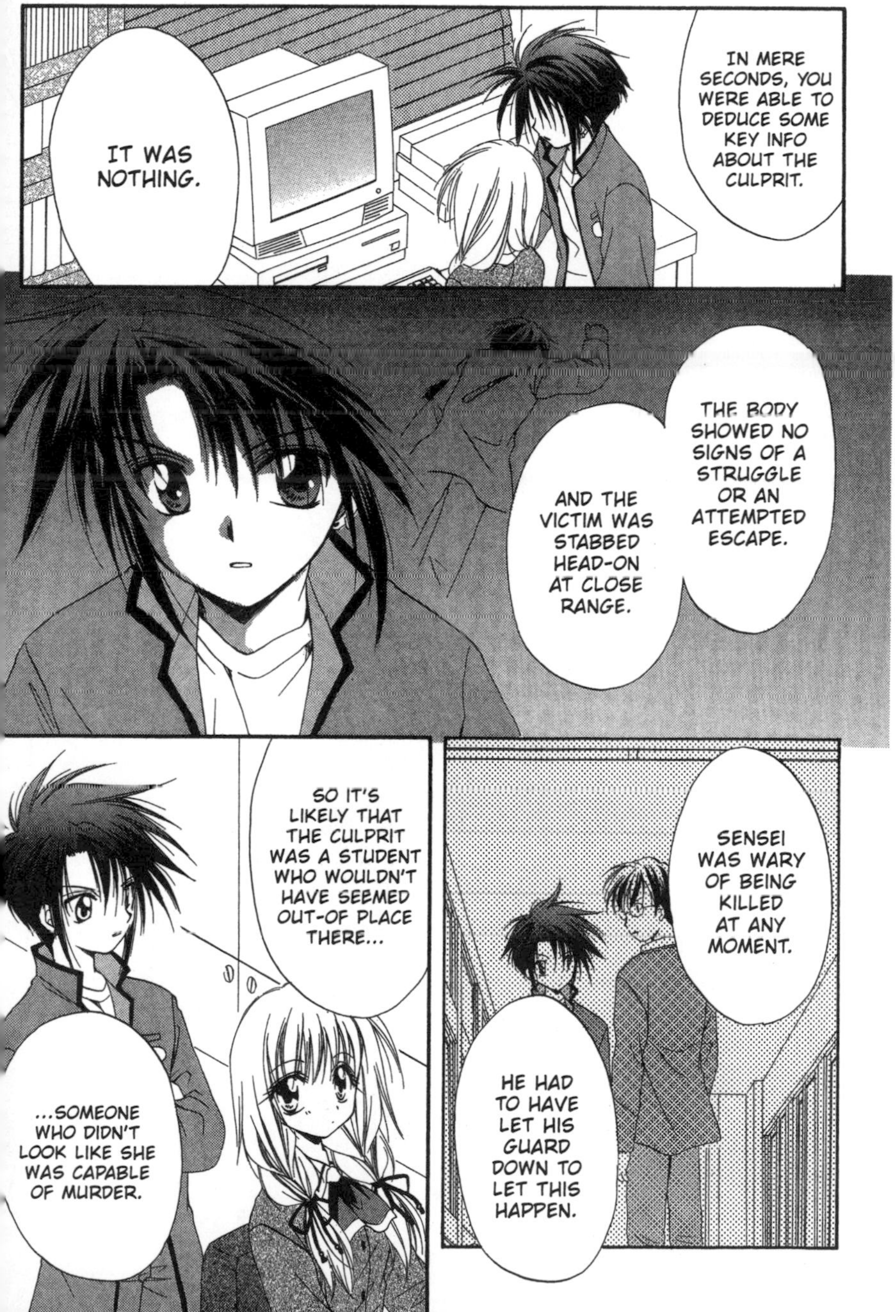
IN MERE SECONDS, YOU WERE ABLE TO DEDUCE SOME KEY INFO ABOUT THE CULPRIT.
IT WAS NOTHING.
THE BODY SHOWED NO SIGNS OF A STRUGGLE OR AN ATTEMPTED ESCAPE.
AND THE VICTIM WAS STABBED HEAD-ON AT CLOSE RANGE.
SENSEI WAS WARY OF BEING KILLED AT ANY MOMENT.
HE HAD TO HAVE LET HIS GUARD DOWN TO LET THIS HAPPEN.
SO IT'S LIKELY THAT THE CULPRIT WAS A STUDENT WHO WOULDN'T HAVE SEEMED OUT-OF PLACE THERE...
...SOMEONE WHO DIDN'T LOOK LIKE SHE WAS CAPABLE OF MURDER.

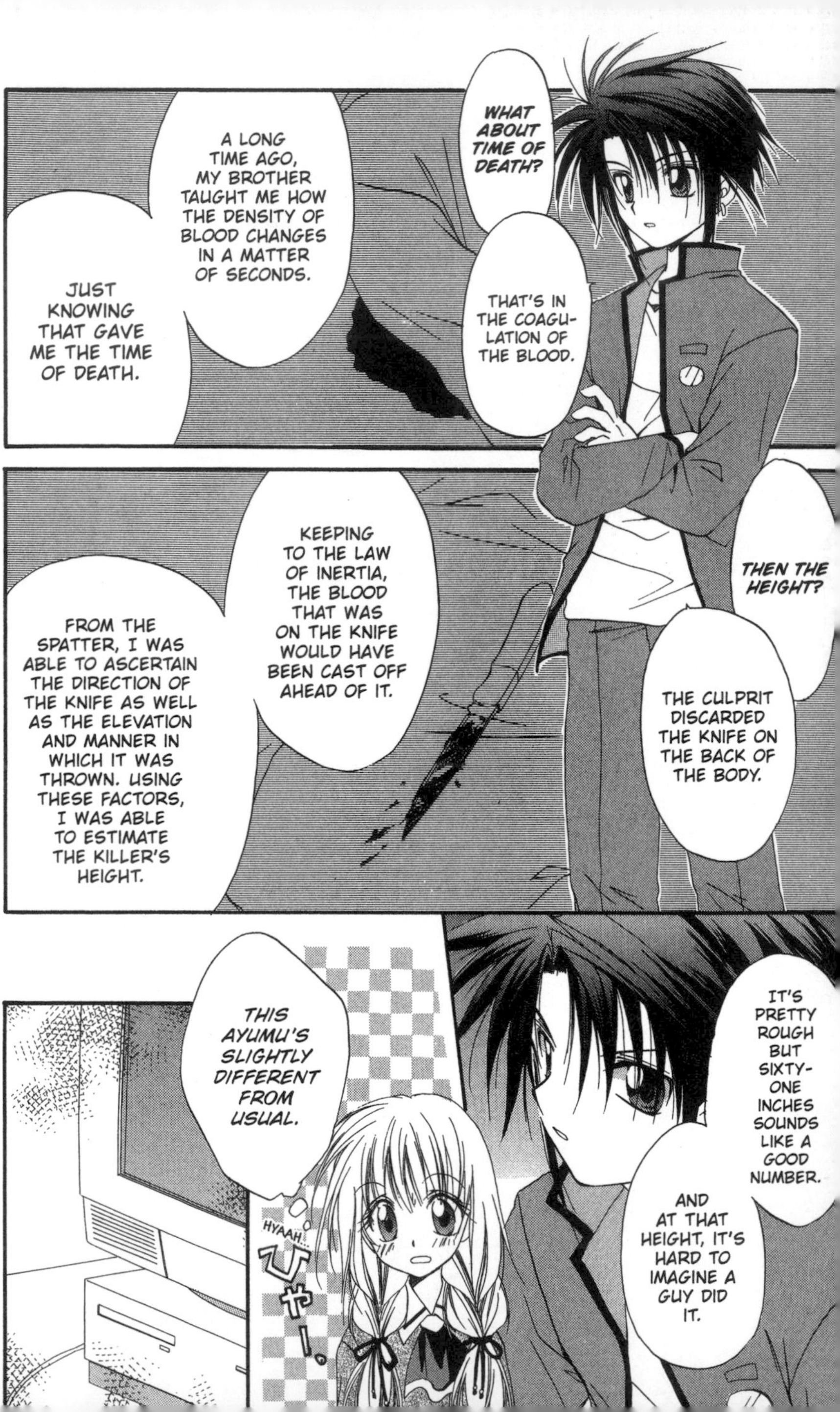
WHAT ABOUT TIME OF DEATH?
THAT'S IN THE COAGULATION OF THE BLOOD.
A LONG TIME AGO, MY BROTHER TAUGHT ME HOW THE DENSITY OF BLOOD CHANGES IN A MATTER OF SECONDS.
JUST KNOWING THAT GAVE ME THE TIME OF DEATH.
THEN THE HEIGHT?
THE CULPRIT DISCARDED THE KNIFE ON THE BACK OF THE BODY.
KEEPING TO THE LAW OF INERTIA, THE BLOOD THAT WAS ON THE KNIFE WOULD HAVE BEEN CAST OFF AHEAD OF IT.
FROM THE SPATTER, I WAS ABLE TO ASCERTAIN THE DIRECTION OF THE KNIFE AS WELL AS THE ELEVATION AND MANNER IN WHICH IT WAS THROWN. USING THESE FACTORS, I WAS ABLE TO ESTIMATE THE KILLER'S HEIGHT.
IT'S PRETTY ROUGH BUT SIXTY-ONE INCHES SOUNDS LIKE A GOOD NUMBER.
AND AT THAT HEIGHT, IT'S HARD TO IMAGINE A GUY DID IT.
THIS AYUMU'S SLIGHTLY DIFFERENT FROM USUAL.
HYAAH...
ひゃー。

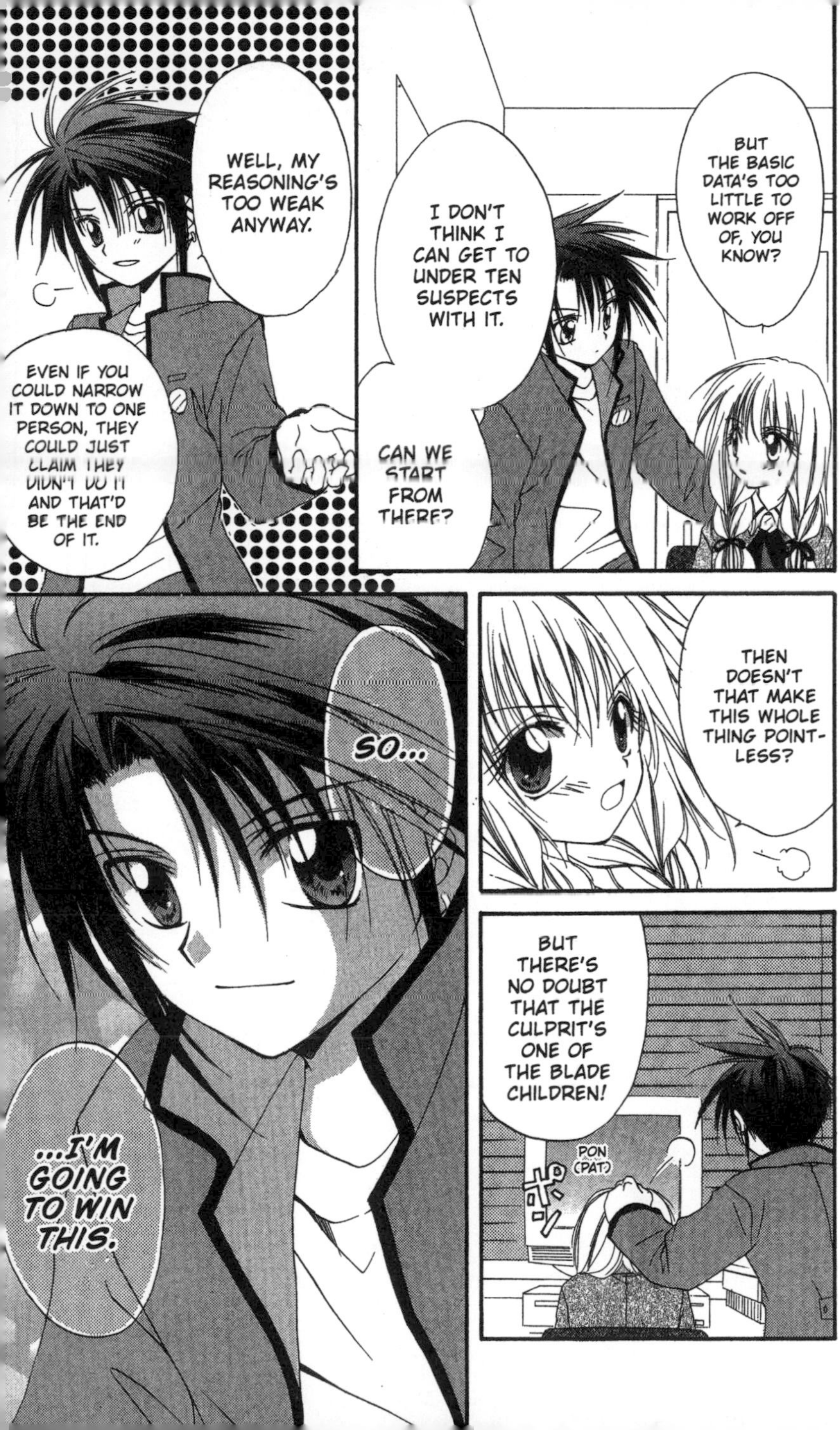
BUT THE BASIC DATA'S TOO LITTLE TO WORK OFF OF, YOU KNOW?
I DON'T THINK I CAN GET TO UNDER TEN SUSPECTS WITH IT.
CAN WE START FROM THERE?
WELL, MY REASONING'S TOO WEAK ANYWAY.
EVEN IF YOU COULD NARROW IT DOWN TO ONE PERSON, THEY COULD JUST CLAIM THEY DIDN'T DO IT AND THAT'D BE THE END OF IT.
THEN DOESN'T THAT MAKE THIS WHOLE THING POINT-LESS?
BUT THERE'S NO DOUBT THAT THE CULPRIT'S ONE OF THE BLADE CHILDREN!
PON (PAT)
SO...
...I'M GOING TO WIN THIS.

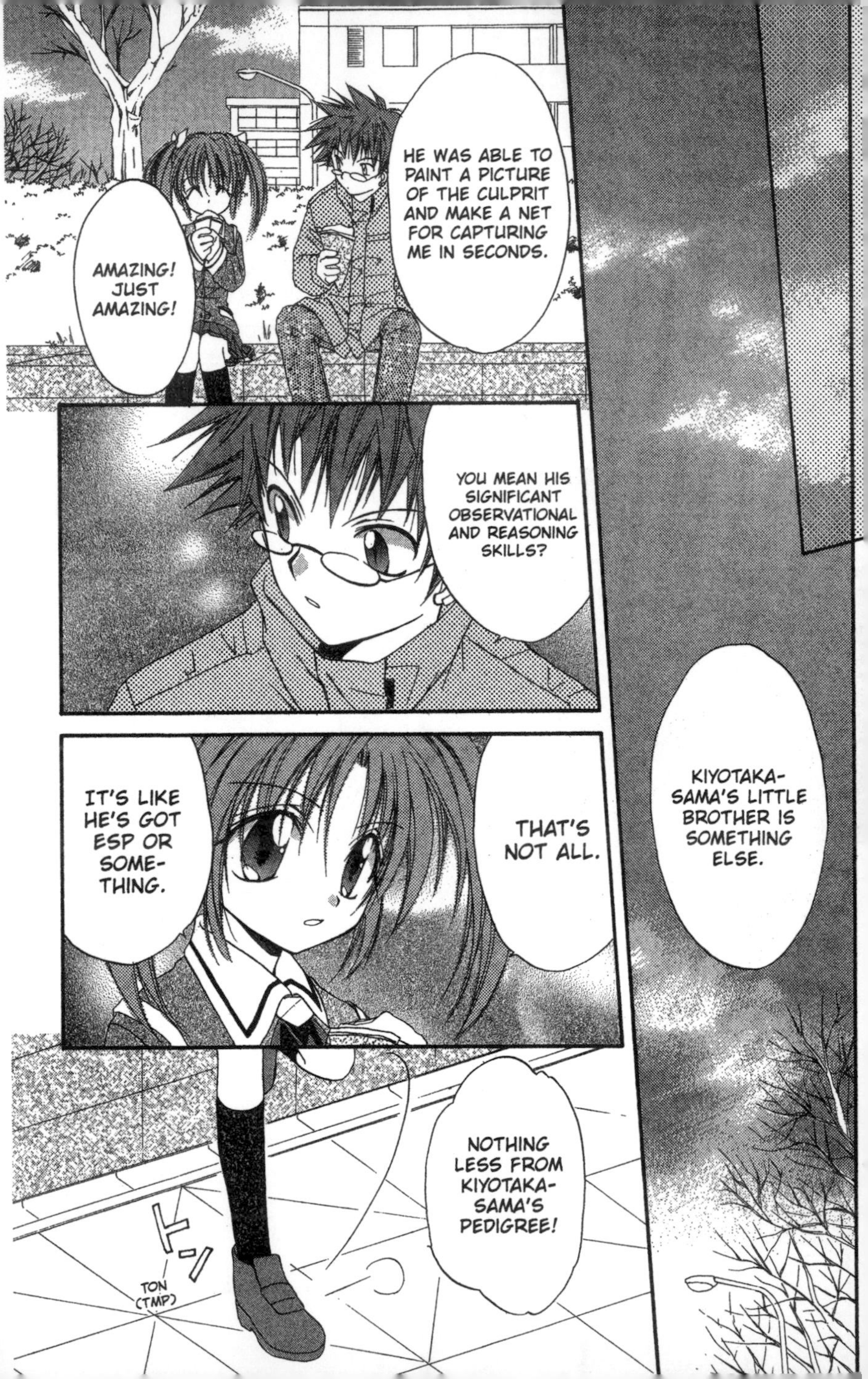
HE WAS ABLE TO PAINT A PICTURE OF THE CULPRIT AND MAKE A NET FOR CAPTURING ME IN SECONDS.
AMAZING! JUST AMAZING!
KIYOTAKA-SAMA'S LITTLE BROTHER IS SOMETHING ELSE.
YOU MEAN HIS SIGNIFICANT OBSERVATIONAL AND REASONING SKILLS?
THAT'S NOT ALL.
IT'S LIKE HE'S GOT ESP OR SOME-THING.
NOTHING LESS FROM KIYOTAKA-SAMA'S PEDIGREE!
TON (TMP)

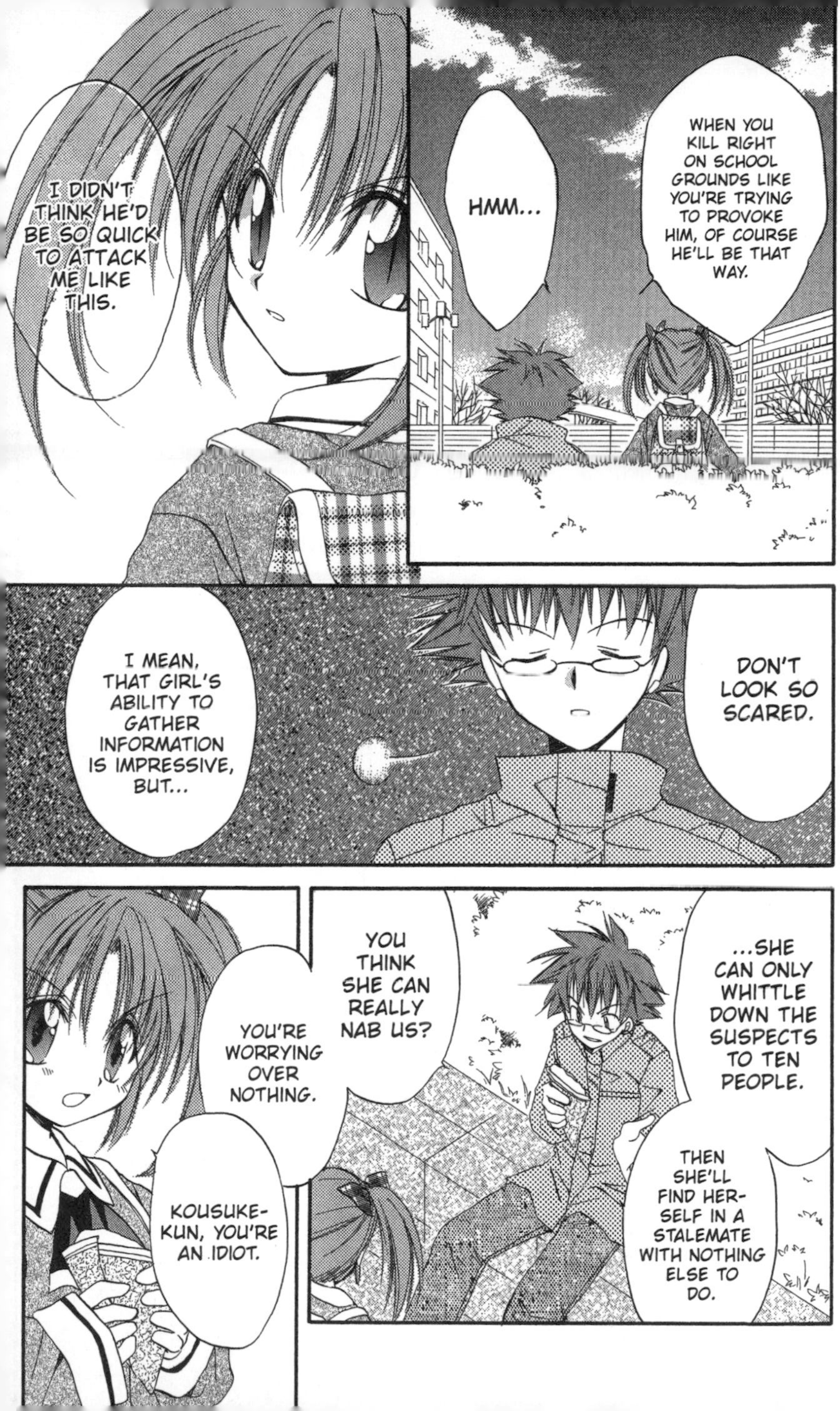
WHEN YOU KILL RIGHT ON SCHOOL GROUNDS LIKE YOU'RE TRYING TO PROVOKE HIM, OF COURSE HE'LL BE THAT WAY.
HMM...
I DIDN'T THINK HE'D BE SO QUICK TO ATTACK ME LIKE THIS.
DON'T LOOK SO SCARED.
I MEAN, THAT GIRL'S ABILITY TO GATHER INFORMATION IS IMPRESSIVE, BUT...
...SHE CAN ONLY WHITTLE DOWN THE SUSPECTS TO TEN PEOPLE.
THEN SHE'LL FIND HER-SELF IN A STALEMATE WITH NOTHING ELSE TO DO.
YOU THINK SHE CAN REALLY NAB US?
YOU'RE WORRYING OVER NOTHING.
KOUSUKE-KUN, YOU'RE AN IDIOT.

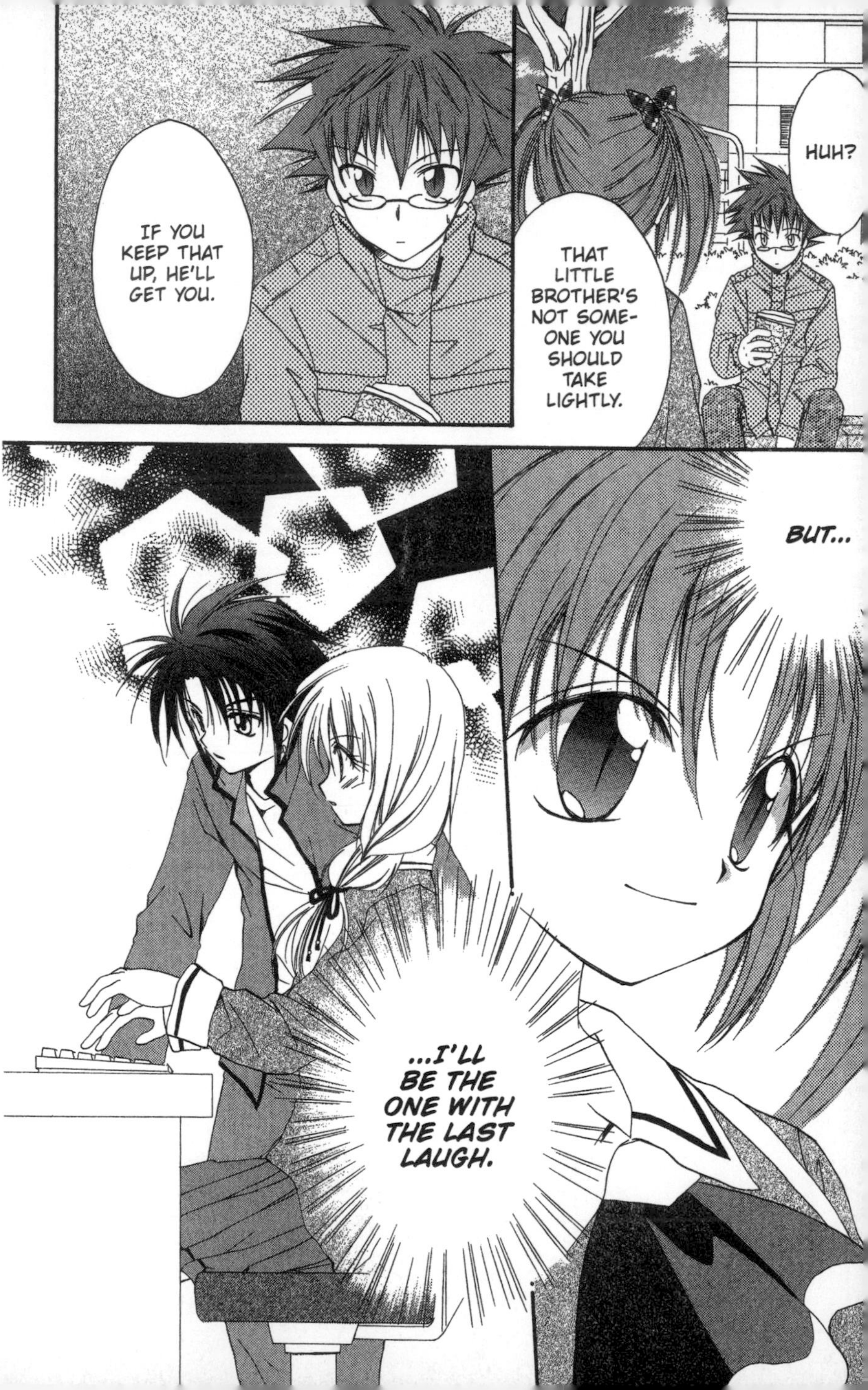
HUH?
THAT LITTLE BROTHER'S NOT SOME-ONE YOU SHOULD TAKE LIGHTLY.
IF YOU KEEP THAT UP, HE'LL GET YOU.
BUT...
...I'LL BE THE ONE WITH THE LAST LAUGH.

THE BONDS OF REASONING

Spiral

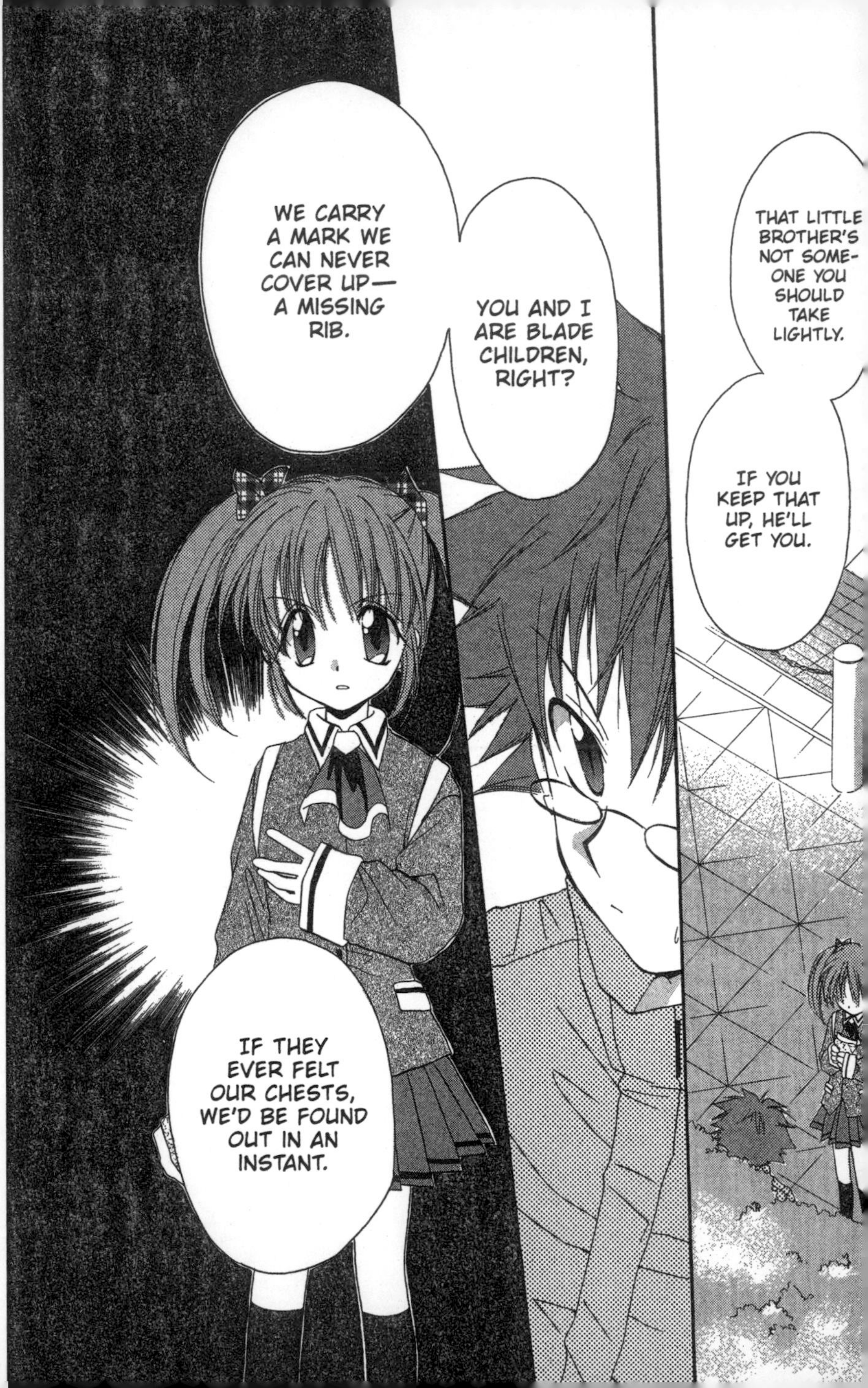
THAT LITTLE BROTHER'S NOT SOME-ONE YOU SHOULD TAKE LIGHTLY.
IF YOU KEEP THAT UP, HE'LL GET YOU.
YOU AND I ARE BLADE CHILDREN, RIGHT?
WE CARRY A MARK WE CAN NEVER COVER UP—A MISSING RIB.
IF THEY EVER FELT OUR CHESTS, WE'D BE FOUND OUT IN AN INSTANT.

CHAPTER THIRTEEN
THROW OFF THE ENCOMPASSING NET

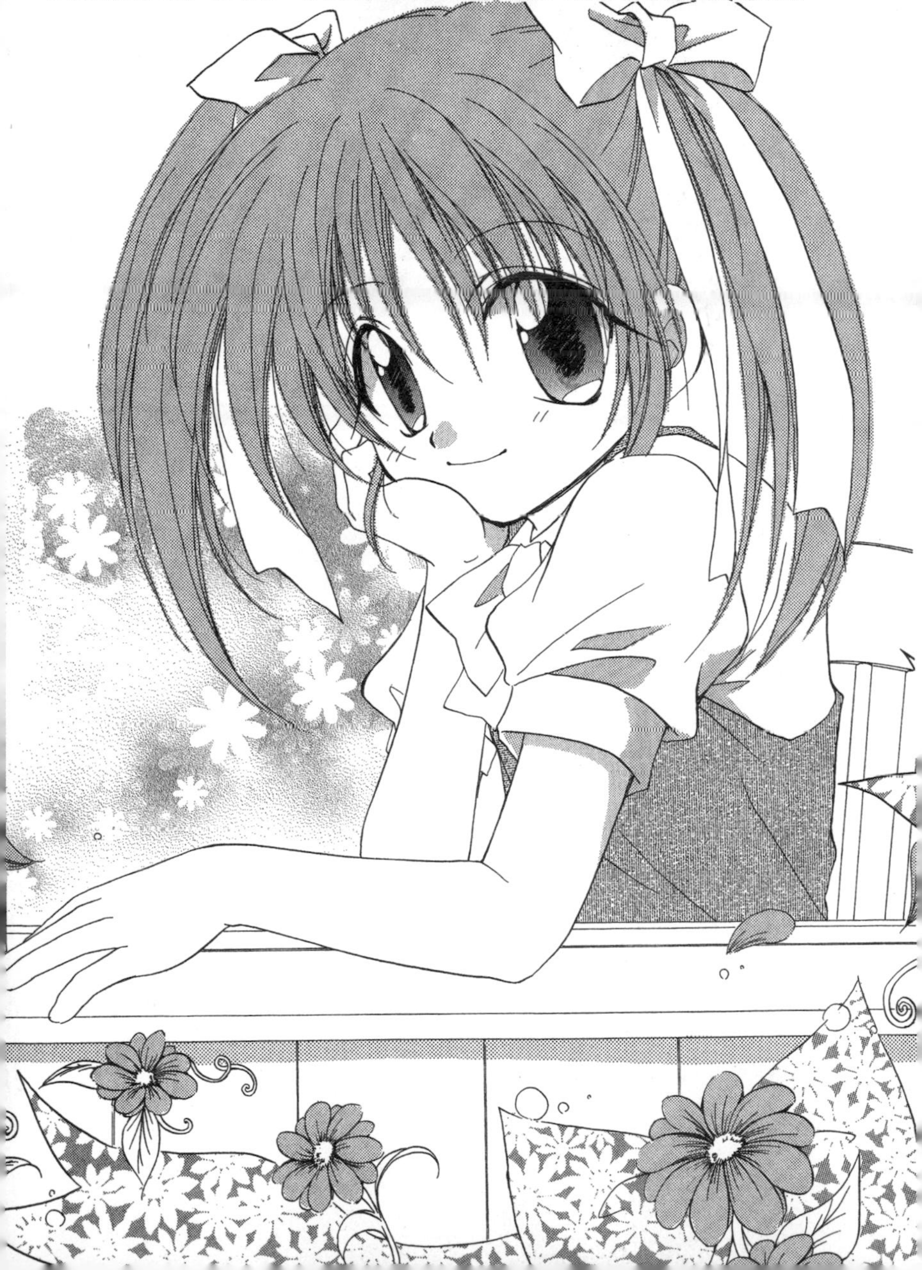

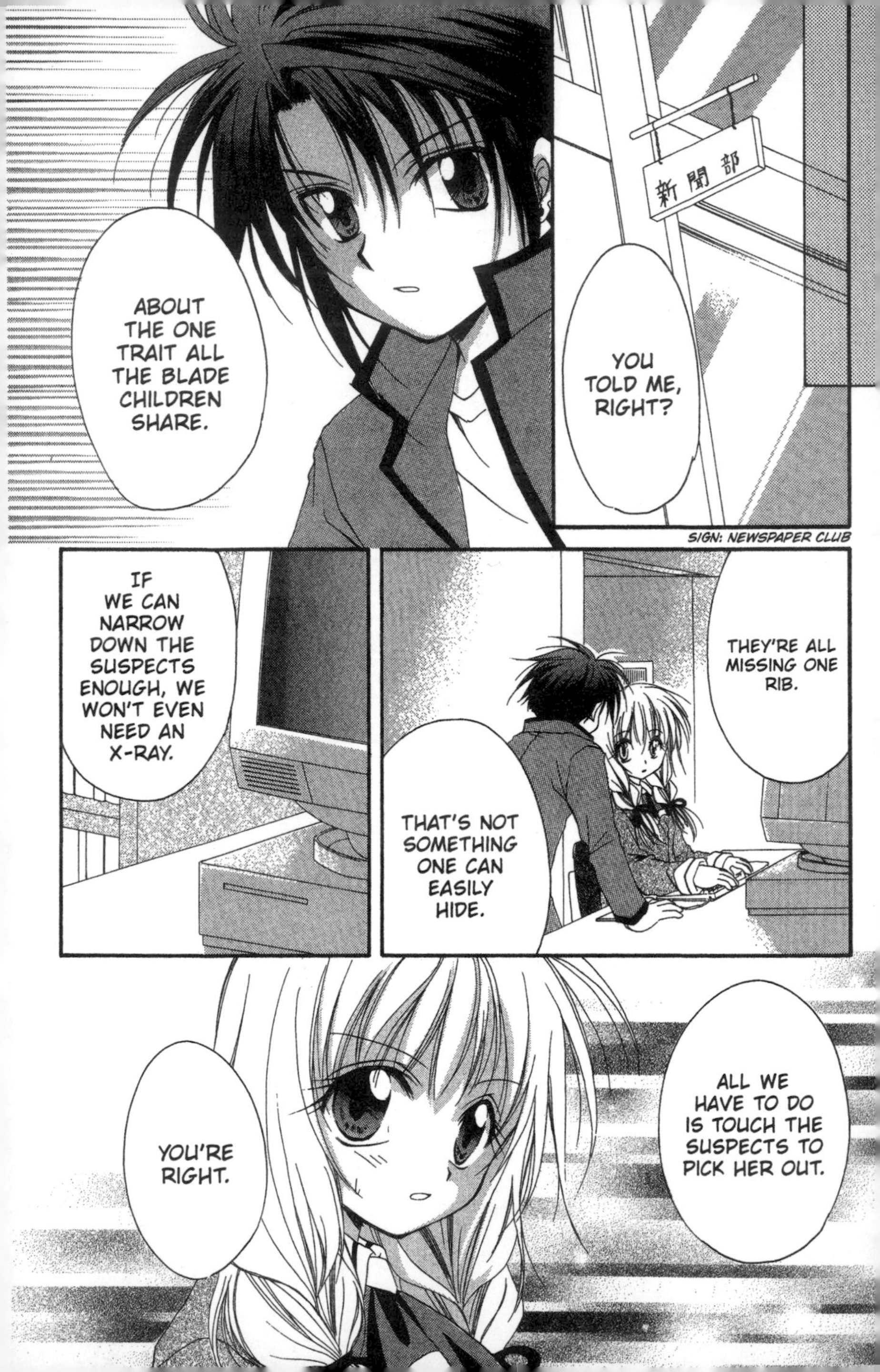
新聞部
YOU TOLD ME, RIGHT?
SIGN: NEWSPAPER CLUB
ABOUT THE ONE TRAIT ALL THE BLADE CHILDREN SHARE.
THEY'RE ALL MISSING ONE RIB.
THAT'S NOT SOMETHING ONE CAN EASILY HIDE.
IF WE CAN NARROW DOWN THE SUSPECTS ENOUGH, WE WON'T EVEN NEED AN X-RAY.
ALL WE HAVE TO DO IS TOUCH THE SUSPECTS TO PICK HER OUT.
YOU'RE RIGHT.

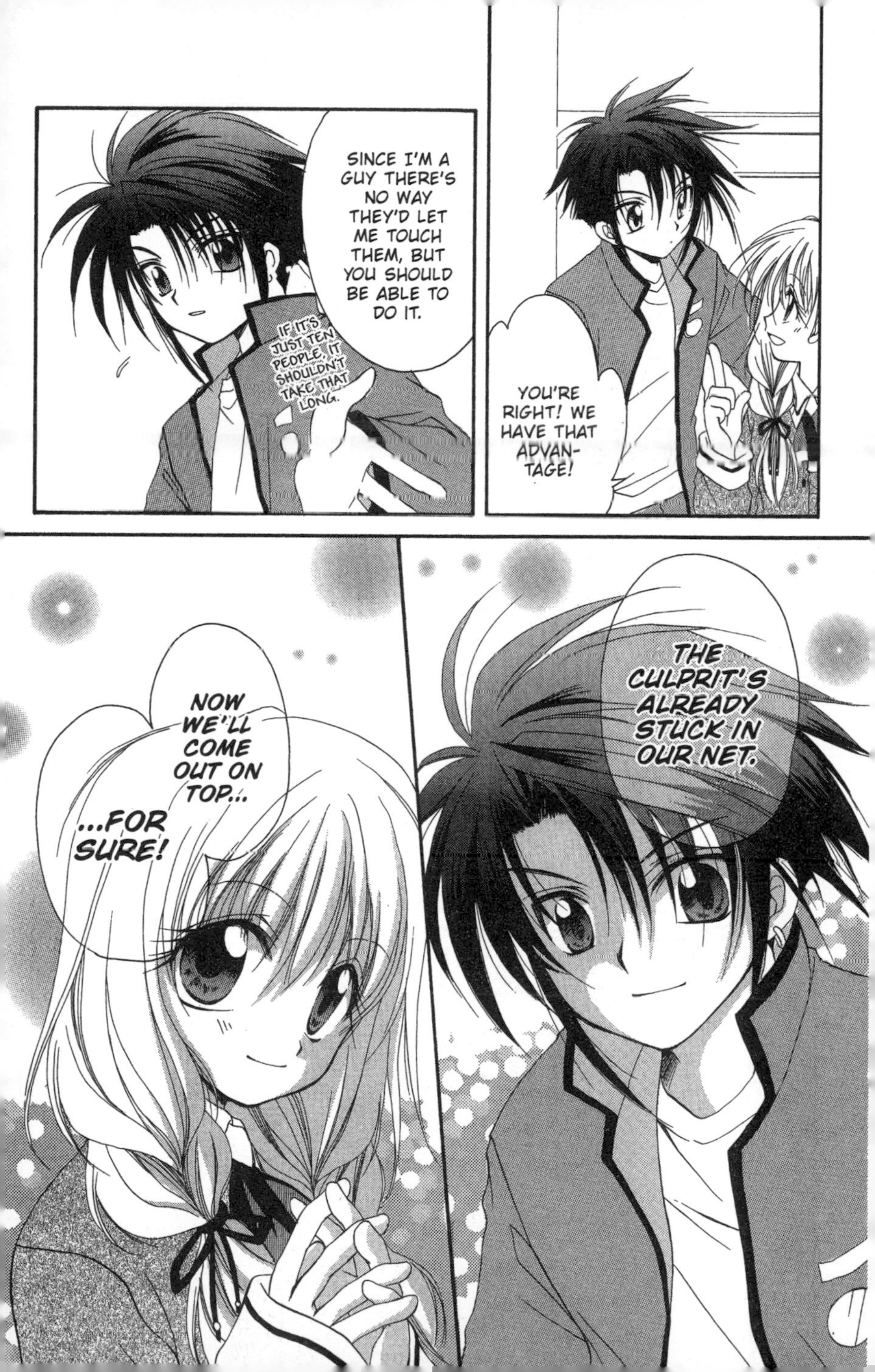
SINCE I'M A GUY THERE'S NO WAY THEY'D LET ME TOUCH THEM, BUT YOU SHOULD BE ABLE TO DO IT.
IF IT'S JUST TEN PEOPLE, IT SHOULDN'T TAKE THAT LONG.
YOU'RE RIGHT! WE HAVE THAT ADVAN-TAGE!
NOW WE'LL COME OUT ON TOP...
...FOR SURE!
THE CULPRIT'S ALREADY STUCK IN OUR NET.

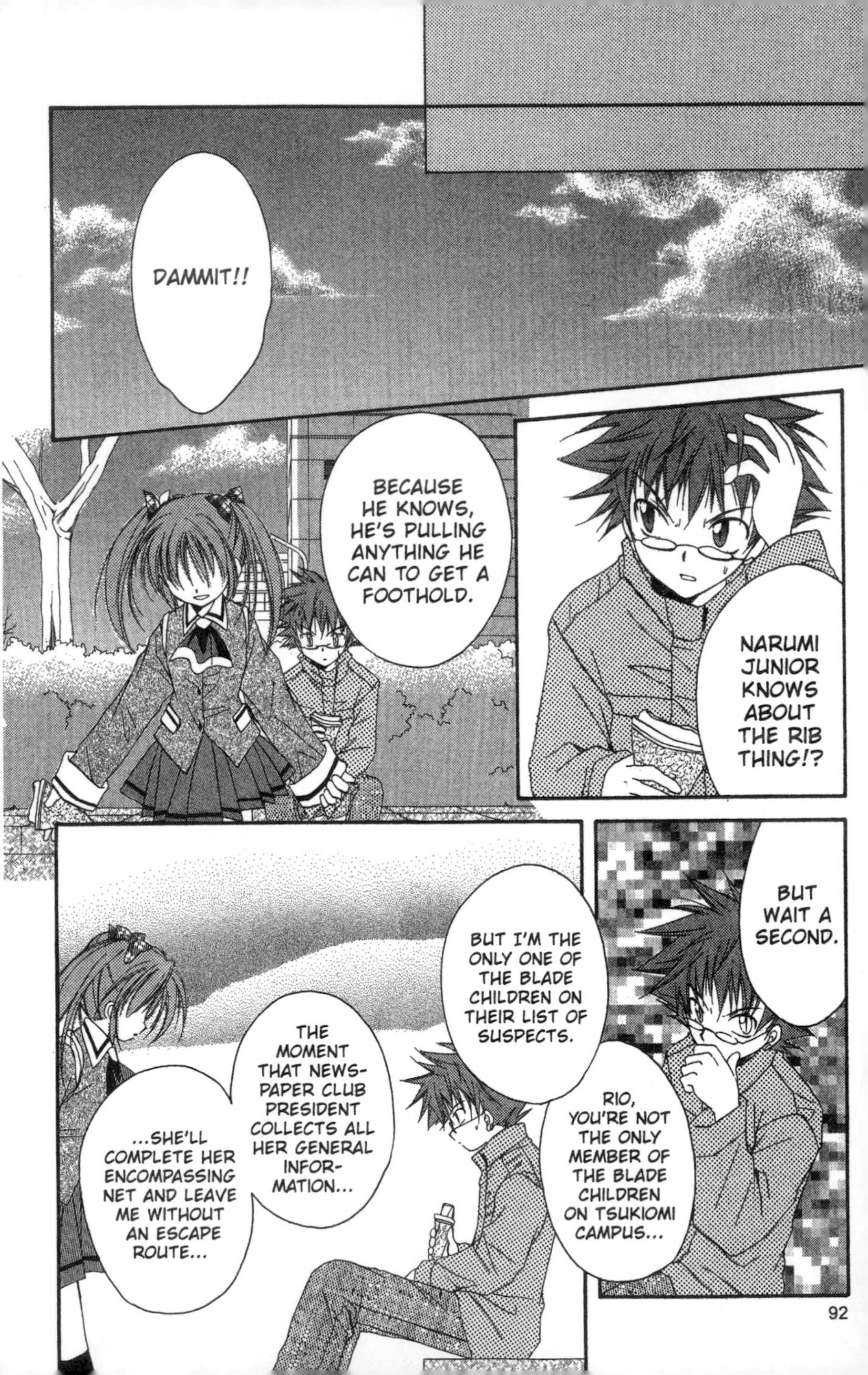
DAMMIT!!
NARUMI JUNIOR KNOWS ABOUT THE RIB THING!?
BECAUSE HE KNOWS, HE'S PULLING ANYTHING HE CAN TO GET A FOOTHOLD.
BUT WAIT A SECOND.
RIO, YOU'RE NOT THE ONLY MEMBER OF THE BLADE CHILDREN ON TSUKIOMI CAMPUS...
BUT I'M THE ONLY ONE OF THE BLADE CHILDREN ON THEIR LIST OF SUSPECTS.
THE MOMENT THAT NEWS-PAPER CLUB PRESIDENT COLLECTS ALL HER GENERAL INFOR-MATION...
...SHE'LL COMPLETE HER ENCOMPASSING NET AND LEAVE ME WITHOUT AN ESCAPE ROUTE...

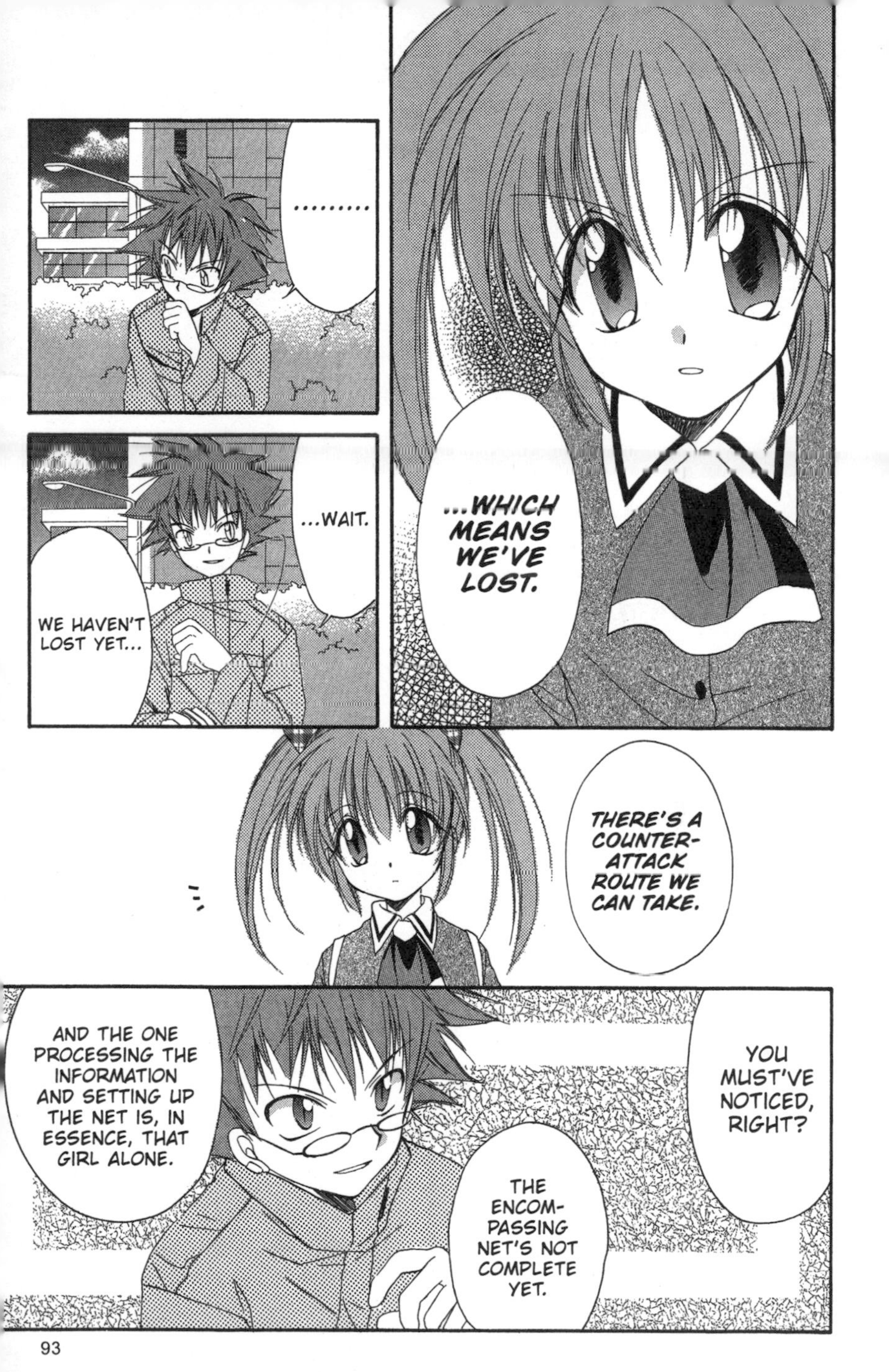
...WHICH MEANS WE'VE LOST.
....
...WAIT.
WE HAVEN'T LOST YET...
THERE'S A COUNTER-ATTACK ROUTE WE CAN TAKE.
YOU MUST'VE NOTICED, RIGHT?
THE ENCOM-PASSING NET'S NOT COMPLETE YET.
AND THE ONE PROCESSING THE INFORMATION AND SETTING UP THE NET IS, IN ESSENCE, THAT GIRL ALONE.

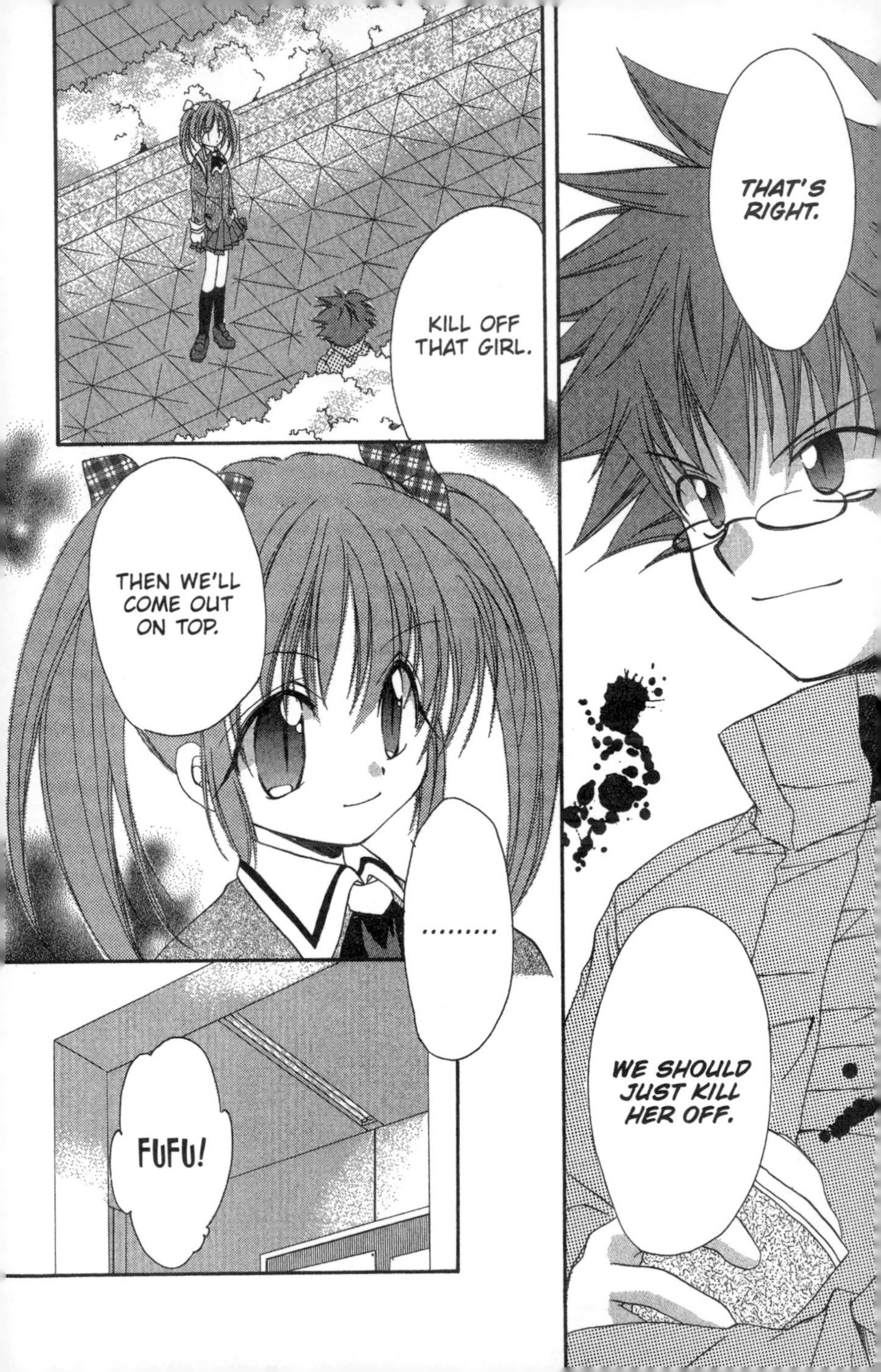
THAT'S RIGHT.
WE SHOULD JUST KILL HER OFF.
KILL OFF THAT GIRL.
THEN WE'LL COME OUT ON TOP.
....
FUFU!

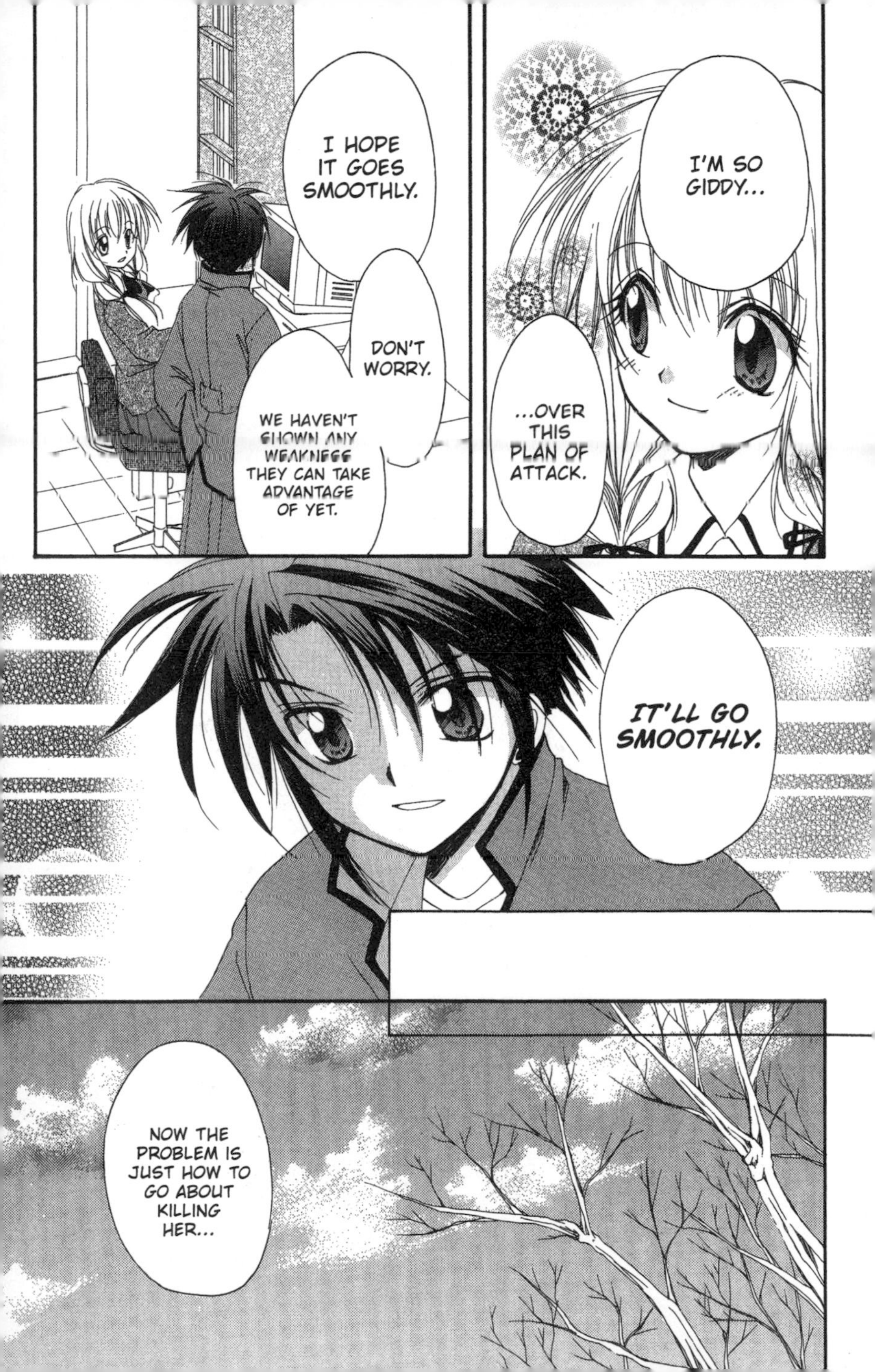
I'M SO GIDDY...
...OVER THIS PLAN OF ATTACK.
I HOPE IT GOES SMOOTHLY.
DON'T WORRY.
WE HAVEN'T SHOWN ANY WEAKNESS THEY CAN TAKE ADVANTAGE OF YET.
IT'LL GO SMOOTHLY.
NOW THE PROBLEM IS JUST HOW TO GO ABOUT KILLING HER...

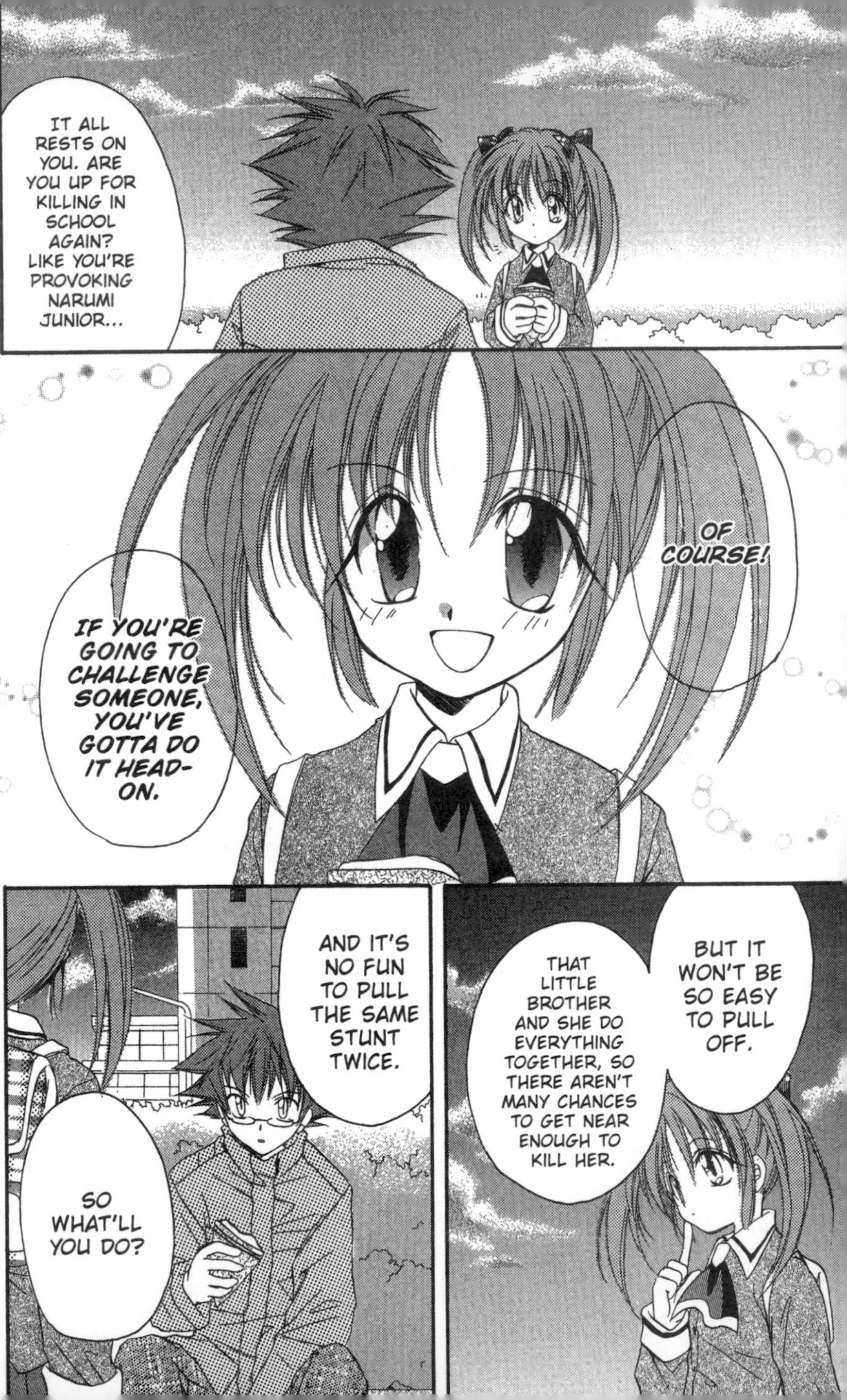

IT ALL RESTS ON YOU. ARE YOU UP FOR KILLING IN SCHOOL AGAIN? LIKE YOU'RE PROVOKING NARUMI JUNIOR...
OF COURSE!
IF YOU'RE GOING TO CHALLENGE SOMEONE, YOU'VE GOTTA DO IT HEAD-ON.
BUT IT WON'T BE SO EASY TO PULL OFF.
THAT LITTLE BROTHER AND SHE DO EVERYTHING TOGETHER, SO THERE AREN'T MANY CHANCES TO GET NEAR ENOUGH TO KILL HER.
AND IT'S NO FUN TO PULL THE SAME STUNT TWICE.
SO WHAT'LL YOU DO?

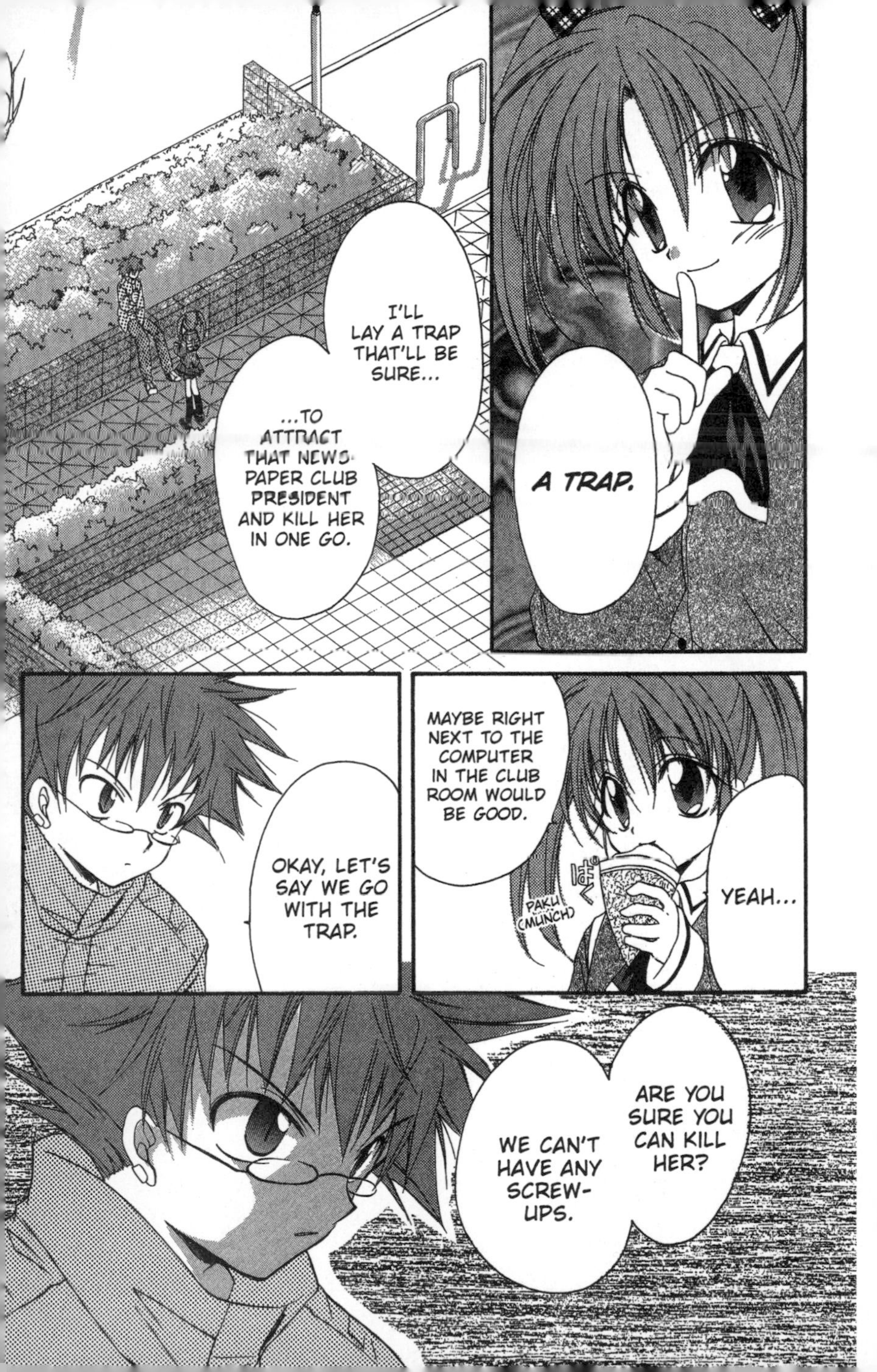
A TRAP.
I'LL LAY A TRAP THAT'LL BE SURE...
...TO ATTRACT THAT NEWS-PAPER CLUB PRESIDENT AND KILL HER IN ONE GO.
YEAH...
MAYBE RIGHT NEXT TO THE COMPUTER IN THE CLUB ROOM WOULD BE GOOD.
ぱく
PAKU (MUNCH)
OKAY, LET'S SAY WE GO WITH THE TRAP.
ARE YOU SURE YOU CAN KILL HER?
WE CAN'T HAVE ANY SCREW-UPS.

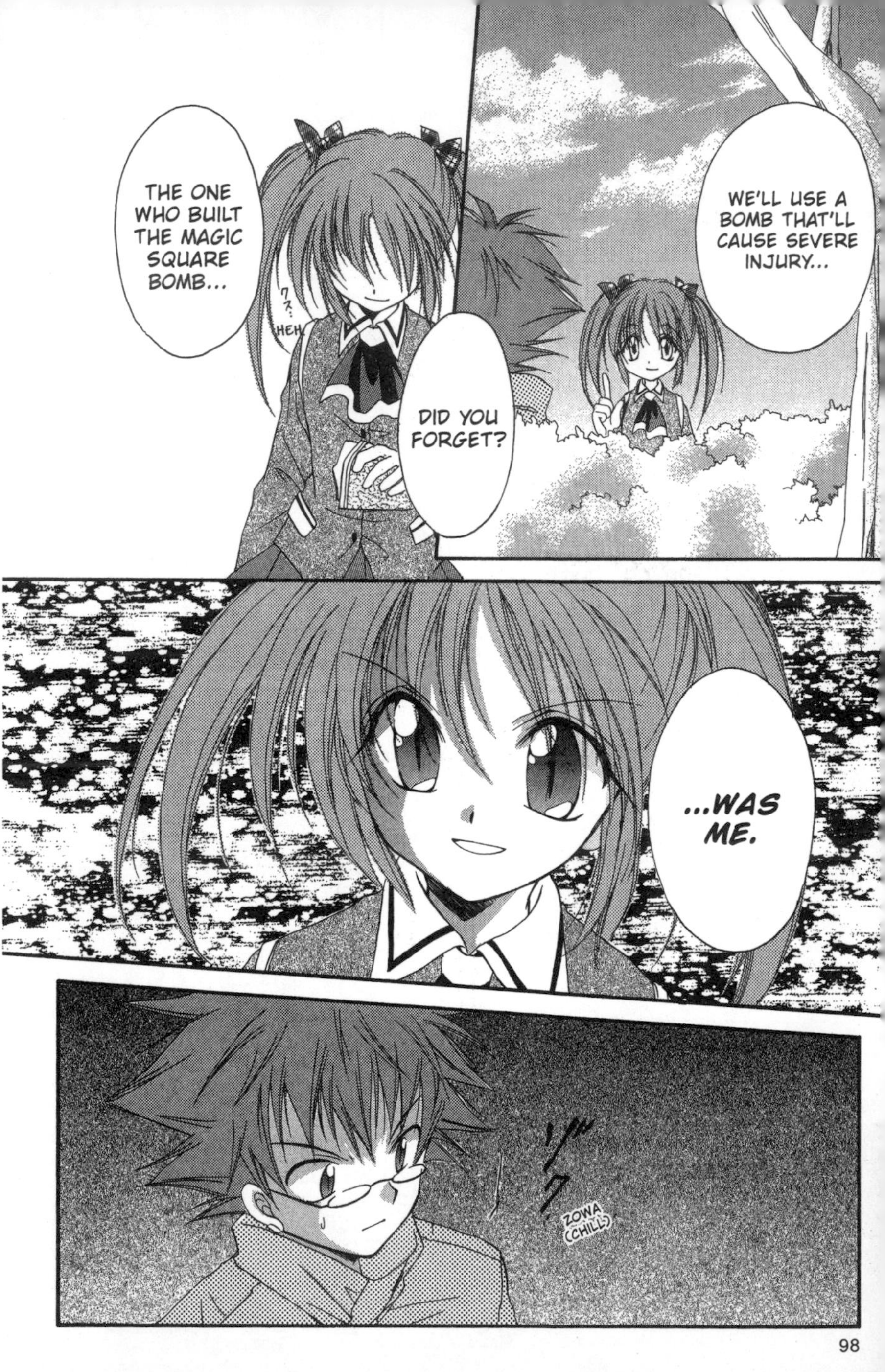
WE'LL USE A BOMB THAT'LL CAUSE SEVERE INJURY...
DID YOU FORGET?
THE ONE WHO BUILT THE MAGIC SQUARE BOMB...
クス…
HEH
...WAS ME.
ゾク
ZOWA (CHILL)

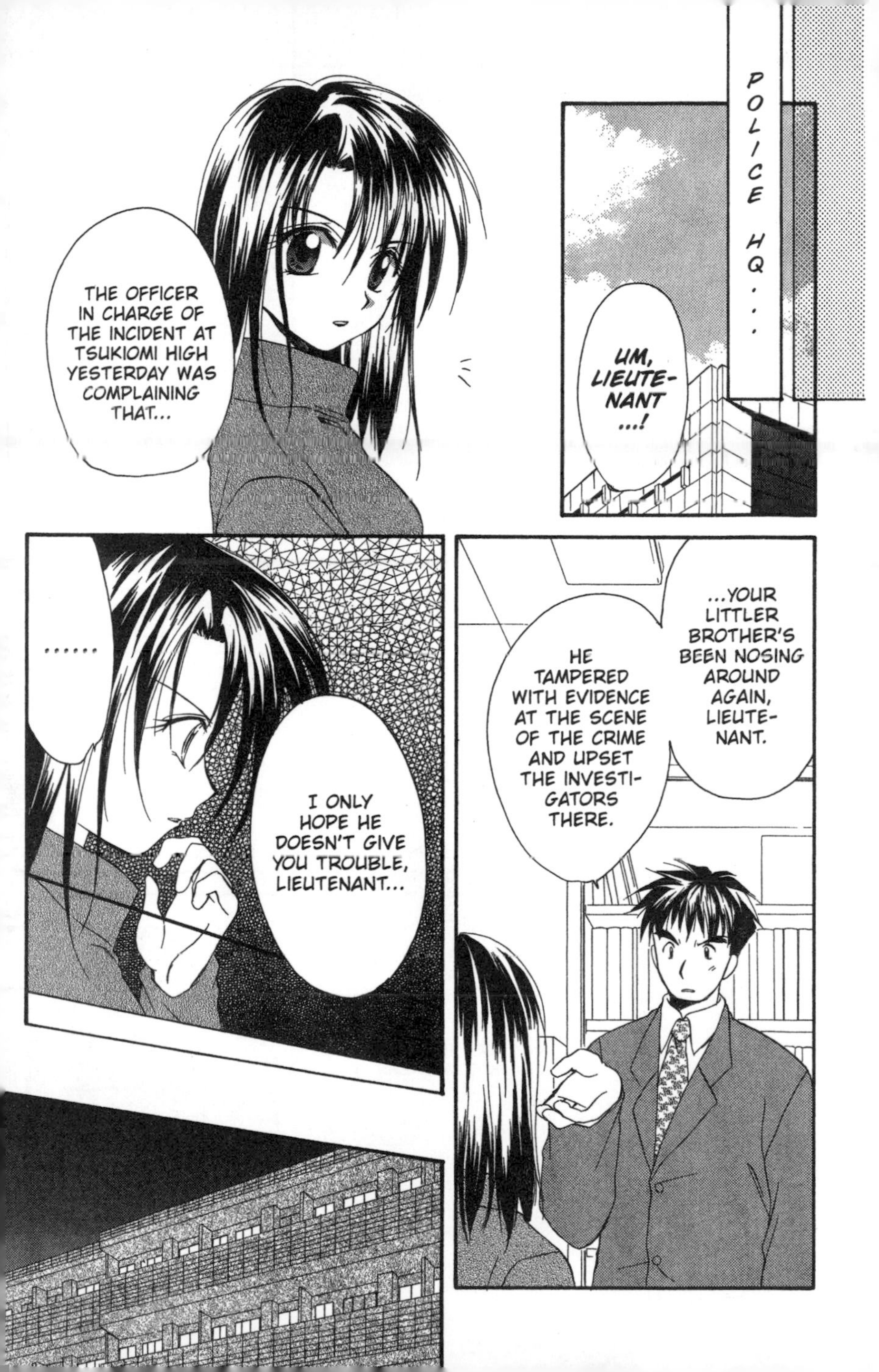
POLICE HQ . . .
UM, LIEUTENANT ...!
THE OFFICER IN CHARGE OF THE INCIDENT AT TSUKIOMI HIGH YESTERDAY WAS COMPLAINING THAT...
...YOUR LITTLER BROTHER'S BEEN NOSING AROUND AGAIN, LIEUTENANT.
HE TAMPERED WITH EVIDENCE AT THE SCENE OF THE CRIME AND UPSET THE INVESTIGATORS THERE.
......
I ONLY HOPE HE DOESN'T GIVE YOU TROUBLE, LIEUTENANT...

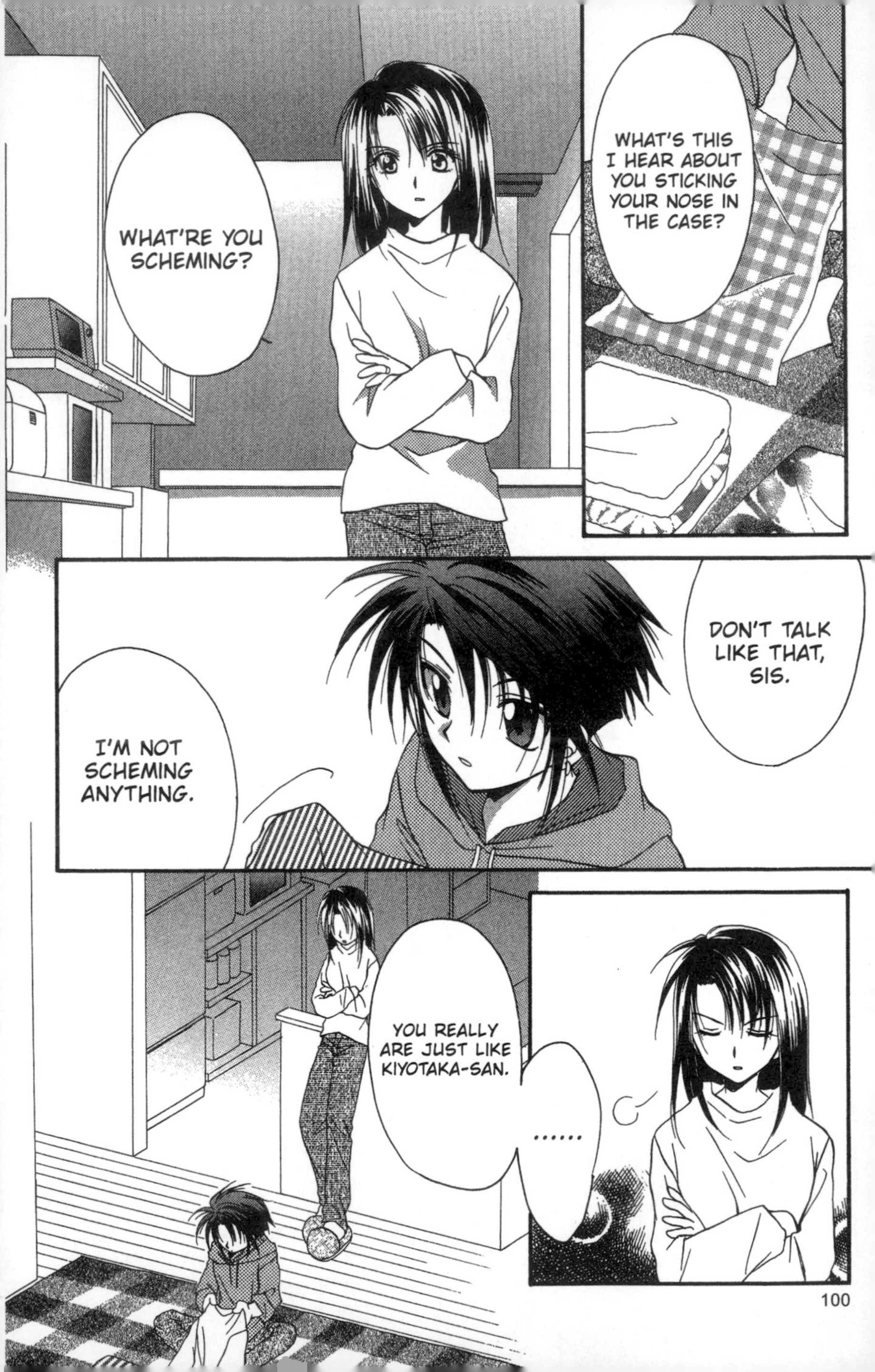
WHAT'S THIS I HEAR ABOUT YOU STICKING YOUR NOSE IN THE CASE?
WHAT'RE YOU SCHEMING?
DON'T TALK LIKE THAT, SIS.
I'M NOT SCHEMING ANYTHING.
......
YOU REALLY ARE JUST LIKE KIYOTAKA-SAN.

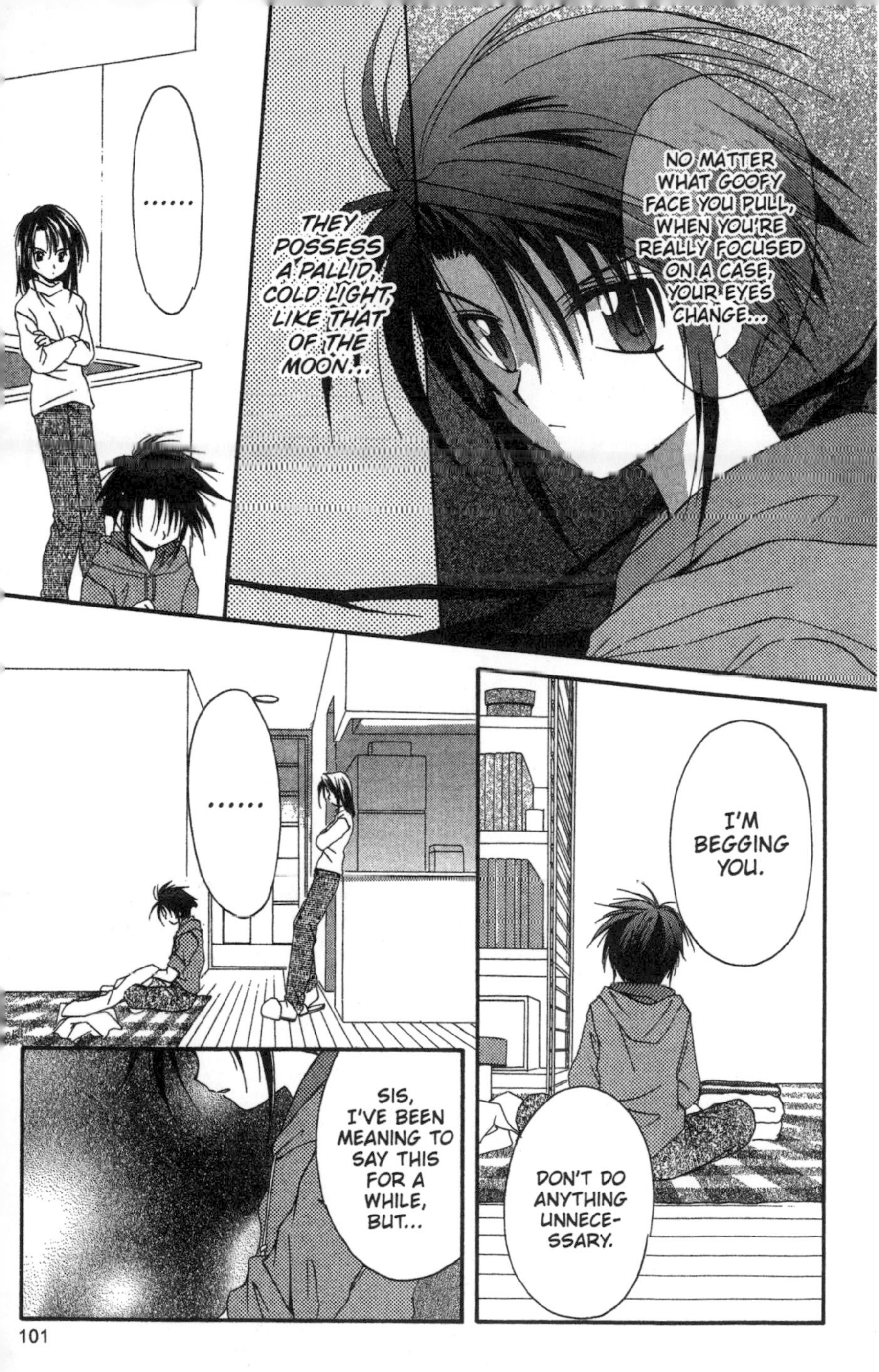
NO MATTER WHAT GOOFY FACE YOU PULL, WHEN YOU'RE REALLY FOCUSED ON A CASE, YOUR EYES CHANGE...
THEY POSSESS A PALLID, COLD LIGHT, LIKE THAT OF THE MOON...
......
I'M BEGGING YOU.
DON'T DO ANYTHING UNNECE-SSARY.
......
SIS, I'VE BEEN MEANING TO SAY THIS FOR A WHILE, BUT...

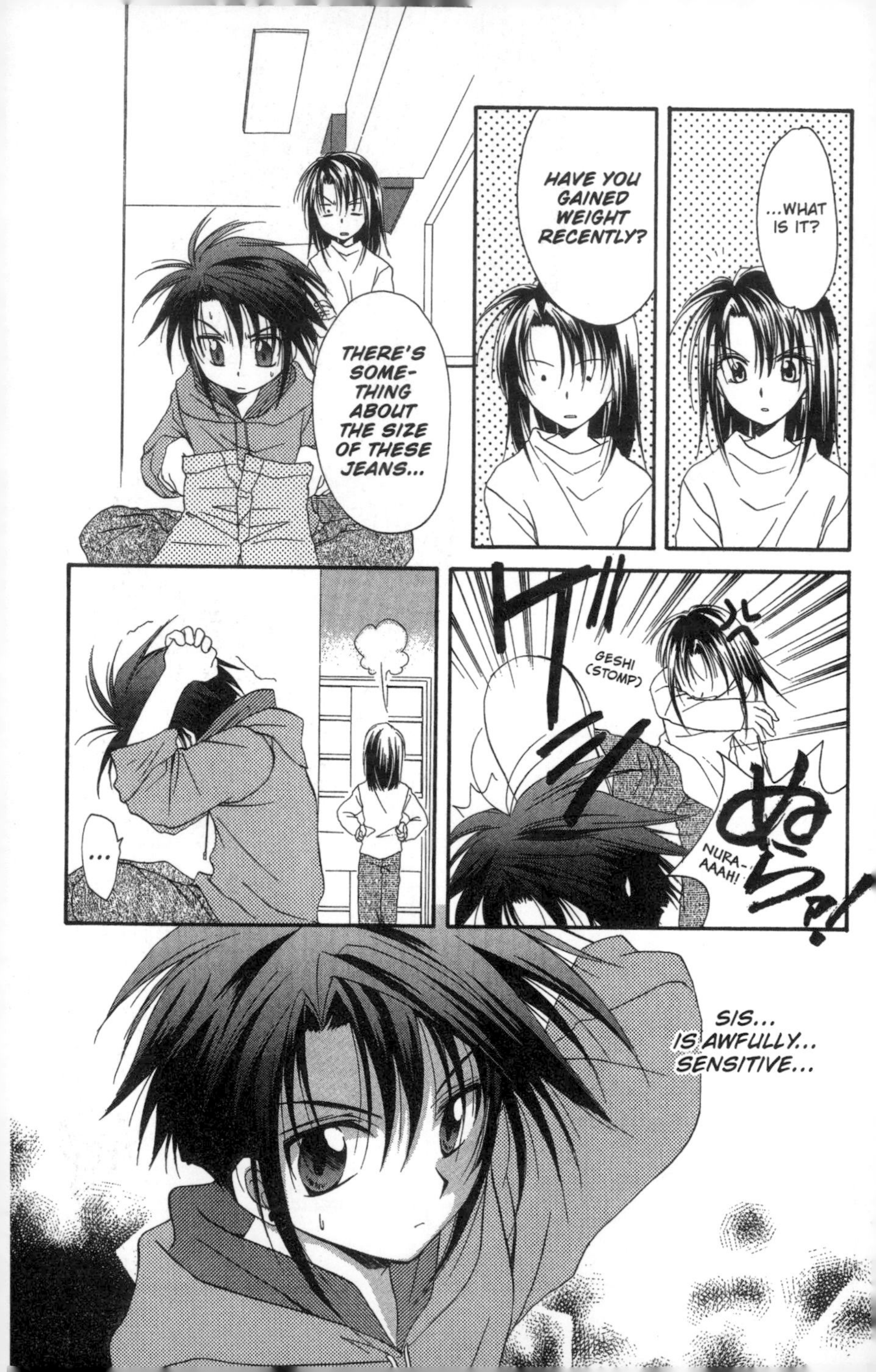
THERE'S SOMETHING ABOUT THE SIZE OF THESE JEANS...
...WHAT IS IT?
HAVE YOU GAINED WEIGHT RECENTLY?
GESHI (STOMP)
NURA-AAAH!
...
SIS... IS AWFULLY... SENSITIVE...

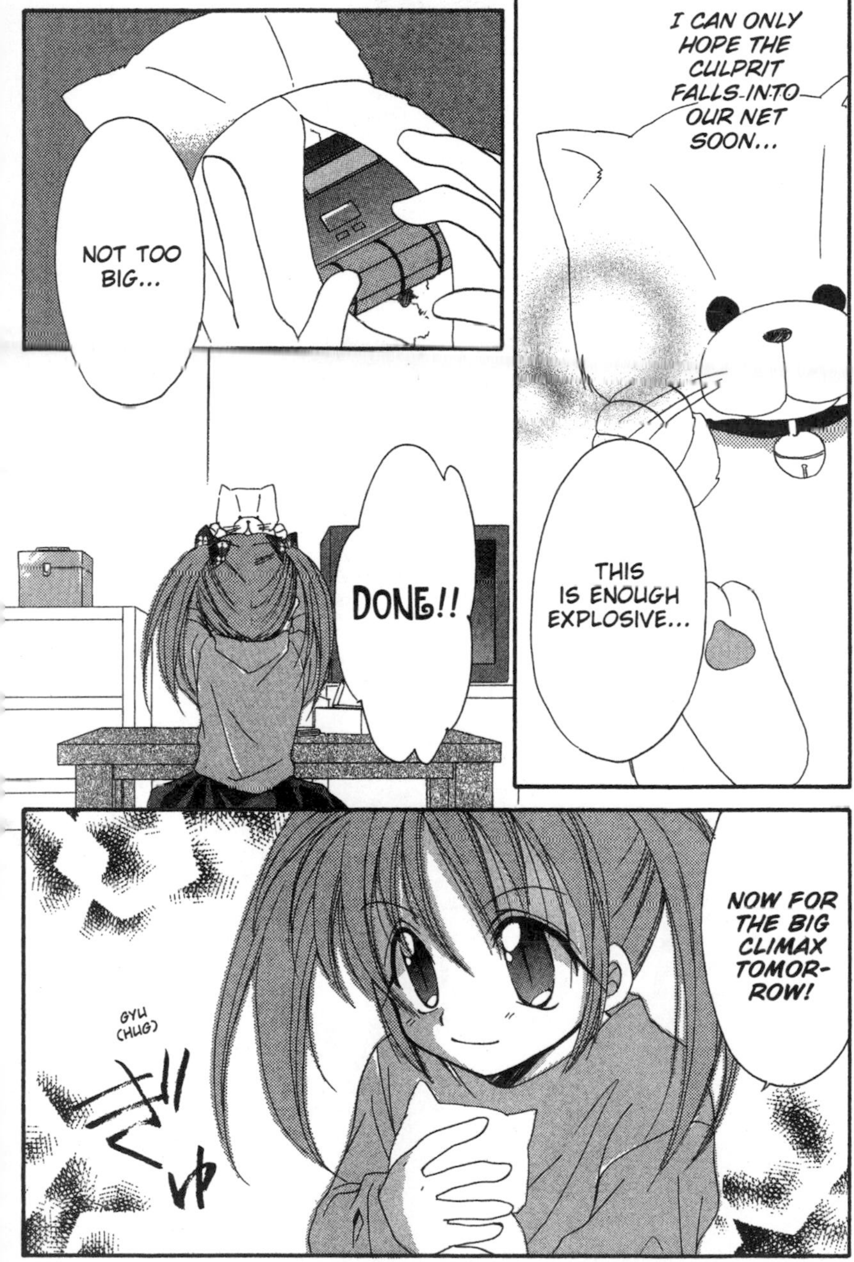
I CAN ONLY HOPE THE CULPRIT FALLS INTO OUR NET SOON...
THIS IS ENOUGH EXPLOSIVE...
NOT TOO BIG...
DONE!!
NOW FOR THE BIG CLIMAX TOMOR-ROW!
GYU (HUG)
ぎゅ

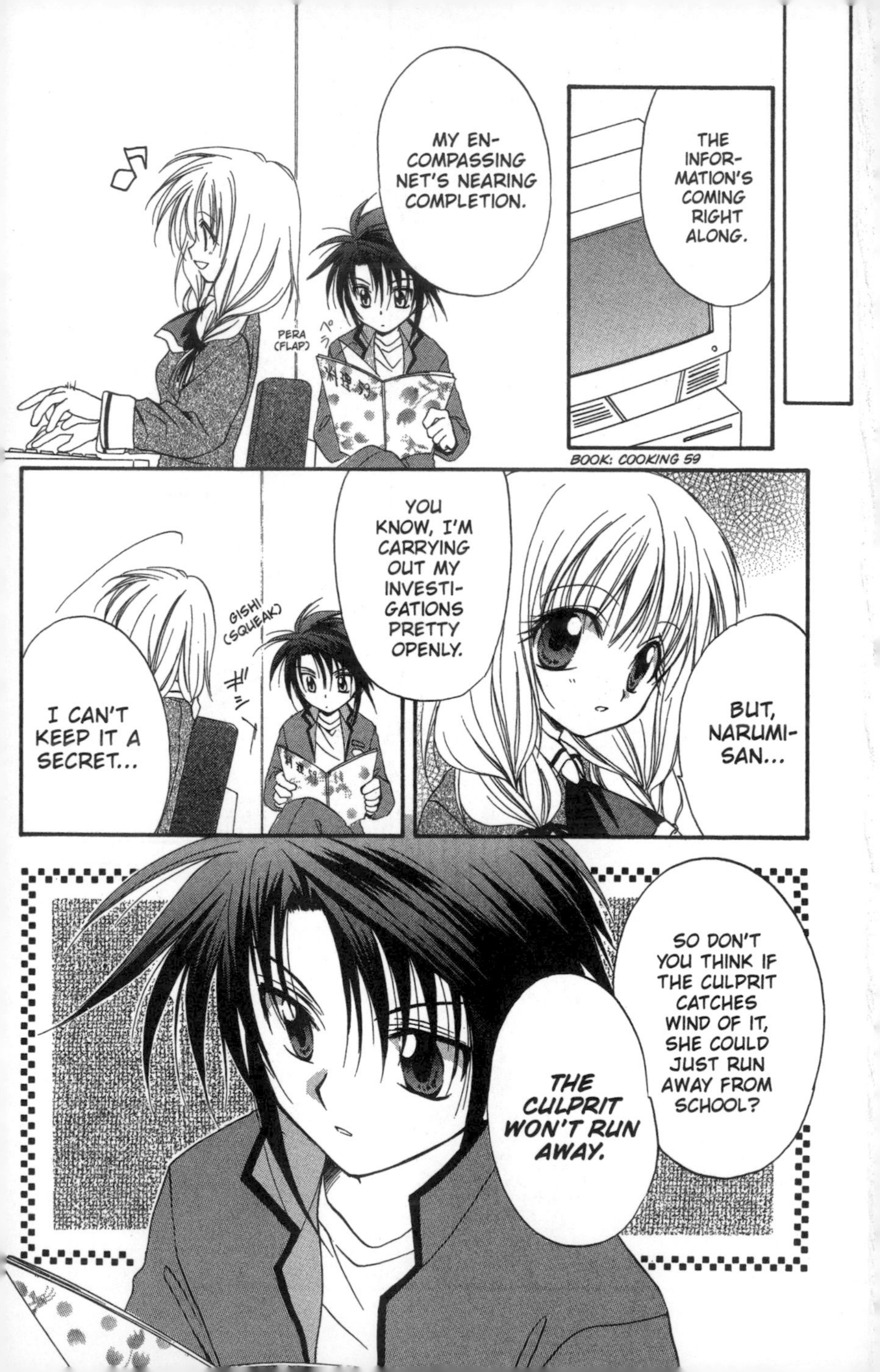
THE INFOR-MATION'S COMING RIGHT ALONG.
MY EN-COMPASSING NET'S NEARING COMPLETION.
PERA (FLAP)
BOOK: COOKING 59
BUT, NARUMI-SAN...
YOU KNOW, I'M CARRYING OUT MY INVESTI-GATIONS PRETTY OPENLY.
GISHI (SQUEAK)
I CAN'T KEEP IT A SECRET...
SO DON'T YOU THINK IF THE CULPRIT CATCHES WIND OF IT, SHE COULD JUST RUN AWAY FROM SCHOOL?
THE CULPRIT WON'T RUN AWAY.

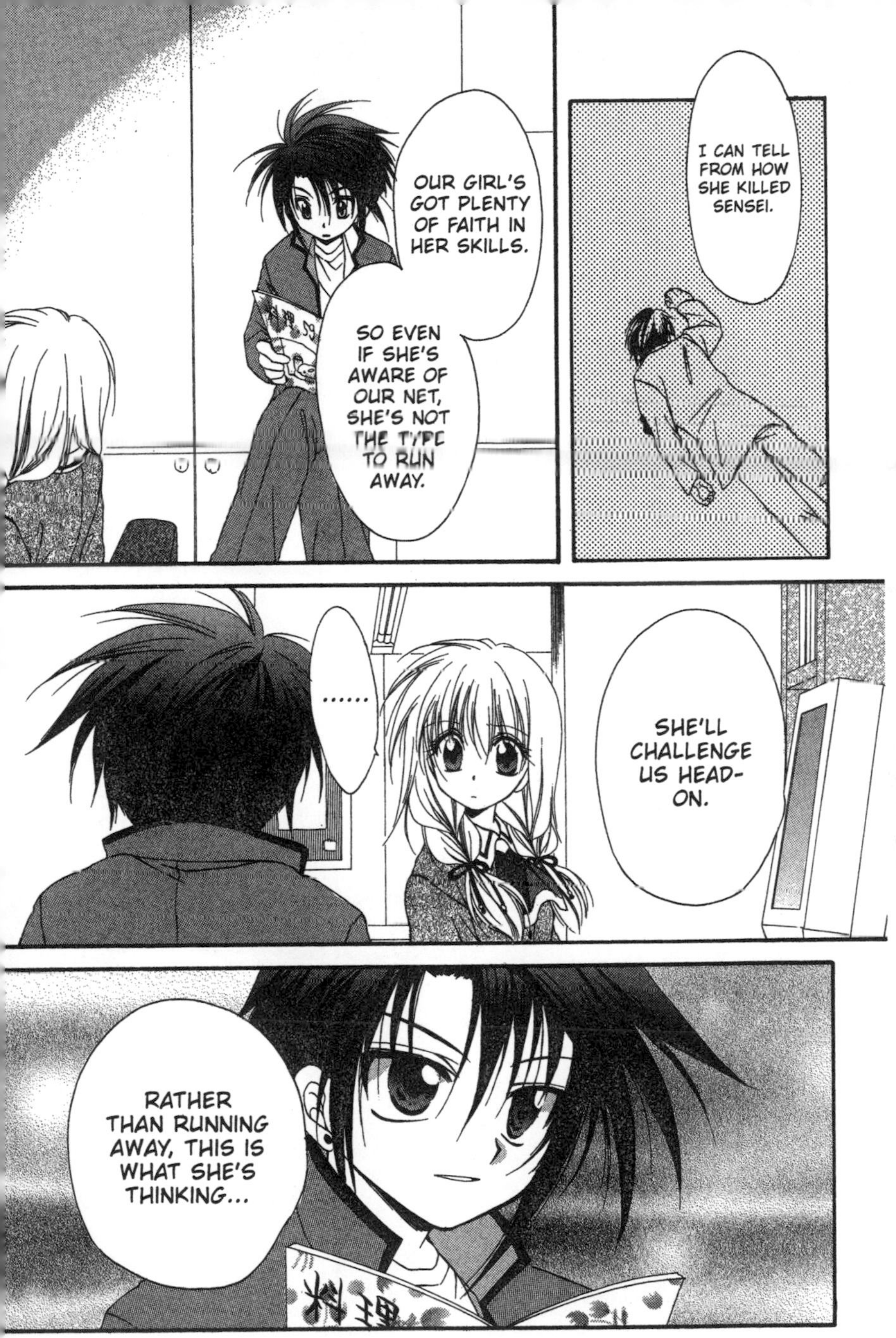
I CAN TELL FROM HOW SHE KILLED SENSEI.
OUR GIRL'S GOT PLENTY OF FAITH IN HER SKILLS.
SO EVEN IF SHE'S AWARE OF OUR NET, SHE'S NOT THE TYPE TO RUN AWAY.
SHE'LL CHALLENGE US HEAD-ON.
......
RATHER THAN RUNNING AWAY, THIS IS WHAT SHE'S THINKING...

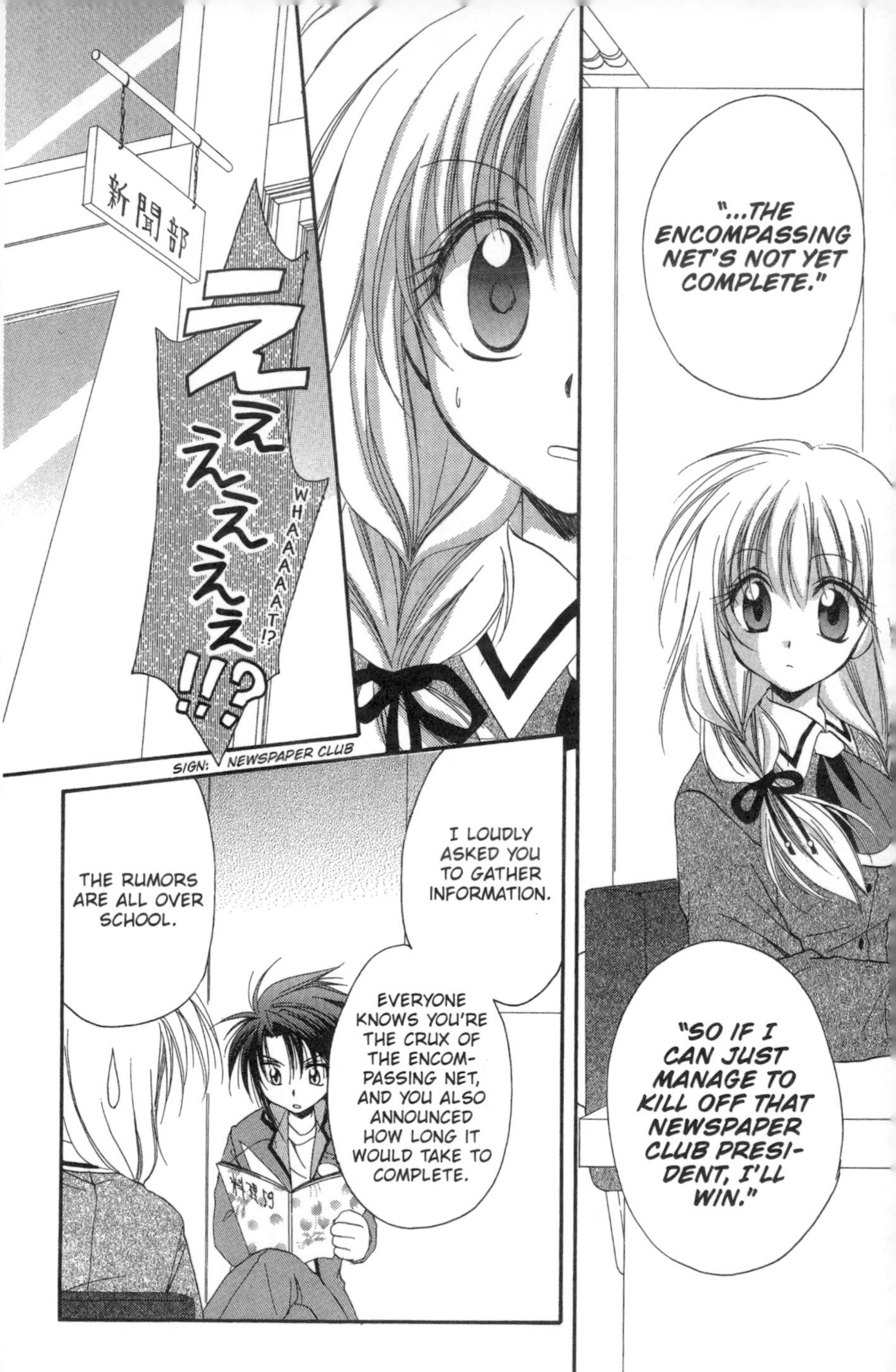
"...THE ENCOMPASSING NET'S NOT YET COMPLETE."
"SO IF I CAN JUST MANAGE TO KILL OFF THAT NEWSPAPER CLUB PRESIDENT, I'LL WIN."
新聞部
えええええ!!?
WHAAAAAT!?
SIGN: NEWSPAPER CLUB
I LOUDLY ASKED YOU TO GATHER INFORMATION.
THE RUMORS ARE ALL OVER SCHOOL.
EVERYONE KNOWS YOU'RE THE CRUX OF THE ENCOMPASSING NET, AND YOU ALSO ANNOUNCED HOW LONG IT WOULD TAKE TO COMPLETE.

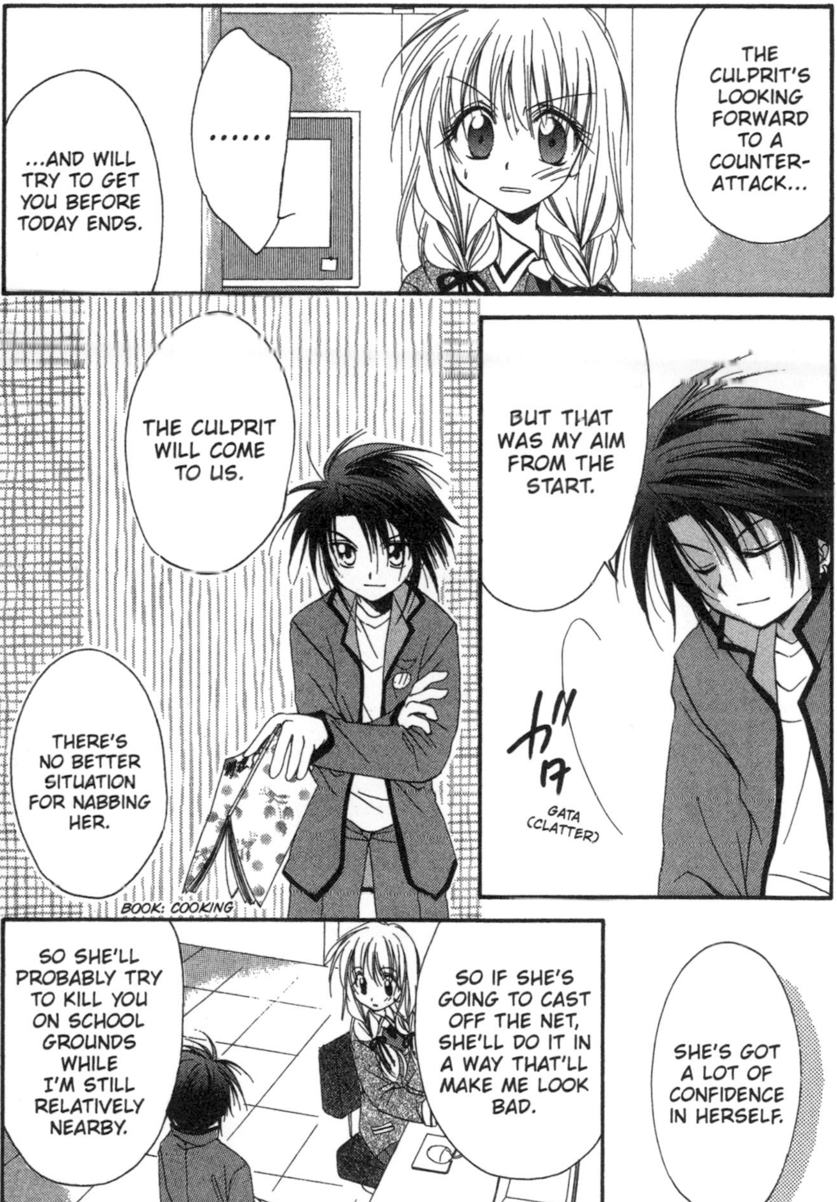
THE CULPRIT'S LOOKING FORWARD TO A COUNTER-ATTACK...
......
...AND WILL TRY TO GET YOU BEFORE TODAY ENDS.
BUT THAT WAS MY AIM FROM THE START.
ガタ
GATA (CLATTER)
THE CULPRIT WILL COME TO US.
THERE'S NO BETTER SITUATION FOR NABBING HER.
BOOK: COOKING
SHE'S GOT A LOT OF CONFIDENCE IN HERSELF.
SO IF SHE'S GOING TO CAST OFF THE NET, SHE'LL DO IT IN A WAY THAT'LL MAKE ME LOOK BAD.
SO SHE'LL PROBABLY TRY TO KILL YOU ON SCHOOL GROUNDS WHILE I'M STILL RELATIVELY NEARBY.

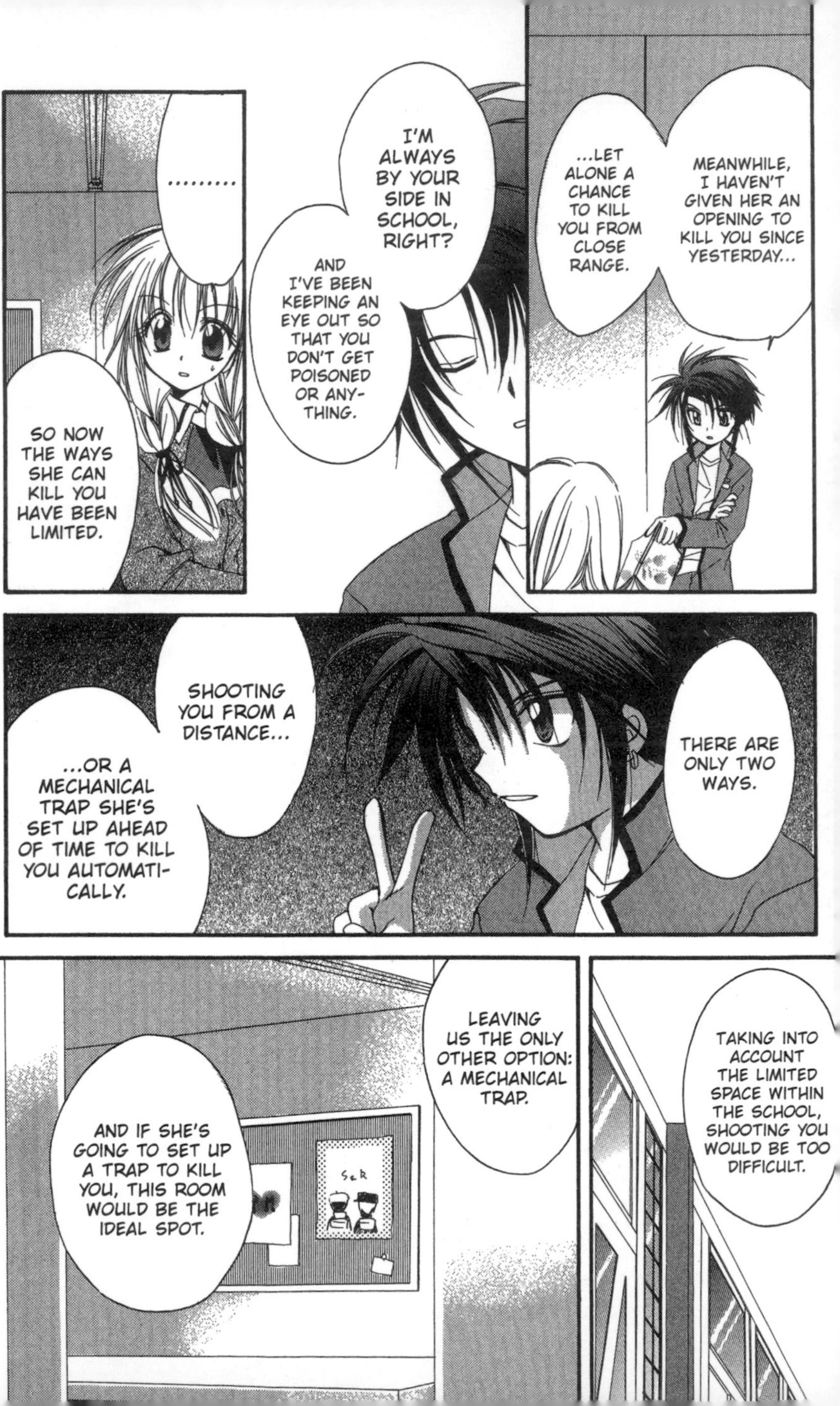
MEANWHILE, I HAVEN'T GIVEN HER AN OPENING TO KILL YOU SINCE YESTERDAY...
...LET ALONE A CHANCE TO KILL YOU FROM CLOSE RANGE.
I'M ALWAYS BY YOUR SIDE IN SCHOOL, RIGHT?
AND I'VE BEEN KEEPING AN EYE OUT SO THAT YOU DON'T GET POISONED OR ANY-THING.
....
SO NOW THE WAYS SHE CAN KILL YOU HAVE BEEN LIMITED.
THERE ARE ONLY TWO WAYS.
SHOOTING YOU FROM A DISTANCE...
...OR A MECHANICAL TRAP SHE'S SET UP AHEAD OF TIME TO KILL YOU AUTOMATI-CALLY.
TAKING INTO ACCOUNT THE LIMITED SPACE WITHIN THE SCHOOL, SHOOTING YOU WOULD BE TOO DIFFICULT.
LEAVING US THE ONLY OTHER OPTION: A MECHANICAL TRAP.
AND IF SHE'S GOING TO SET UP A TRAP TO KILL YOU, THIS ROOM WOULD BE THE IDEAL SPOT.

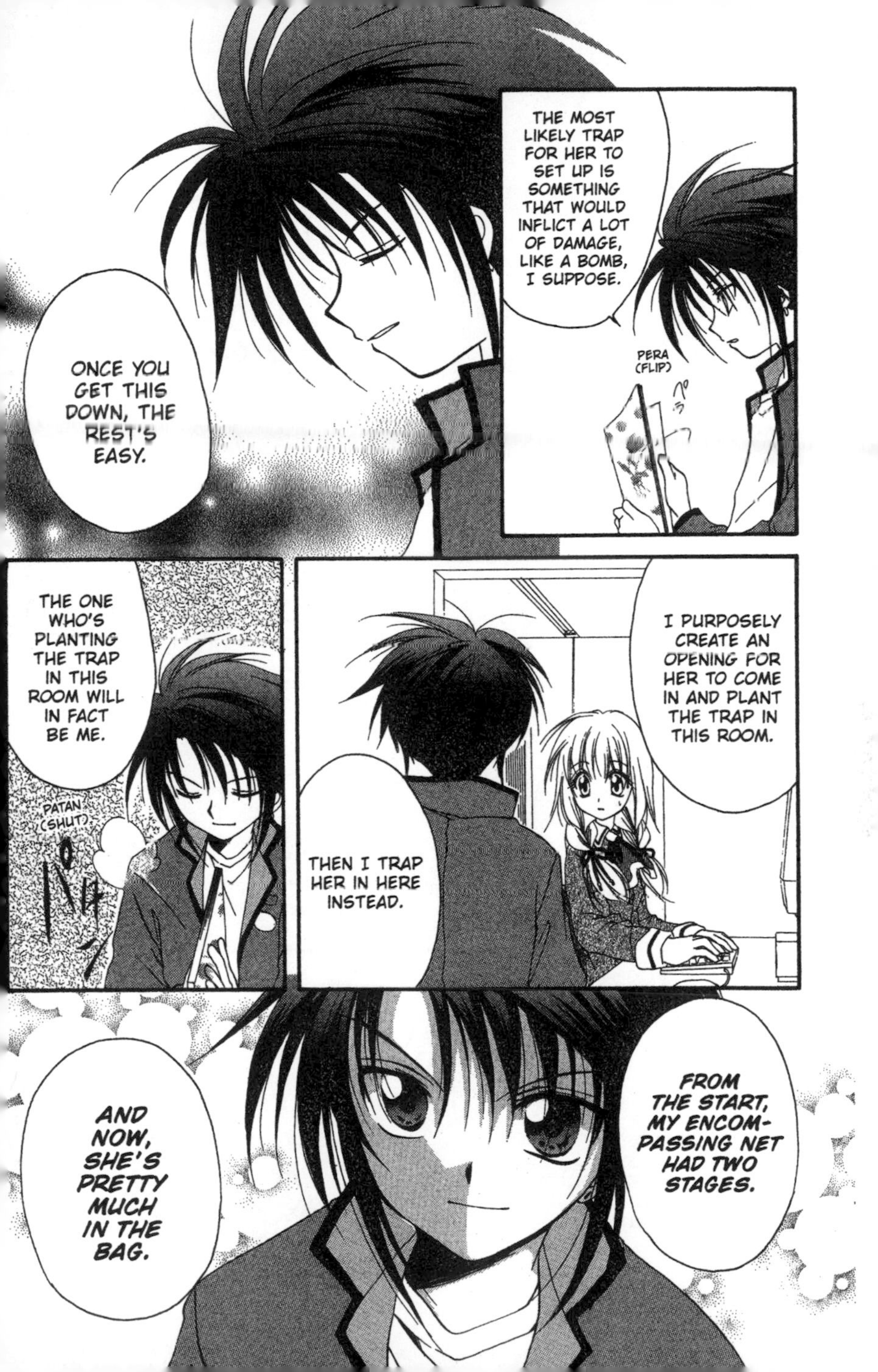
THE MOST LIKELY TRAP FOR HER TO SET UP IS SOMETHING THAT WOULD INFLICT A LOT OF DAMAGE, LIKE A BOMB, I SUPPOSE.
PERA (FLIP)
ONCE YOU GET THIS DOWN, THE REST'S EASY.
I PURPOSELY CREATE AN OPENING FOR HER TO COME IN AND PLANT THE TRAP IN THIS ROOM.
THEN I TRAP HER IN HERE INSTEAD.
THE ONE WHO'S PLANTING THE TRAP IN THIS ROOM WILL IN FACT BE ME.
PATAN (SHUT)
FROM THE START, MY ENCOM-PASSING NET HAD TWO STAGES.
AND NOW, SHE'S PRETTY MUCH IN THE BAG.

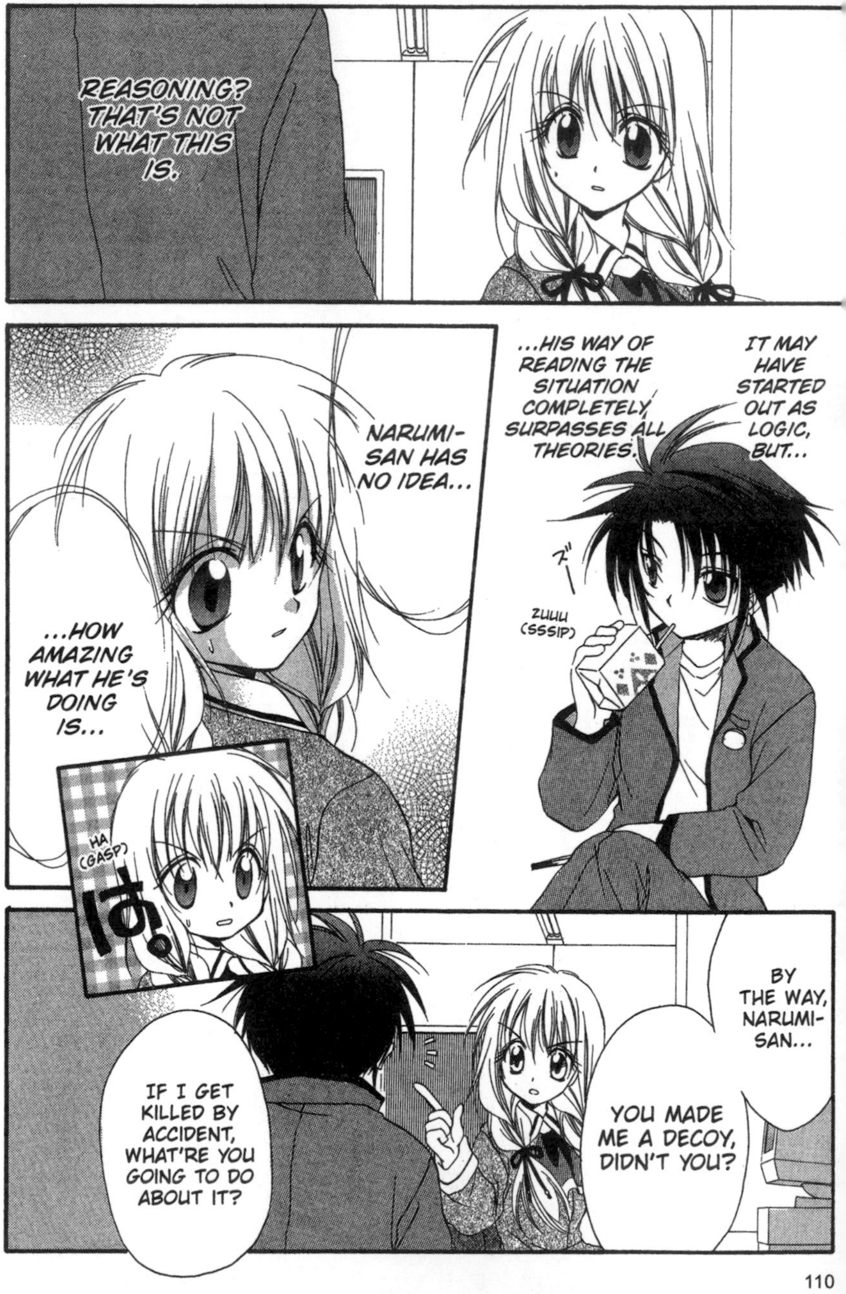
REASONING? THAT'S NOT WHAT THIS IS.
IT MAY HAVE STARTED OUT AS LOGIC, BUT...
...HIS WAY OF READING THE SITUATION COMPLETELY SURPASSES ALL THEORIES.
ズー
ZUUU (SSSIP)
NARUMI-SAN HAS NO IDEA...
...HOW AMAZING WHAT HE'S DOING IS...
は。
HA (GASP)
BY THE WAY, NARUMI-SAN...
YOU MADE ME A DECOY, DIDN'T YOU?
IF I GET KILLED BY ACCIDENT, WHAT'RE YOU GOING TO DO ABOUT IT?

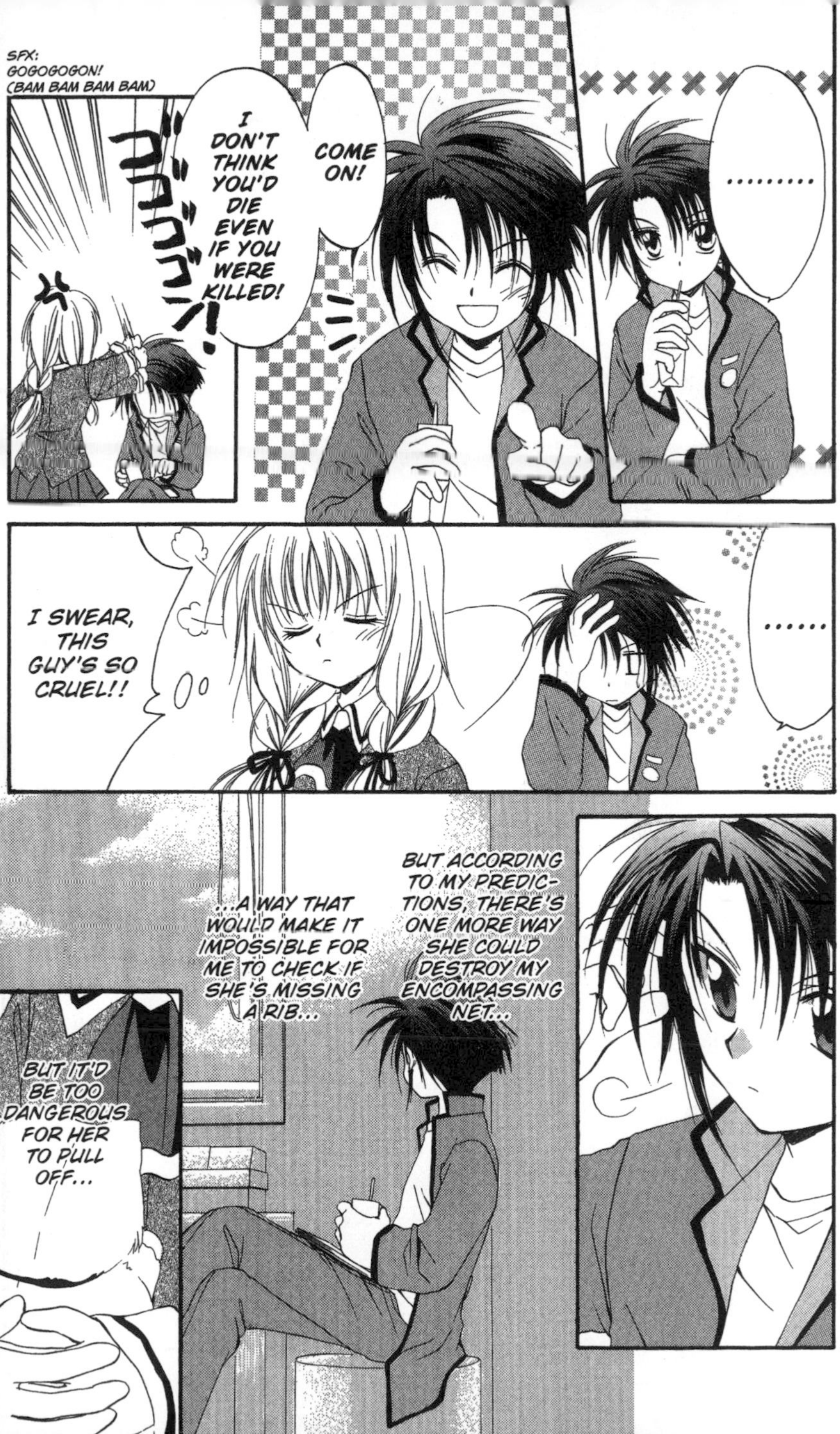
....
COME ON!
I DON'T THINK YOU'D DIE EVEN IF YOU WERE KILLED!
SFX: GOGOGOGON! (BAM BAM BAM BAM)
......
I SWEAR, THIS GUY'S SO CRUEL!!
BUT ACCORDING TO MY PREDICTIONS, THERE'S ONE MORE WAY SHE COULD DESTROY MY ENCOMPASSING NET...
...A WAY THAT WOULD MAKE IT IMPOSSIBLE FOR ME TO CHECK IF SHE'S MISSING A RIB...
BUT IT'D BE TOO DANGEROUS FOR HER TO PULL OFF...

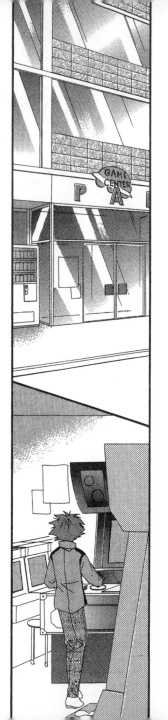

WOULD THAT BE POSSI- BLE IN REALITY?

TE
(TMP)
TE
TE

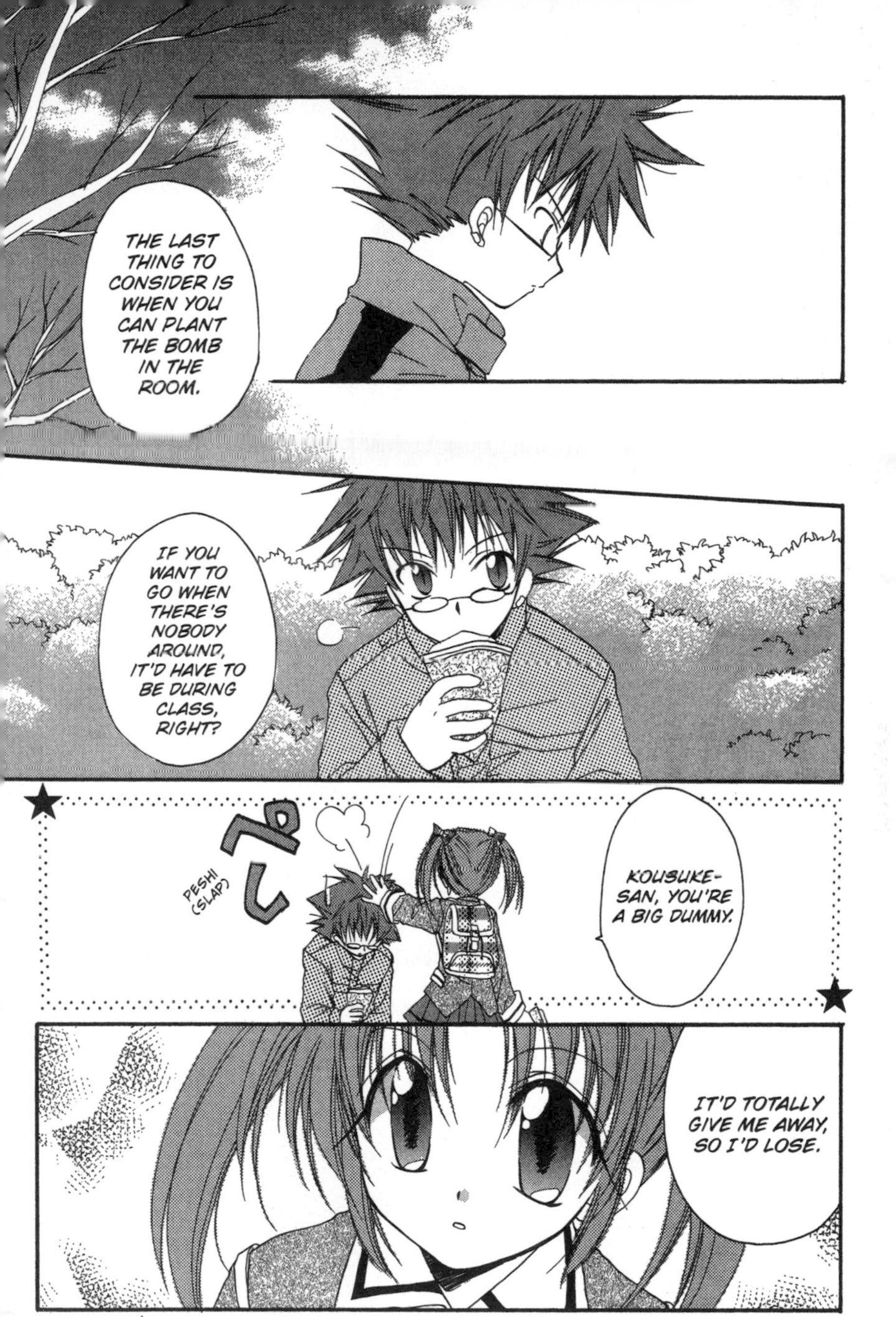
THE LAST THING TO CONSIDER IS WHEN YOU CAN PLANT THE BOMB IN THE ROOM.
IF YOU WANT TO GO WHEN THERE'S NOBODY AROUND, IT'D HAVE TO BE DURING CLASS, RIGHT?
KOUSUKE-SAN, YOU'RE A BIG DUMMY.
PESHI (SLAP)
IT'D TOTALLY GIVE ME AWAY, SO I'D LOSE.

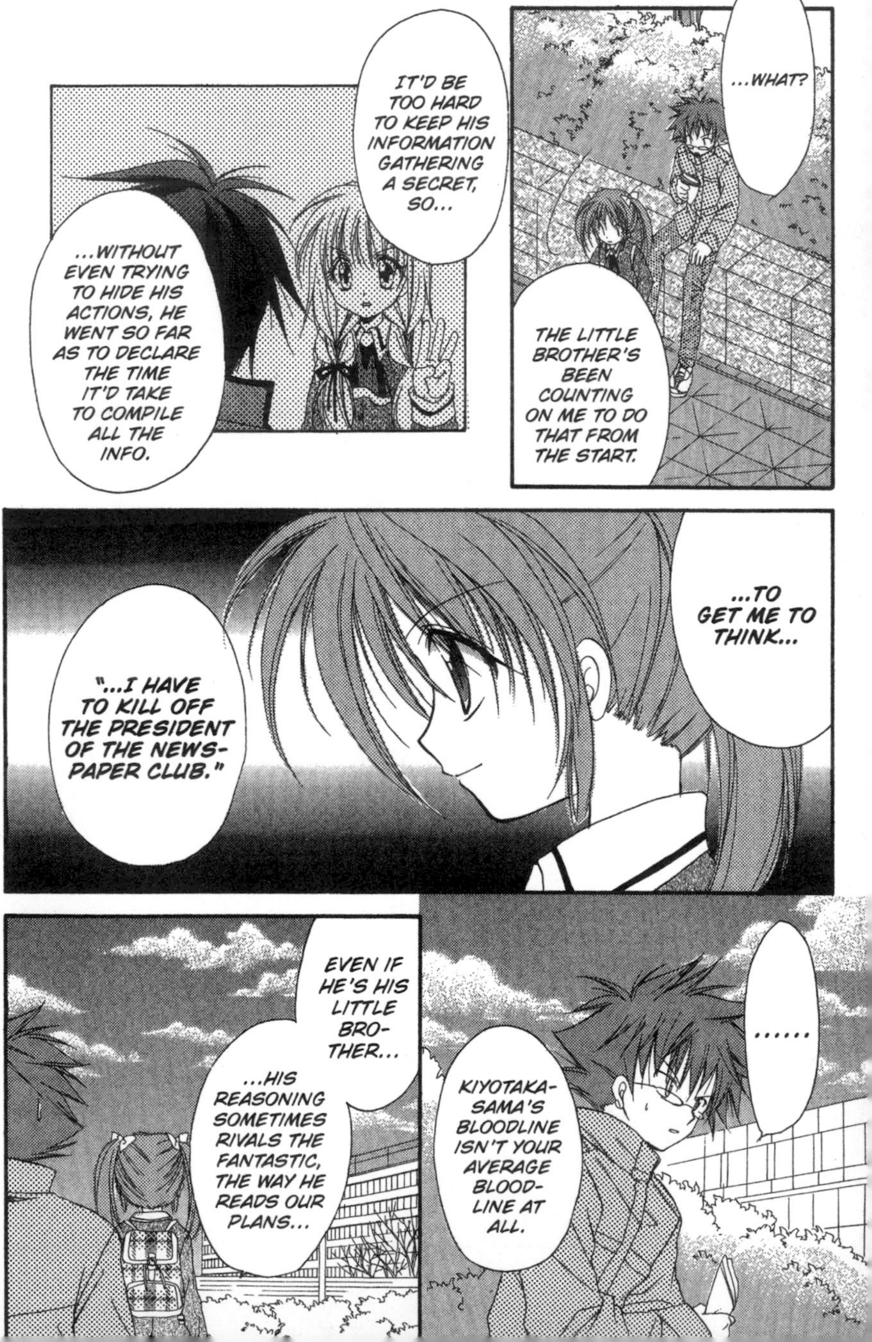
...WHAT?
THE LITTLE BROTHER'S BEEN COUNTING ON ME TO DO THAT FROM THE START.
IT'D BE TOO HARD TO KEEP HIS INFORMATION GATHERING A SECRET, SO...
...WITHOUT EVEN TRYING TO HIDE HIS ACTIONS, HE WENT SO FAR AS TO DECLARE THE TIME IT'D TAKE TO COMPILE ALL THE INFO.
...TO GET ME TO THINK...
"...I HAVE TO KILL OFF THE PRESIDENT OF THE NEWS-PAPER CLUB."
......
KIYOTAKA-SAMA'S BLOODLINE ISN'T YOUR AVERAGE BLOOD-LINE AT ALL.
EVEN IF HE'S HIS LITTLE BRO-THER...
...HIS REASONING SOMETIMES RIVALS THE FANTASTIC, THE WAY HE READS OUR PLANS...

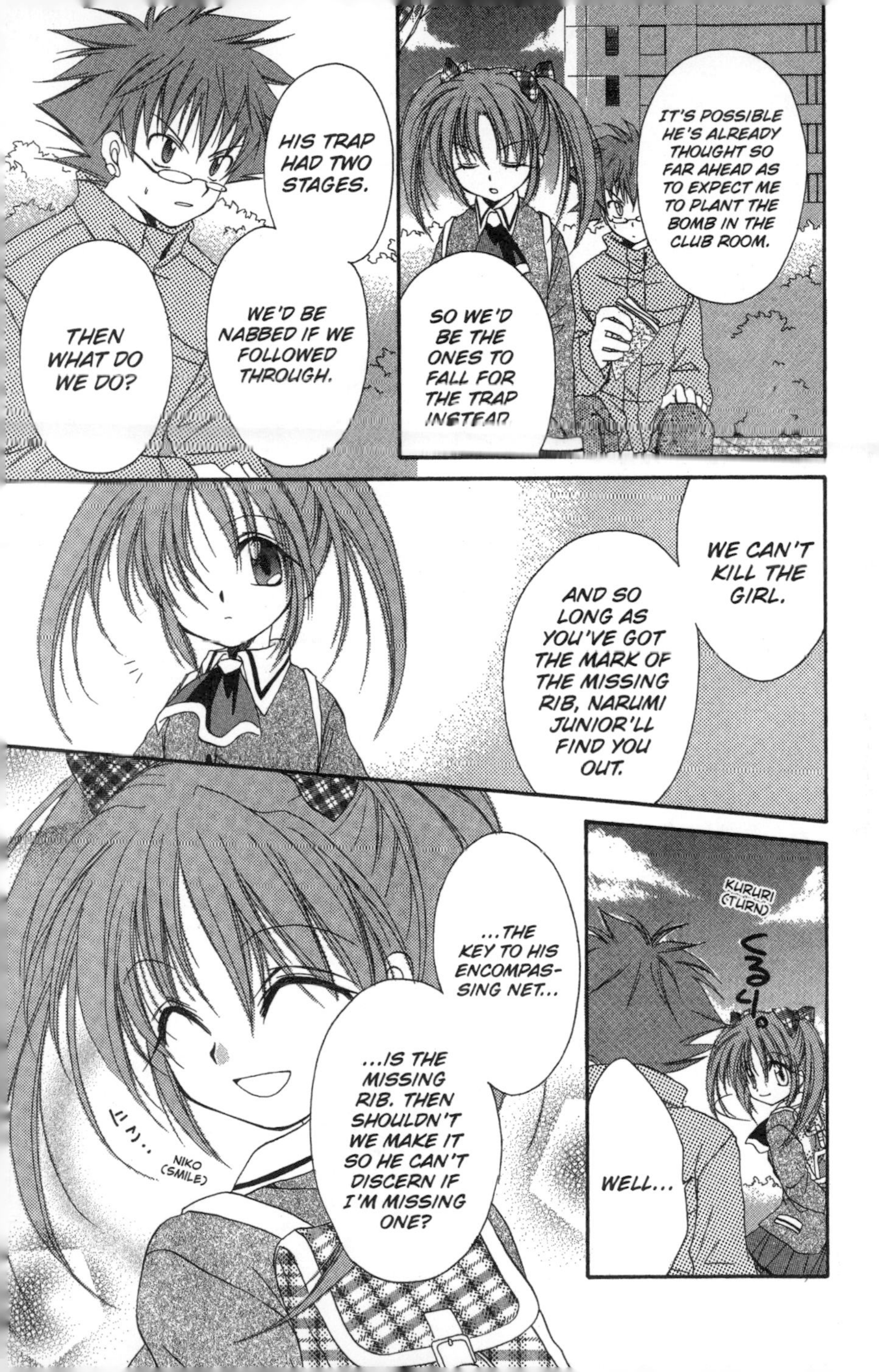
IT'S POSSIBLE HE'S ALREADY THOUGHT SO FAR AHEAD AS TO EXPECT ME TO PLANT THE BOMB IN THE CLUB ROOM.
SO WE'D BE THE ONES TO FALL FOR THE TRAP INSTEAD
HIS TRAP HAD TWO STAGES.
WE'D BE NABBED IF WE FOLLOWED THROUGH.
THEN WHAT DO WE DO?
WE CAN'T KILL THE GIRL.
AND SO LONG AS YOU'VE GOT THE MARK OF THE MISSING RIB, NARUMI JUNIOR'LL FIND YOU OUT.
KURURI (TURN)
WELL...
...THE KEY TO HIS ENCOMPAS-SING NET...
...IS THE MISSING RIB. THEN SHOULDN'T WE MAKE IT SO HE CAN'T DISCERN IF I'M MISSING ONE?
NIKO (SMILE)

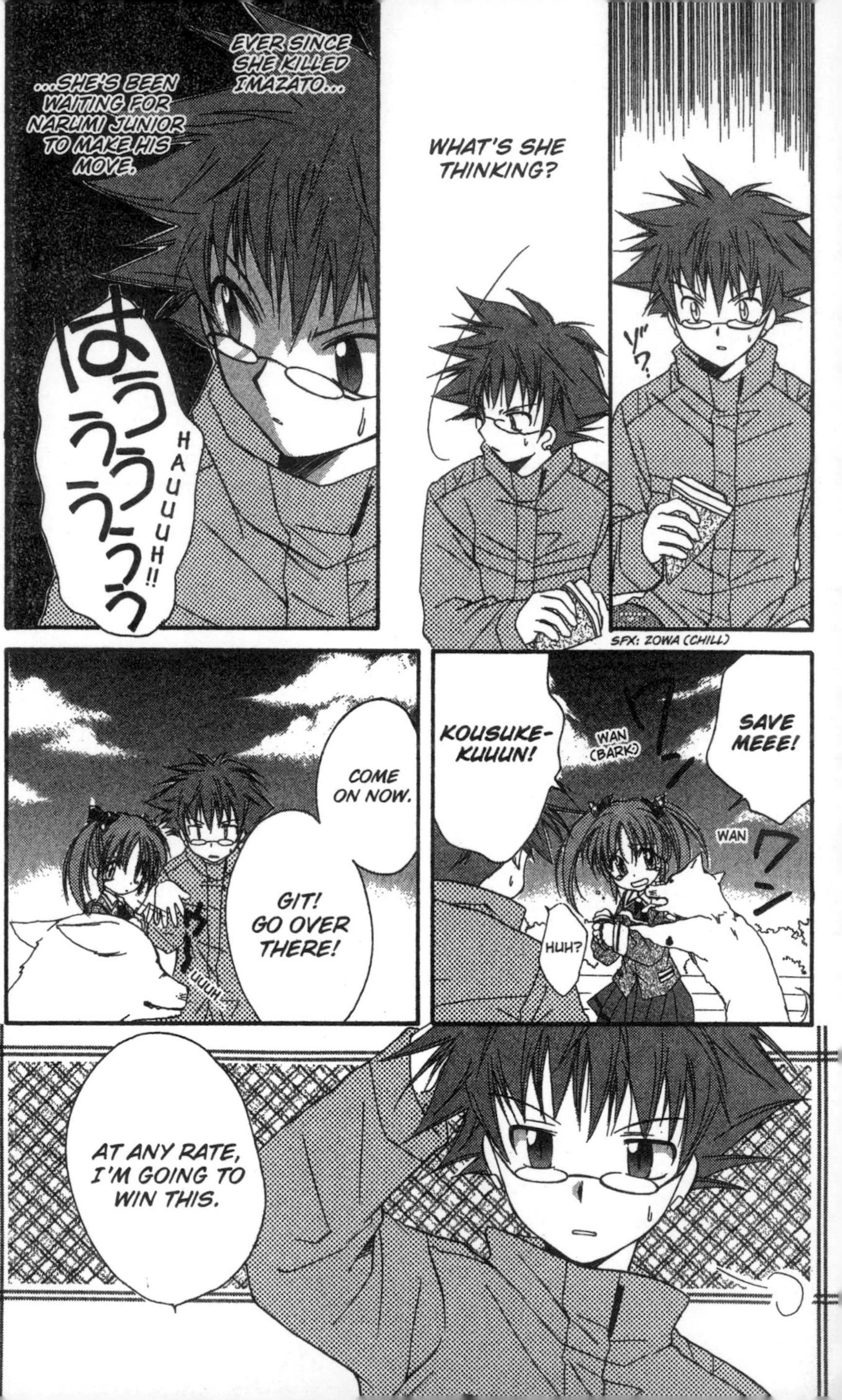
SFX: ZOWA (CHILL)
WHAT'S SHE THINKING?
EVER SINCE SHE KILLED IMAZATO...
...SHE'S BEEN WAITING FOR NARUMI JUNIOR TO MAKE HIS MOVE.
HAUUUUH!!
SAVE MEEE!
WAN (BARK)
KOUSUKE-KUUUN!
WAN
HUH?
COME ON NOW.
GIT! GO OVER THERE!
UUUH...
AT ANY RATE, I'M GOING TO WIN THIS.

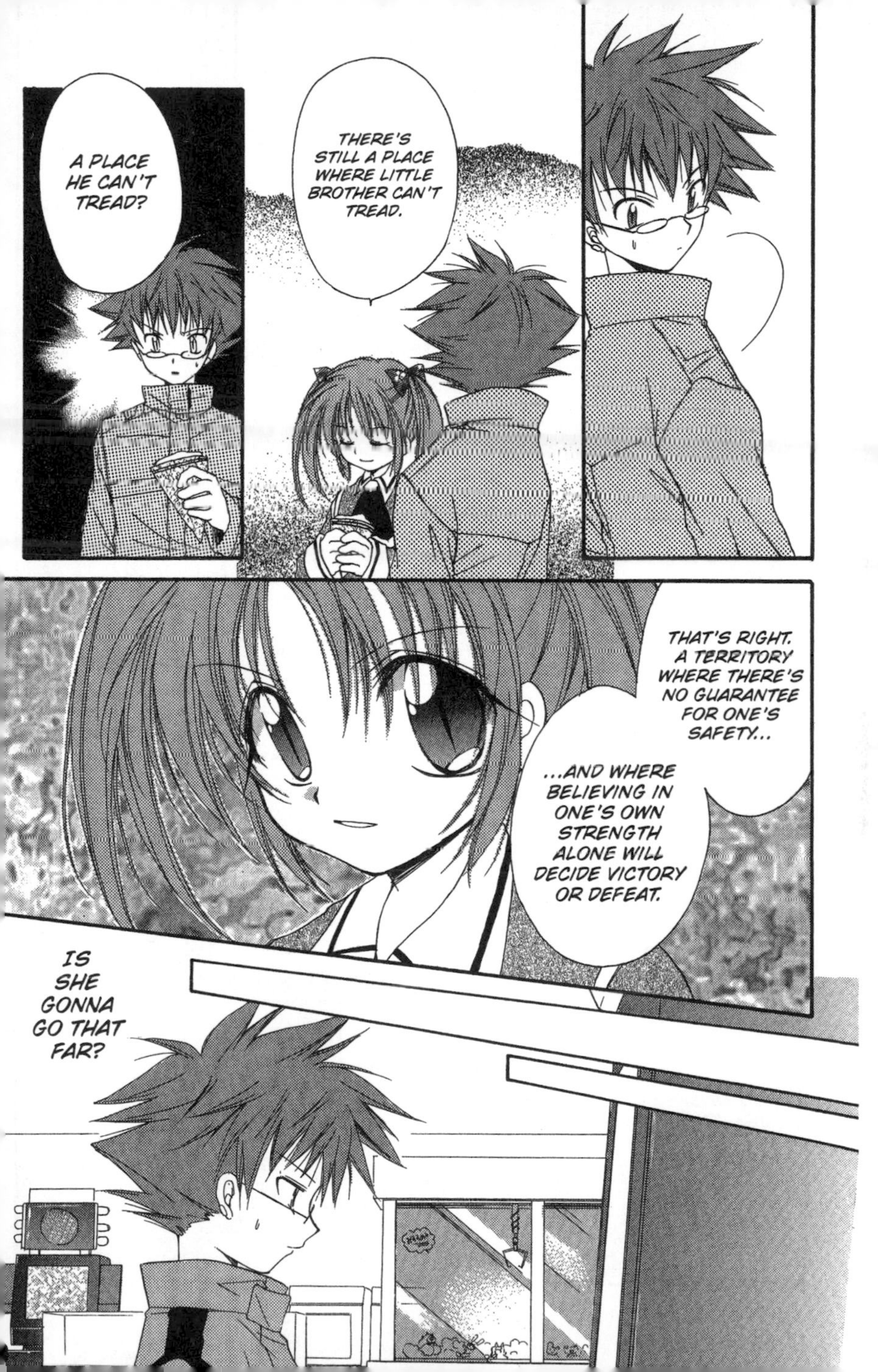
THERE'S STILL A PLACE WHERE LITTLE BROTHER CAN'T TREAD.
A PLACE HE CAN'T TREAD?
THAT'S RIGHT. A TERRITORY WHERE THERE'S NO GUARANTEE FOR ONE'S SAFETY...
...AND WHERE BELIEVING IN ONE'S OWN STRENGTH ALONE WILL DECIDE VICTORY OR DEFEAT.
IS SHE GONNA GO THAT FAR?

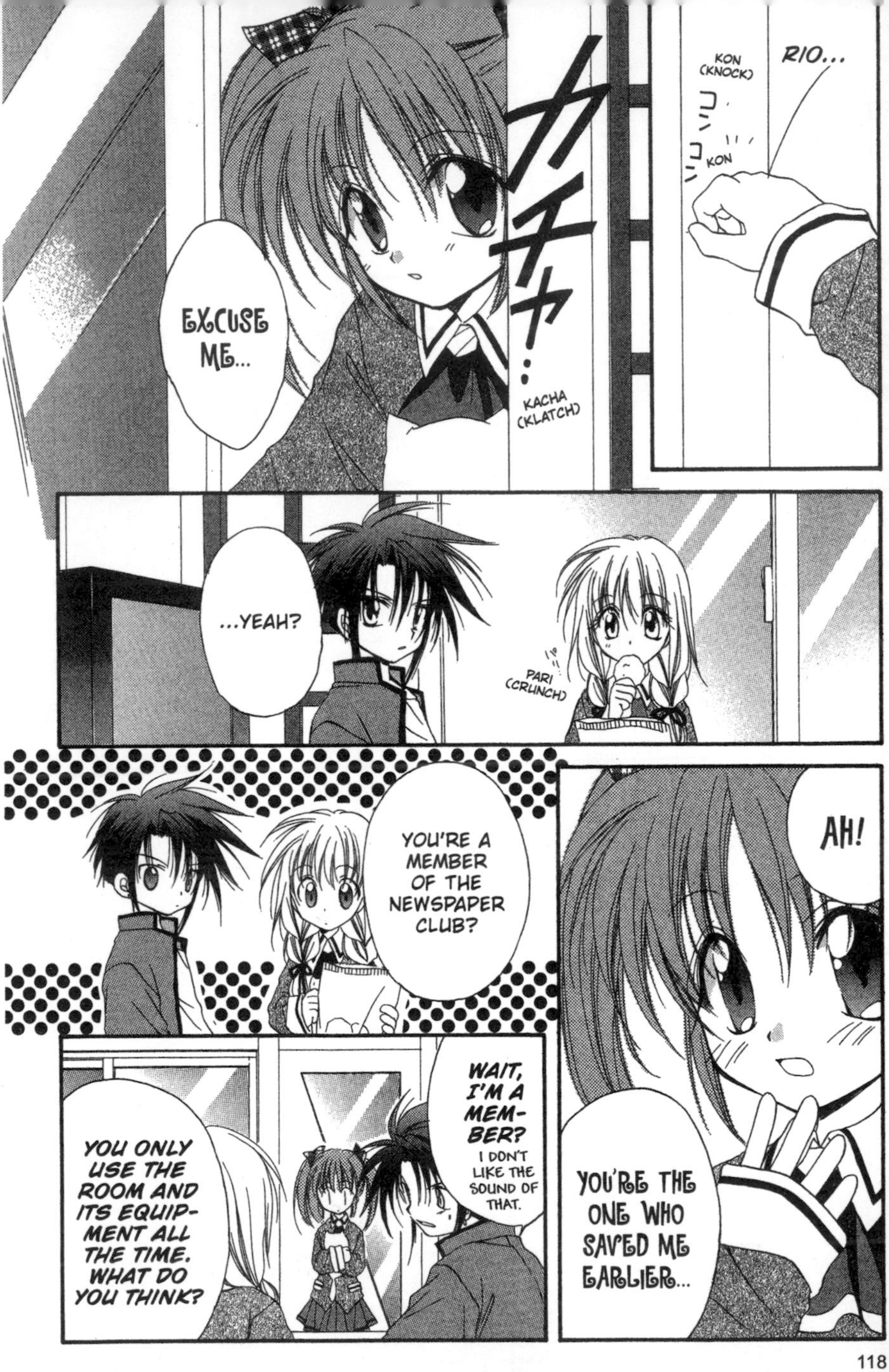
RIO...
KON (KNOCK)
KON
KACHA (KLATCH)
EXCUSE ME...
PARI (CRUNCH)
...YEAH?
AH!
YOU'RE THE ONE WHO SAVED ME EARLIER...
YOU'RE A MEMBER OF THE NEWSPAPER CLUB?
WAIT, I'M A MEMBER?
I DON'T LIKE THE SOUND OF THAT.
YOU ONLY USE THE ROOM AND ITS EQUIPMENT ALL THE TIME. WHAT DO YOU THINK?

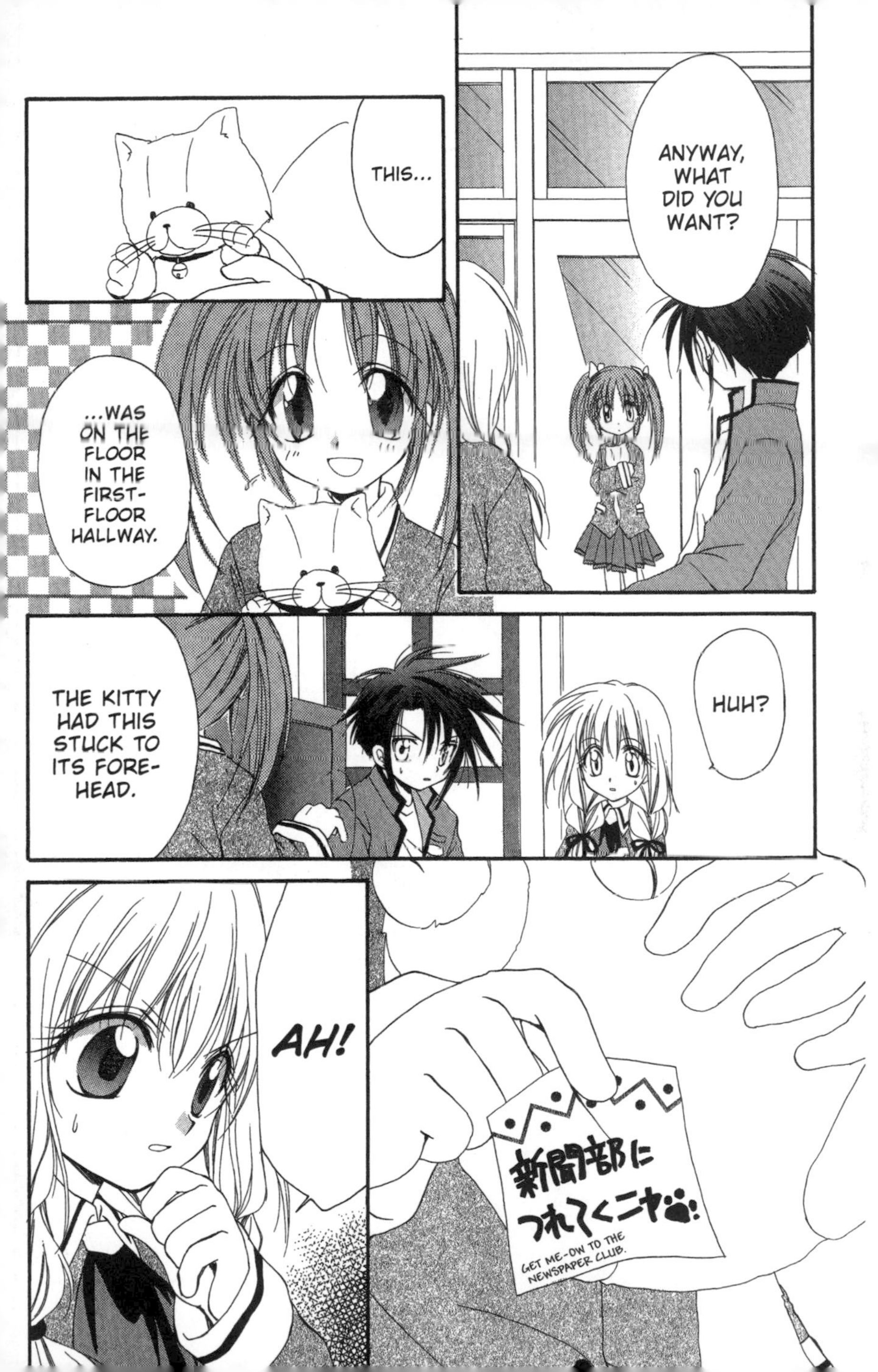
ANYWAY, WHAT DID YOU WANT?
THIS...
...WAS ON THE FLOOR IN THE FIRST-FLOOR HALLWAY.
HUH?
THE KITTY HAD THIS STUCK TO ITS FORE-HEAD.
新聞部につれてくニャ!
GET ME-OW TO THE NEWSPAPER CLUB.
AH!

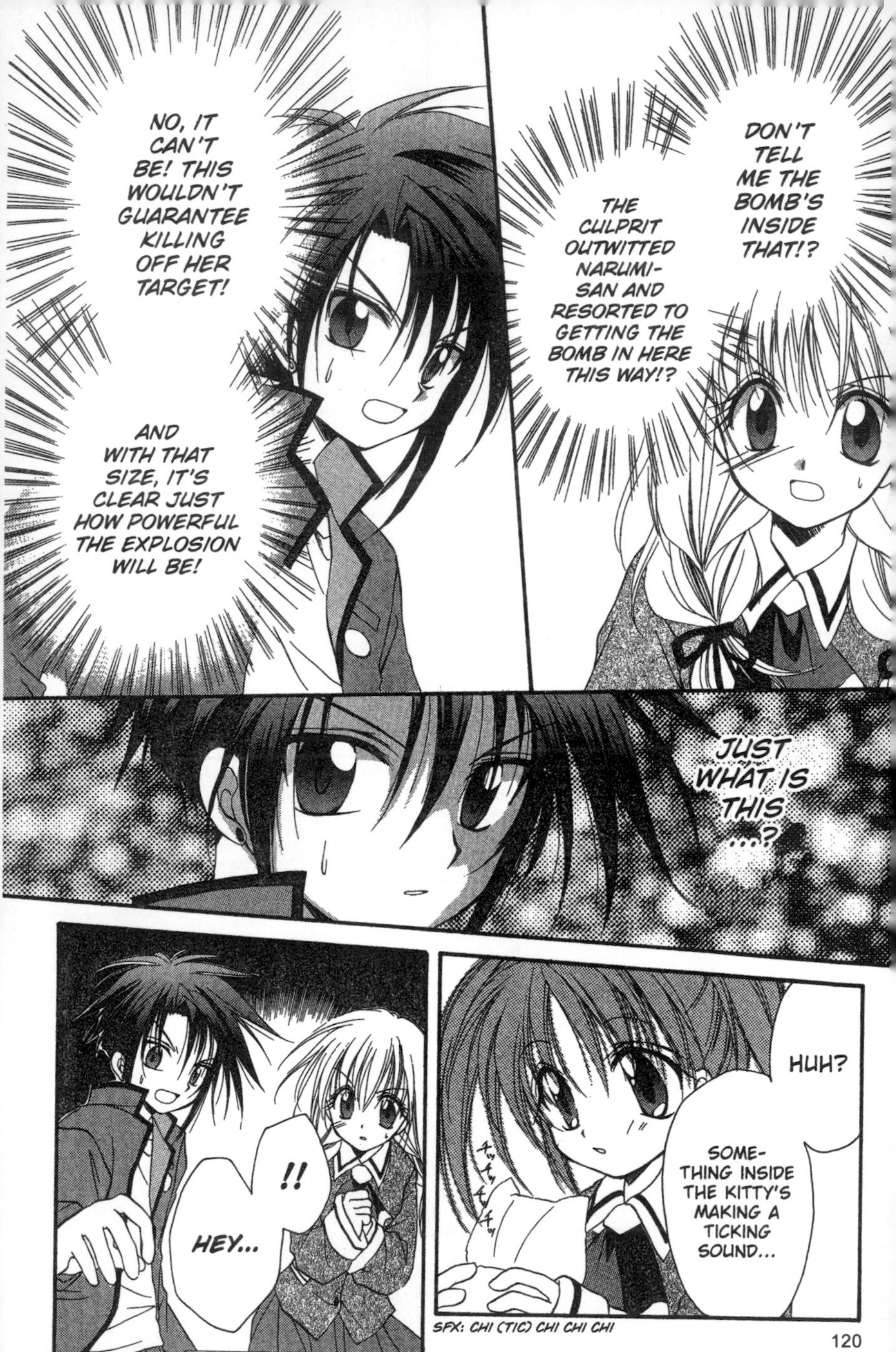
DON'T TELL ME THE BOMB'S INSIDE THAT!?
THE CULPRIT OUTWITTED NARUMI-SAN AND RESORTED TO GETTING THE BOMB IN HERE THIS WAY!?
NO, IT CAN'T BE! THIS WOULDN'T GUARANTEE KILLING OFF HER TARGET!
AND WITH THAT SIZE, IT'S CLEAR JUST HOW POWERFUL THE EXPLOSION WILL BE!
JUST WHAT IS THIS ...?
HUH?
SOME-THING INSIDE THE KITTY'S MAKING A TICKING SOUND...
!!
HEY...

SFX: CHI (TIC) CHI CHI CHI

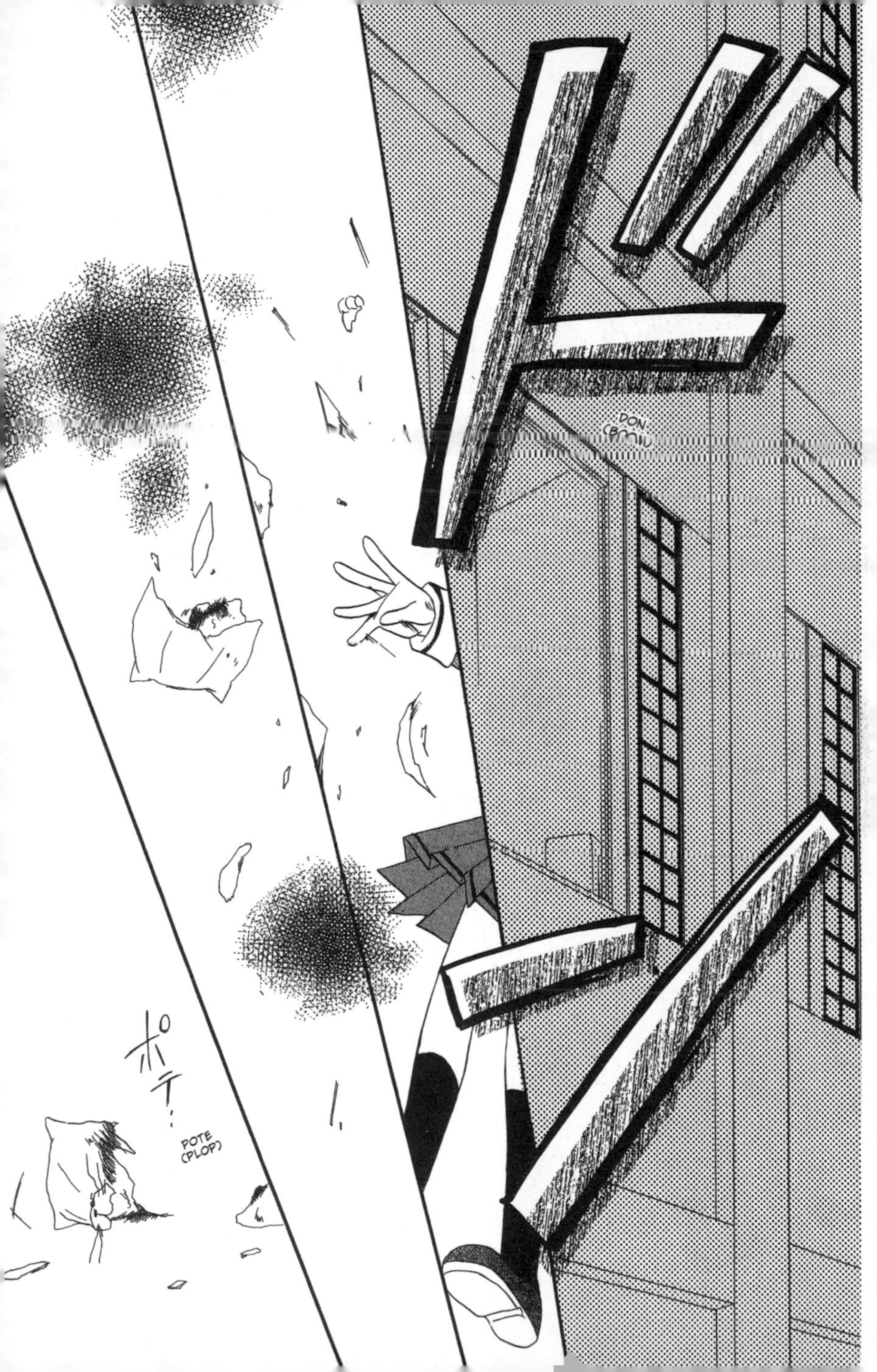
ドン
DON (BAM!)
ポテ
POTE (PLOP)

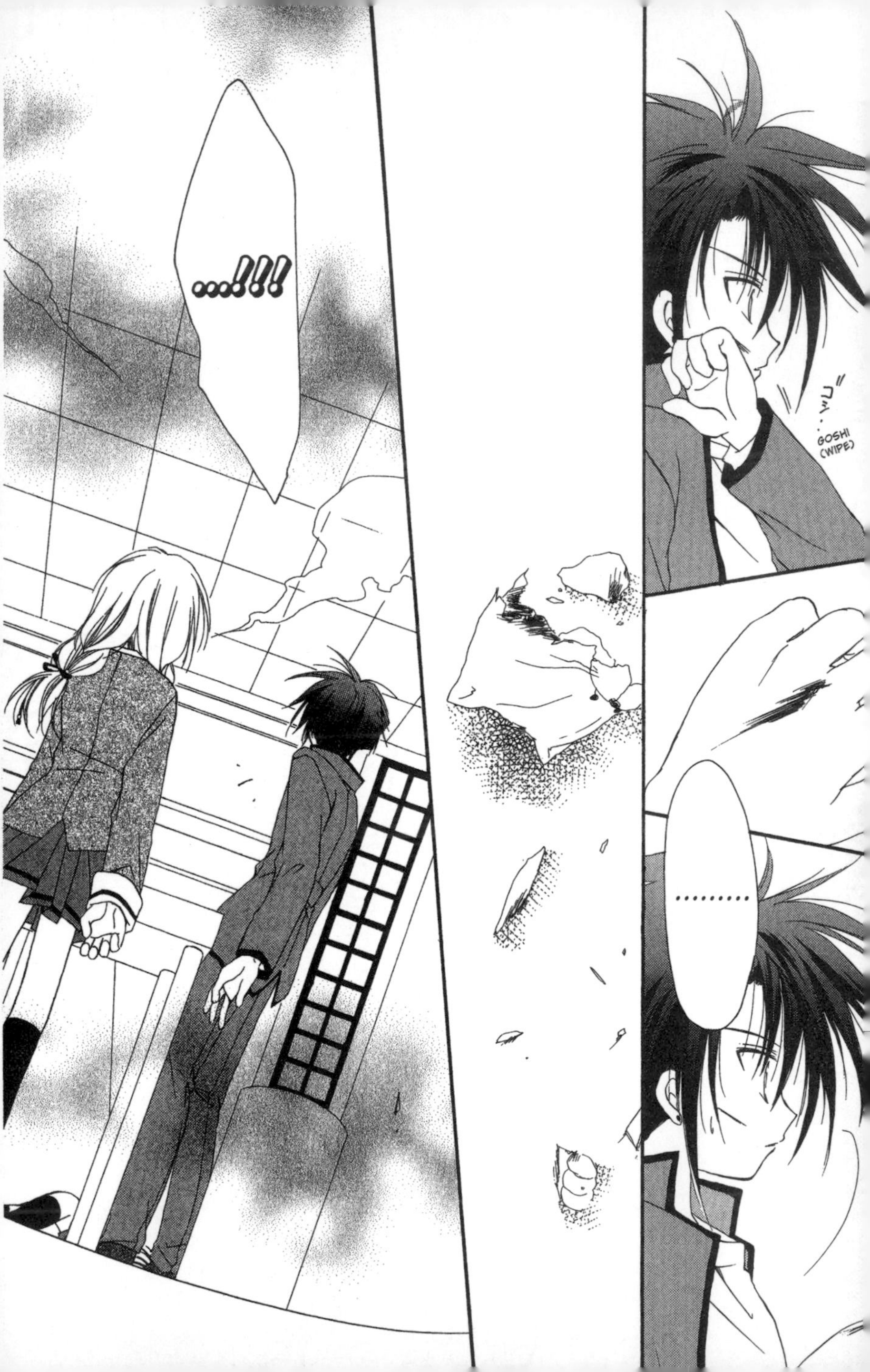
GOSHI (WIPE)
....
...!!!

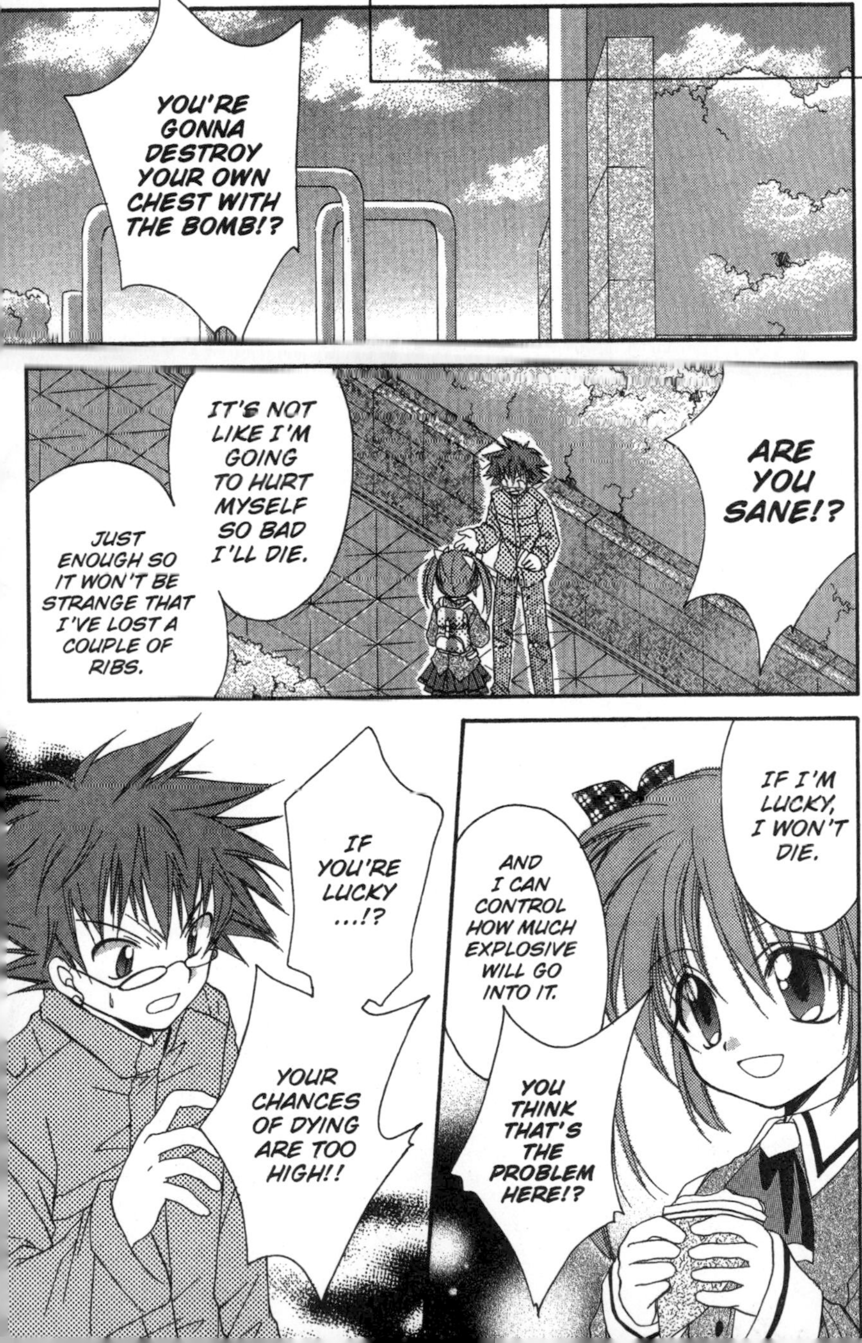
YOU'RE GONNA DESTROY YOUR OWN CHEST WITH THE BOMB!?
ARE YOU SANE!?
IT'S NOT LIKE I'M GOING TO HURT MYSELF SO BAD I'LL DIE.
JUST ENOUGH SO IT WON'T BE STRANGE THAT I'VE LOST A COUPLE OF RIBS.
IF I'M LUCKY, I WON'T DIE.
AND I CAN CONTROL HOW MUCH EXPLOSIVE WILL GO INTO IT.
YOU THINK THAT'S THE PROBLEM HERE!?
IF YOU'RE LUCKY ...!?
YOUR CHANCES OF DYING ARE TOO HIGH!!

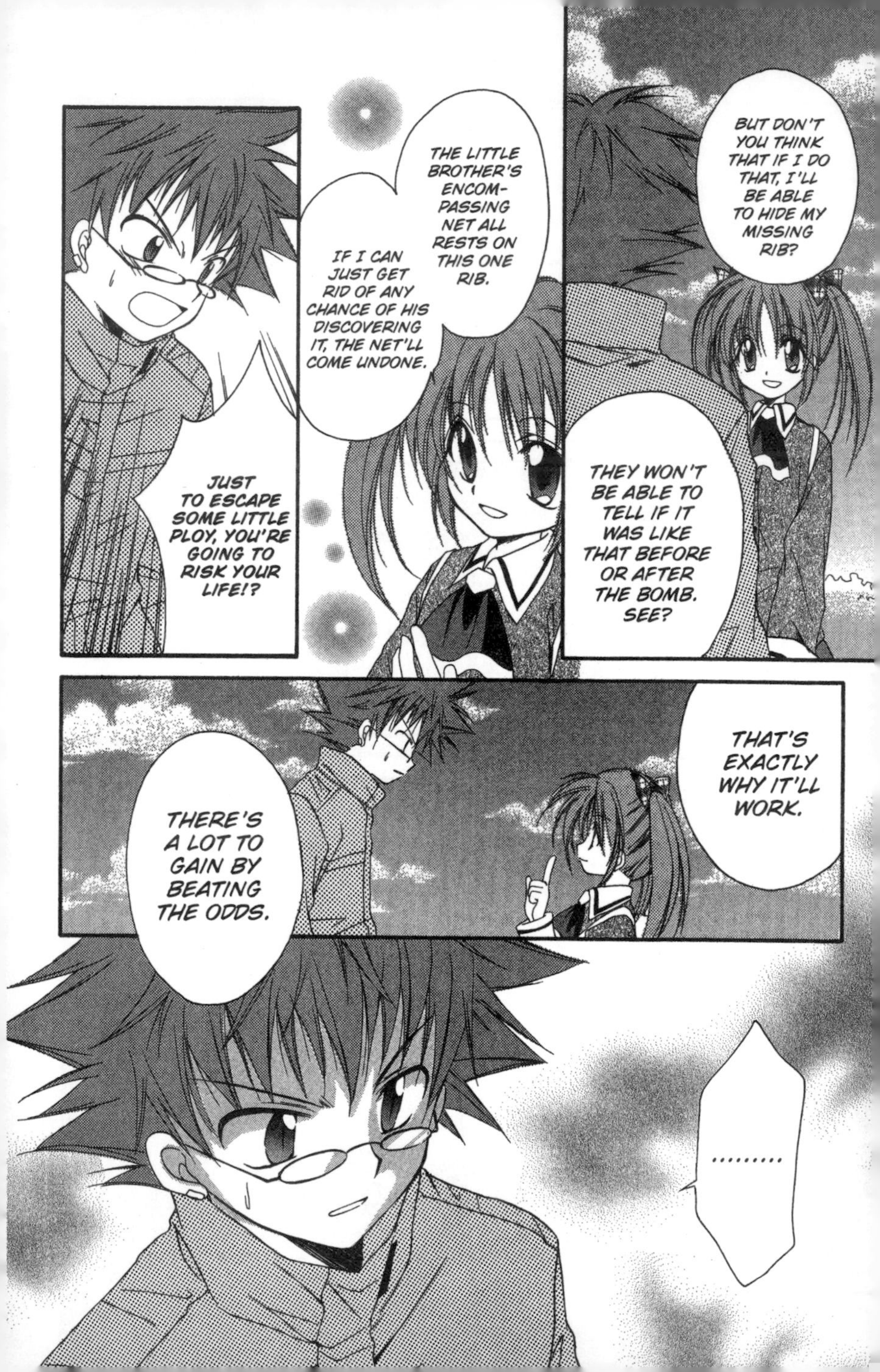
BUT DON'T YOU THINK THAT IF I DO THAT, I'LL BE ABLE TO HIDE MY MISSING RIB?
THEY WON'T BE ABLE TO TELL IF IT WAS LIKE THAT BEFORE OR AFTER THE BOMB. SEE?
THE LITTLE BROTHER'S ENCOM-PASSING NET ALL RESTS ON THIS ONE RIB.
IF I CAN JUST GET RID OF ANY CHANCE OF HIS DISCOVERING IT, THE NET'LL COME UNDONE.
JUST TO ESCAPE SOME LITTLE PLOY, YOU'RE GOING TO RISK YOUR LIFE!?
THAT'S EXACTLY WHY IT'LL WORK.
THERE'S A LOT TO GAIN BY BEATING THE ODDS.
....

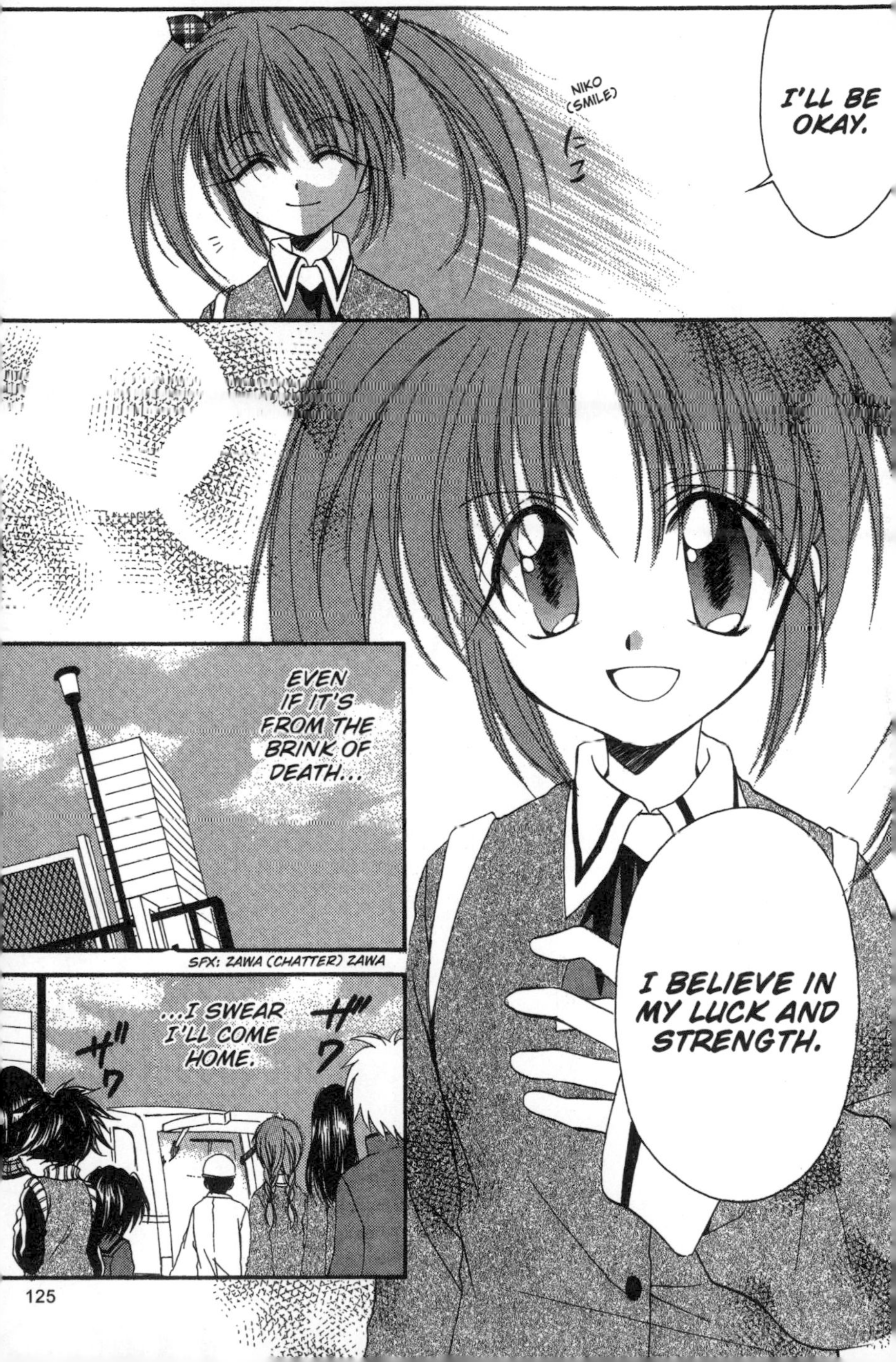
I'LL BE OKAY.
NIKO (SMILE)
I BELIEVE IN MY LUCK AND STRENGTH.
EVEN IF IT'S FROM THE BRINK OF DEATH...
SFX: ZAWA (CHATTER) ZAWA
ザワ
ザワ
...I SWEAR I'LL COME HOME.

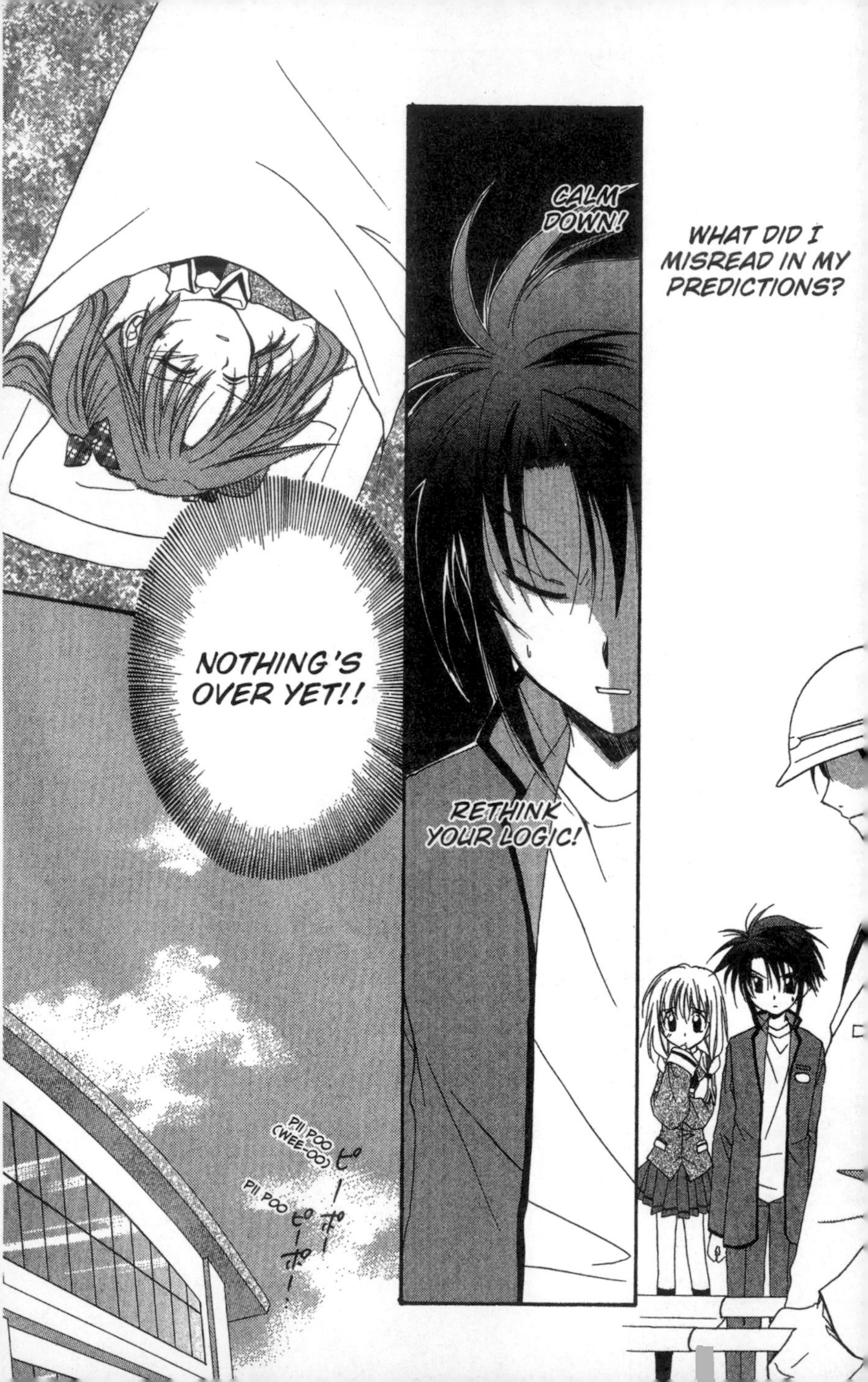
WHAT DID I MISREAD IN MY PREDICTIONS?
CALM DOWN!
RETHINK YOUR LOGIC!
NOTHING'S OVER YET!!
PII POO (WEE-OO)
PII POO

Spiral

THE BONDS OF REASONING

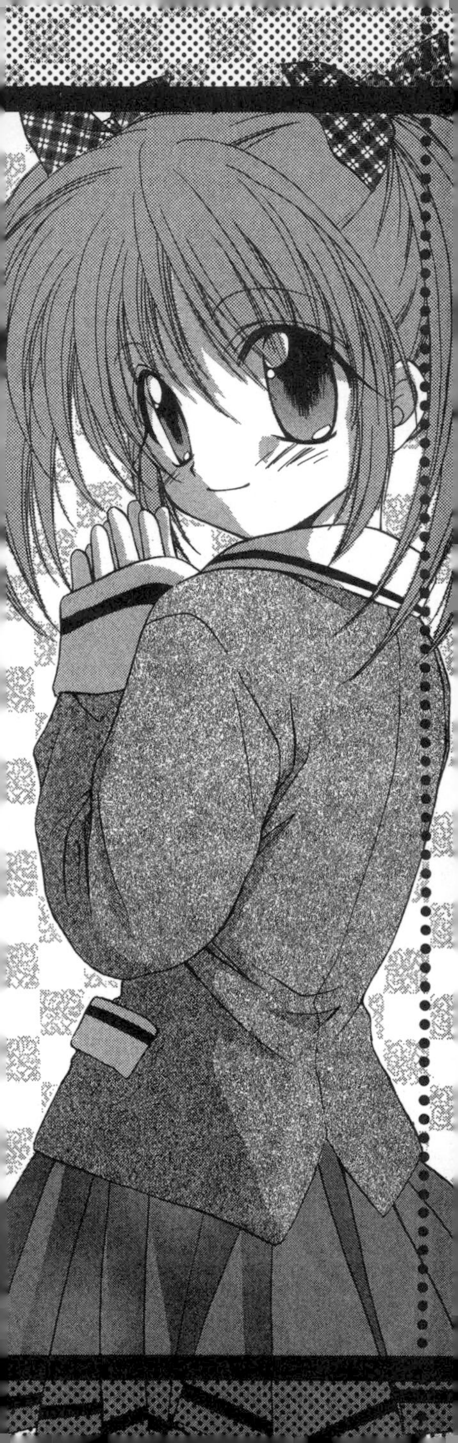

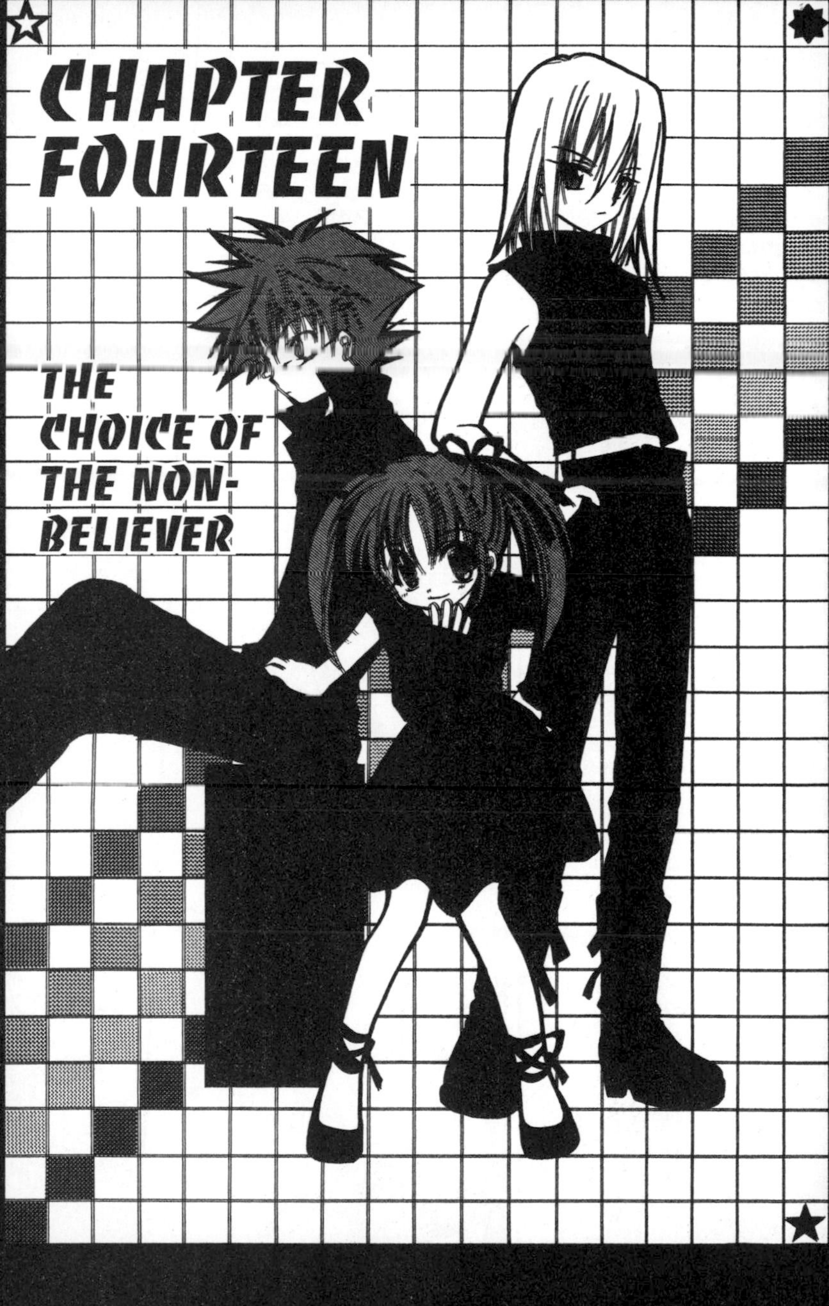
CHAPTER FOURTEEN
THE CHOICE OF THE NON-BELIEVER

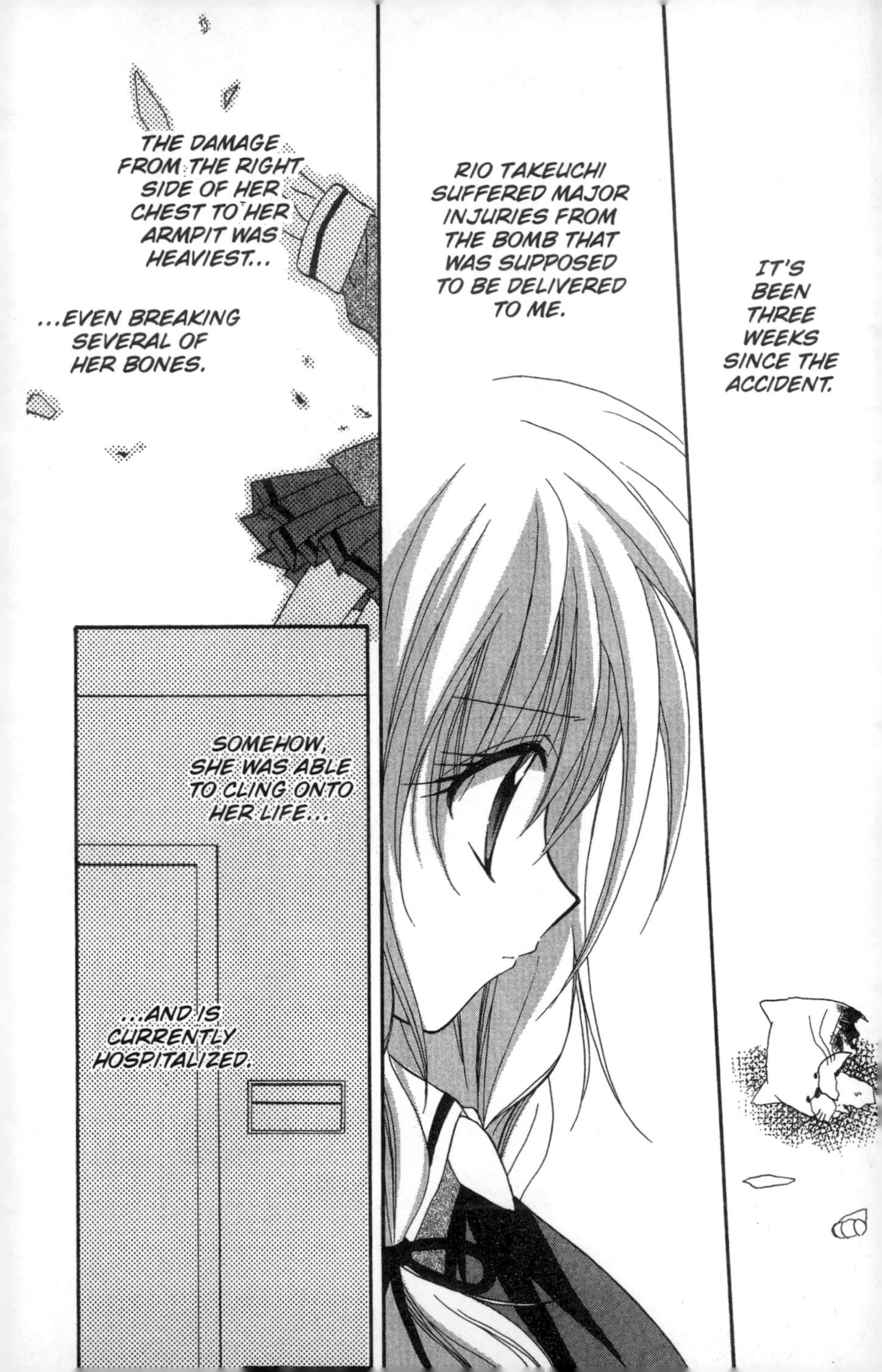
IT'S BEEN THREE WEEKS SINCE THE ACCIDENT.
RIO TAKEUCHI SUFFERED MAJOR INJURIES FROM THE BOMB THAT WAS SUPPOSED TO BE DELIVERED TO ME.
THE DAMAGE FROM THE RIGHT SIDE OF HER CHEST TO HER ARMPIT WAS HEAVIEST...
...EVEN BREAKING SEVERAL OF HER BONES.
SOMEHOW, SHE WAS ABLE TO CLING ONTO HER LIFE...
...AND IS CURRENTLY HOSPITALIZED.

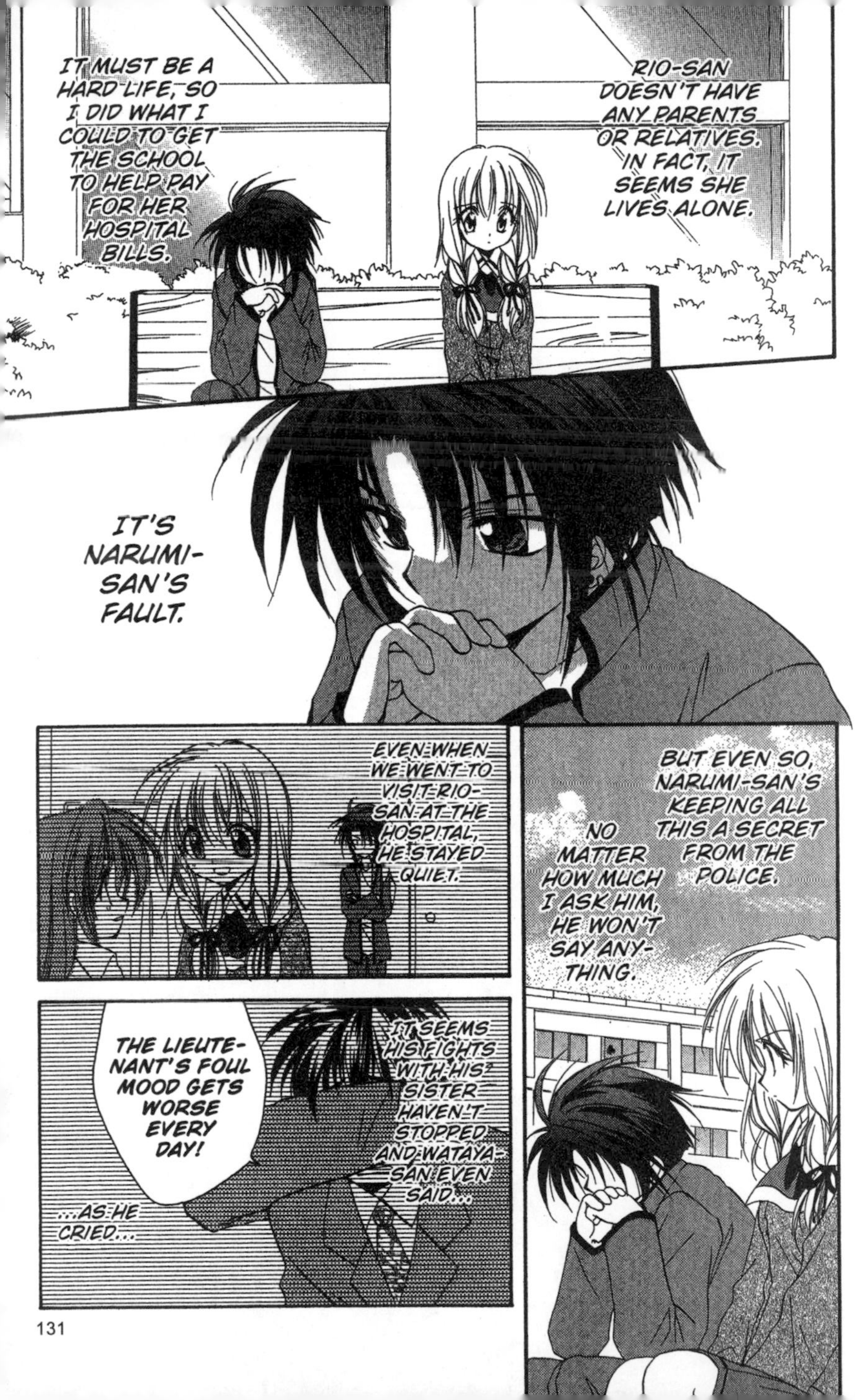
RIO-SAN DOESN'T HAVE ANY PARENTS OR RELATIVES. IN FACT, IT SEEMS SHE LIVES ALONE.
IT MUST BE A HARD LIFE, SO I DID WHAT I COULD TO GET THE SCHOOL TO HELP PAY FOR HER HOSPITAL BILLS.
IT'S NARUMI-SAN'S FAULT.
BUT EVEN SO, NARUMI-SAN'S KEEPING ALL THIS A SECRET FROM THE POLICE.
NO MATTER HOW MUCH I ASK HIM, HE WON'T SAY ANY-THING.
EVEN WHEN WE WENT TO VISIT RIO-SAN AT THE HOSPITAL, HE STAYED QUIET.
IT SEEMS HIS FIGHTS WITH HIS SISTER HAVEN'T STOPPED AND WATAYA-SAN EVEN SAID...
THE LIEUTE-NANT'S FOUL MOOD GETS WORSE EVERY DAY!
...AS HE CRIED...

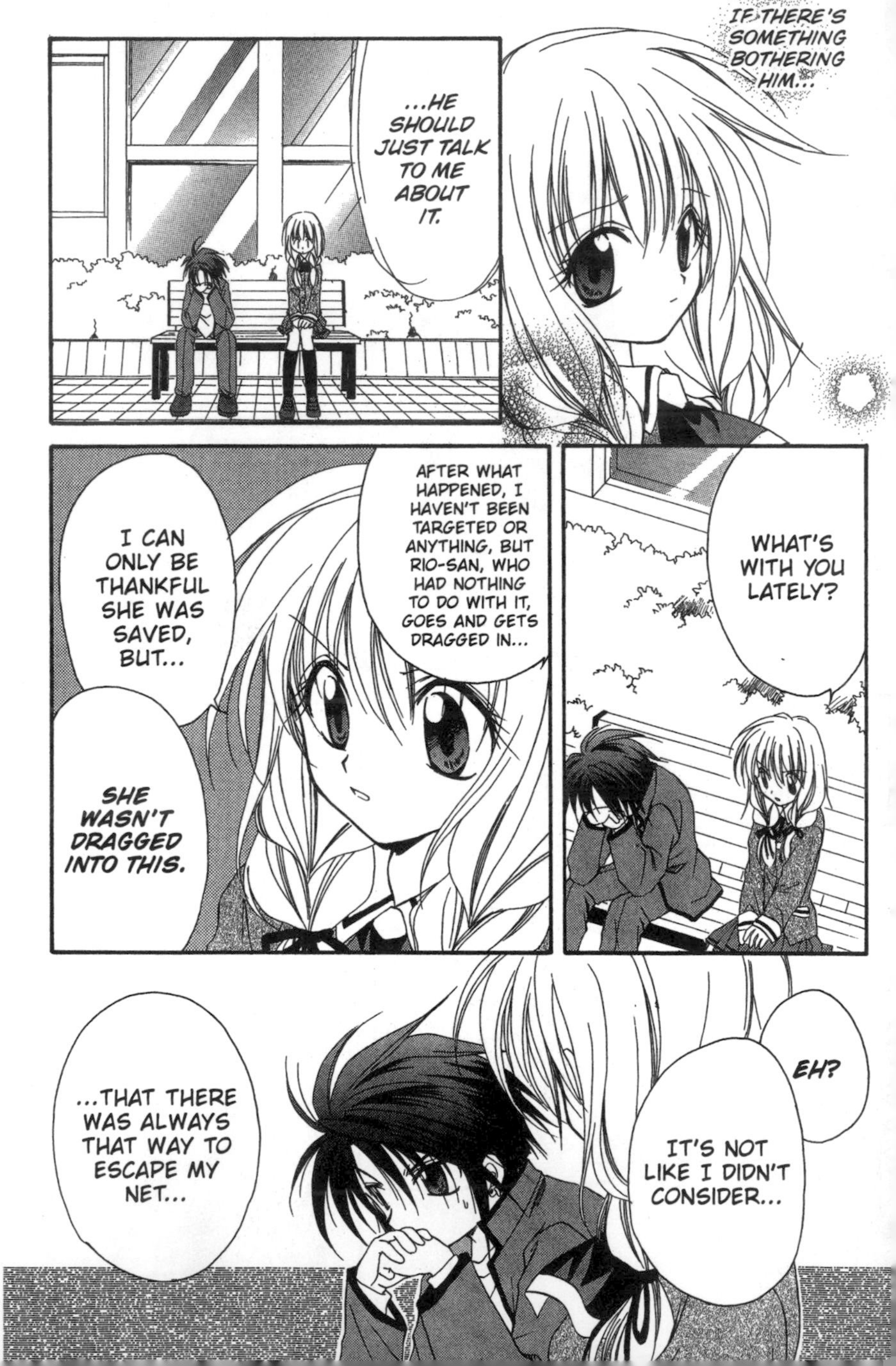
IF THERE'S SOMETHING BOTHERING HIM...
...HE SHOULD JUST TALK TO ME ABOUT IT.
WHAT'S WITH YOU LATELY?
AFTER WHAT HAPPENED, I HAVEN'T BEEN TARGETED OR ANYTHING, BUT RIO-SAN, WHO HAD NOTHING TO DO WITH IT, GOES AND GETS DRAGGED IN...
I CAN ONLY BE THANKFUL SHE WAS SAVED, BUT...
SHE WASN'T DRAGGED INTO THIS.
EH?
IT'S NOT LIKE I DIDN'T CONSIDER...
...THAT THERE WAS ALWAYS THAT WAY TO ESCAPE MY NET...

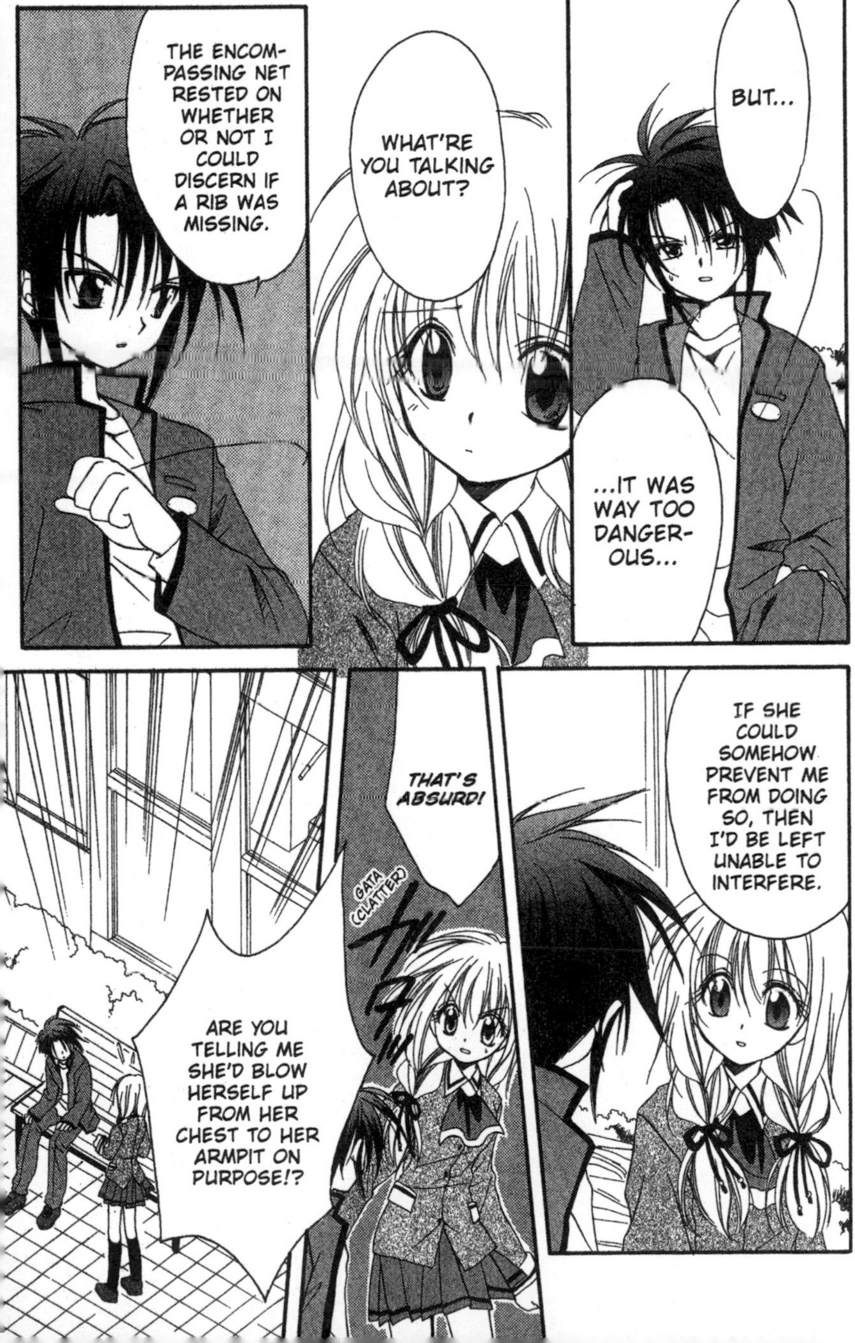
BUT...
...IT WAS WAY TOO DANGER-OUS...
WHAT'RE YOU TALKING ABOUT?
THE ENCOM-PASSING NET RESTED ON WHETHER OR NOT I COULD DISCERN IF A RIB WAS MISSING.
IF SHE COULD SOMEHOW PREVENT ME FROM DOING SO, THEN I'D BE LEFT UNABLE TO INTERFERE.
THAT'S ABSURD!
GATA (CLATTER)
ARE YOU TELLING ME SHE'D BLOW HERSELF UP FROM HER CHEST TO HER ARMPIT ON PURPOSE!?

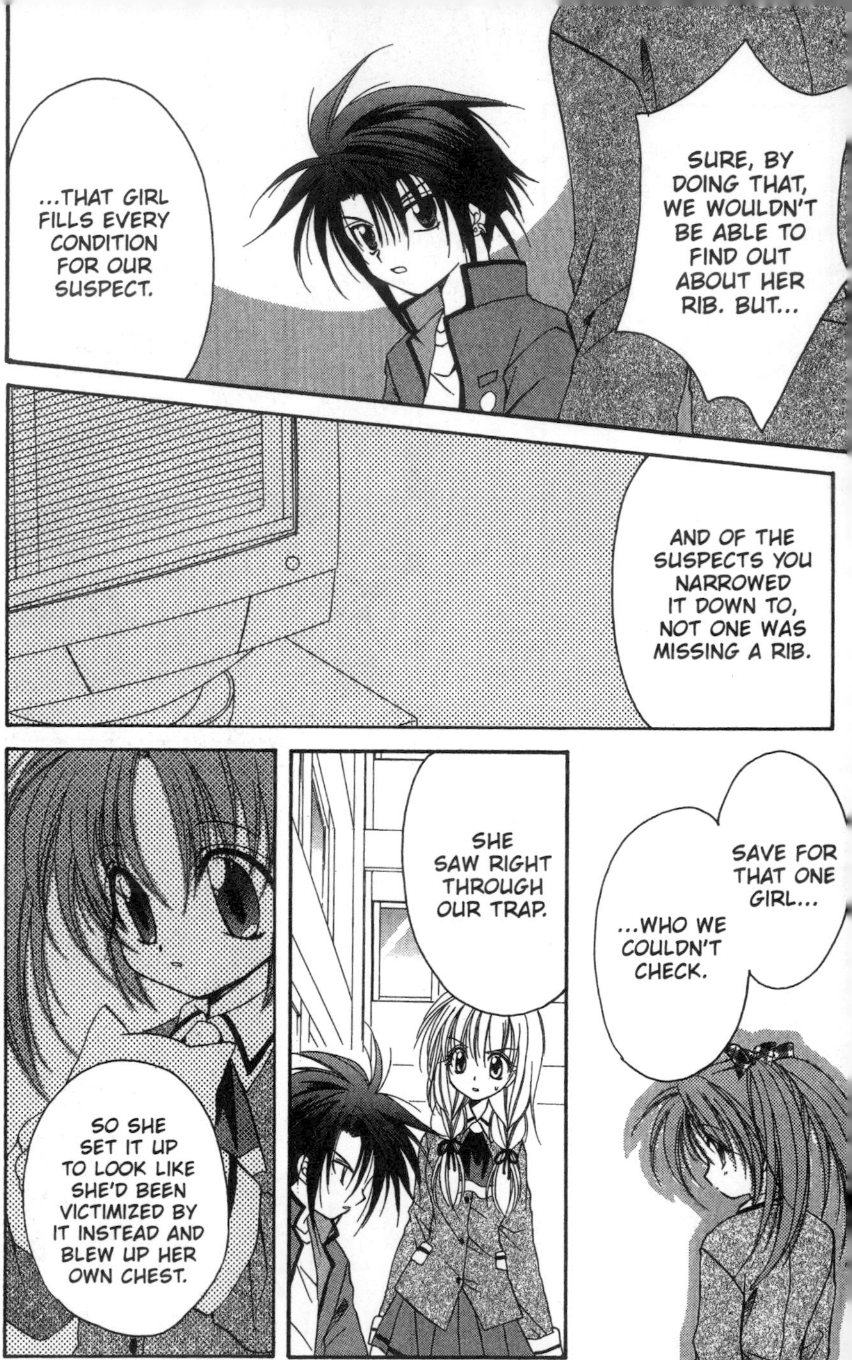
SURE, BY DOING THAT, WE WOULDN'T BE ABLE TO FIND OUT ABOUT HER RIB. BUT...
...THAT GIRL FILLS EVERY CONDITION FOR OUR SUSPECT.
AND OF THE SUSPECTS YOU NARROWED IT DOWN TO, NOT ONE WAS MISSING A RIB.
SAVE FOR THAT ONE GIRL...
...WHO WE COULDN'T CHECK.
SHE SAW RIGHT THROUGH OUR TRAP.
SO SHE SET IT UP TO LOOK LIKE SHE'D BEEN VICTIMIZED BY IT INSTEAD AND BLEW UP HER OWN CHEST.

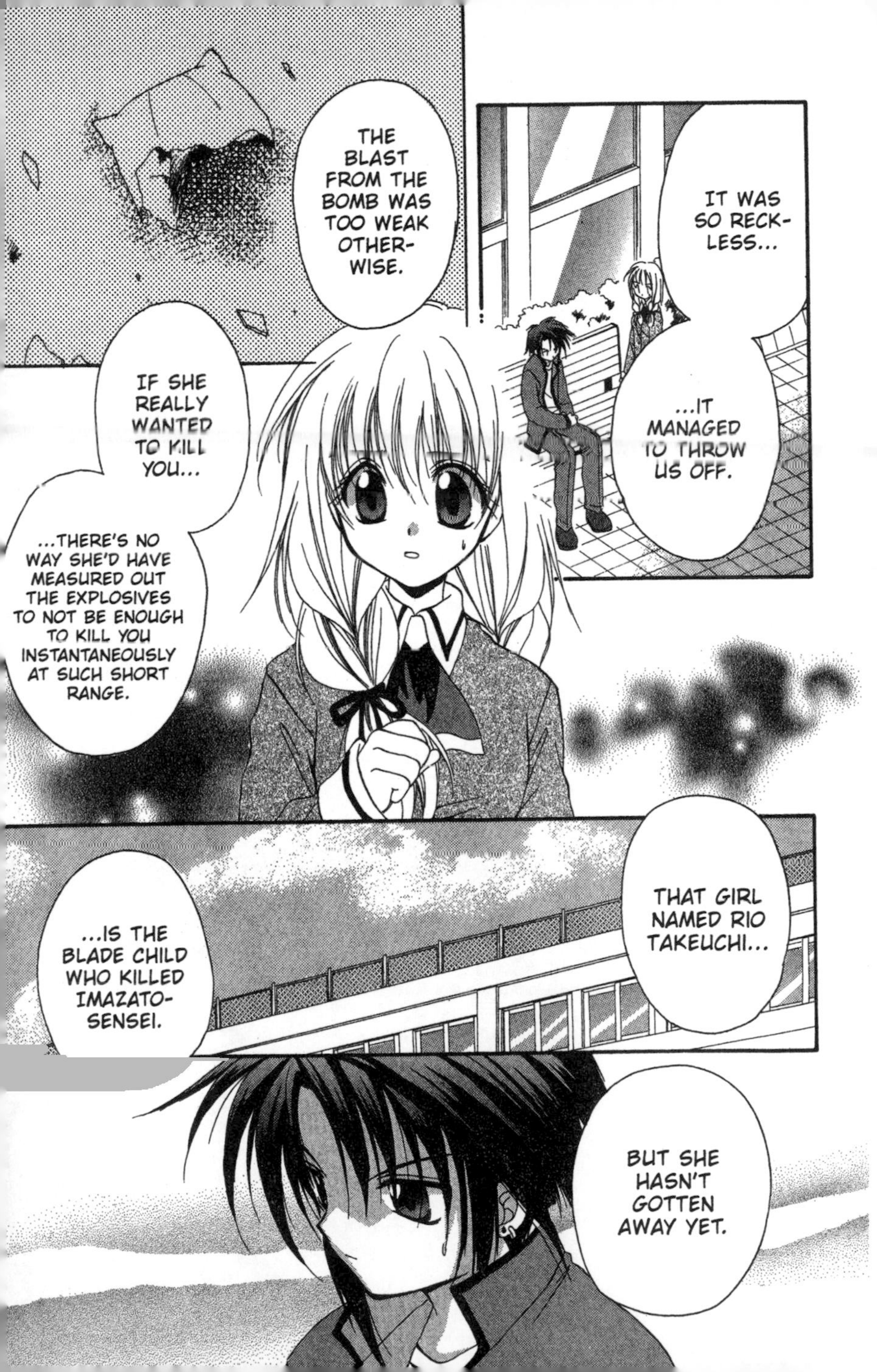
IT WAS SO RECKLESS...
...IT MANAGED TO THROW US OFF.
THE BLAST FROM THE BOMB WAS TOO WEAK OTHERWISE.
IF SHE REALLY WANTED TO KILL YOU...
...THERE'S NO WAY SHE'D HAVE MEASURED OUT THE EXPLOSIVES TO NOT BE ENOUGH TO KILL YOU INSTANTANEOUSLY AT SUCH SHORT RANGE.
THAT GIRL NAMED RIO TAKEUCHI...
...IS THE BLADE CHILD WHO KILLED IMAZATO-SENSEI.
BUT SHE HASN'T GOTTEN AWAY YET.

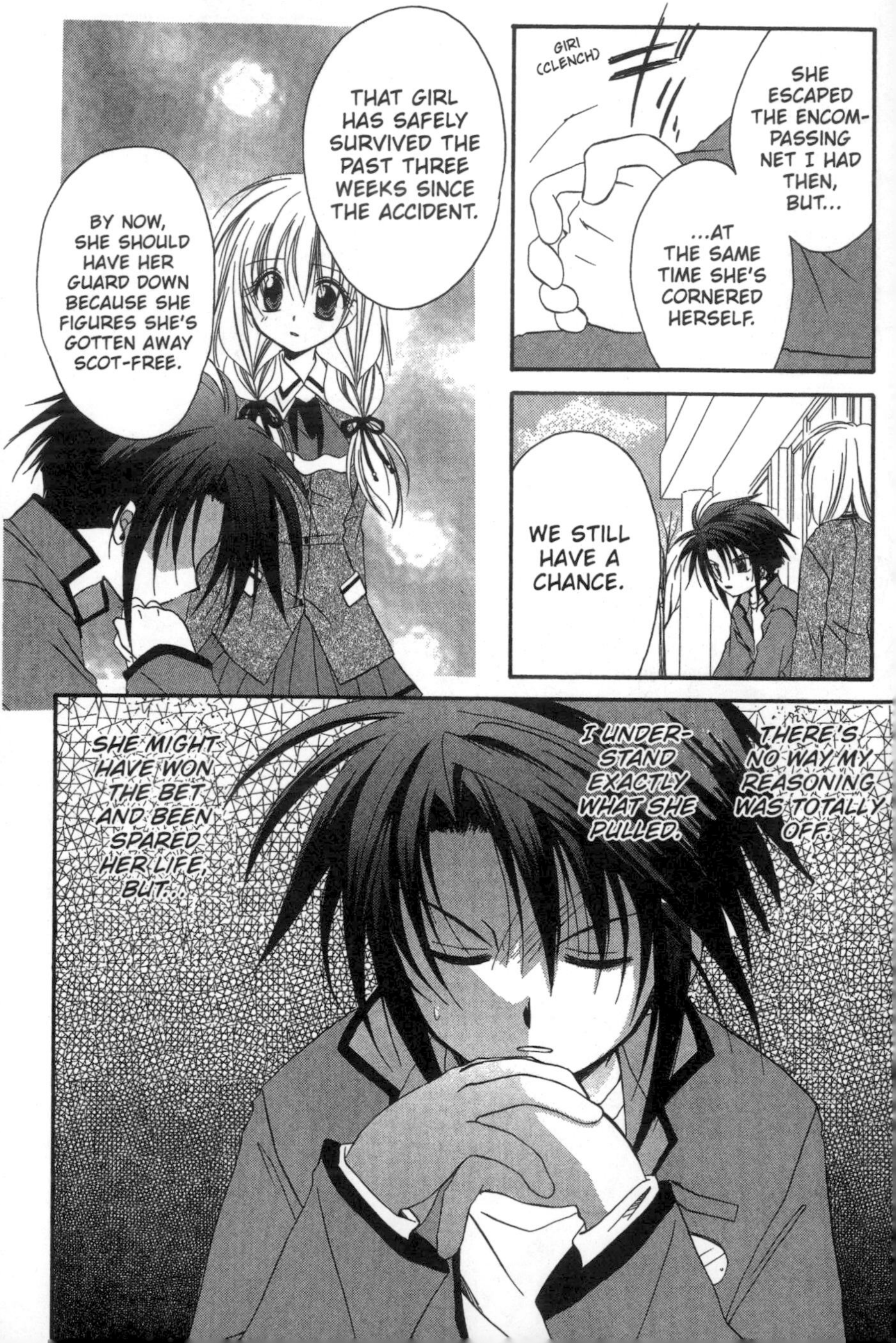
SHE ESCAPED THE ENCOM-PASSING NET I HAD THEN, BUT...
GIRI (CLENCH)
...AT THE SAME TIME SHE'S CORNERED HERSELF.
WE STILL HAVE A CHANCE.
THAT GIRL HAS SAFELY SURVIVED THE PAST THREE WEEKS SINCE THE ACCIDENT.
BY NOW, SHE SHOULD HAVE HER GUARD DOWN BECAUSE SHE FIGURES SHE'S GOTTEN AWAY SCOT-FREE.
THERE'S NO WAY MY REASONING WAS TOTALLY OFF.
I UNDER-STAND EXACTLY WHAT SHE PULLED.
SHE MIGHT HAVE WON THE BET AND BEEN SPARED HER LIFE, BUT...

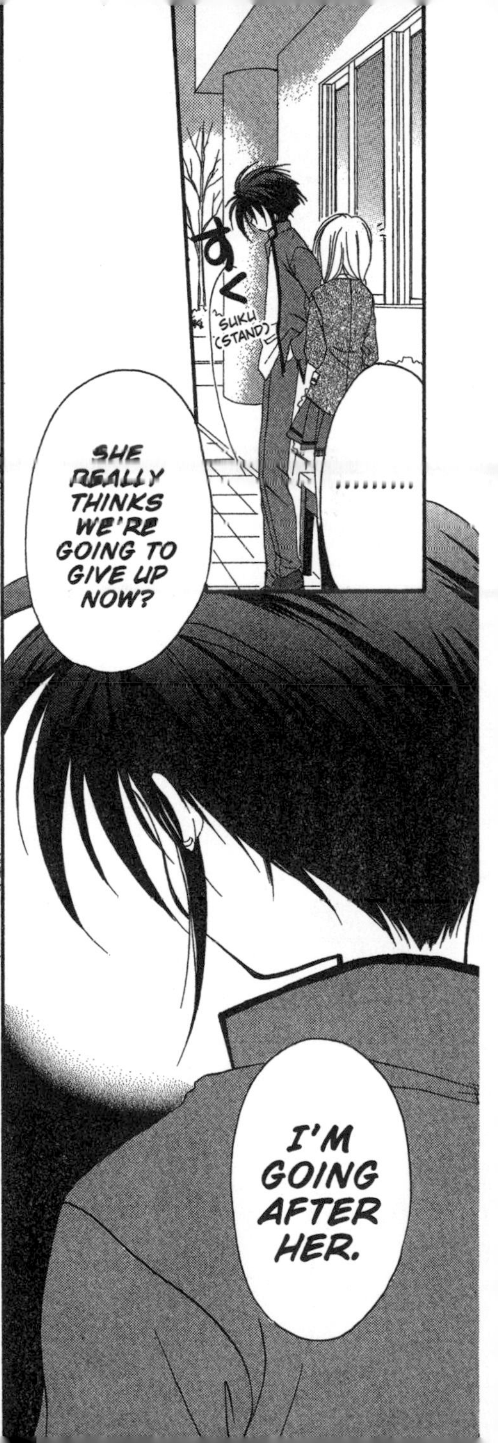
すく
SUKU (STAND)
....
SHE REALLY THINKS WE'RE GOING TO GIVE UP NOW?
I'M GOING AFTER HER.
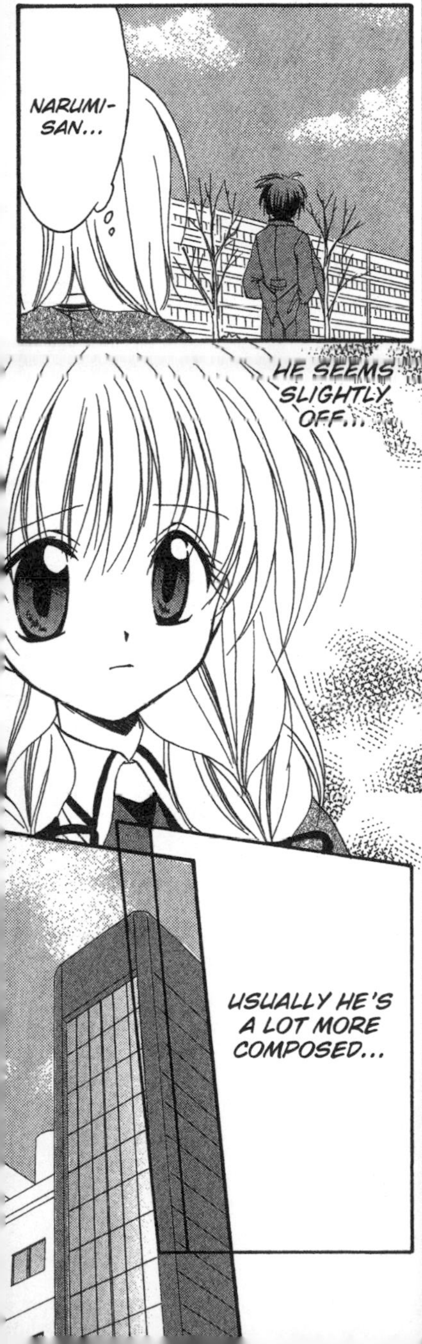
NARUMI-SAN...
HE SEEMS SLIGHTLY OFF...
USUALLY HE'S A LOT MORE COMPOSED...

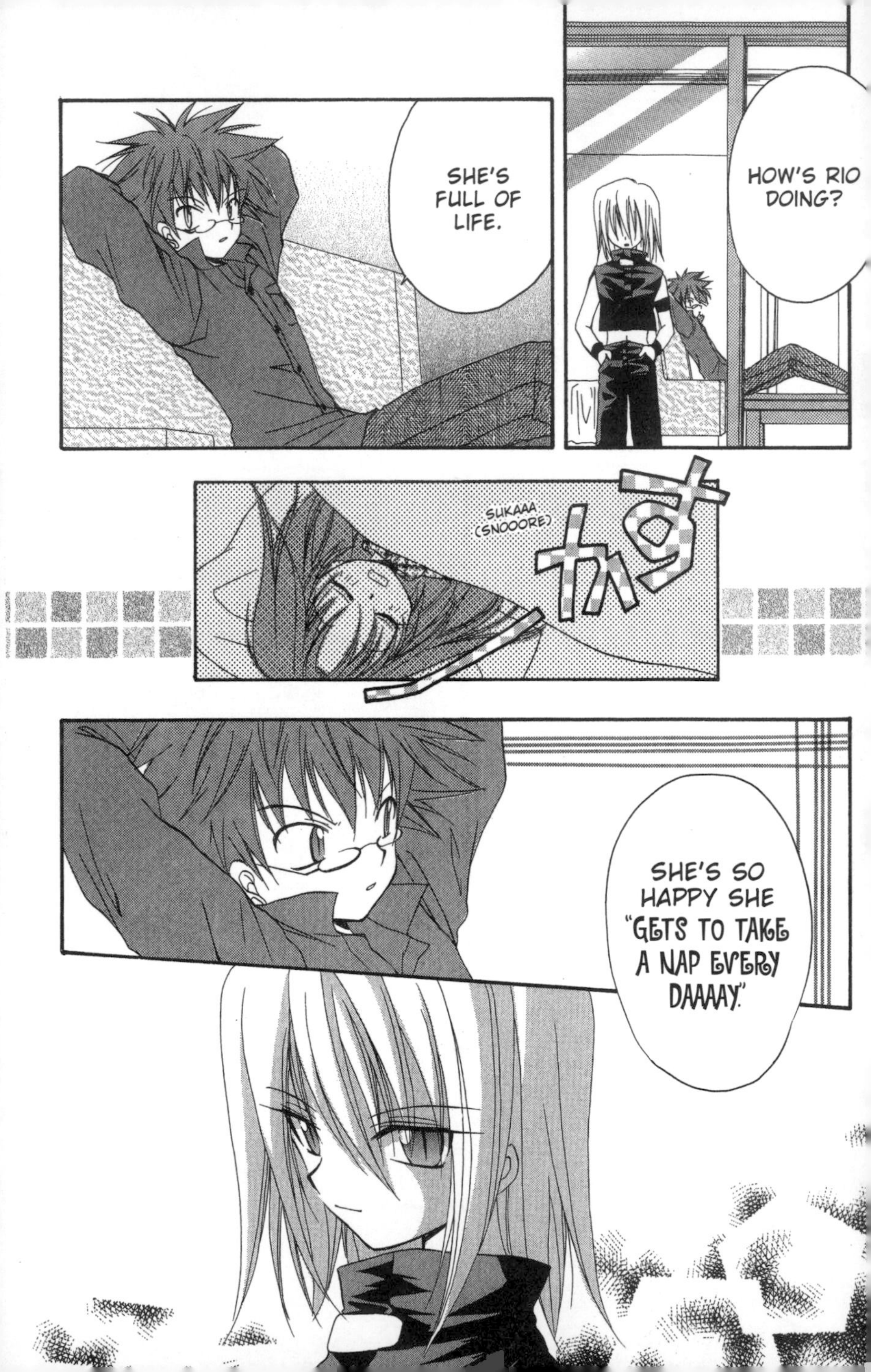
HOW'S RIO DOING?
SHE'S FULL OF LIFE.
SUKAAA (SNOOORE)
かぁ
SHE'S SO HAPPY SHE "GETS TO TAKE A NAP EVERY DAAAAY."

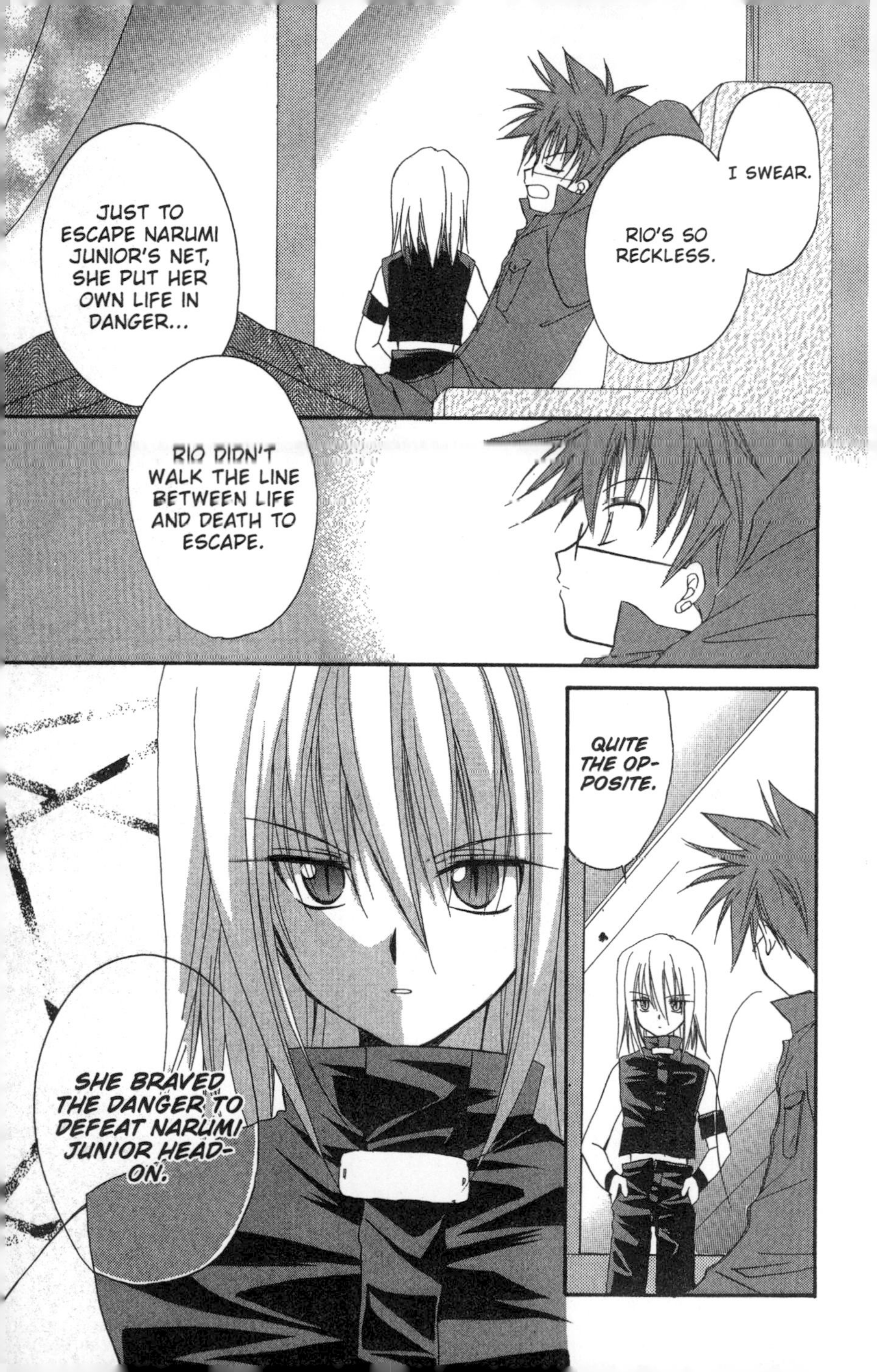
I SWEAR.
RIO'S SO RECKLESS.
JUST TO ESCAPE NARUMI JUNIOR'S NET, SHE PUT HER OWN LIFE IN DANGER...
RIO DIDN'T WALK THE LINE BETWEEN LIFE AND DEATH TO ESCAPE.
QUITE THE OP-POSITE.
SHE BRAVED THE DANGER TO DEFEAT NARUMI JUNIOR HEAD-ON.

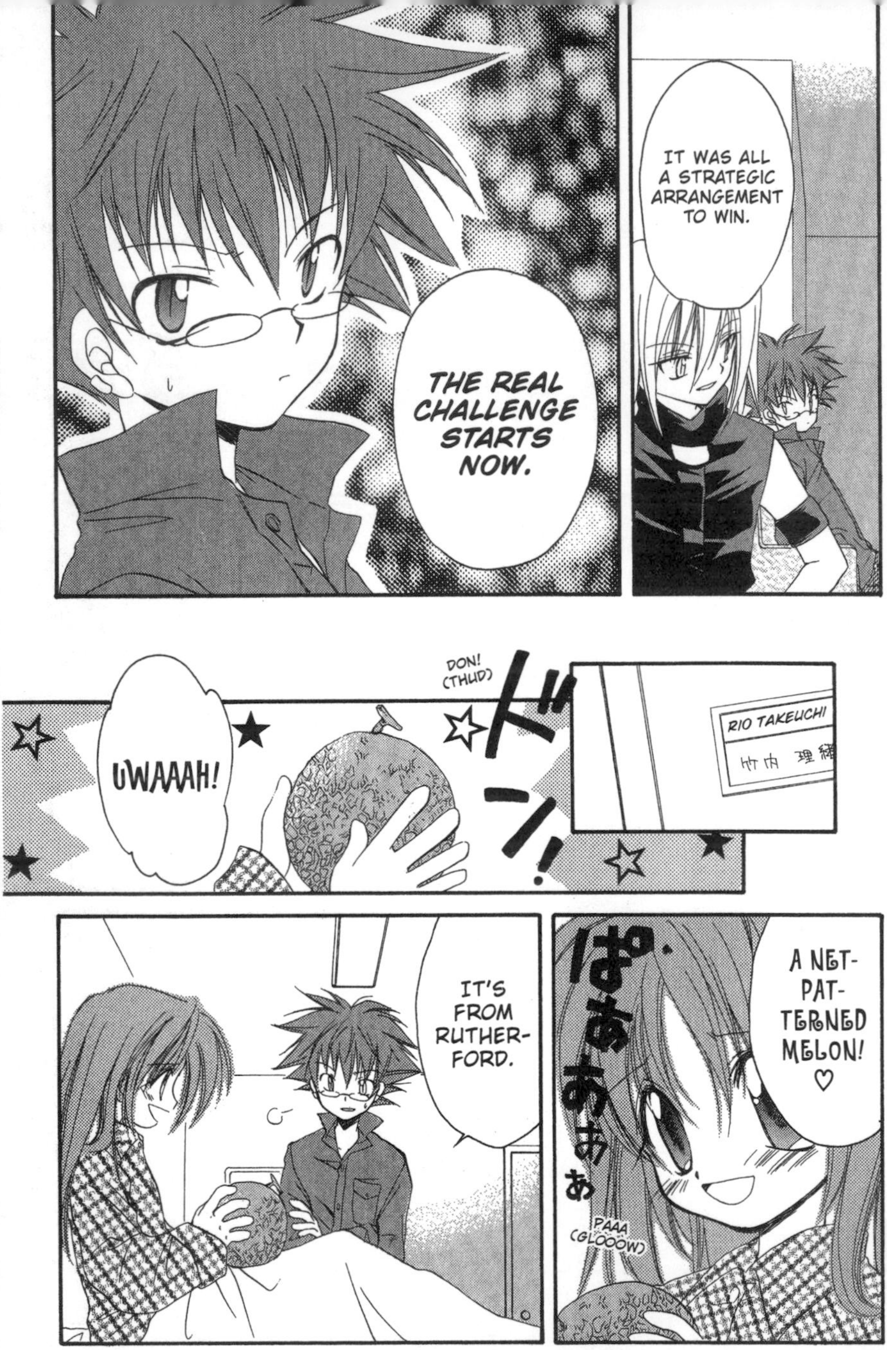
IT WAS ALL A STRATEGIC ARRANGEMENT TO WIN.
THE REAL CHALLENGE STARTS NOW.
RIO TAKEUCHI
竹内 理
DON! (THUD)
ドン!
UWAAAH!
ぱあああ
PAAA (GLOOOW)
A NET-PATTERNED MELON! ♡
IT'S FROM RUTHERFORD.

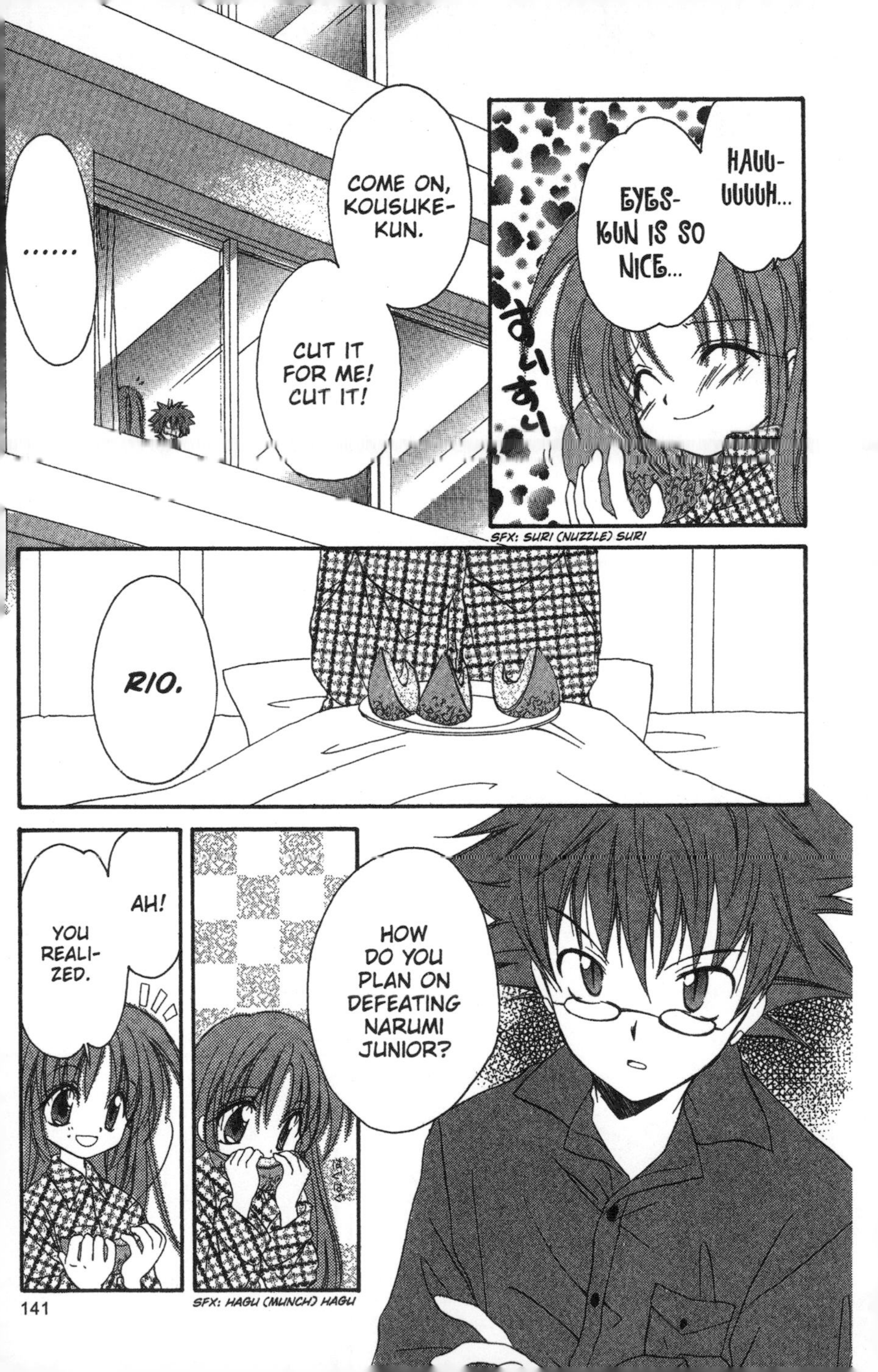
HAUU-UUUUH...
EYES-KUN IS SO NICE...
SFX: SURI (NUZZLE) SURI
COME ON, KOUSUKE-KUN.
CUT IT FOR ME! CUT IT!
......
RIO.
HOW DO YOU PLAN ON DEFEATING NARUMI JUNIOR?
SFX: HAGU (MUNCH) HAGU
AH!
YOU REALI-ZED.

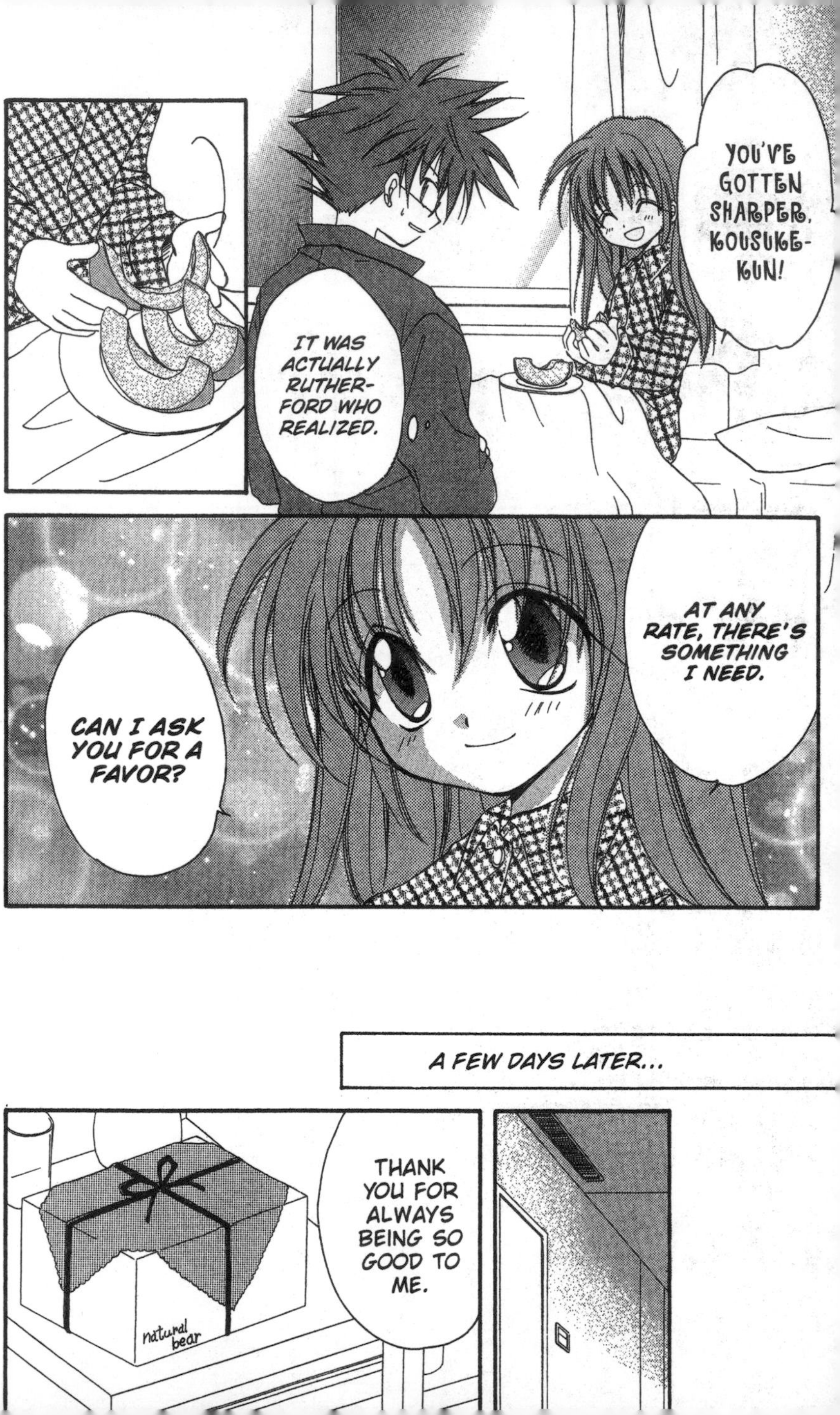
YOU'VE GOTTEN SHARPER, KOUSUKE-KUN!
IT WAS ACTUALLY RUTHER-FORD WHO REALIZED.
AT ANY RATE, THERE'S SOMETHING I NEED.
CAN I ASK YOU FOR A FAVOR?
A FEW DAYS LATER...
THANK YOU FOR ALWAYS BEING SO GOOD TO ME.
natural bear

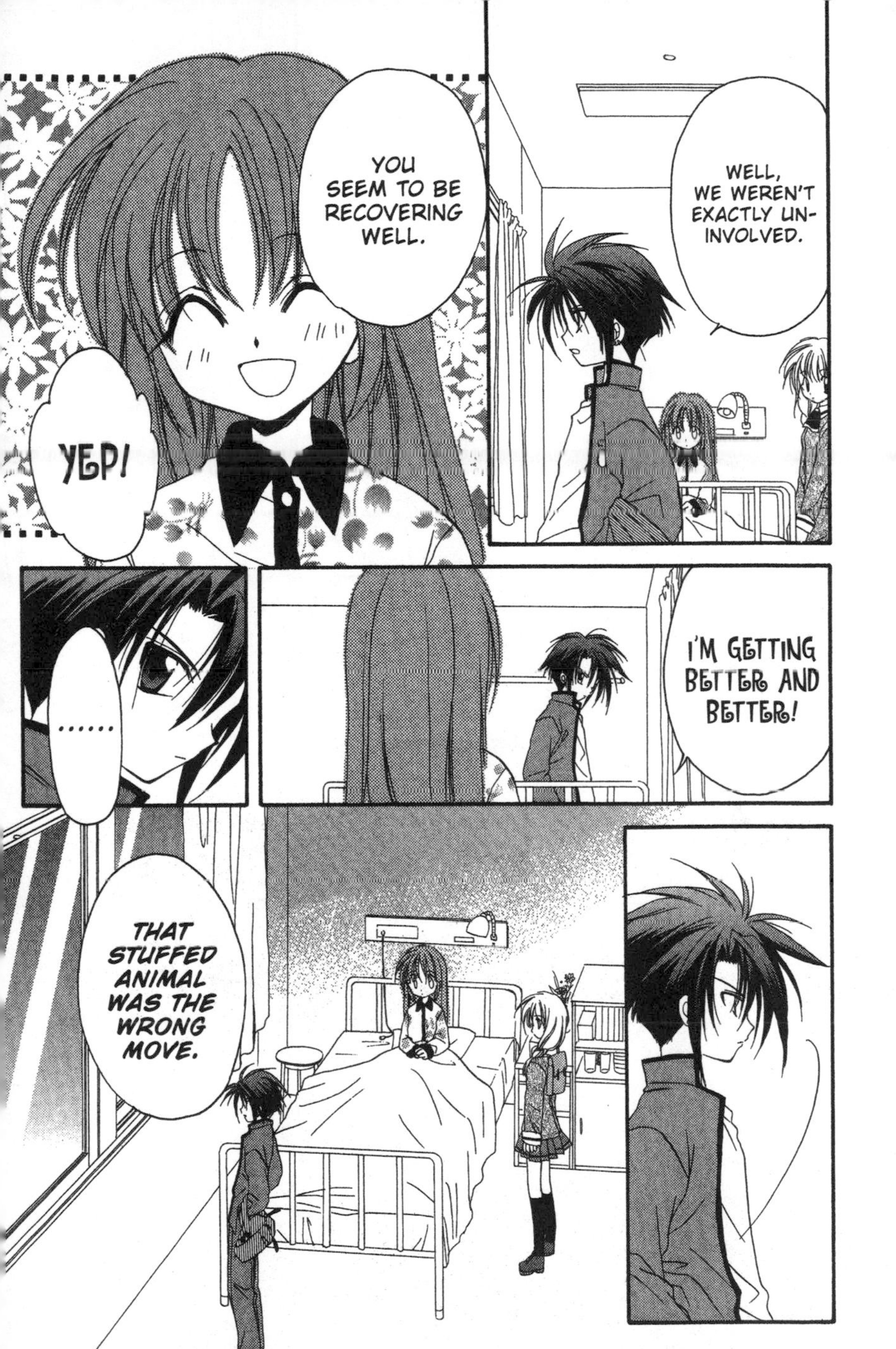
WELL, WE WEREN'T EXACTLY UN-INVOLVED.
YOU SEEM TO BE RECOVERING WELL.
YEP!
I'M GETTING BETTER AND BETTER!
......
THAT STUFFED ANIMAL WAS THE WRONG MOVE.

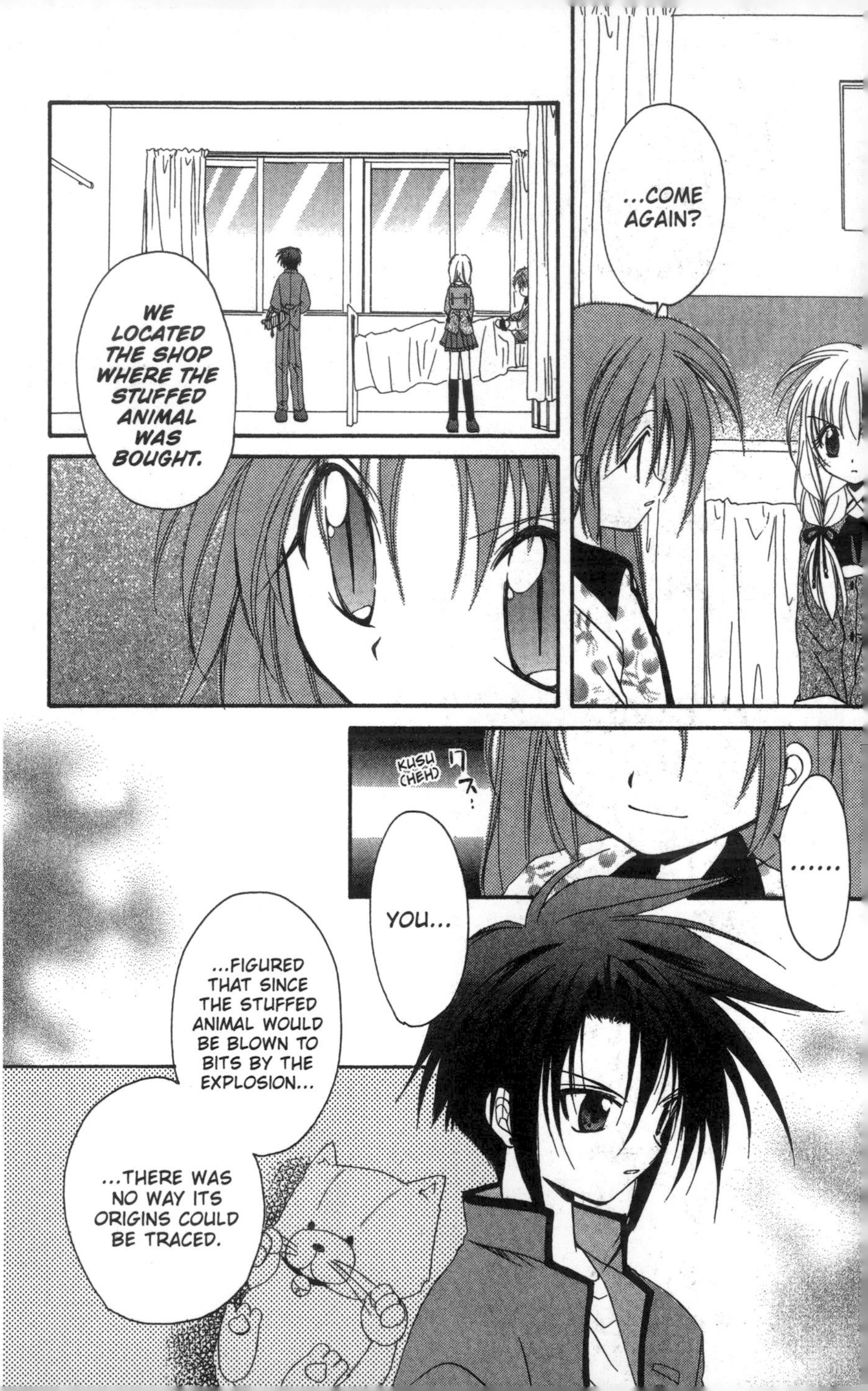
...COME AGAIN?
WE LOCATED THE SHOP WHERE THE STUFFED ANIMAL WAS BOUGHT.
......
KUSU (HEH)
YOU...
...FIGURED THAT SINCE THE STUFFED ANIMAL WOULD BE BLOWN TO BITS BY THE EXPLOSION...
...THERE WAS NO WAY ITS ORIGINS COULD BE TRACED.

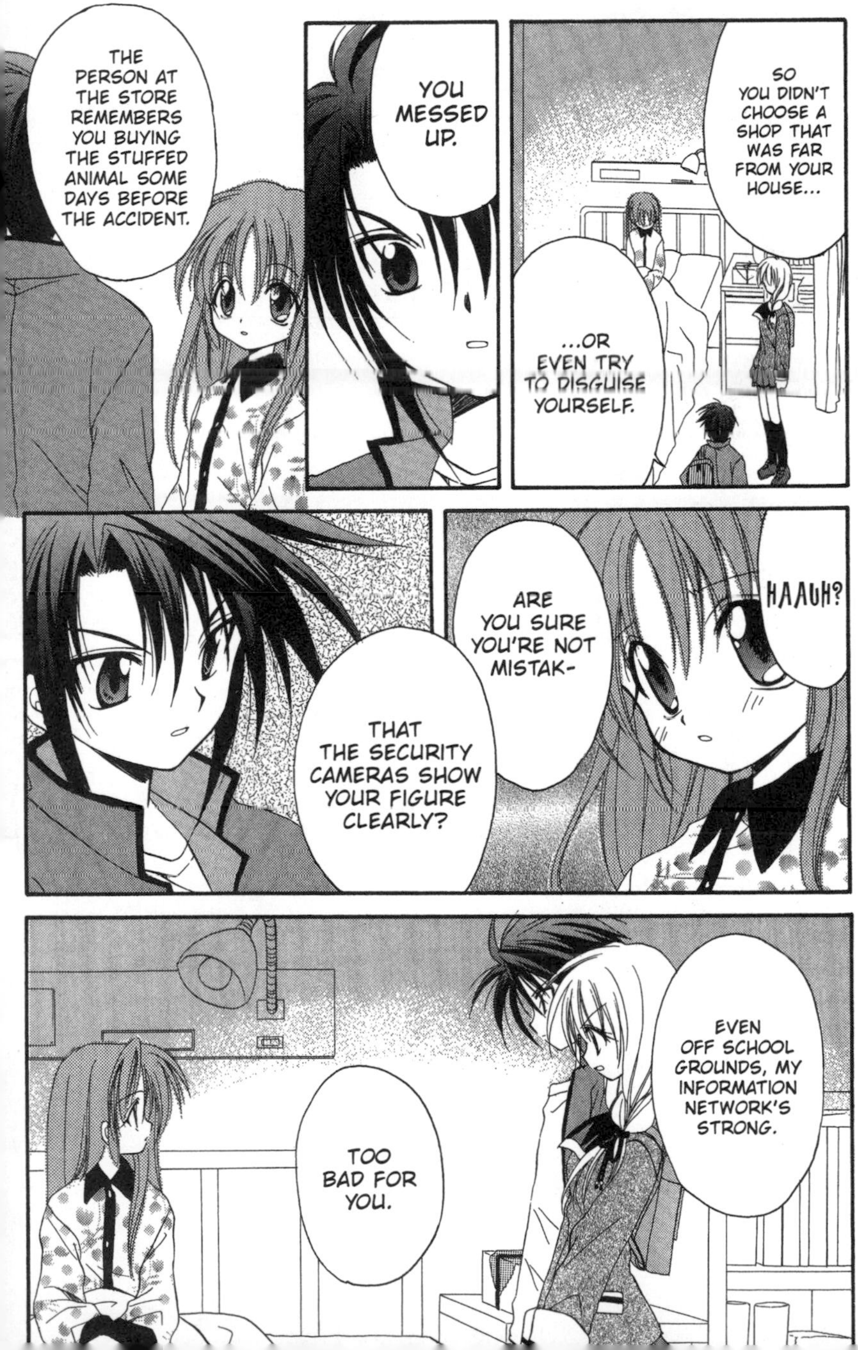
SO YOU DIDN'T CHOOSE A SHOP THAT WAS FAR FROM YOUR HOUSE...
...OR EVEN TRY TO DISGUISE YOURSELF.
YOU MESSED UP.
THE PERSON AT THE STORE REMEMBERS YOU BUYING THE STUFFED ANIMAL SOME DAYS BEFORE THE ACCIDENT.
HAAUH?
ARE YOU SURE YOU'RE NOT MISTAK-
THAT THE SECURITY CAMERAS SHOW YOUR FIGURE CLEARLY?
EVEN OFF SCHOOL GROUNDS, MY INFORMATION NETWORK'S STRONG.
TOO BAD FOR YOU.

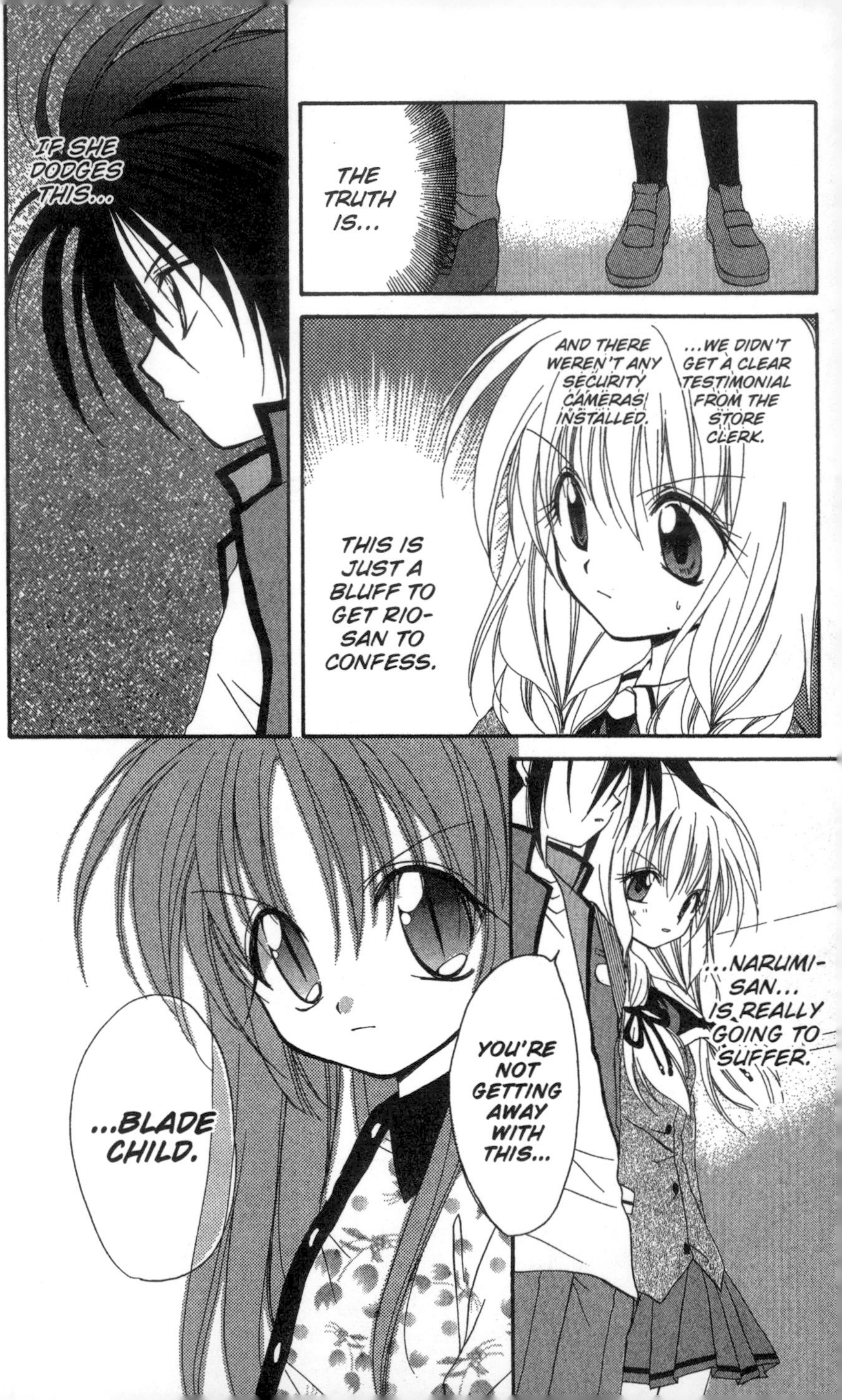
THE TRUTH IS...
...WE DIDN'T GET A CLEAR TESTIMONIAL FROM THE STORE CLERK.
AND THERE WEREN'T ANY SECURITY CAMERAS INSTALLED.
THIS IS JUST A BLUFF TO GET RIO-SAN TO CONFESS.
IF SHE DODGES THIS...
...NARUMI-SAN... IS REALLY GOING TO SUFFER.
YOU'RE NOT GETTING AWAY WITH THIS...
...BLADE CHILD.

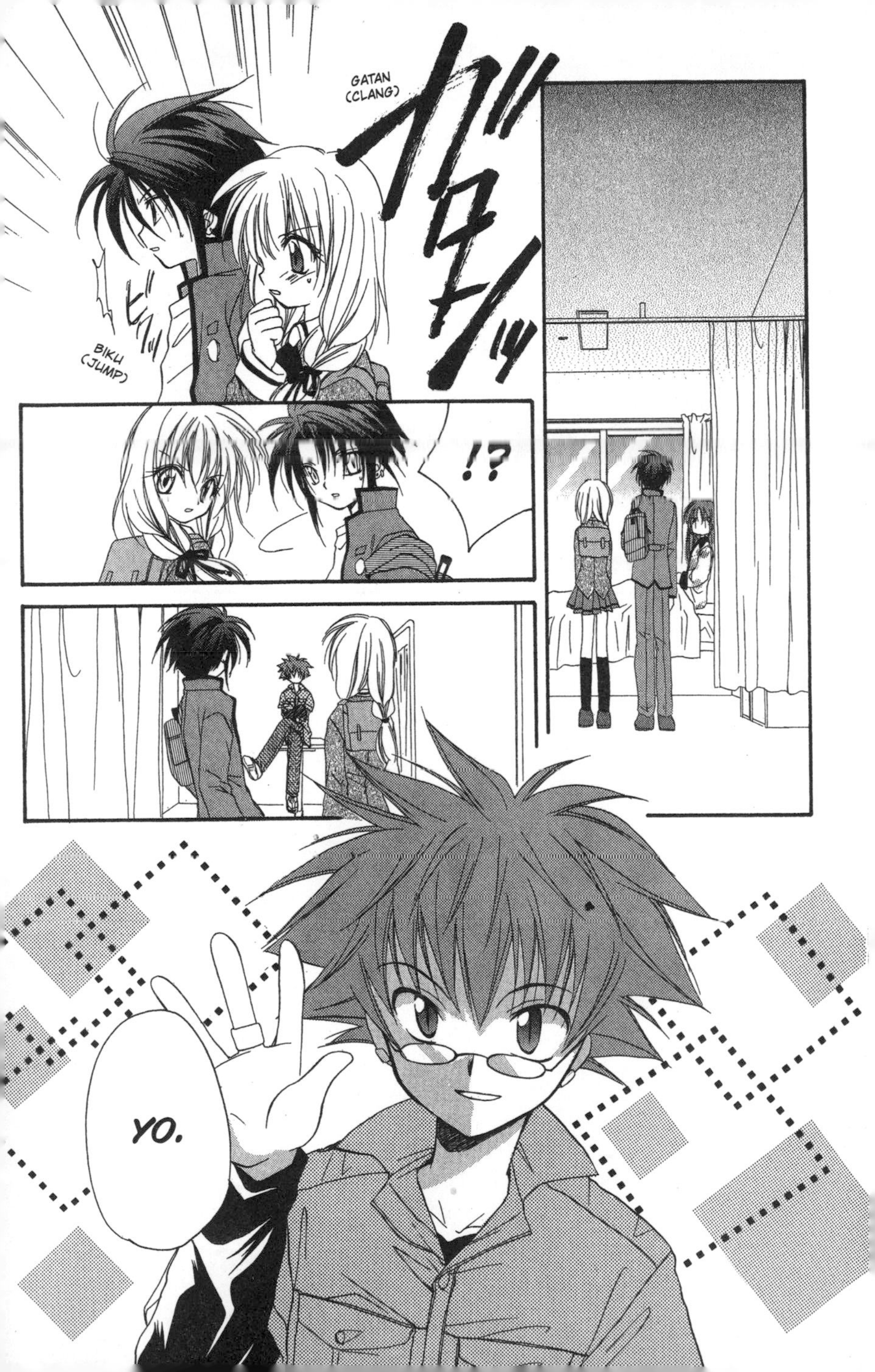
GATAN (CLANG)
BIKU (JUMP)
!?
YO.

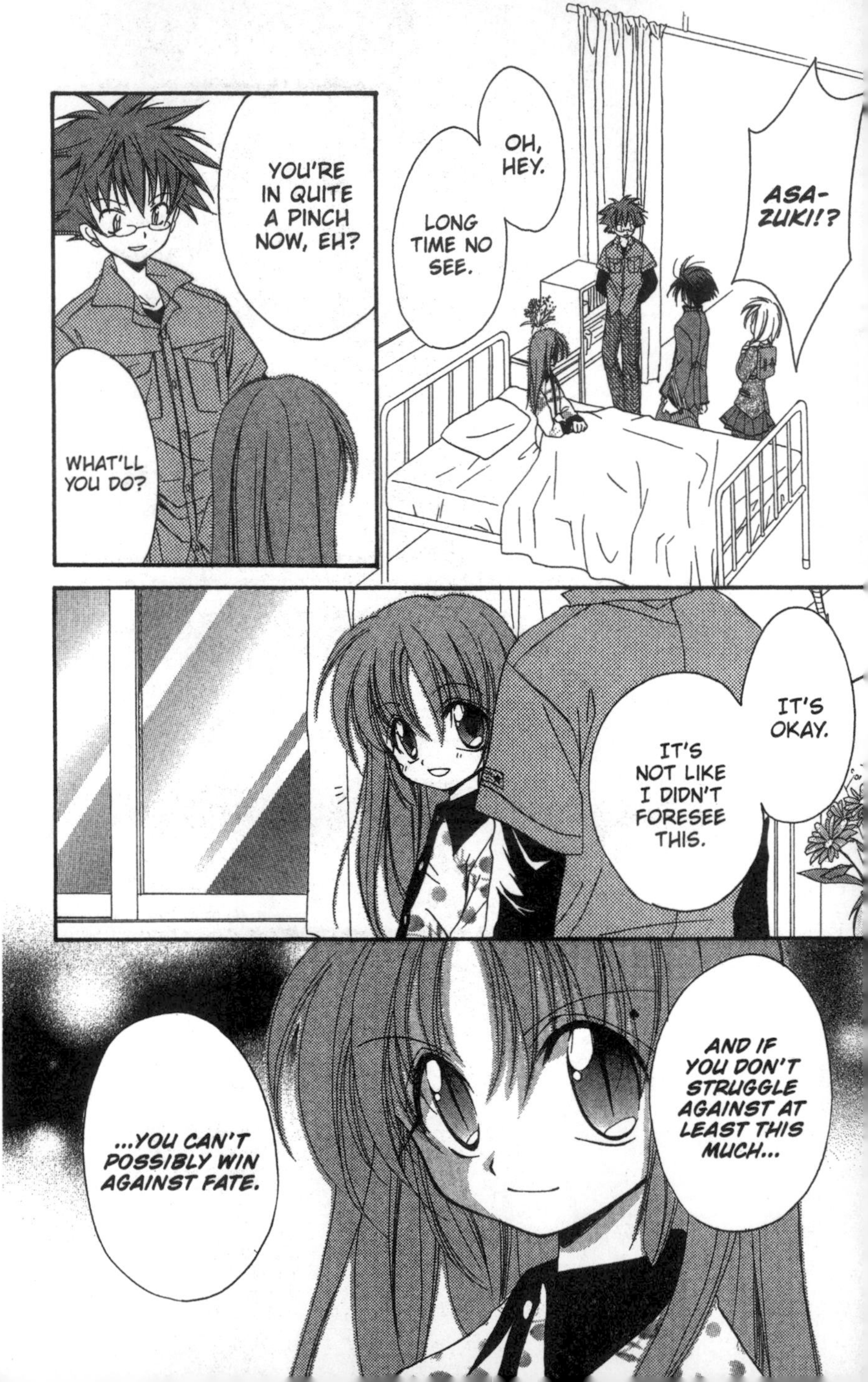
ASA-ZUKI!?
OH, HEY.
LONG TIME NO SEE.
YOU'RE IN QUITE A PINCH NOW, EH?
WHAT'LL YOU DO?
IT'S OKAY.
IT'S NOT LIKE I DIDN'T FORESEE THIS.
AND IF YOU DON'T STRUGGLE AGAINST AT LEAST THIS MUCH...
...YOU CAN'T POSSIBLY WIN AGAINST FATE.

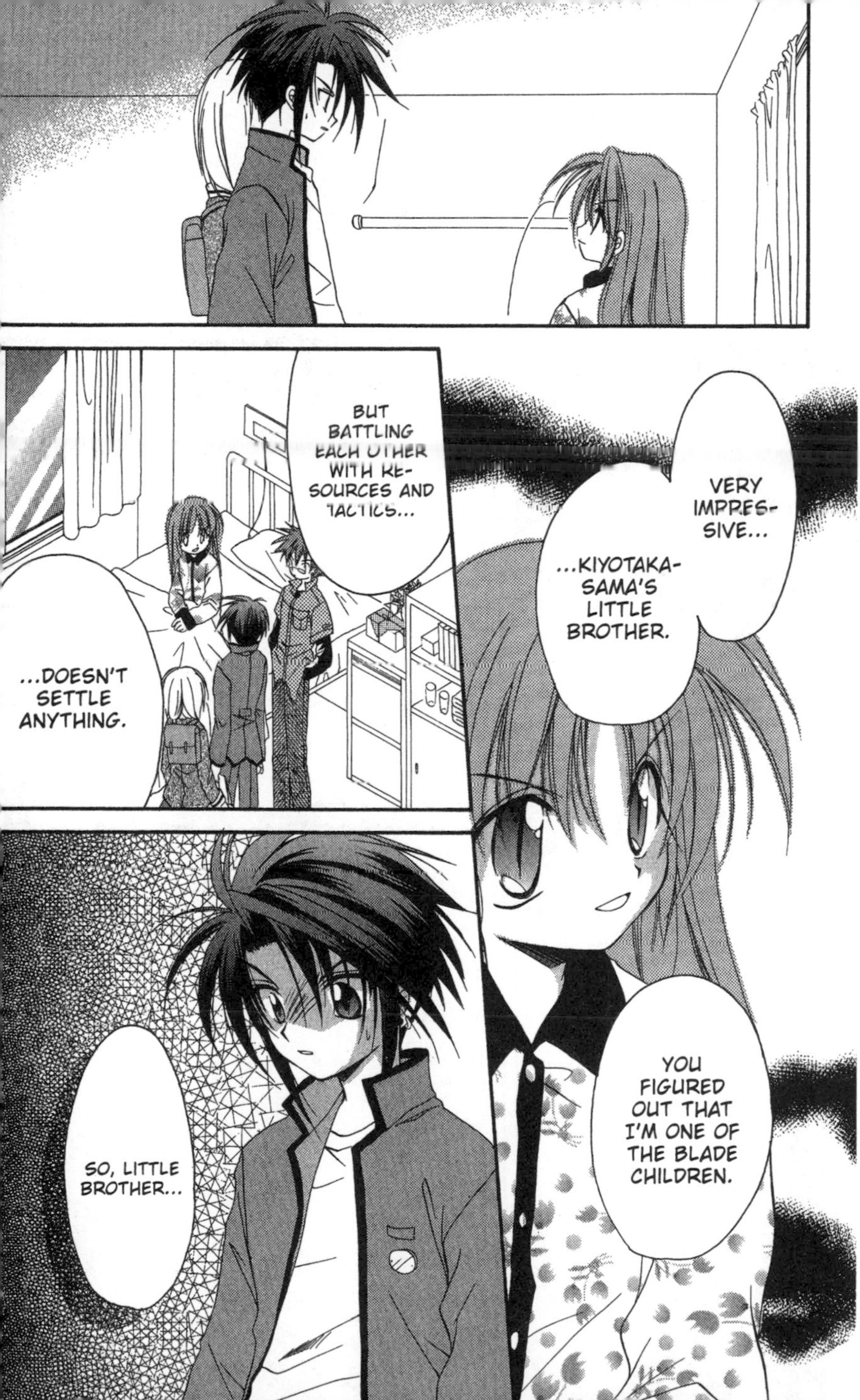
VERY IMPRES-SIVE...
...KIYOTAKA-SAMA'S LITTLE BROTHER.
YOU FIGURED OUT THAT I'M ONE OF THE BLADE CHILDREN.
BUT BATTLING EACH OTHER WITH RE-SOURCES AND TACTICS...
...DOESN'T SETTLE ANYTHING.
SO, LITTLE BROTHER...

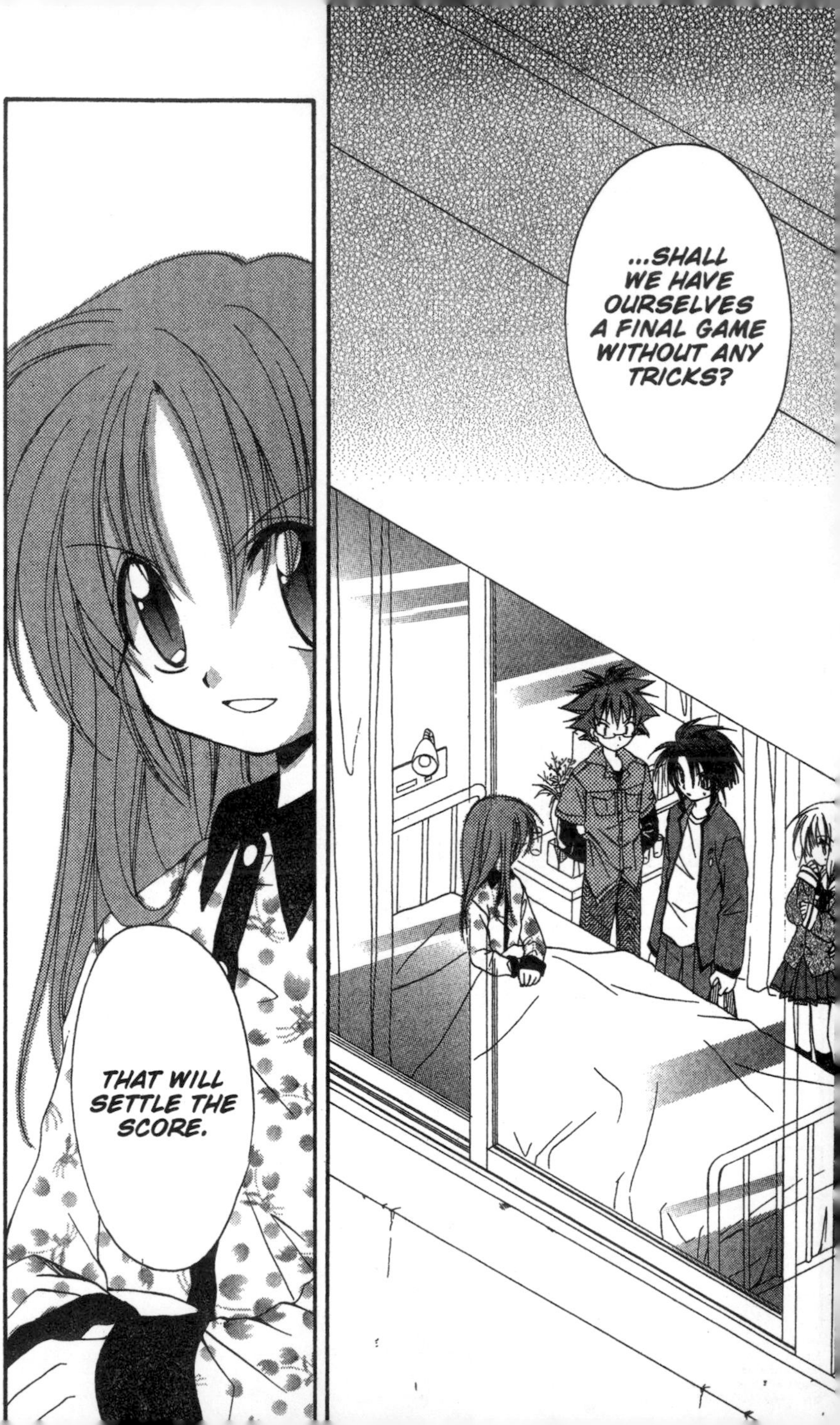
...SHALL WE HAVE OURSELVES A FINAL GAME WITHOUT ANY TRICKS?
THAT WILL SETTLE THE SCORE.

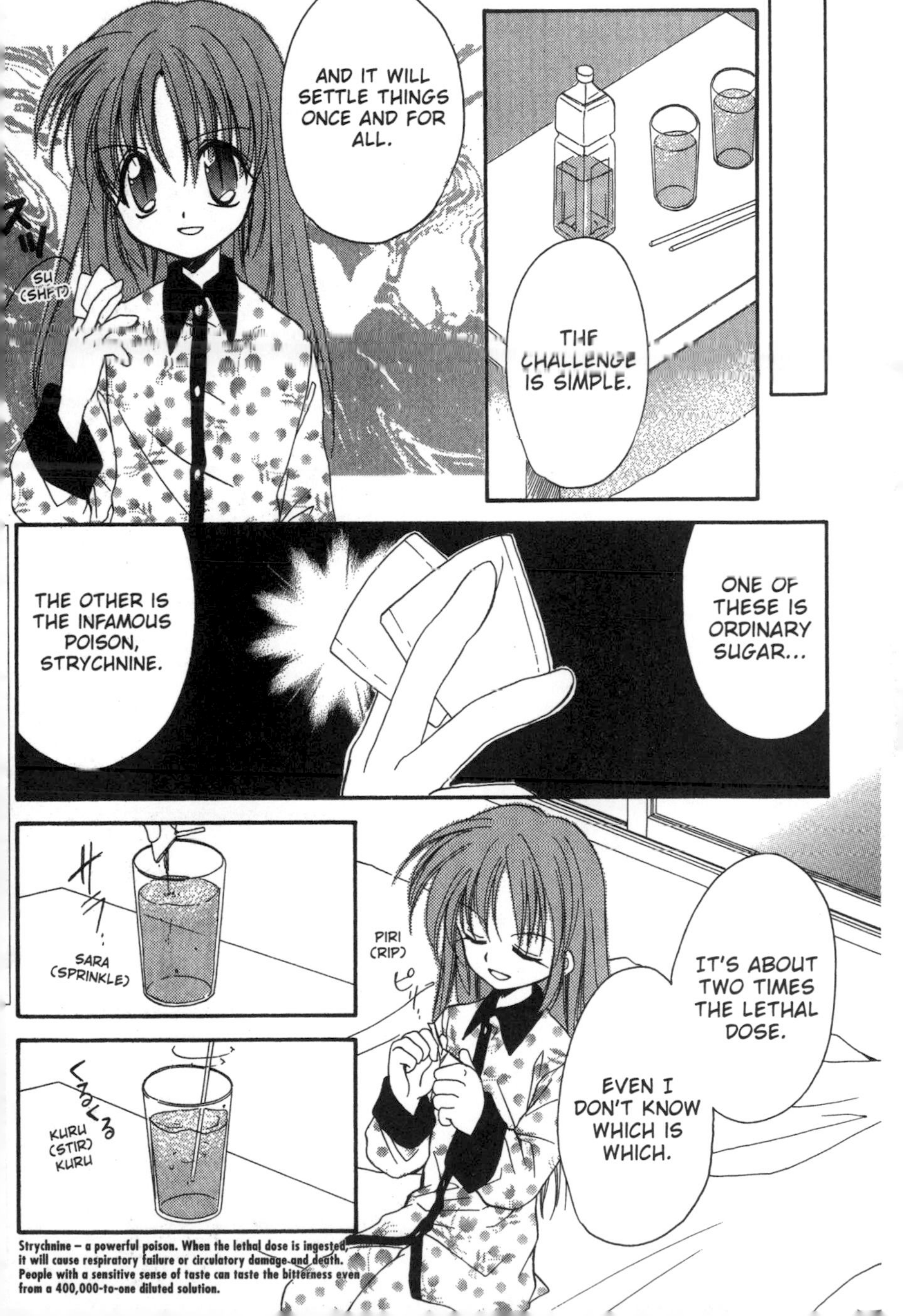
THE CHALLENGE IS SIMPLE.
AND IT WILL SETTLE THINGS ONCE AND FOR ALL.
SU (SHFT)
ONE OF THESE IS ORDINARY SUGAR...
THE OTHER IS THE INFAMOUS POISON, STRYCHNINE.
PIRI (RIP)
IT'S ABOUT TWO TIMES THE LETHAL DOSE.
EVEN I DON'T KNOW WHICH IS WHICH.
SARA (SPRINKLE)
KURU (STIR) KURU

Strychnine – a powerful poison. When the lethal dose is ingested, it will cause respiratory failure or circulatory damage and death. People with a sensitive sense of taste can taste the bitterness even from a 400,000-to-one diluted solution.

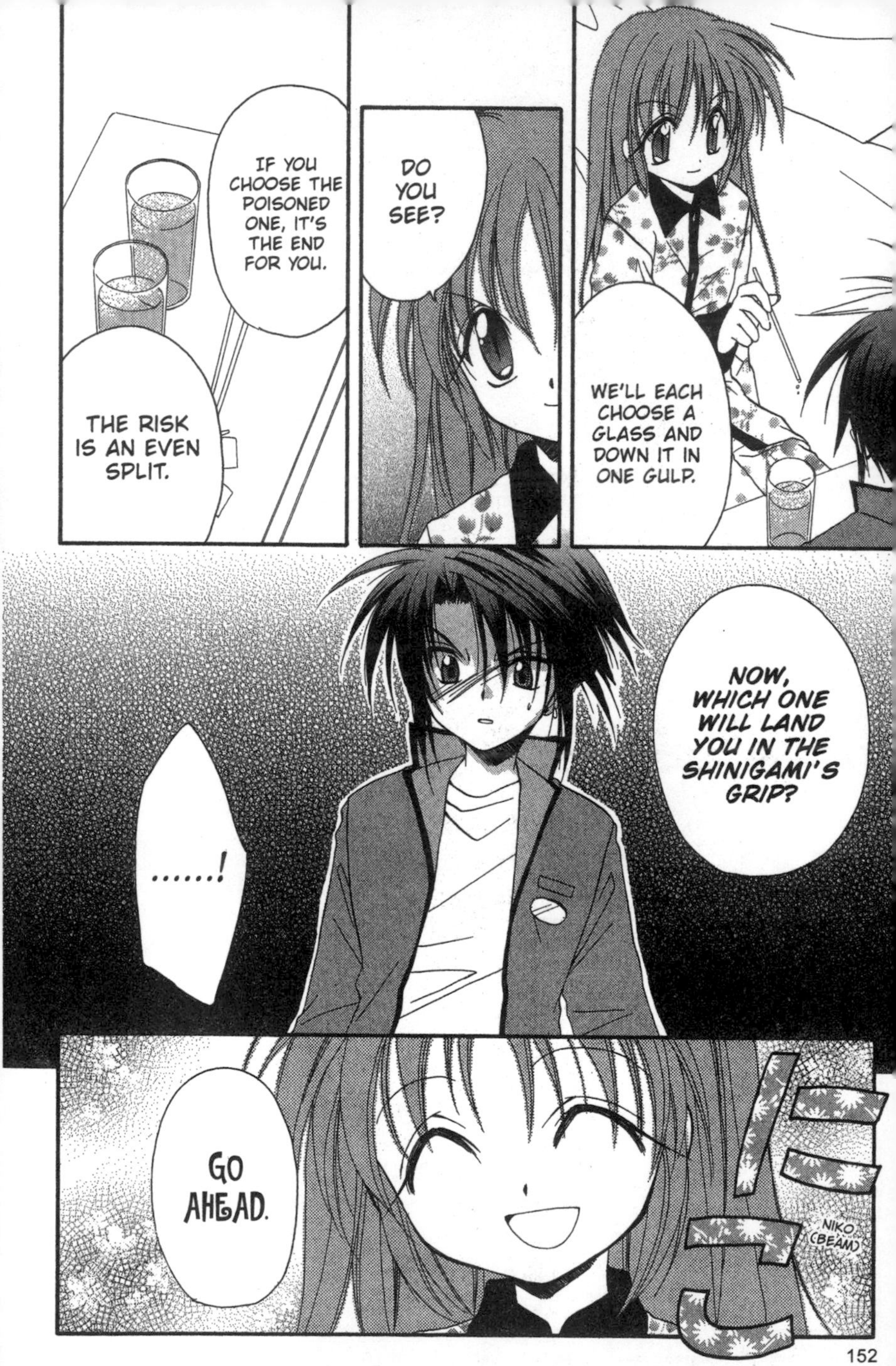
WE'LL EACH CHOOSE A GLASS AND DOWN IT IN ONE GULP.
DO YOU SEE?
IF YOU CHOOSE THE POISONED ONE, IT'S THE END FOR YOU.
THE RISK IS AN EVEN SPLIT.
NOW, WHICH ONE WILL LAND YOU IN THE SHINIGAMI'S GRIP?
......!
NIKO (BEAM)
GO AHEAD.

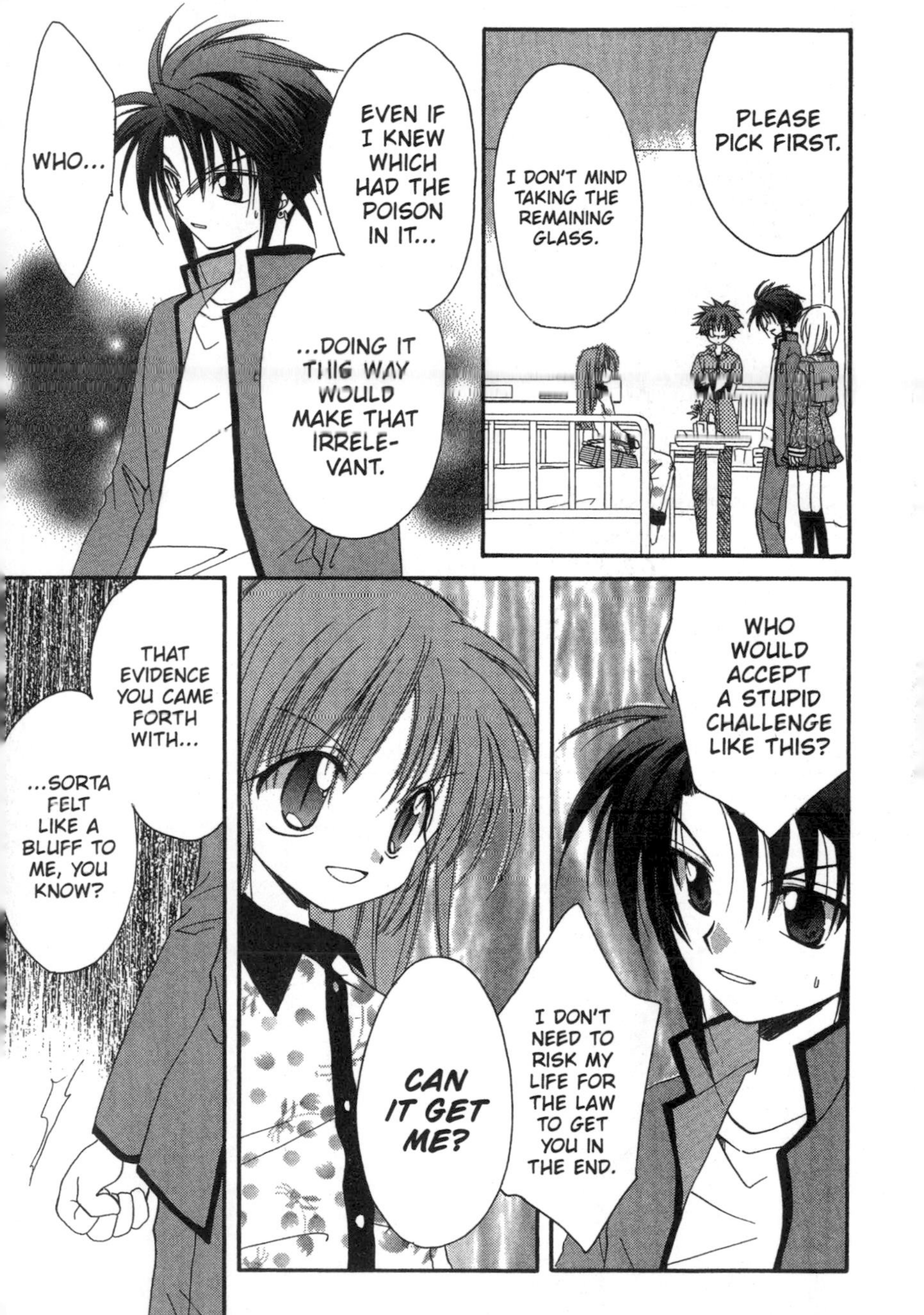
PLEASE PICK FIRST.
I DON'T MIND TAKING THE REMAINING GLASS.
EVEN IF I KNEW WHICH HAD THE POISON IN IT...
...DOING IT THIS WAY WOULD MAKE THAT IRRELE- VANT.
WHO...
WHO WOULD ACCEPT A STUPID CHALLENGE LIKE THIS?
I DON'T NEED TO RISK MY LIFE FOR THE LAW TO GET YOU IN THE END.
CAN IT GET ME?
THAT EVIDENCE YOU CAME FORTH WITH...
...SORTA FELT LIKE A BLUFF TO ME, YOU KNOW?

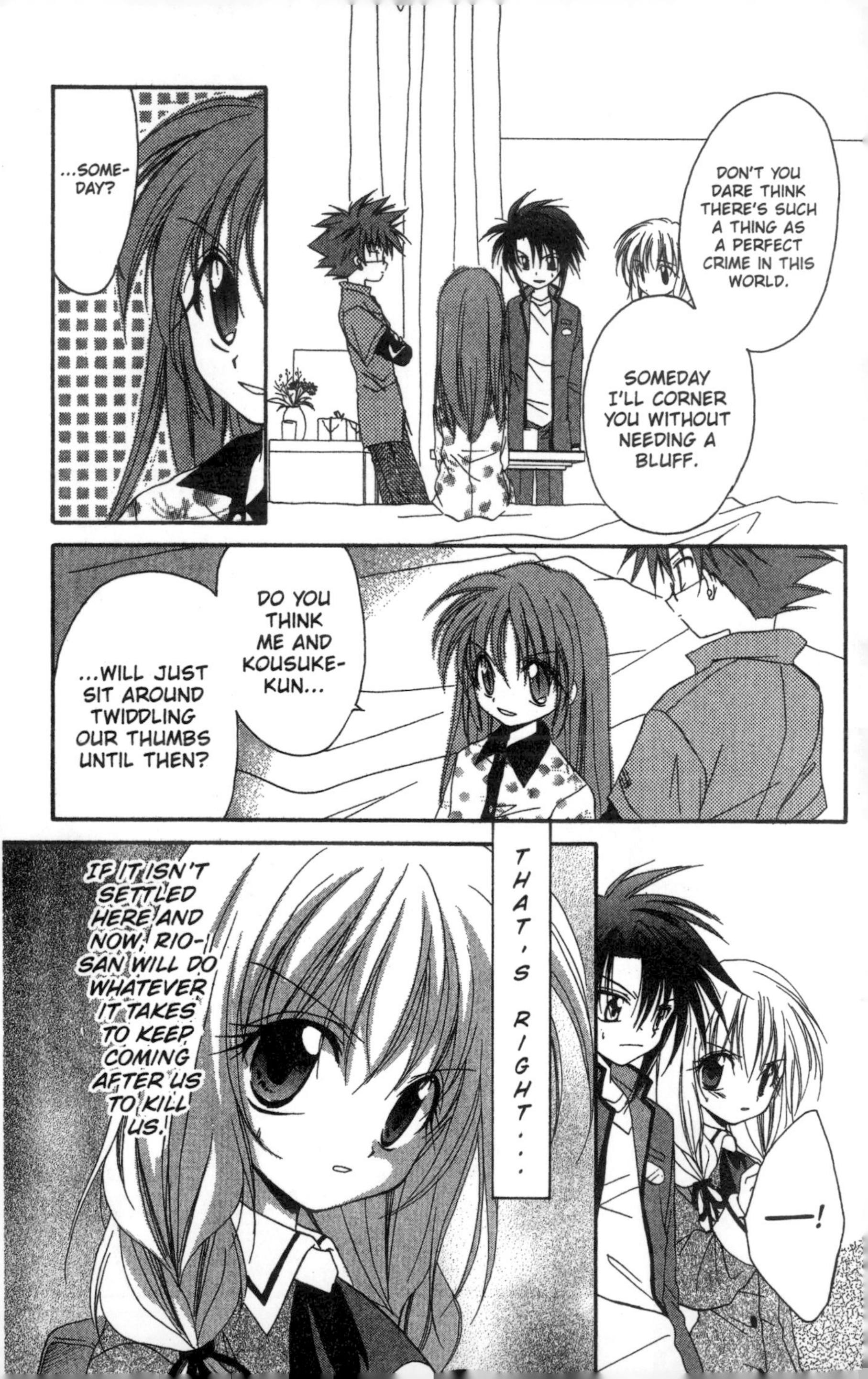
DON'T YOU DARE THINK THERE'S SUCH A THING AS A PERFECT CRIME IN THIS WORLD.
SOMEDAY I'LL CORNER YOU WITHOUT NEEDING A BLUFF.
...SOME-DAY?
DO YOU THINK ME AND KOUSUKE-KUN...
...WILL JUST SIT AROUND TWIDDLING OUR THUMBS UNTIL THEN?
THAT'S RIGHT...
—!
IF IT ISN'T SETTLED HERE AND NOW, RIO-SAN WILL DO WHATEVER IT TAKES TO KEEP COMING AFTER US TO KILL US!

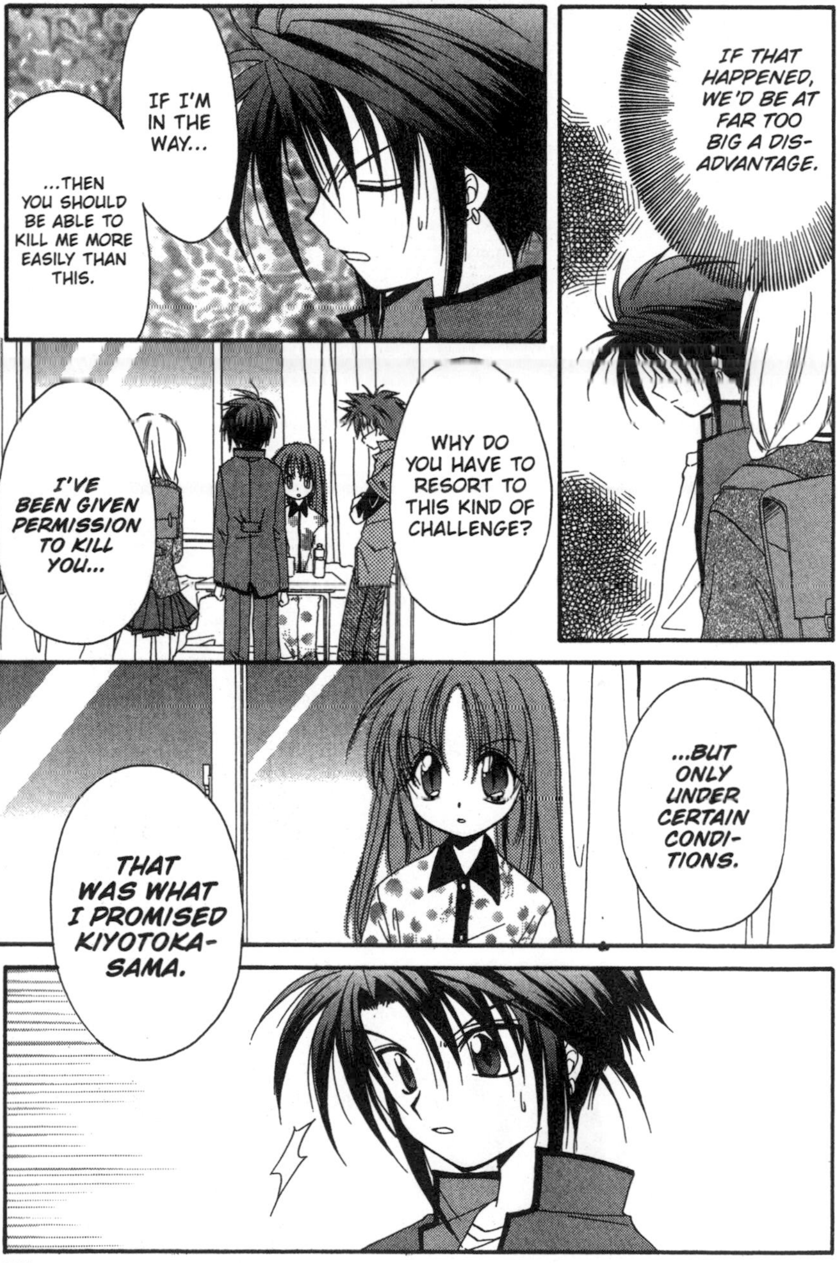
IF THAT HAPPENED, WE'D BE AT FAR TOO BIG A DIS-ADVANTAGE.
IF I'M IN THE WAY...
...THEN YOU SHOULD BE ABLE TO KILL ME MORE EASILY THAN THIS.
WHY DO YOU HAVE TO RESORT TO THIS KIND OF CHALLENGE?
I'VE BEEN GIVEN PERMISSION TO KILL YOU...
...BUT ONLY UNDER CERTAIN CONDI-TIONS.
THAT WAS WHAT I PROMISED KIYOTOKA-SAMA.

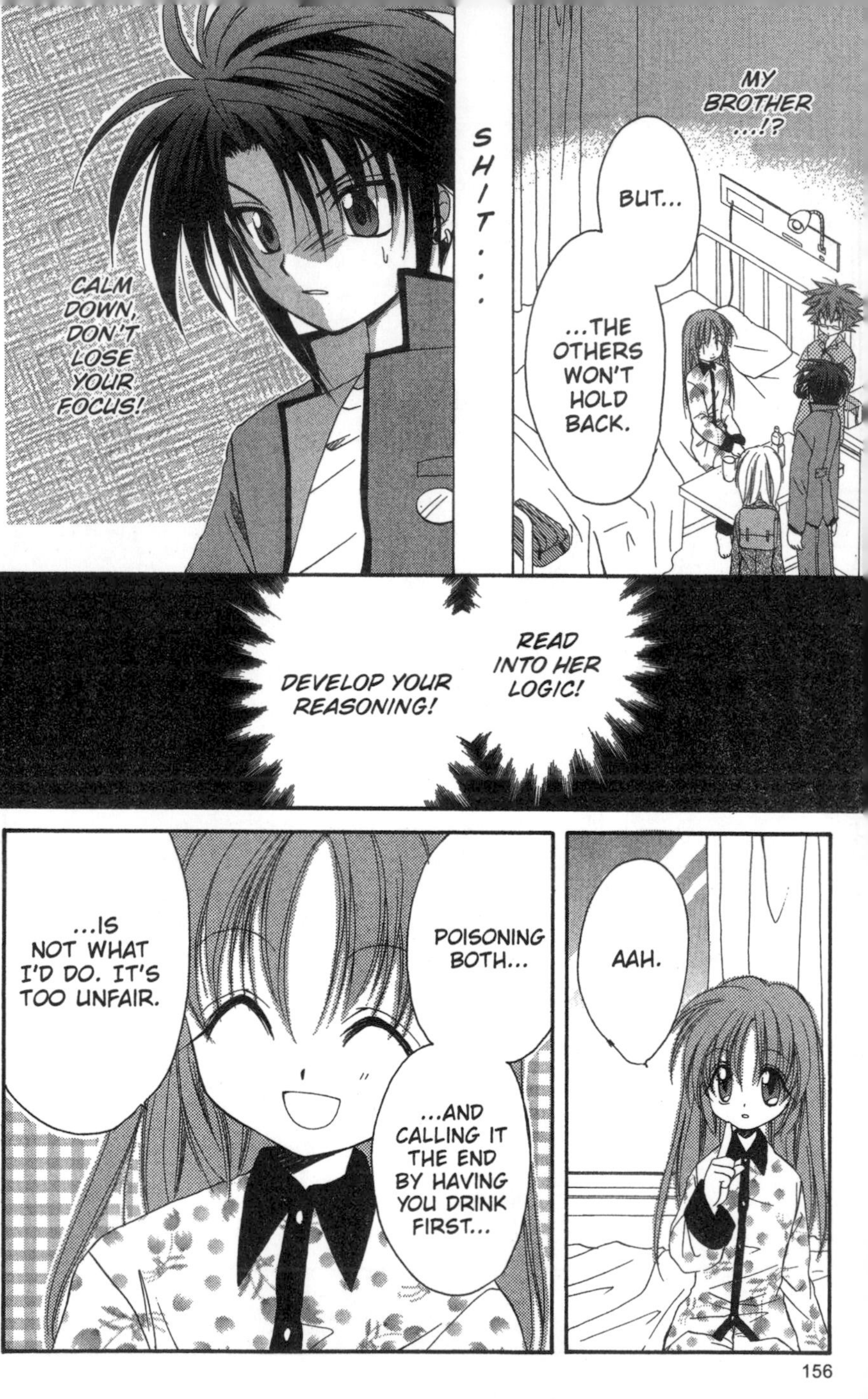
MY BROTHER ...!?
BUT...
...THE OTHERS WON'T HOLD BACK.
SHIT...
CALM DOWN, DON'T LOSE YOUR FOCUS!
READ INTO HER LOGIC!
DEVELOP YOUR REASONING!
AAH.
POISONING BOTH...
...AND CALLING IT THE END BY HAVING YOU DRINK FIRST...
...IS NOT WHAT I'D DO. IT'S TOO UNFAIR.

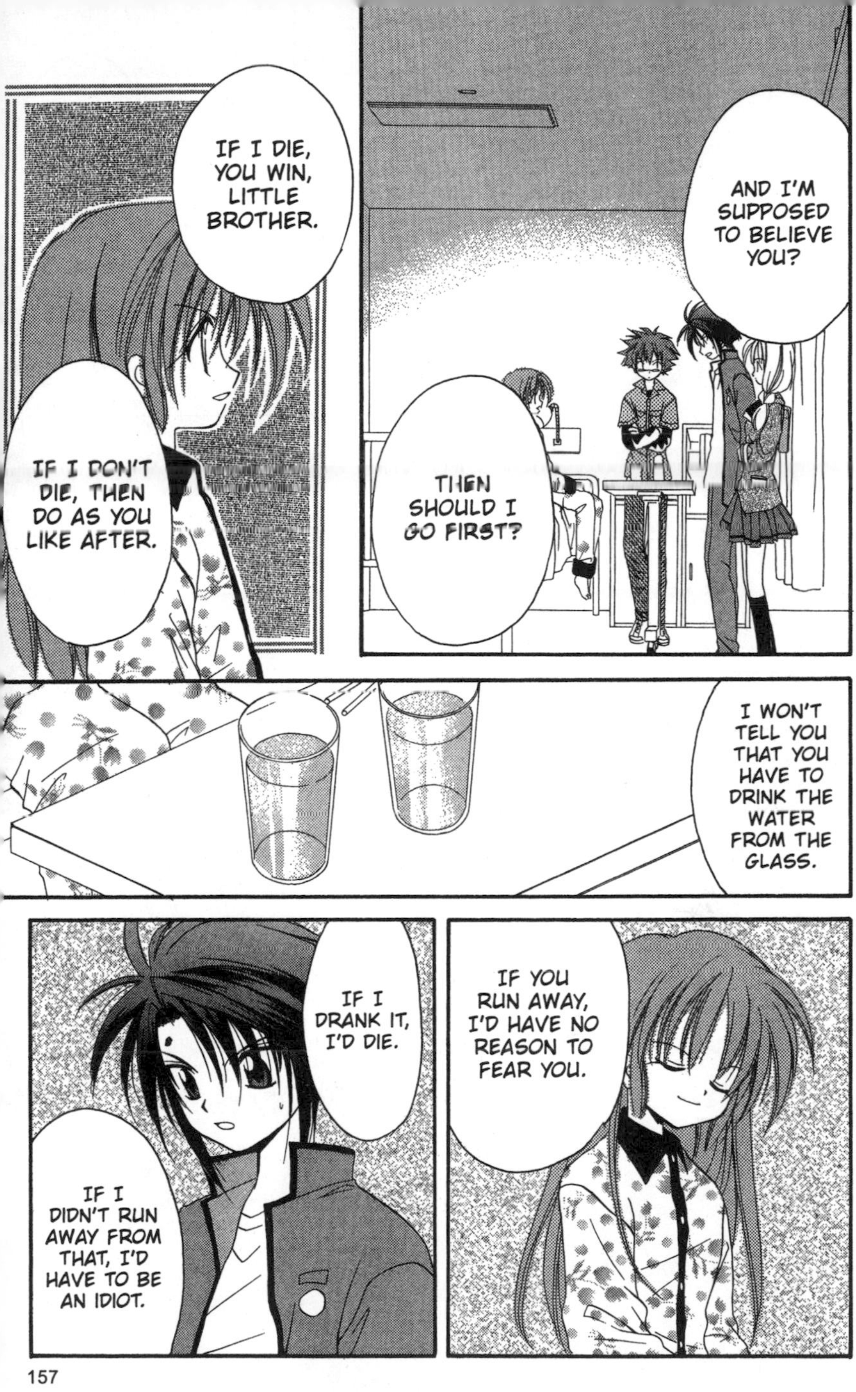
AND I'M SUPPOSED TO BELIEVE YOU?
THEN SHOULD I GO FIRST?
IF I DIE, YOU WIN, LITTLE BROTHER.
IF I DON'T DIE, THEN DO AS YOU LIKE AFTER.
I WON'T TELL YOU THAT YOU HAVE TO DRINK THE WATER FROM THE GLASS.
IF YOU RUN AWAY, I'D HAVE NO REASON TO FEAR YOU.
IF I DRANK IT, I'D DIE.
IF I DIDN'T RUN AWAY FROM THAT, I'D HAVE TO BE AN IDIOT.

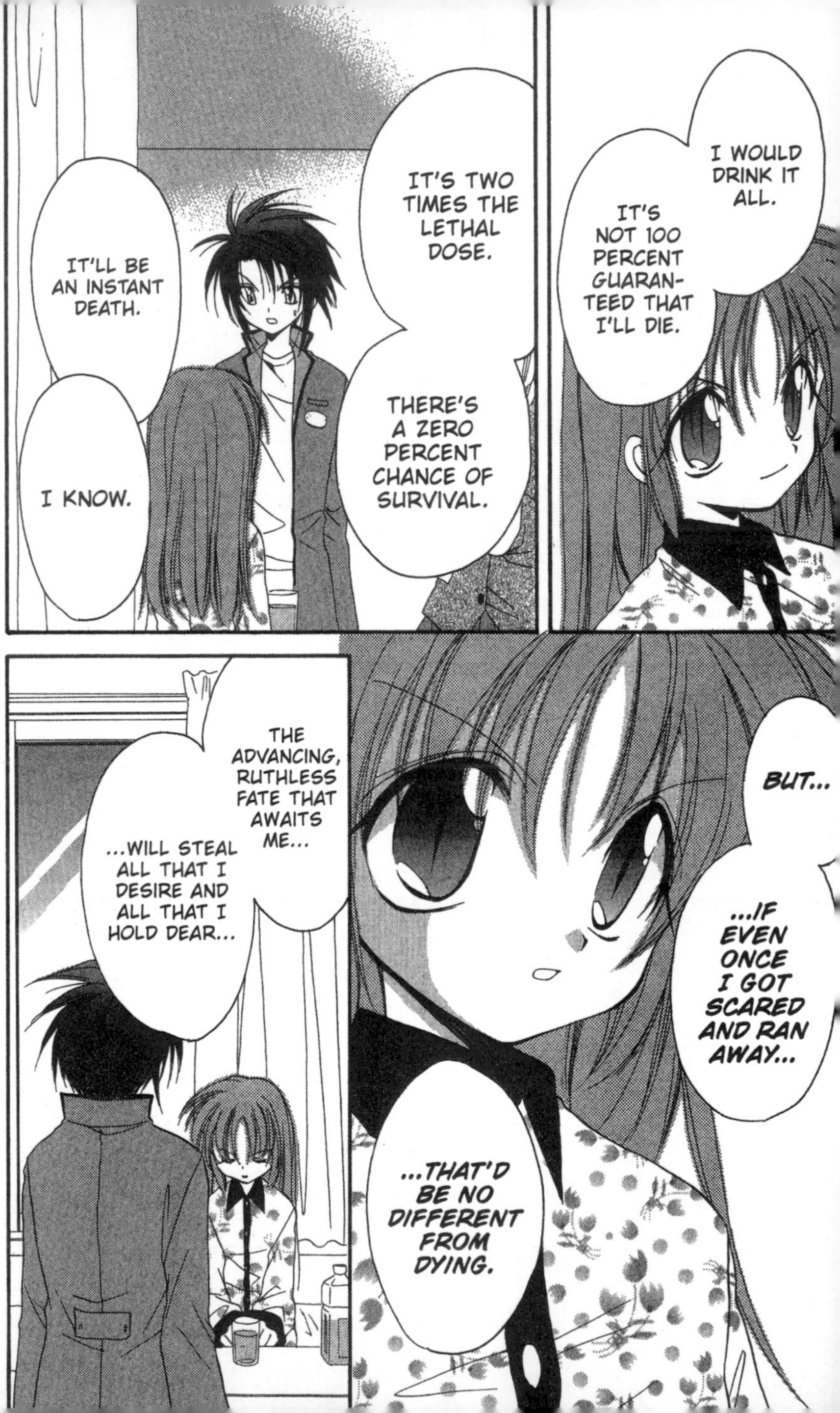
I WOULD DRINK IT ALL.
IT'S NOT 100 PERCENT GUARANTEED THAT I'LL DIE.
IT'S TWO TIMES THE LETHAL DOSE.
THERE'S A ZERO PERCENT CHANCE OF SURVIVAL.
IT'LL BE AN INSTANT DEATH.
I KNOW.
BUT...
...IF EVEN ONCE I GOT SCARED AND RAN AWAY...
...THAT'D BE NO DIFFERENT FROM DYING.
THE ADVANCING, RUTHLESS FATE THAT AWAITS ME...
...WILL STEAL ALL THAT I DESIRE AND ALL THAT I HOLD DEAR...

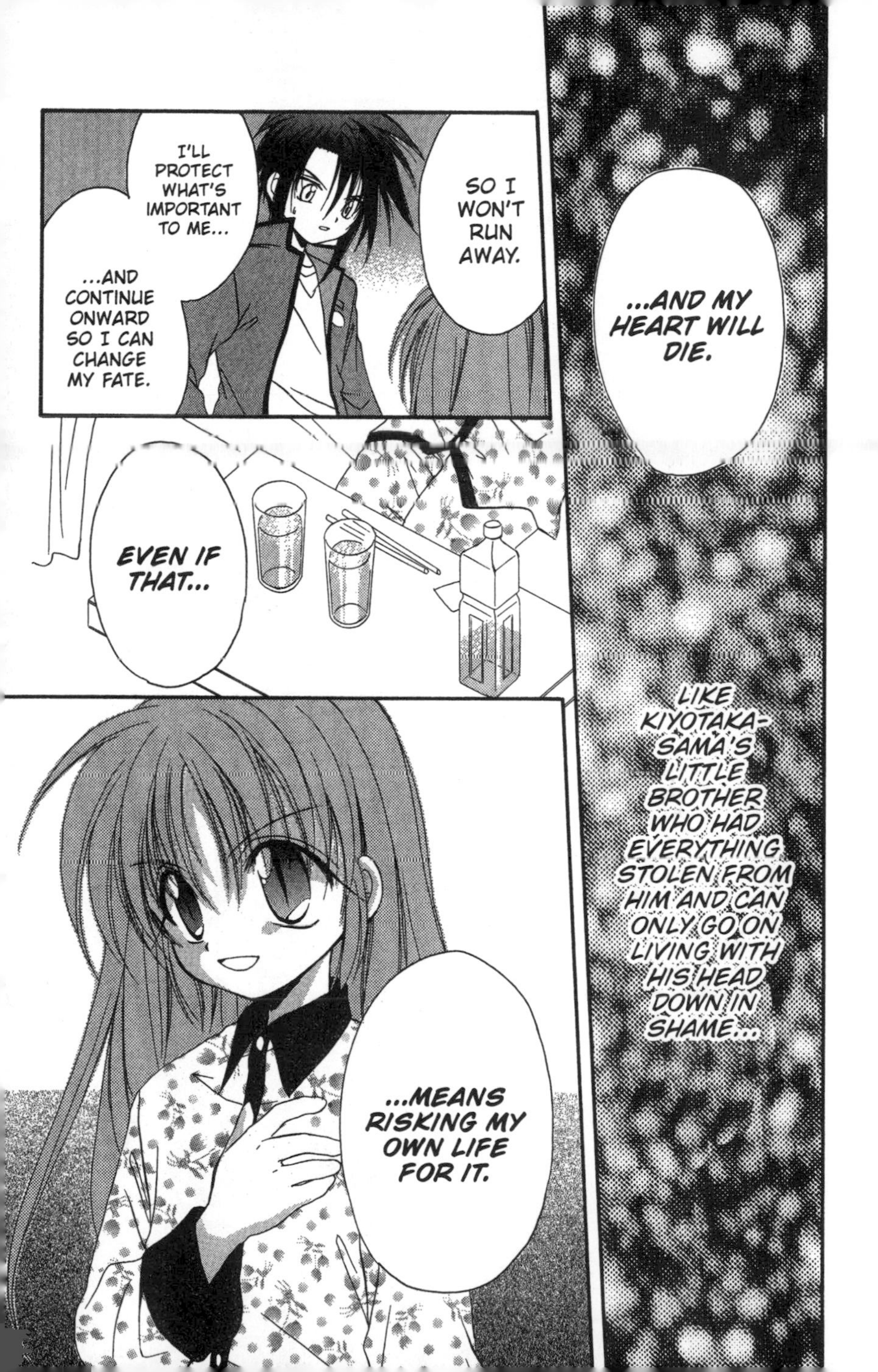
...AND MY HEART WILL DIE.
LIKE KIYOTAKA-SAMA'S LITTLE BROTHER WHO HAD EVERYTHING STOLEN FROM HIM AND CAN ONLY GO ON LIVING WITH HIS HEAD DOWN IN SHAME...
SO I WON'T RUN AWAY.
I'LL PROTECT WHAT'S IMPORTANT TO ME...
...AND CONTINUE ONWARD SO I CAN CHANGE MY FATE.
EVEN IF THAT...
...MEANS RISKING MY OWN LIFE FOR IT.

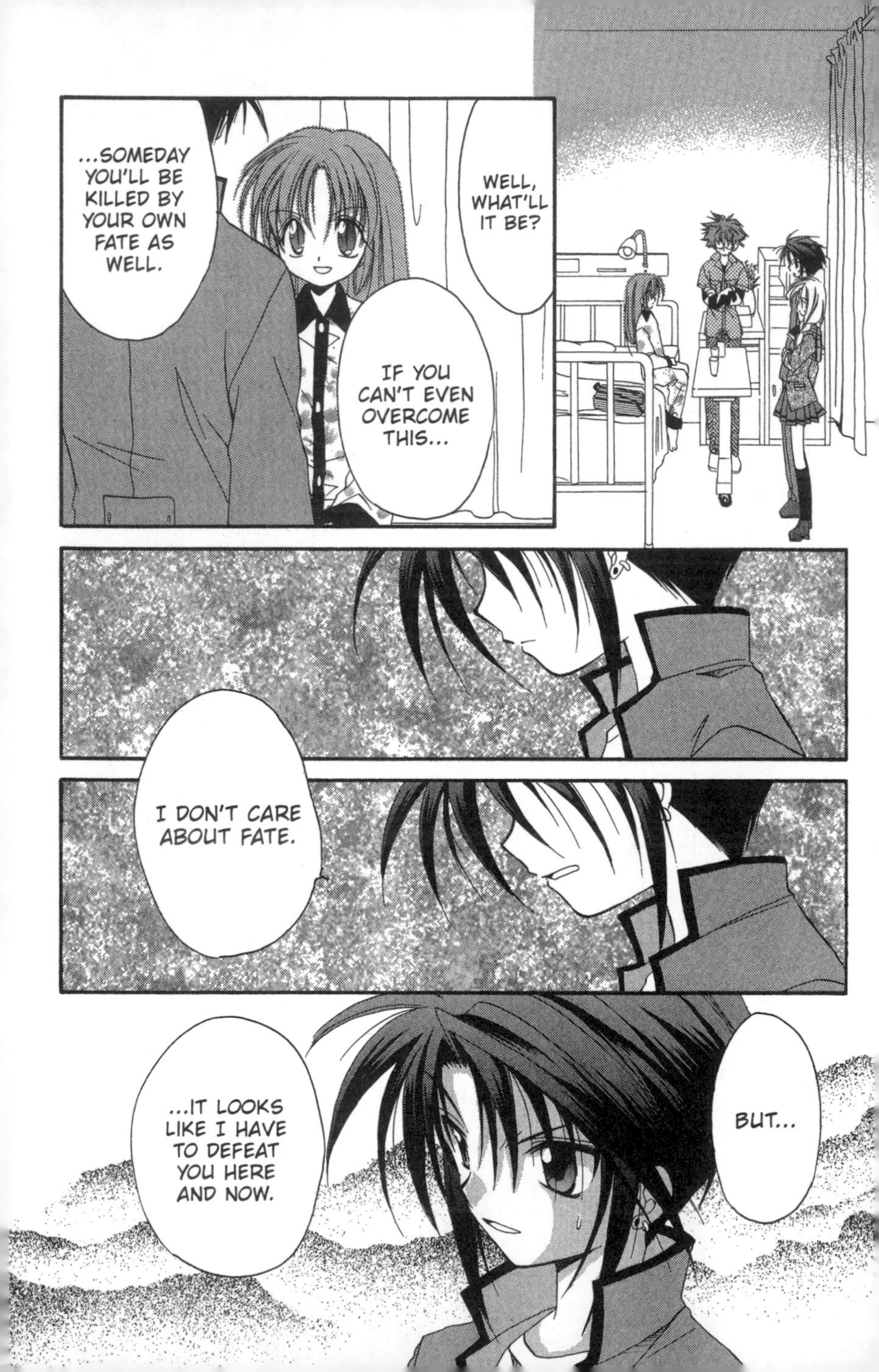
WELL, WHAT'LL IT BE?
IF YOU CAN'T EVEN OVERCOME THIS...
...SOMEDAY YOU'LL BE KILLED BY YOUR OWN FATE AS WELL.
I DON'T CARE ABOUT FATE.
BUT...
...IT LOOKS LIKE I HAVE TO DEFEAT YOU HERE AND NOW.

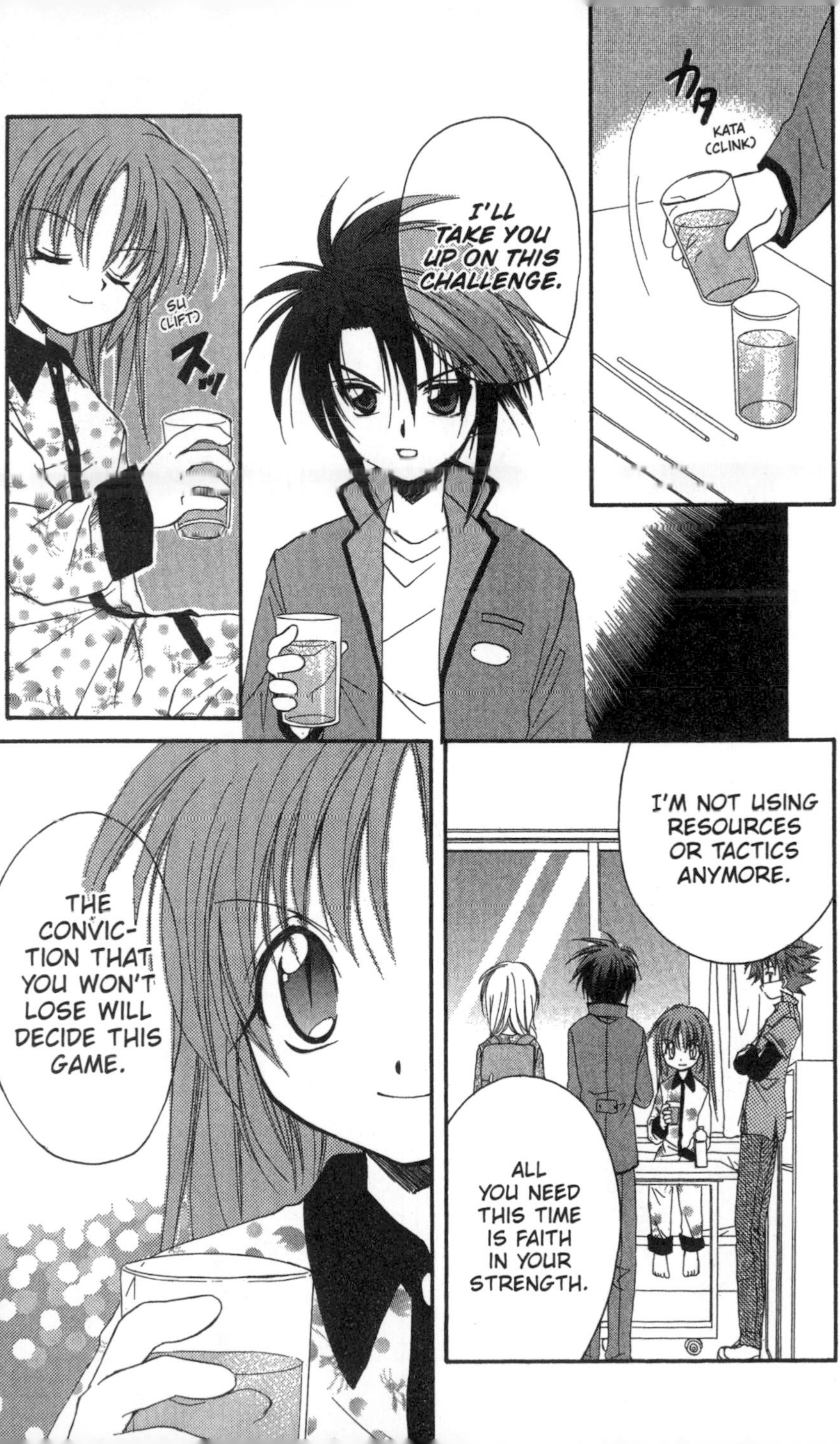
カタ
KATA (CLINK)
I'LL TAKE YOU UP ON THIS CHALLENGE.
SU (LIFT)
スッ
I'M NOT USING RESOURCES OR TACTICS ANYMORE.
ALL YOU NEED THIS TIME IS FAITH IN YOUR STRENGTH.
THE CONVICTION THAT YOU WON'T LOSE WILL DECIDE THIS GAME.

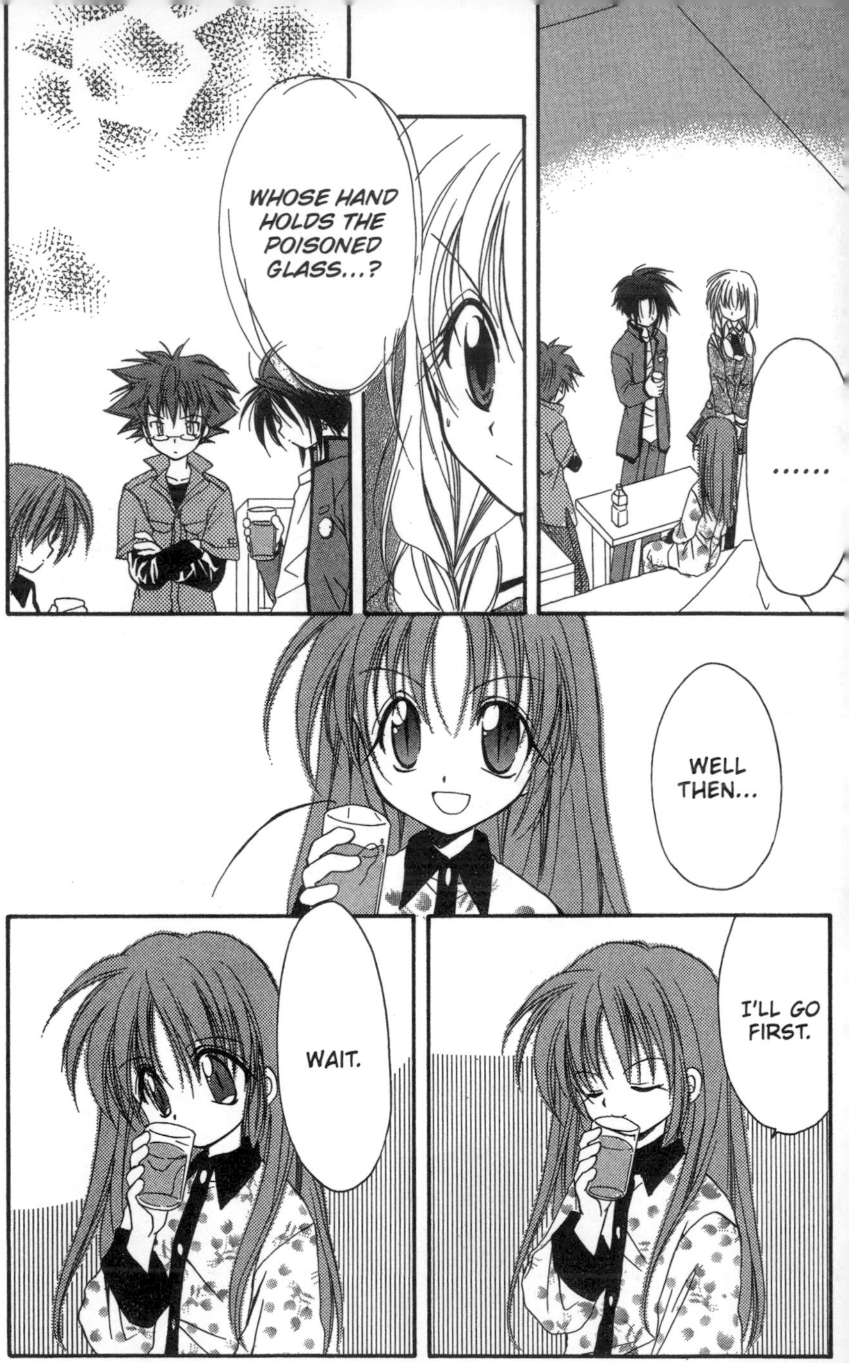
......
WHOSE HAND HOLDS THE POISONED GLASS...?
WELL THEN...
I'LL GO FIRST.
WAIT.

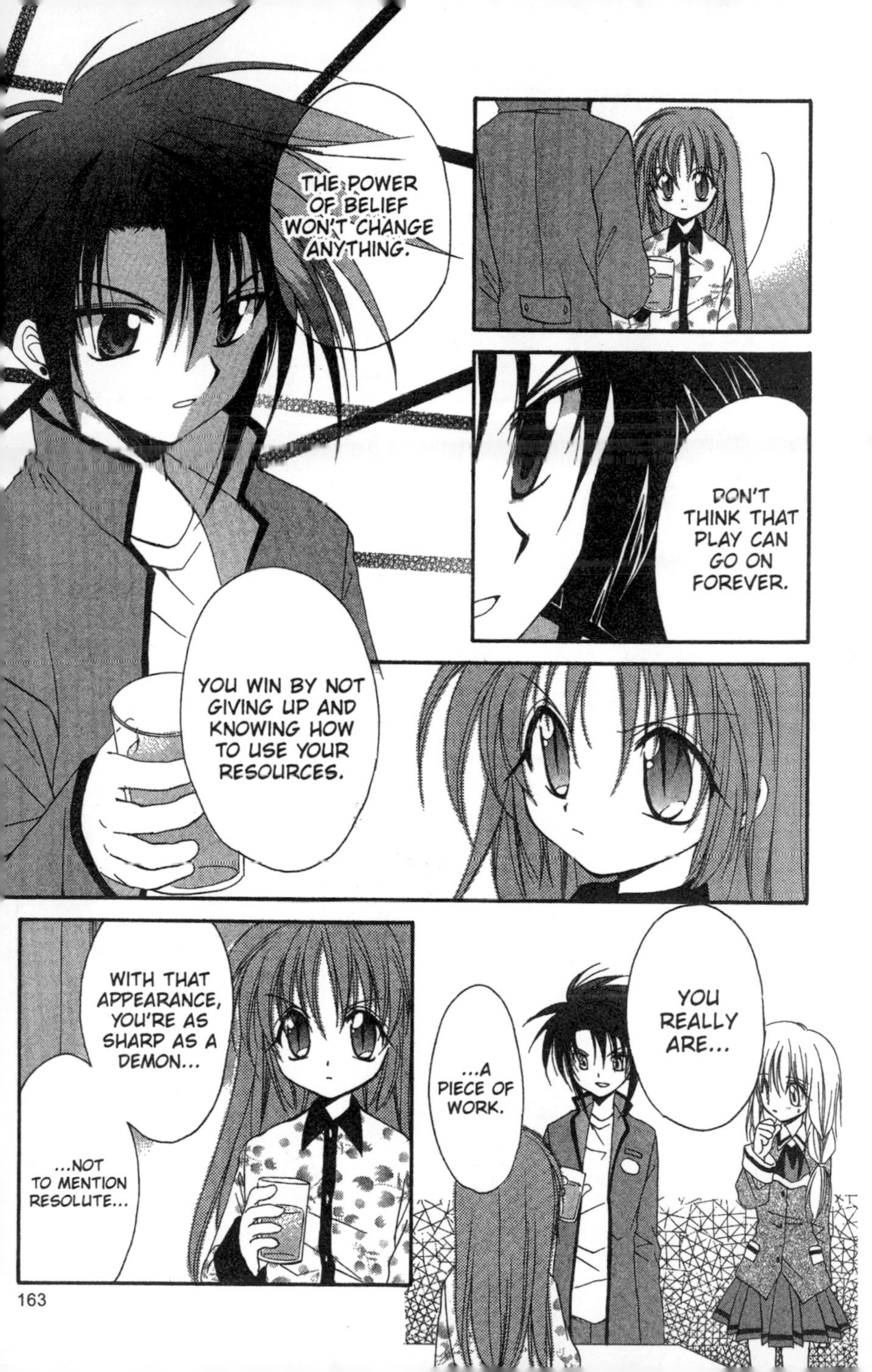
DON'T THINK THAT PLAY CAN GO ON FOREVER.
THE POWER OF BELIEF WON'T CHANGE ANYTHING.
YOU WIN BY NOT GIVING UP AND KNOWING HOW TO USE YOUR RESOURCES.
YOU REALLY ARE...
...A PIECE OF WORK.
WITH THAT APPEARANCE, YOU'RE AS SHARP AS A DEMON...
...NOT TO MENTION RESOLUTE...

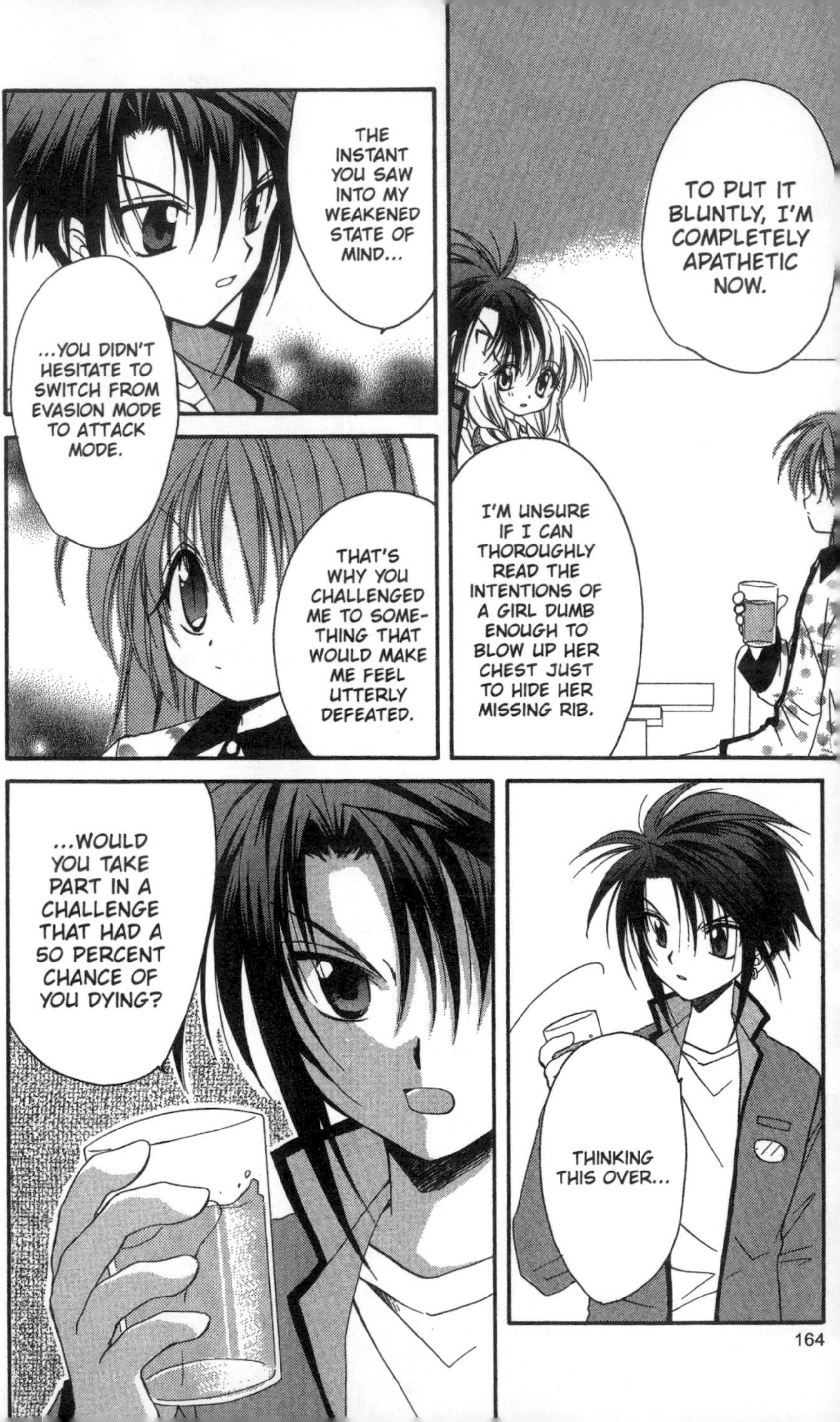
TO PUT IT BLUNTLY, I'M COMPLETELY APATHETIC NOW.
I'M UNSURE IF I CAN THOROUGHLY READ THE INTENTIONS OF A GIRL DUMB ENOUGH TO BLOW UP HER CHEST JUST TO HIDE HER MISSING RIB.
THE INSTANT YOU SAW INTO MY WEAKENED STATE OF MIND...
...YOU DIDN'T HESITATE TO SWITCH FROM EVASION MODE TO ATTACK MODE.
THAT'S WHY YOU CHALLENGED ME TO SOME-THING THAT WOULD MAKE ME FEEL UTTERLY DEFEATED.
THINKING THIS OVER...
...WOULD YOU TAKE PART IN A CHALLENGE THAT HAD A 50 PERCENT CHANCE OF YOU DYING?

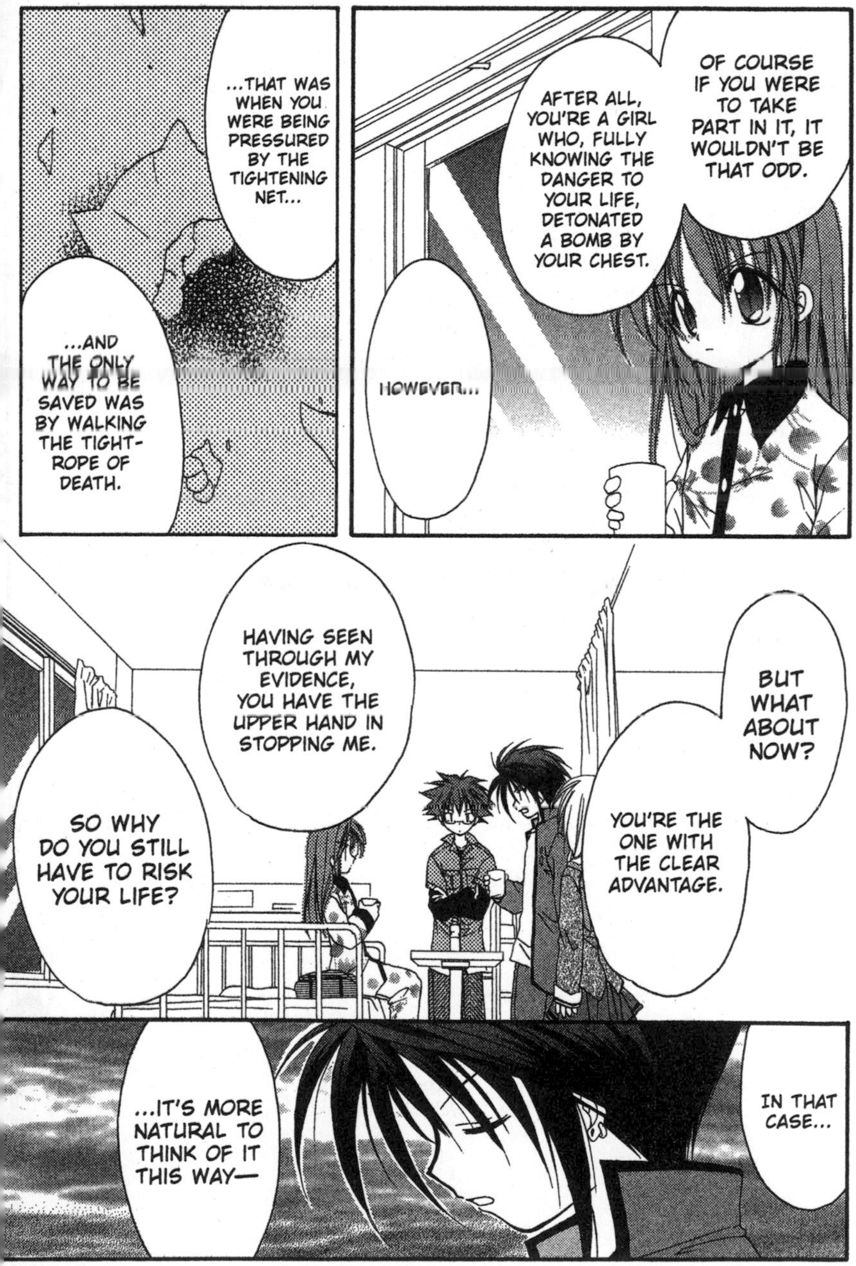
OF COURSE IF YOU WERE TO TAKE PART IN IT, IT WOULDN'T BE THAT ODD.
AFTER ALL, YOU'RE A GIRL WHO, FULLY KNOWING THE DANGER TO YOUR LIFE, DETONATED A BOMB BY YOUR CHEST.
HOWEVER...
...THAT WAS WHEN YOU WERE BEING PRESSURED BY THE TIGHTENING NET...
...AND THE ONLY WAY TO BE SAVED WAS BY WALKING THE TIGHT-ROPE OF DEATH.
BUT WHAT ABOUT NOW?
YOU'RE THE ONE WITH THE CLEAR ADVANTAGE.
HAVING SEEN THROUGH MY EVIDENCE, YOU HAVE THE UPPER HAND IN STOPPING ME.
SO WHY DO YOU STILL HAVE TO RISK YOUR LIFE?
IN THAT CASE...
...IT'S MORE NATURAL TO THINK OF IT THIS WAY—

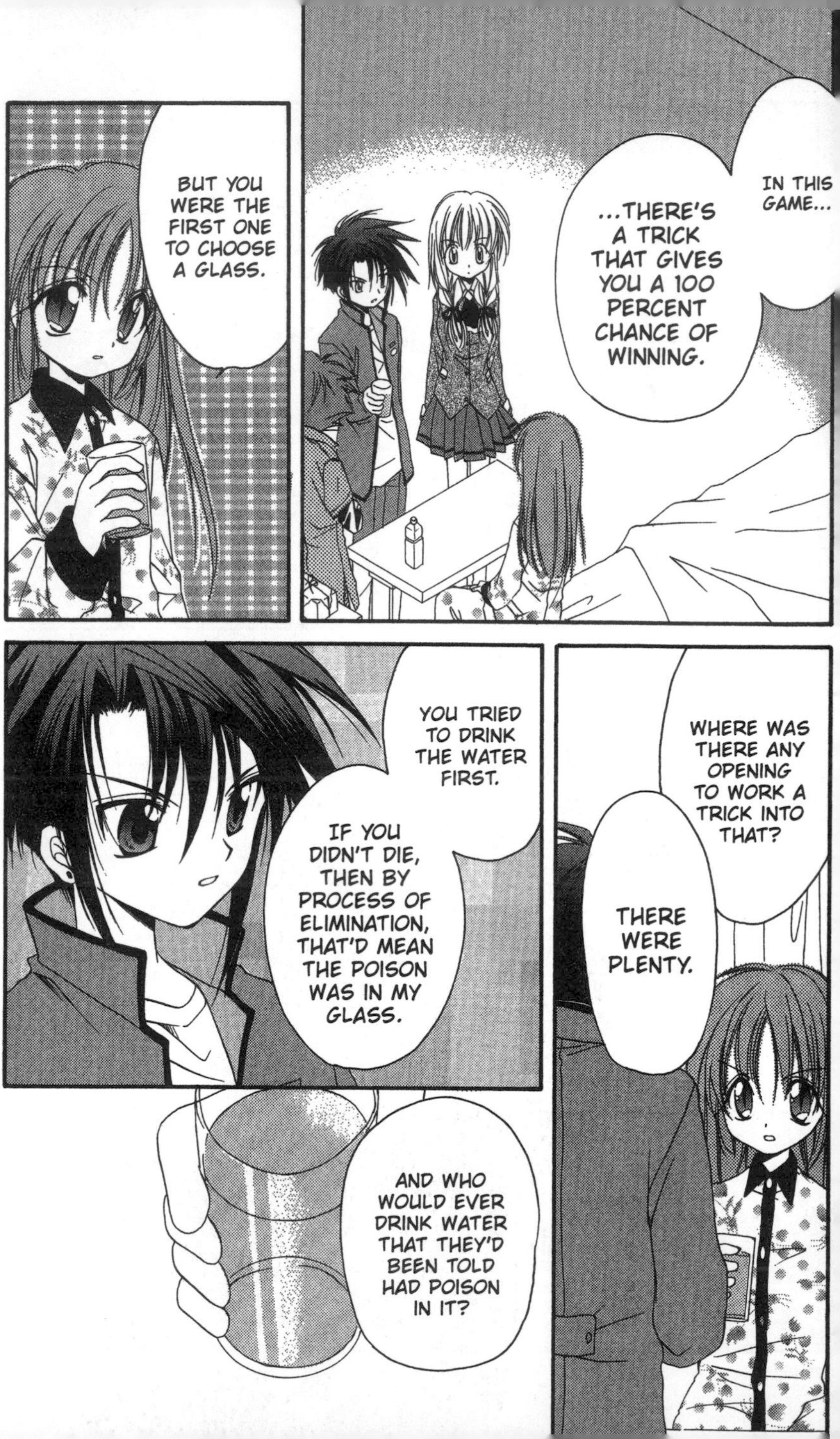
IN THIS GAME...
...THERE'S A TRICK THAT GIVES YOU A 100 PERCENT CHANCE OF WINNING.
BUT YOU WERE THE FIRST ONE TO CHOOSE A GLASS.
WHERE WAS THERE ANY OPENING TO WORK A TRICK INTO THAT?
THERE WERE PLENTY.
YOU TRIED TO DRINK THE WATER FIRST.
IF YOU DIDN'T DIE, THEN BY PROCESS OF ELIMINATION, THAT'D MEAN THE POISON WAS IN MY GLASS.
AND WHO WOULD EVER DRINK WATER THAT THEY'D BEEN TOLD HAD POISON IN IT?

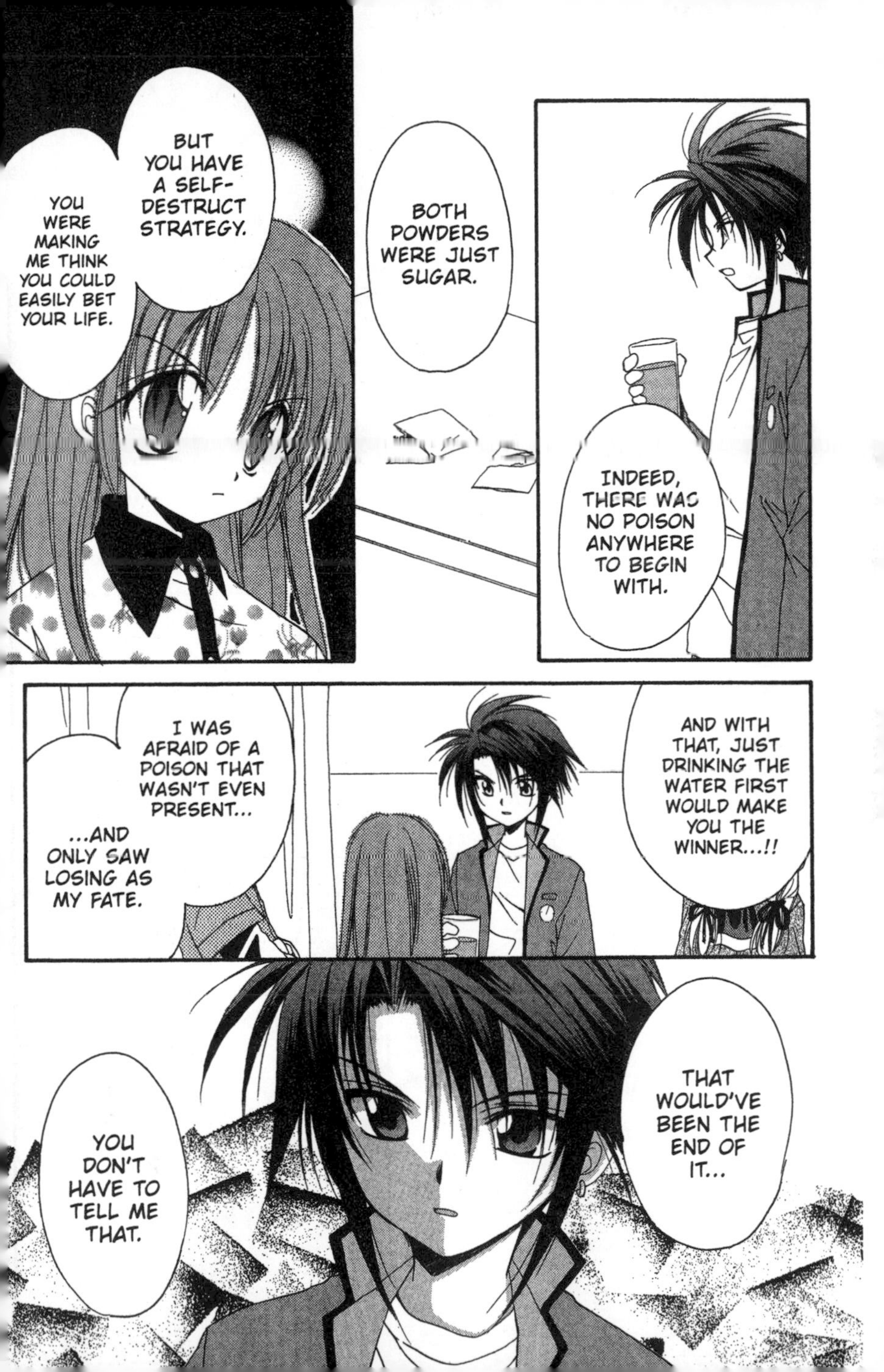
INDEED, THERE WAS NO POISON ANYWHERE TO BEGIN WITH.
BOTH POWDERS WERE JUST SUGAR.
BUT YOU HAVE A SELF-DESTRUCT STRATEGY.
YOU WERE MAKING ME THINK YOU COULD EASILY BET YOUR LIFE.
AND WITH THAT, JUST DRINKING THE WATER FIRST WOULD MAKE YOU THE WINNER...!!
I WAS AFRAID OF A POISON THAT WASN'T EVEN PRESENT...
...AND ONLY SAW LOSING AS MY FATE.
THAT WOULD'VE BEEN THE END OF IT...
YOU DON'T HAVE TO TELL ME THAT.

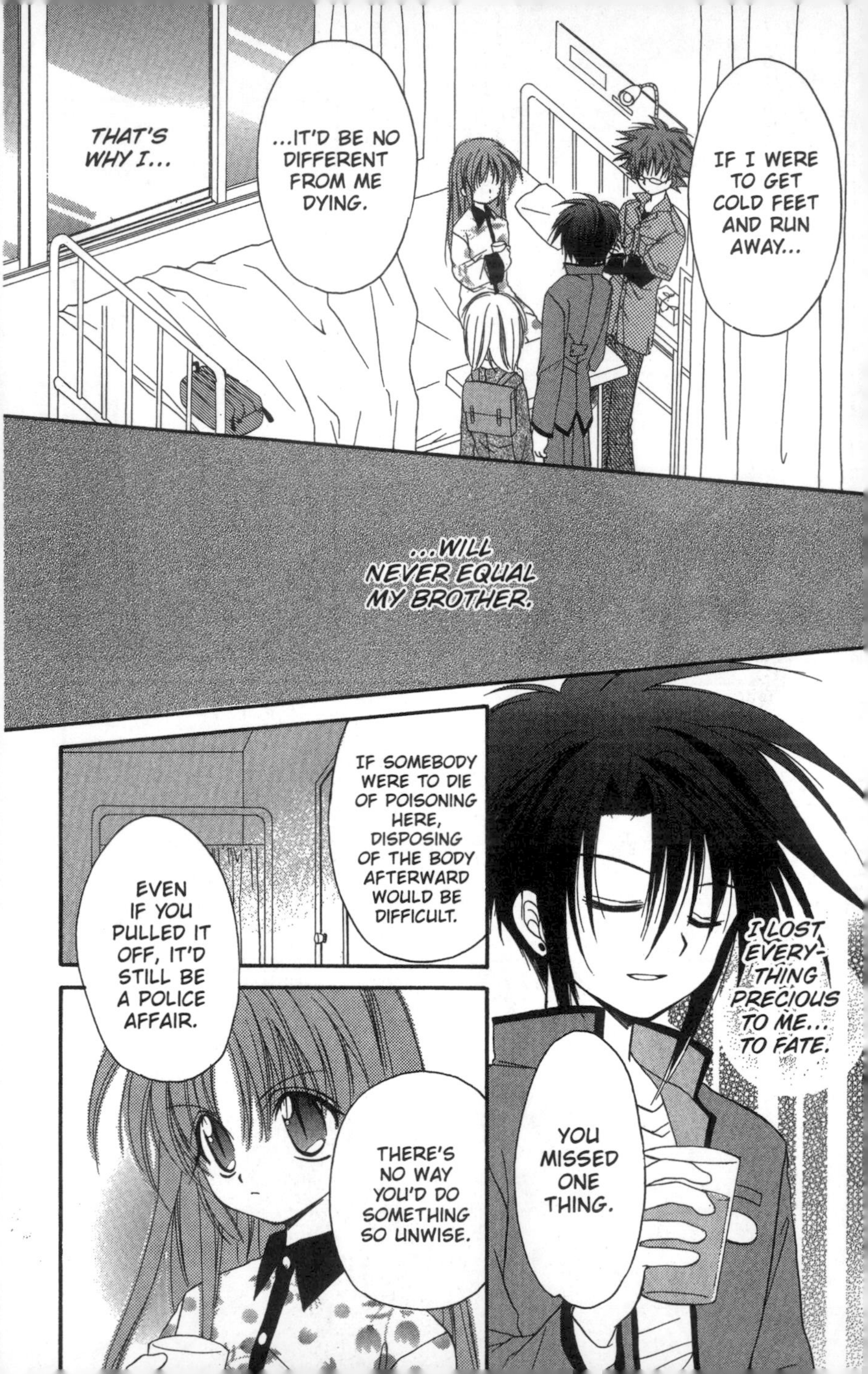
IF I WERE TO GET COLD FEET AND RUN AWAY...
...IT'D BE NO DIFFERENT FROM ME DYING.
THAT'S WHY I...
...WILL NEVER EQUAL MY BROTHER.
IF SOMEBODY WERE TO DIE OF POISONING HERE, DISPOSING OF THE BODY AFTERWARD WOULD BE DIFFICULT.
EVEN IF YOU PULLED IT OFF, IT'D STILL BE A POLICE AFFAIR.
THERE'S NO WAY YOU'D DO SOMETHING SO UNWISE.
I LOST EVERY-THING PRECIOUS TO ME... TO FATE.
YOU MISSED ONE THING.

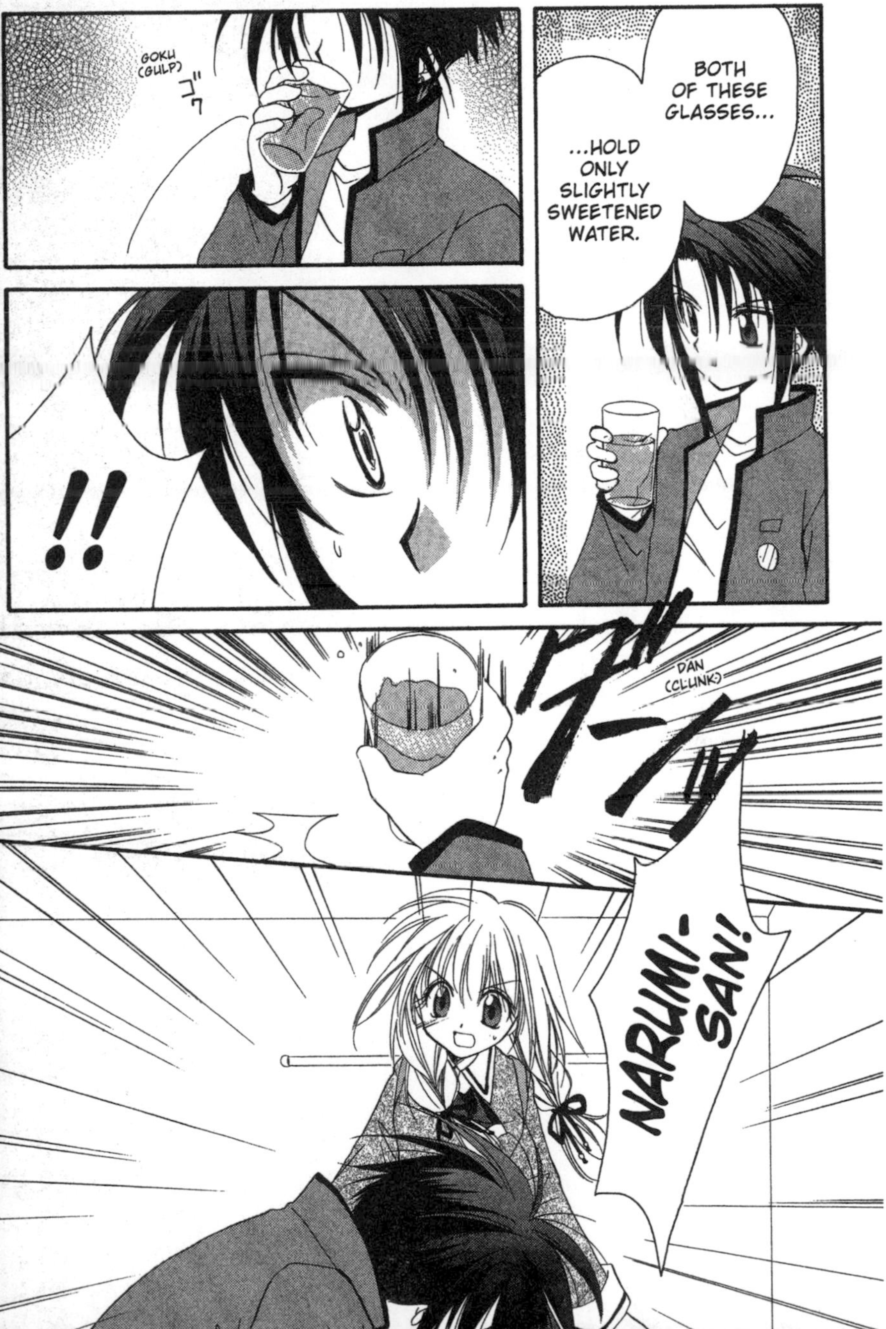
BOTH OF THESE GLASSES...
...HOLD ONLY SLIGHTLY SWEETENED WATER.
GOKU (GULP)
!!
DAN (CLUNK)
NARUMI-SAN!

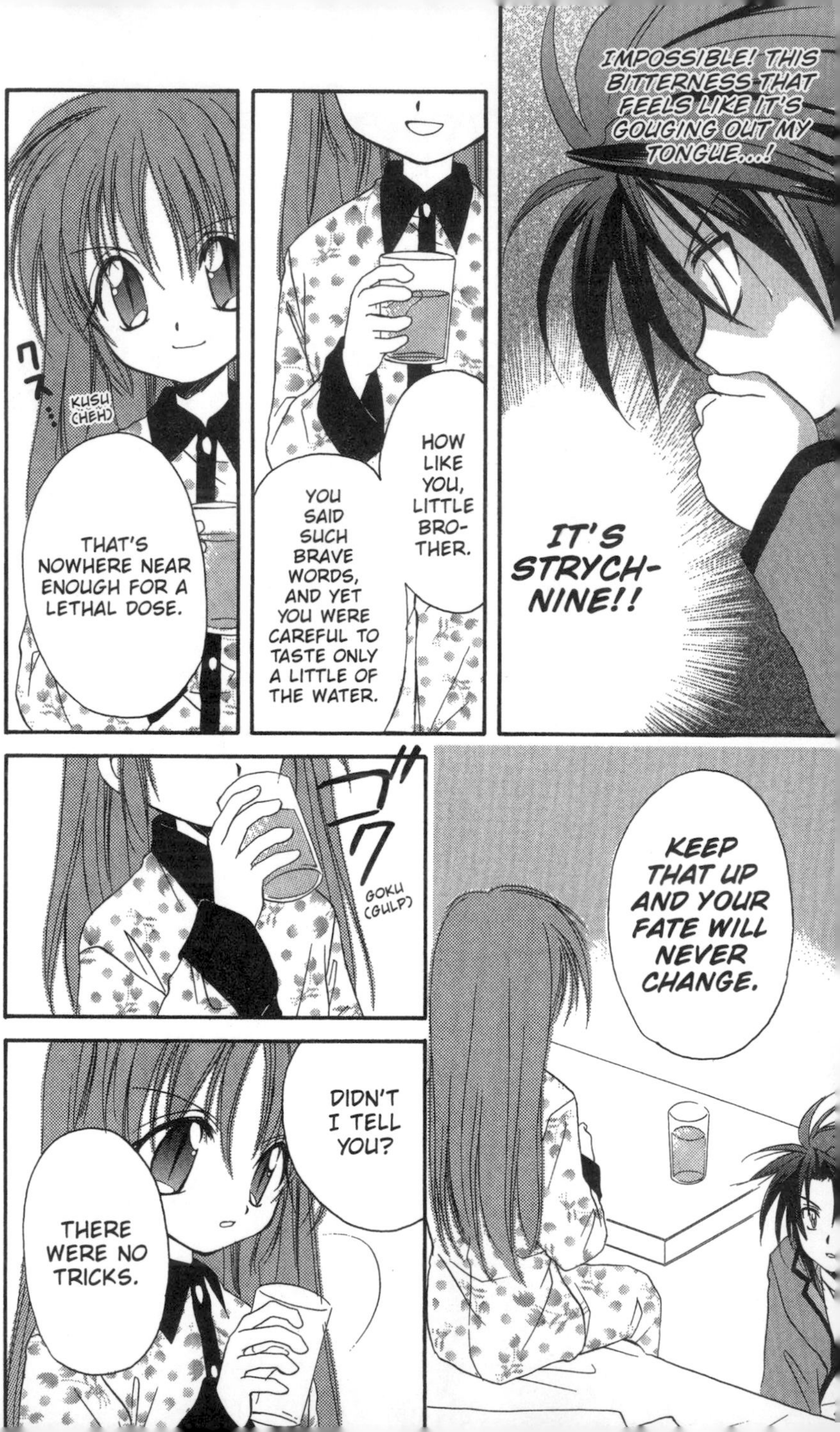

IMPOSSIBLE! THIS BITTERNESS THAT FEELS LIKE IT'S GOUGING OUT MY TONGUE...!
IT'S STRYCH-NINE!!
HOW LIKE YOU, LITTLE BRO-THER.
YOU SAID SUCH BRAVE WORDS, AND YET YOU WERE CAREFUL TO TASTE ONLY A LITTLE OF THE WATER.
クス…
KUSU (HEH)
THAT'S NOWHERE NEAR ENOUGH FOR A LETHAL DOSE.
KEEP THAT UP AND YOUR FATE WILL NEVER CHANGE.
ゴク
GOKU (GULP)
DIDN'T I TELL YOU?
THERE WERE NO TRICKS.

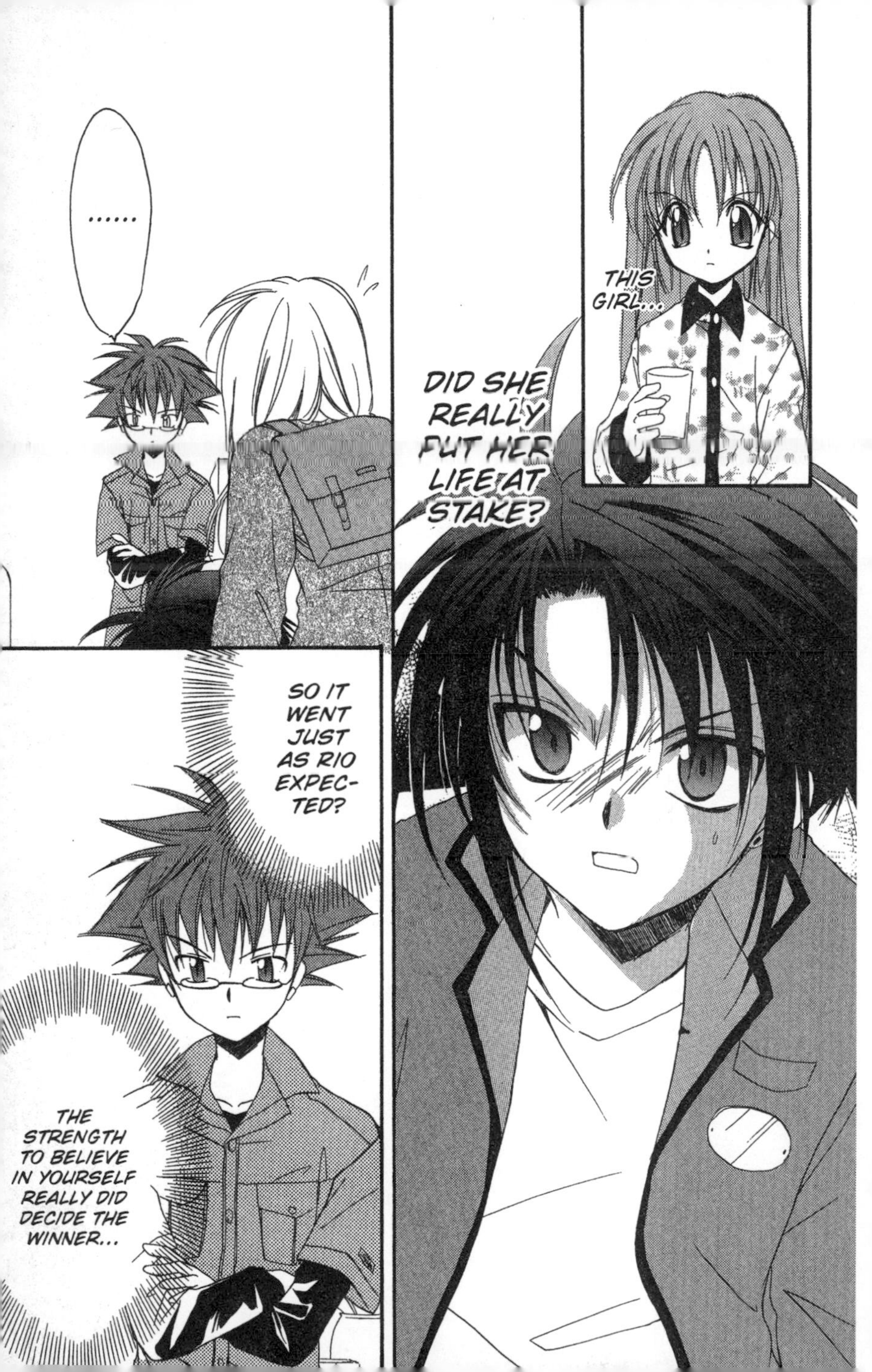
THIS GIRL...
DID SHE REALLY PUT HER LIFE AT STAKE?
......
SO IT WENT JUST AS RIO EXPEC-TED?
THE STRENGTH TO BELIEVE IN YOURSELF REALLY DID DECIDE THE WINNER...

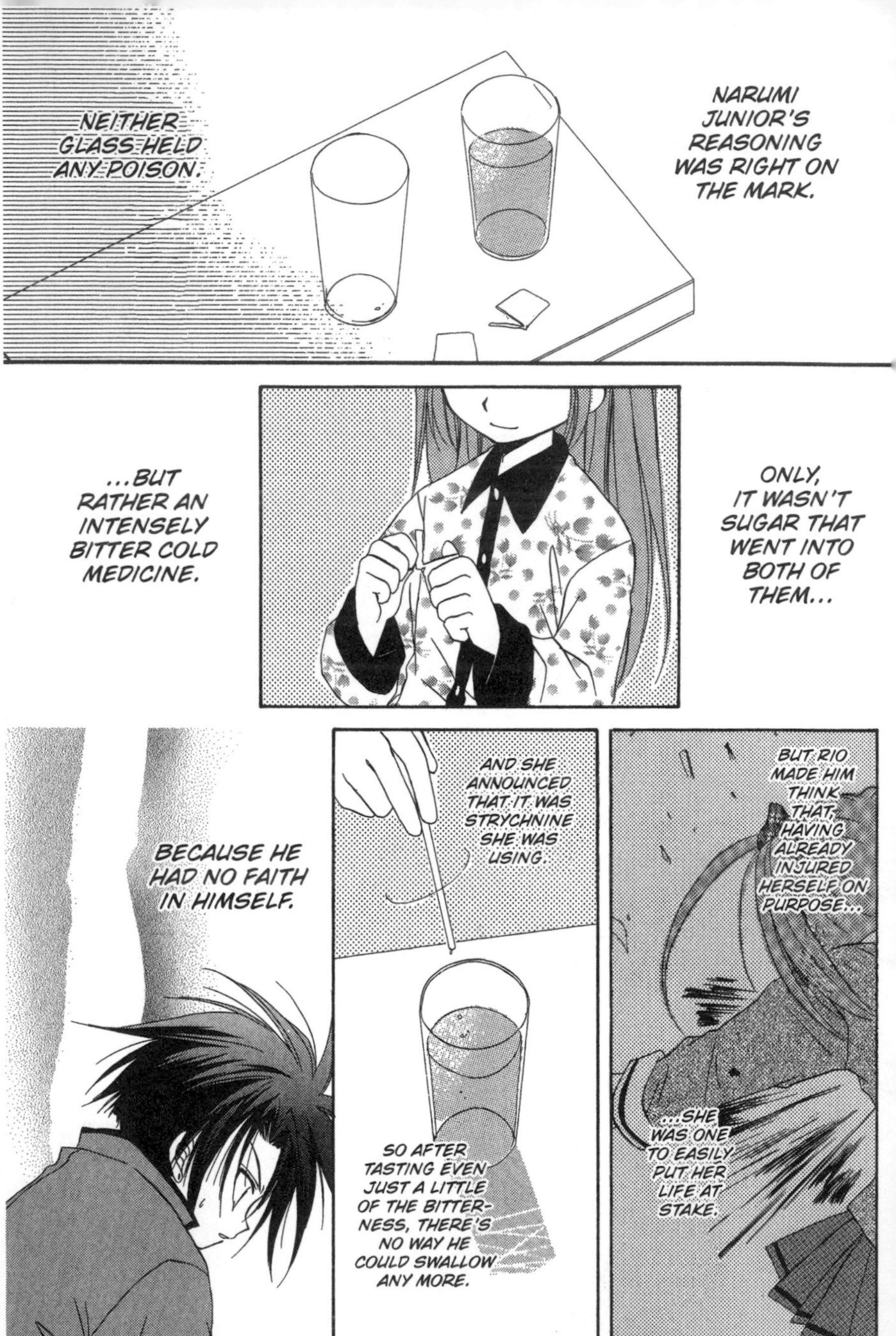
NARUMI JUNIOR'S REASONING WAS RIGHT ON THE MARK.
NEITHER GLASS HELD ANY POISON.
ONLY, IT WASN'T SUGAR THAT WENT INTO BOTH OF THEM...
...BUT RATHER AN INTENSELY BITTER COLD MEDICINE.
BUT RIO MADE HIM THINK THAT, HAVING ALREADY INJURED HERSELF ON PURPOSE...
...SHE WAS ONE TO EASILY PUT HER LIFE AT STAKE.
AND SHE ANNOUNCED THAT IT WAS STRYCHNINE SHE WAS USING.
SO AFTER TASTING EVEN JUST A LITTLE OF THE BITTER-NESS, THERE'S NO WAY HE COULD SWALLOW ANY MORE.
BECAUSE HE HAD NO FAITH IN HIMSELF.

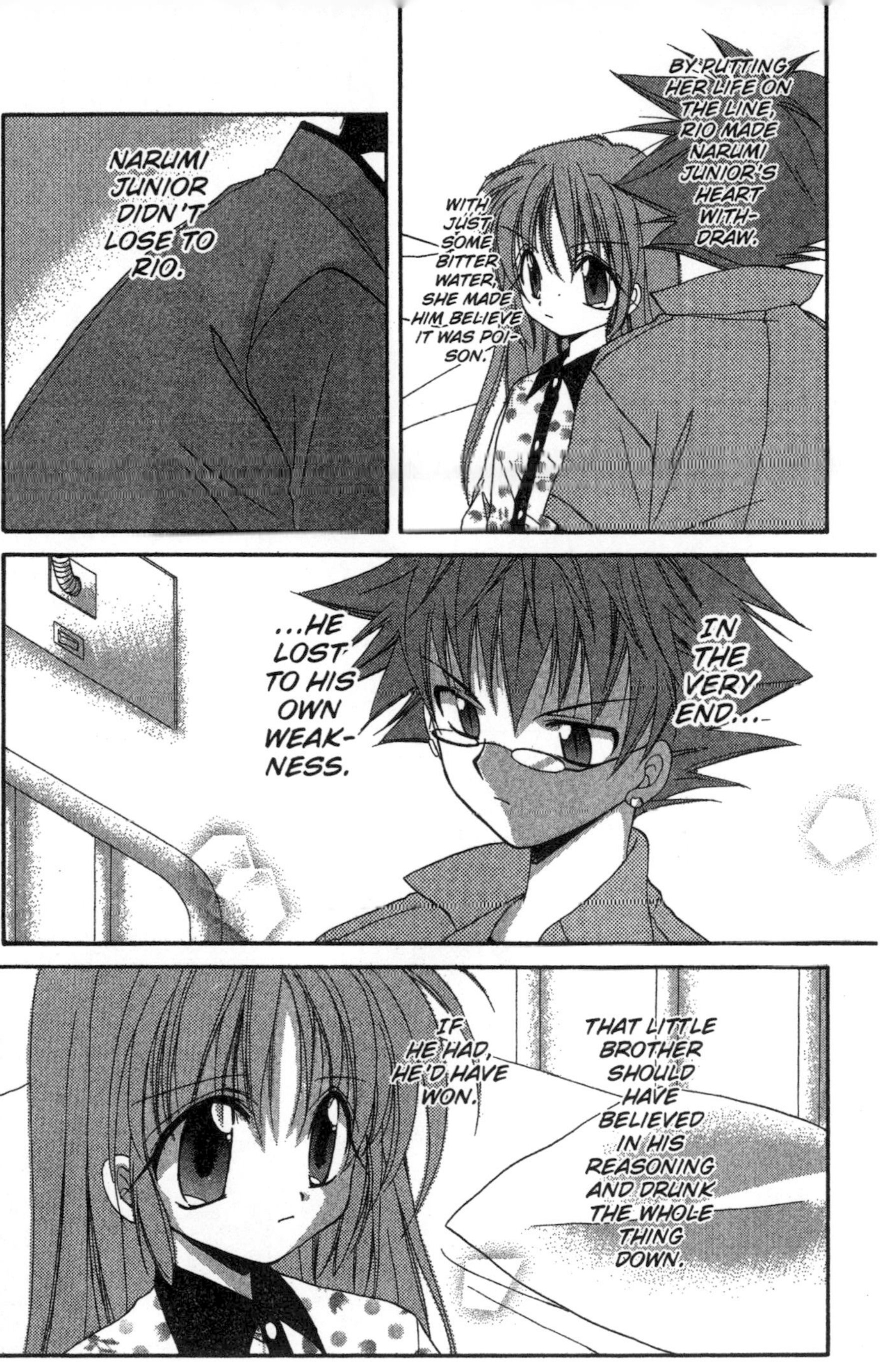
BY PUTTING HER LIFE ON THE LINE, RIO MADE NARUMI JUNIOR'S HEART WITH-DRAW.
WITH JUST SOME BITTER WATER, SHE MADE HIM BELIEVE IT WAS POI-SON.
NARUMI JUNIOR DIDN'T LOSE TO RIO.
IN THE VERY END...
...HE LOST TO HIS OWN WEAK-NESS.
THAT LITTLE BROTHER SHOULD HAVE BELIEVED IN HIS REASONING AND DRUNK THE WHOLE THING DOWN.
IF HE HAD, HE'D HAVE WON.

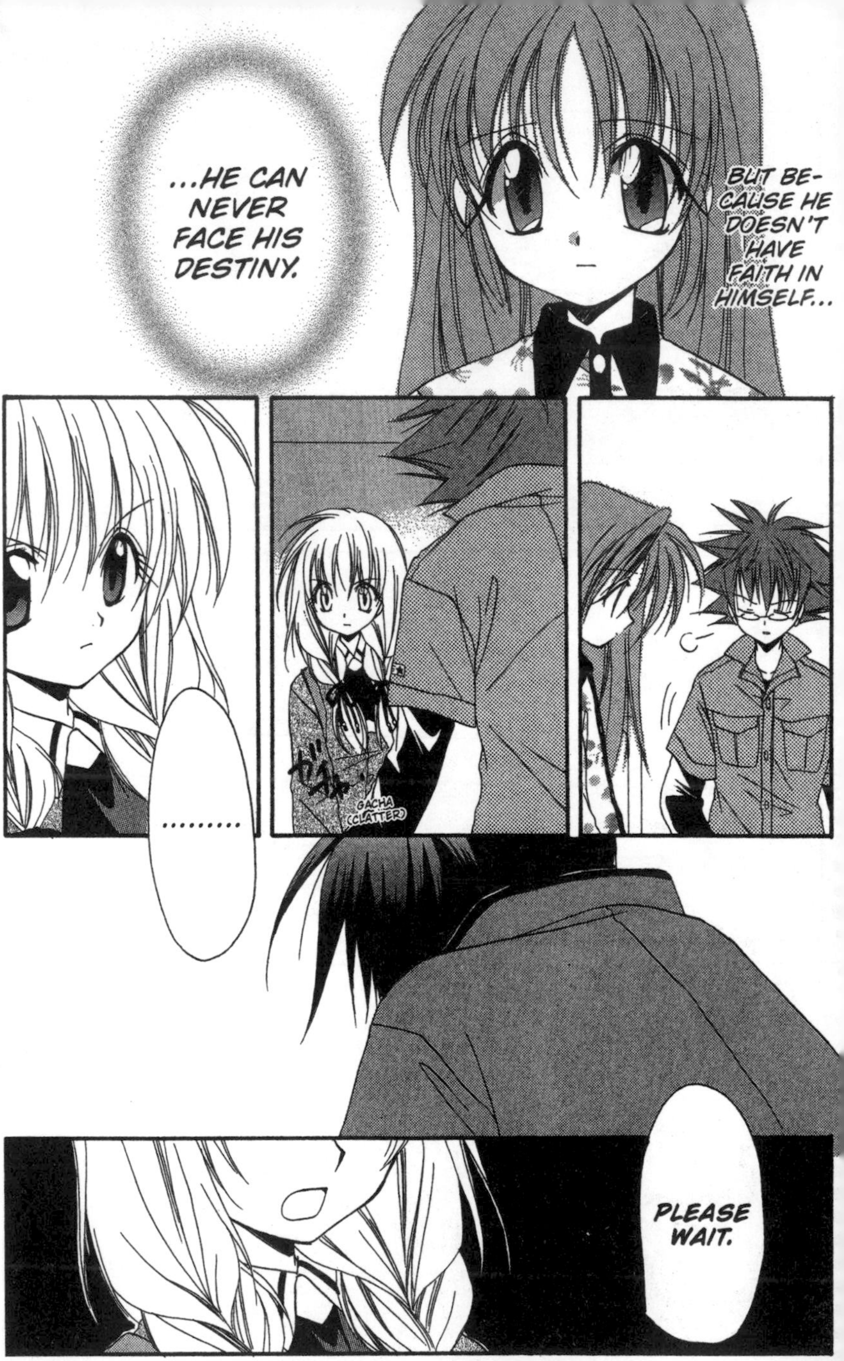
BUT BE-CAUSE HE DOESN'T HAVE FAITH IN HIMSELF...
...HE CAN NEVER FACE HIS DESTINY.
GACHA (CLATTER)
....
PLEASE WAIT.

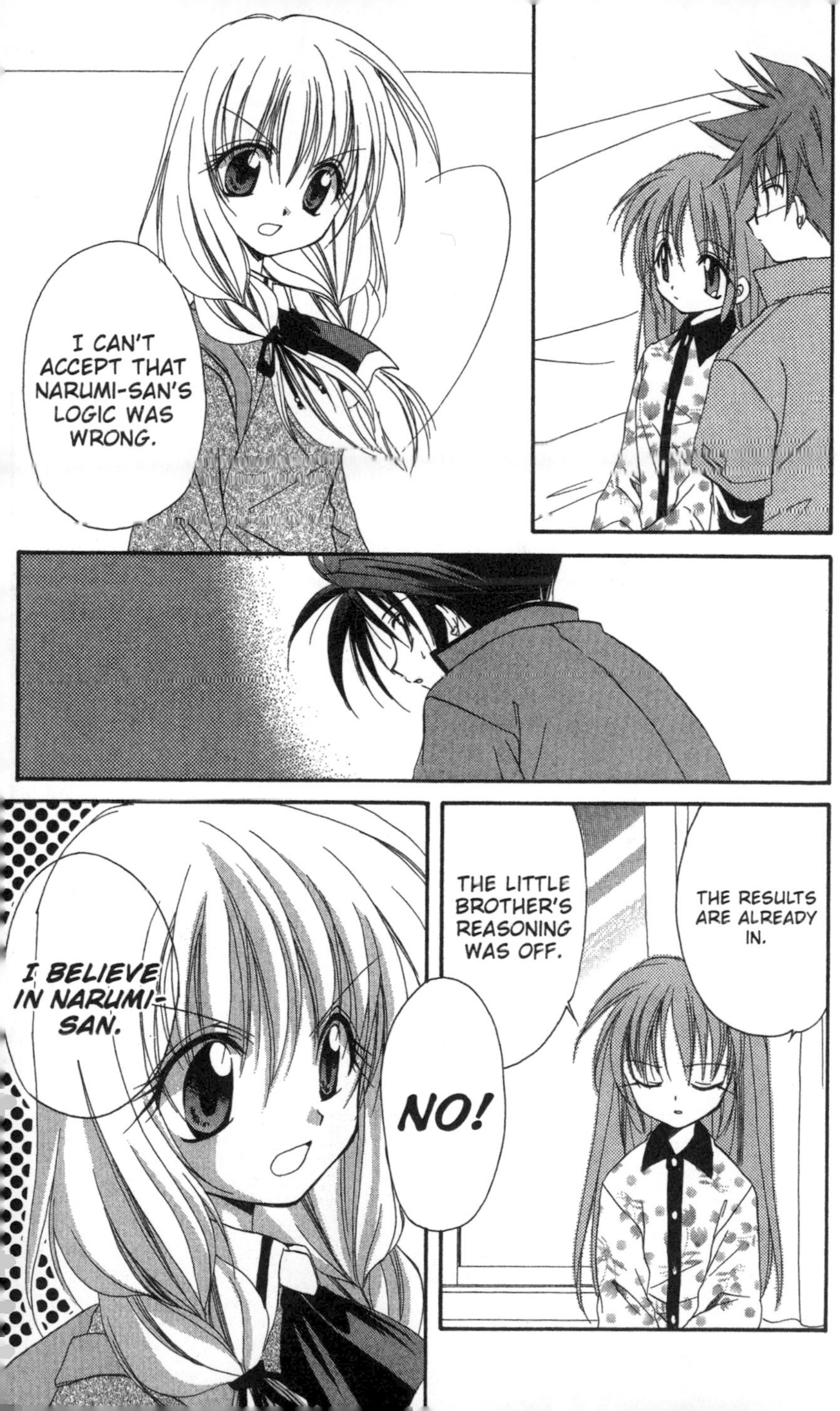
I CAN'T ACCEPT THAT NARUMI-SAN'S LOGIC WAS WRONG.
THE RESULTS ARE ALREADY IN.
THE LITTLE BROTHER'S REASONING WAS OFF.
NO!
I BELIEVE IN NARUMI-SAN.

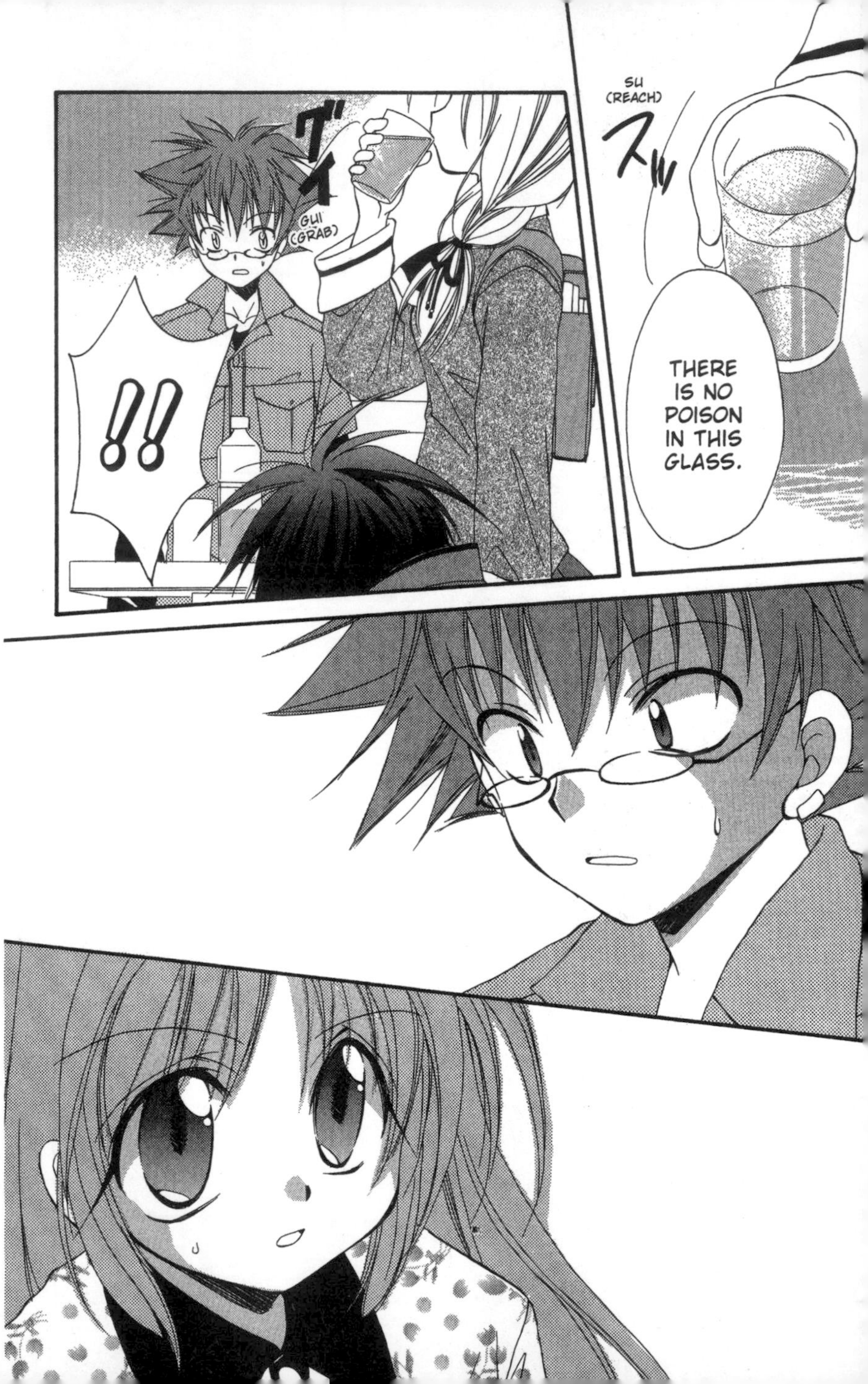
SU (REACH)
スッ
THERE IS NO POISON IN THIS GLASS.
グイ
GUI (GRAB)
!!

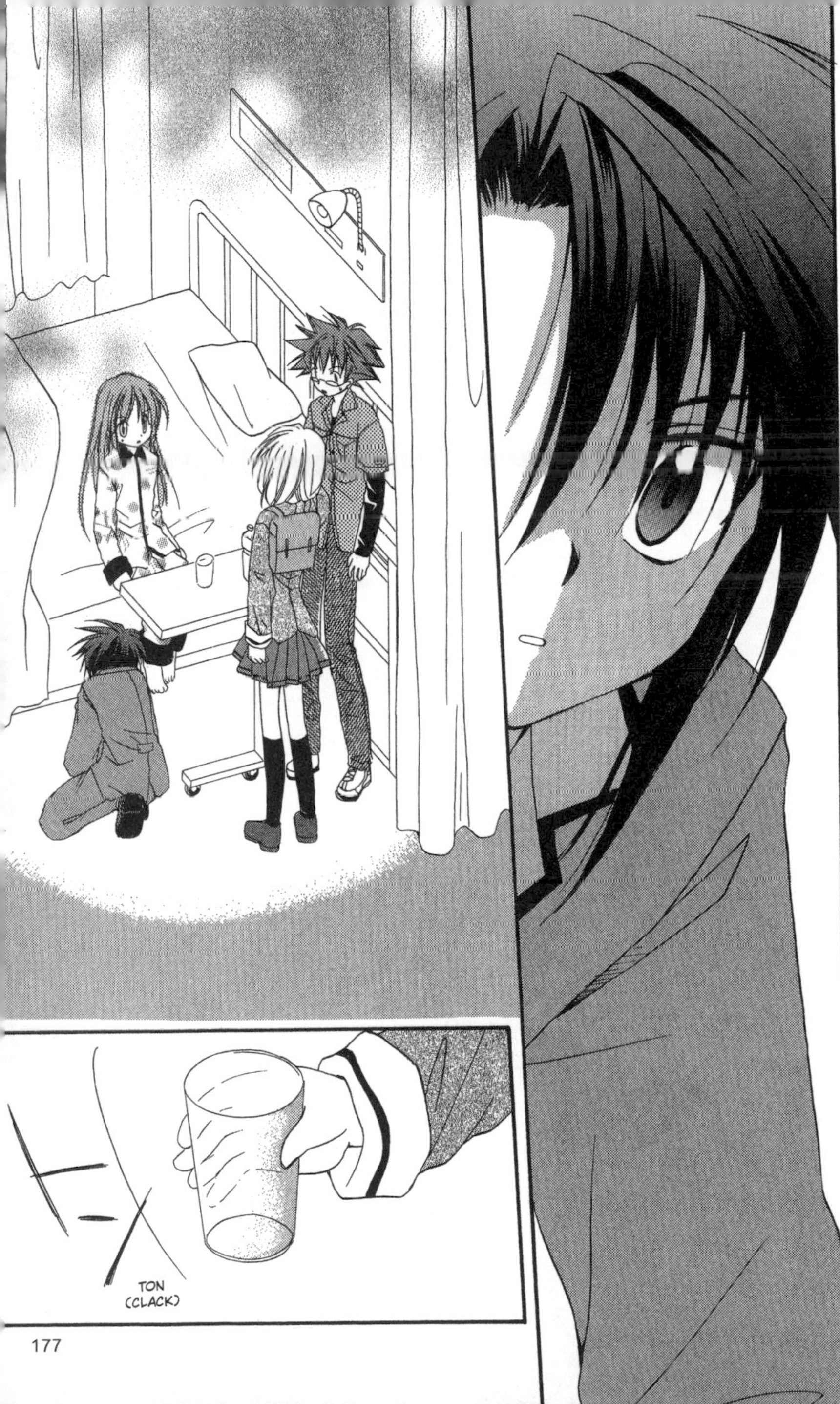
TON
(CLACK)

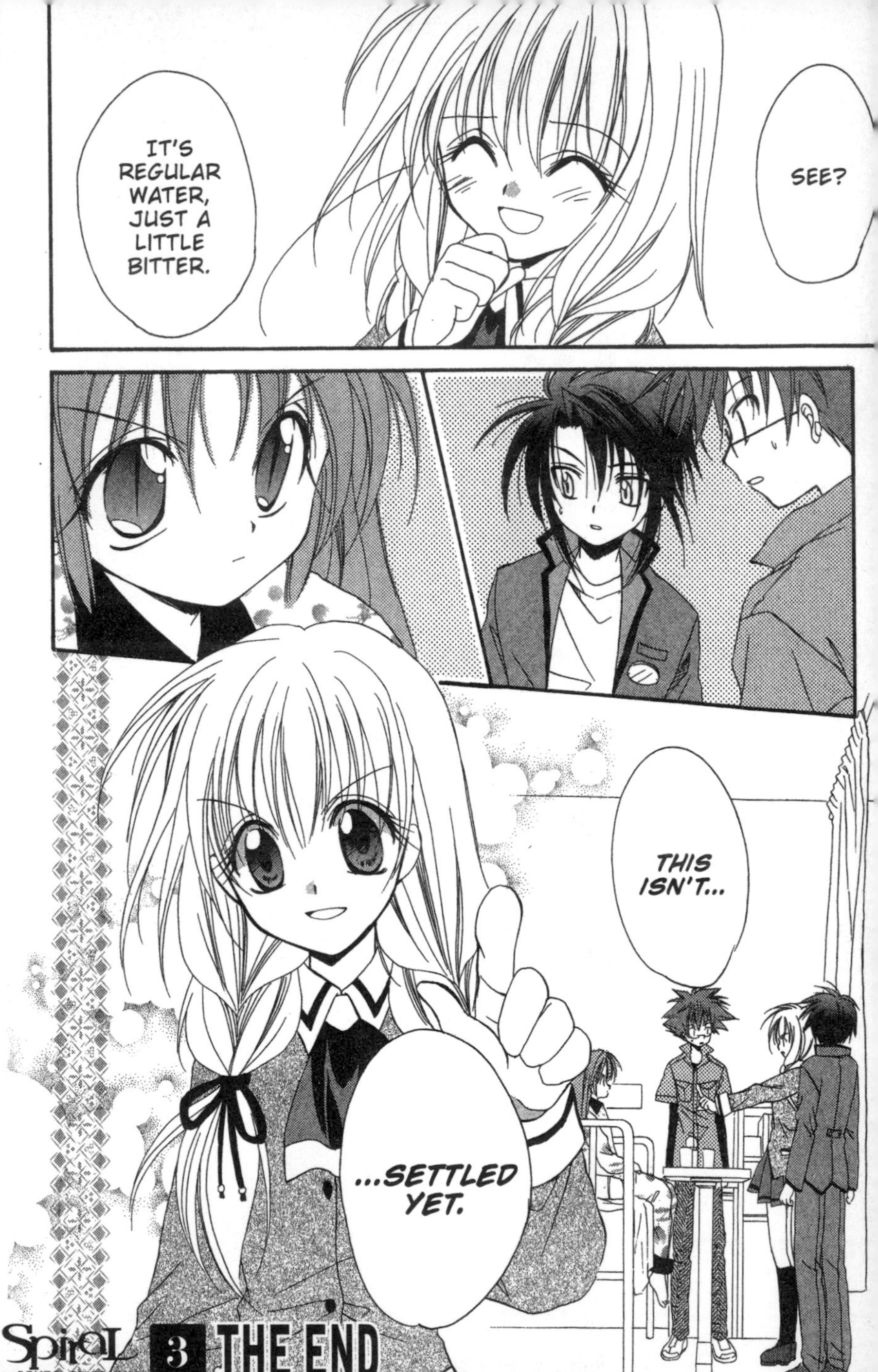
SEE?
IT'S REGULAR WATER, JUST A LITTLE BITTER.
THIS ISN'T...
...SETTLED YET.
Spiral
THE BONDS OF REASONING
3 THE END

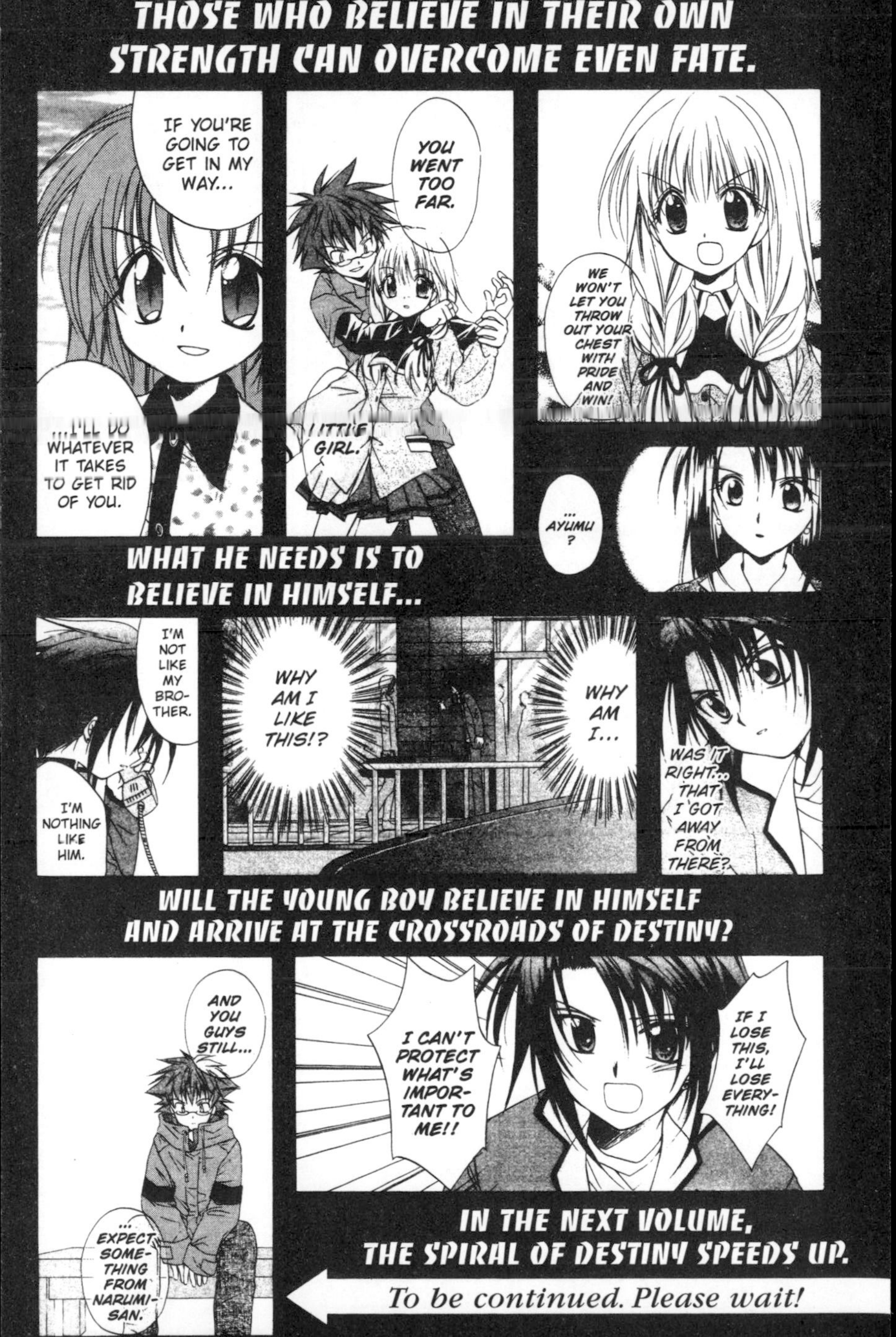
THOSE WHO BELIEVE IN THEIR OWN STRENGTH CAN OVERCOME EVEN FATE.
WE WON'T LET YOU THROW OUT YOUR CHEST WITH PRIDE AND WIN!
YOU WENT TOO FAR.
LITTLE GIRL.
IF YOU'RE GOING TO GET IN MY WAY...
...I'LL DO WHATEVER IT TAKES TO GET RID OF YOU.
...AYUMU?
WHAT HE NEEDS IS TO BELIEVE IN HIMSELF...
WAS IT RIGHT... THAT I GOT AWAY FROM THERE?
WHY AM I...
WHY AM I LIKE THIS!?
I'M NOT LIKE MY BRO-THER.
I'M NOTHING LIKE HIM.
WILL THE YOUNG BOY BELIEVE IN HIMSELF AND ARRIVE AT THE CROSSROADS OF DESTINY?
IF I LOSE THIS, I'LL LOSE EVERY-THING!
I CAN'T PROTECT WHAT'S IMPOR-TANT TO ME!!
AND YOU GUYS STILL...
...EXPECT SOME-THING FROM NARUMI-SAN.
IN THE NEXT VOLUME, THE SPIRAL OF DESTINY SPEEDS UP.
To be continued. Please wait!

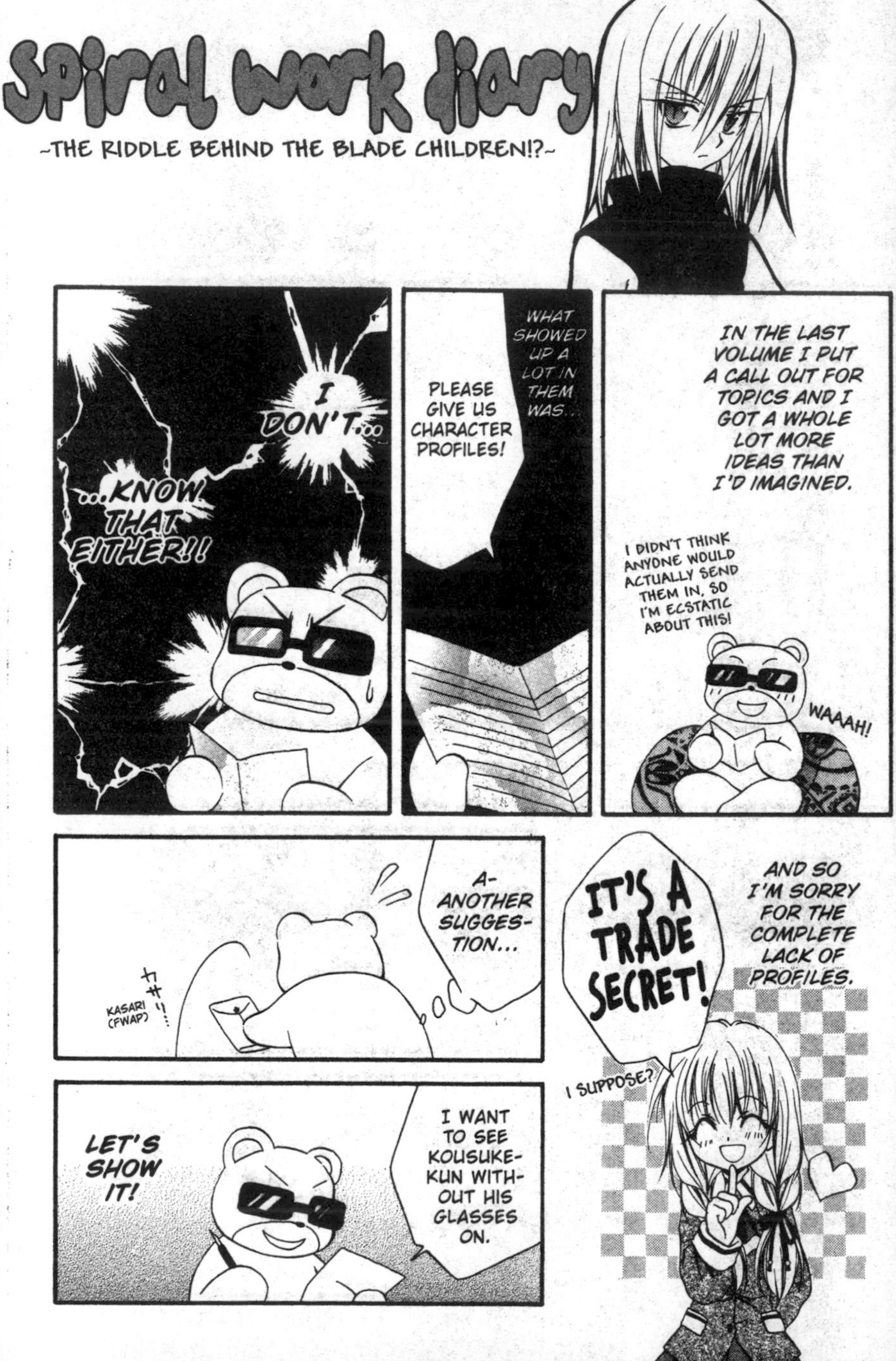
Spiral work diary
~THE RIDDLE BEHIND THE BLADE CHILDREN!?~
IN THE LAST VOLUME I PUT A CALL OUT FOR TOPICS AND I GOT A WHOLE LOT MORE IDEAS THAN I'D IMAGINED.
I DIDN'T THINK ANYONE WOULD ACTUALLY SEND THEM IN, SO I'M ECSTATIC ABOUT THIS!
WAAAH!
WHAT SHOWED UP A LOT IN THEM WAS...
PLEASE GIVE US CHARACTER PROFILES!
I DON'T...
...KNOW THAT EITHER!!
AND SO I'M SORRY FOR THE COMPLETE LACK OF PROFILES.
IT'S A TRADE SECRET!
I SUPPOSE?
A- ANOTHER SUGGESTION...
カサリ…
KASARI (FWAP)
I WANT TO SEE KOUSUKE-KUN WITHOUT HIS GLASSES ON.
LET'S SHOW IT!

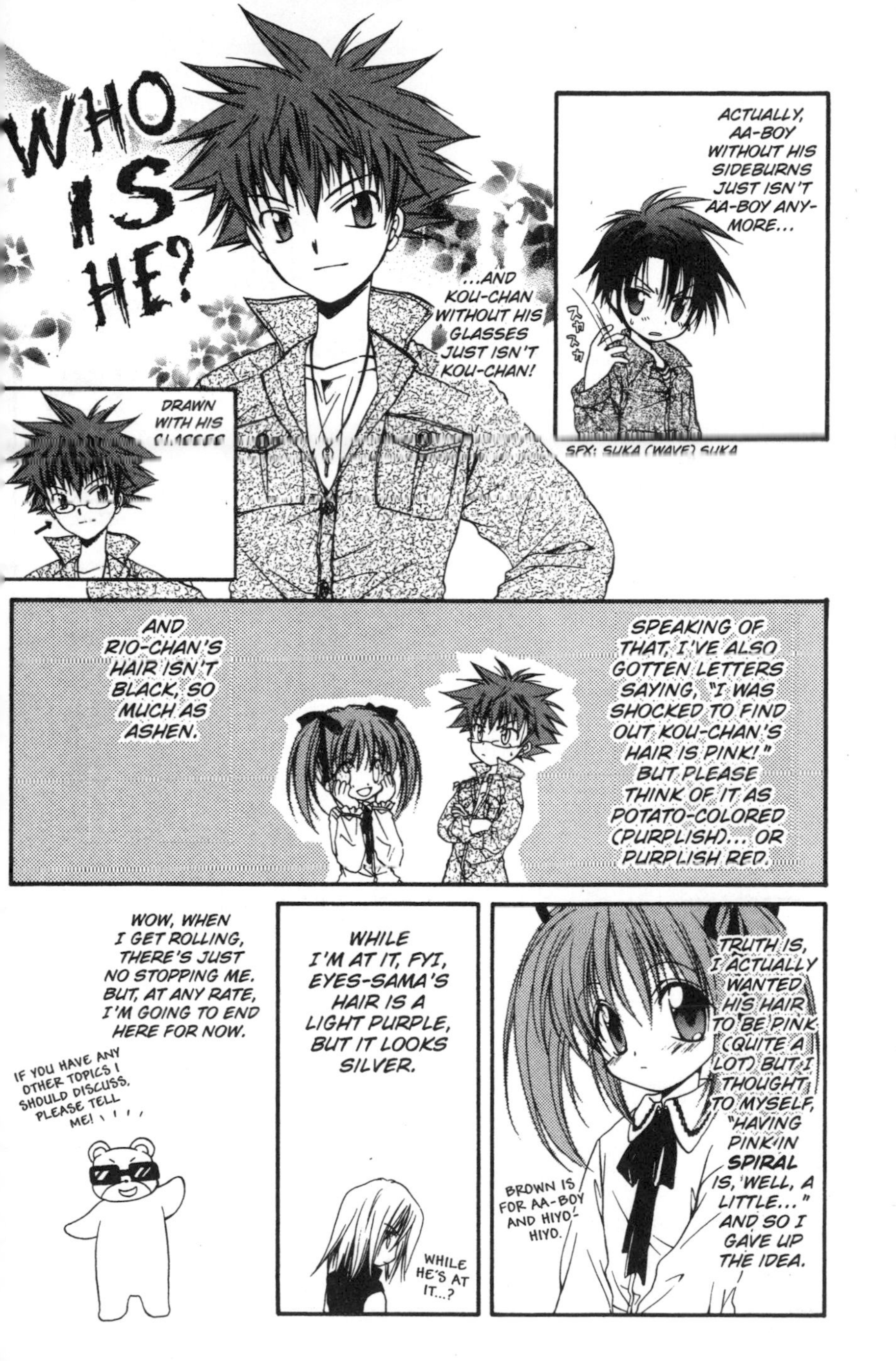
ACTUALLY, AA-BOY WITHOUT HIS SIDEBURNS JUST ISN'T AA-BOY ANYMORE...
スカスカ
SFX: SUKA (WAVE) SUKA
WHO IS HE?
...AND KOU-CHAN WITHOUT HIS GLASSES JUST ISN'T KOU-CHAN!
DRAWN WITH HIS GLASSES
SPEAKING OF THAT, I'VE ALSO GOTTEN LETTERS SAYING, "I WAS SHOCKED TO FIND OUT KOU-CHAN'S HAIR IS PINK!" BUT PLEASE THINK OF IT AS POTATO-COLORED (PURPLISH)... OR PURPLISH RED.
AND RIO-CHAN'S HAIR ISN'T BLACK, SO MUCH AS ASHEN.
TRUTH IS, I ACTUALLY WANTED HIS HAIR TO BE PINK (QUITE A LOT) BUT I THOUGHT TO MYSELF, "HAVING PINK IN SPIRAL IS, WELL, A LITTLE..." AND SO I GAVE UP THE IDEA.
BROWN IS FOR AA-BOY AND HIYO-HIYO.
WHILE I'M AT IT, FYI, EYES-SAMA'S HAIR IS A LIGHT PURPLE, BUT IT LOOKS SILVER.
WHILE HE'S AT IT...?
WOW, WHEN I GET ROLLING, THERE'S JUST NO STOPPING ME. BUT, AT ANY RATE, I'M GOING TO END HERE FOR NOW.
IF YOU HAVE ANY OTHER TOPICS I SHOULD DISCUSS, PLEASE TELL ME!

Thanks for every time, this is the writer, Kyo Shiro-daira. Thanks to everyone's support, the comic's made it to the third volume. It moves me some. I'm happy that it's increasing in volumes like this.

Now then, a new and powerful character showed up in this third volume, and the story's become something that just won't let up. When this happens, I find myself (as the writer) wanting to tell Ayumu and Hiyo, "L-Let's take this a little easier, shall we?"

Of course, they don't listen to a thing I say as they keep moving forward (and of course making their situation even more convoluted and tangled. Aah...). So it doesn't seem the hardships will be ceasing anytime soon.

That's why even I don't know what will happen next, and it really makes my heart beat faster. Are wit, bravery, and the strength to believe in yourself enough to overcome all hardships? Please keep your eyes peeled.

The story's changed so that *Spiral* has been labeled as a mystery manga, but it's turning out to be a mystery manga quite unlike the typical ones found on the shelves. I wonder if there are any readers who feel "this kind of mystery just doesn't exist."

When I'm told that, I say that indeed, you already know who committed the crime, there's no impossible crime that is miraculously solved, and murder doesn't always happen so it isn't your typical mystery at all. So maybe it'd be more fitting to say it's a "showdown manga." Only, through the showdowns, I'm trying to write the "reasoning" out to be the actions.

By obtaining certain information about your opponents you can infer their actions, set up traps, and get out of traps. Isn't following this chain of thoughts and actions one part of the fun behind mysteries?

To you readers out there, just what is the fun behind mystery in your opinion? I'd appreciate it if you could tell me for future reference.

Lastly, this is always advertised in the comic but GANGAN's website (http://www.enix.co.jp/gangan) is still serializing the *Spiral: The Bonds of Reasoning* side-story novel. The side-story novel is a short mystery series focusing on Kiyotaka Narumi working as a detective, and it's been constructed to stand independently from the main story.

Even if you don't read it, you can still understand the main story so there's no problem. But if you give it a go, you might make some unexpected discoveries! So to those who have access to it, please check it out.

Since the side-story novel is written in time with the sale of the comic for the most part, if you can access it while it's out, you could also do the bonus "whodunit" quiz. I'd also be happy if you took up the challenge.

Well, I'll be hoping to see you again in Volume Four.

KYO SHIRODAIRA

Spiral 3

THE BONDS OF REASONING Omake!

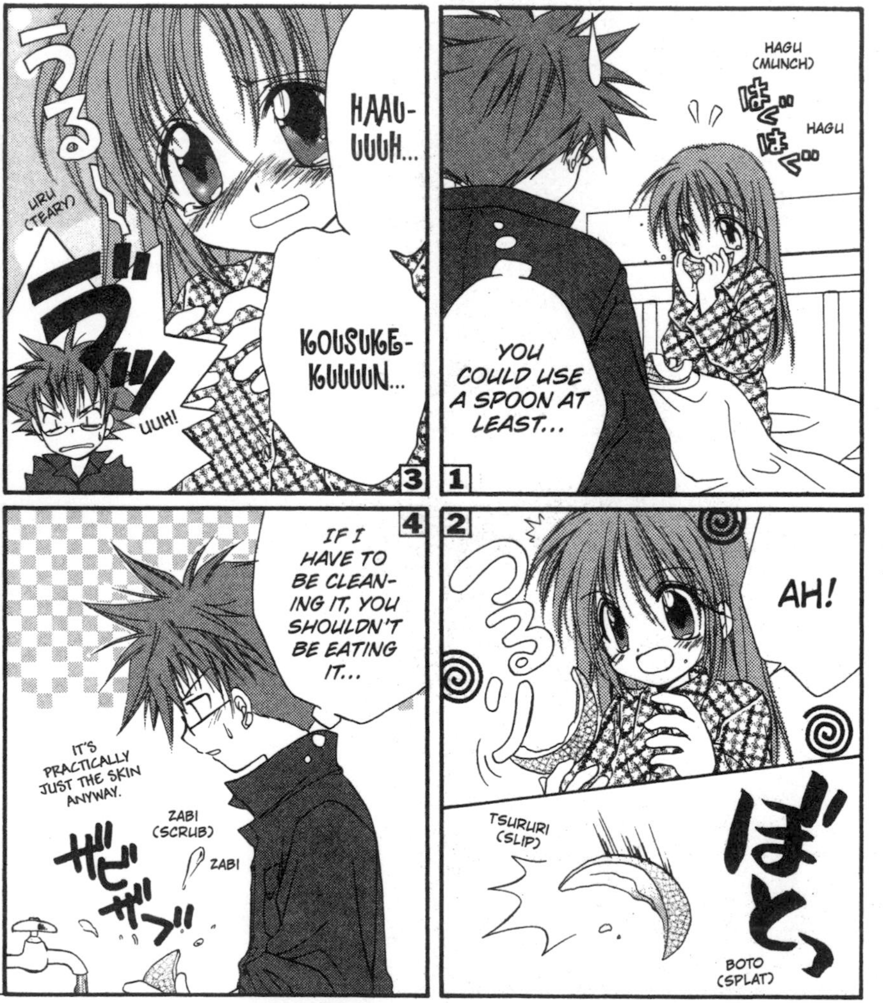
HAGU (MUNCH)
はぐはぐ
HAGU
YOU COULD USE A SPOON AT LEAST...
AH!
つるり
TSURURI (SLIP)
ぼとっ
BOTO (SPLAT)
HAAU-UUUH...
KOUSUKE-KUUUUN...
うる～
URU (TEARY)
UUH!
IF I HAVE TO BE CLEANING IT, YOU SHOULDN'T BE EATING IT...
IT'S PRACTICALLY JUST THE SKIN ANYWAY.
ZABI (SCRUB)
ZABI
ザビザブ

TRANSLATOR'S NOTES

p31
Mikans are seedless citrus fruits similar to mandarin oranges.

p77
"Check" is called out during a game of chess when one is making a direct attack on the opponent's king. It implies that victory is only one move away for the attacker.

p78
A girl's **three sizes** are her bust, waist, and hip measurements.

p84
The **law of inertia** states that the tendency of a body in motion is to stay in motion unless acted on by an outside force.

p140
The **net-patterned melon** Rutherford gives to Rio is probably one variety of muskmelon, which is cultivated by some Japanese farmers as a luxury fruit. One can cost hundreds of dollars, and is often regarded as a perfect gift.

p152
A **shinigami** is a Japanese god of death or grim reaper.

MOST JAPANESE EDITIONS OF MANGA ARE SOLD WITH DUST JACKETS. ON THE FLAPS OF THE JACKET, YOU CAN OFTEN FIND COMMENTARY BY THE CREATORS. SINCE THIS EDITION DOES NOT HAVE A JACKET, WE THOUGHT WE'D COMPILE EITA MIZUNO-SENSEI'S JACKET COMMENTS FOR VOLS. 1-3 OF **SPIRAL: THE BONDS OF REASONING** HERE FOR YOUR READING PLEASURE. ENJOY!

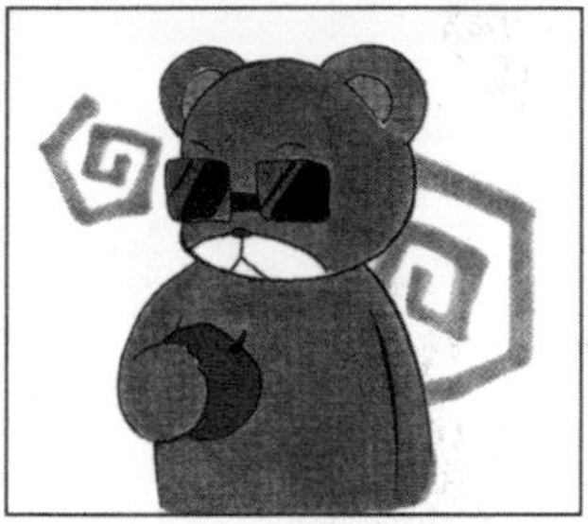

EITA MIZUNO

Somehow, even without any confidence in myself, I got a tankoubon out. I'm both happy and sad about that. I'm a newbie but I'll still do my best to draw stuff that everyone can enjoy, so I really appreciate your encouragement and support.

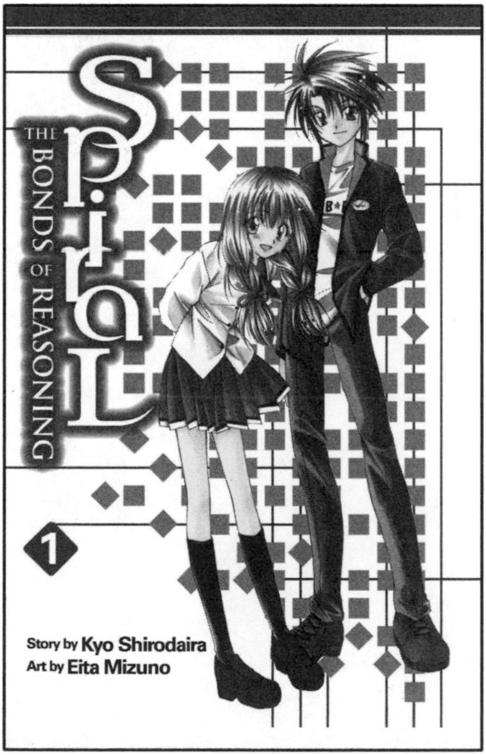
Spiral
THE BONDS OF REASONING
1
Story by Kyo Shirodaira
Art by Eita Mizuno

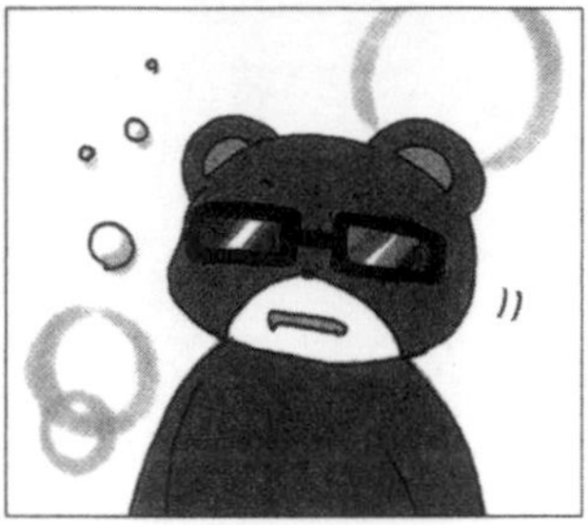

EITA MIZUNO

Even though decreasing my sleep time by one hour gives me more time to do things I like to do (like games and stuff), I can't deny that one of the things I like is sleeping.

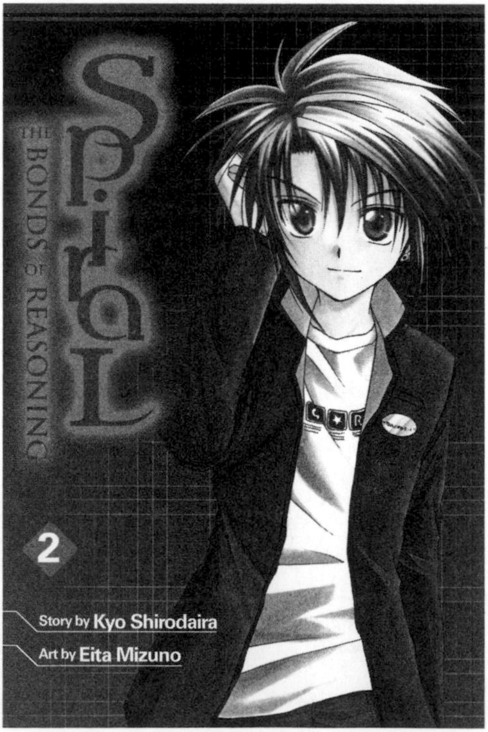

SpiraL
THE BONDS OF REASONING
2
Story by Kyo Shirodaira
Art by Eita Mizuno

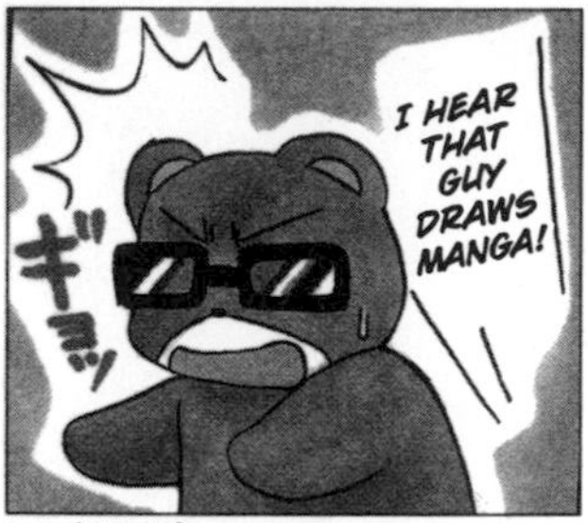
I HEAR THAT GUY DRAWS MANGA!
ギョッ
GYO (SHOCK)

EITA MIZUNO

Whenever somebody learns that I draw manga, the response is almost always "Oh, cool!" (Why?) But since I'm no good at being told that, I do my best to keep my profession under wraps. And that makes me a very mysterious person.

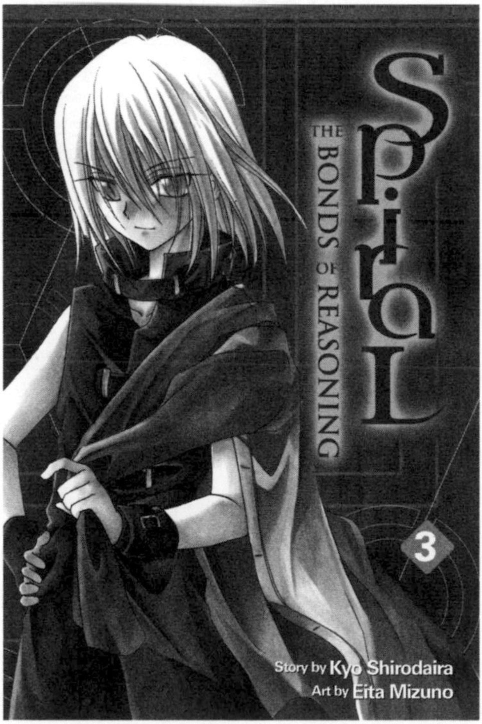
SPIRAL
THE BONDS OF REASONING
3
Story by Kyo Shirodaira
Art by Eita Mizuno

SPIRAL
The Bonds of Reasoning
3

by Kyo Shirodaira and Eita Mizuno

Translation: Christine Schilling
Lettering: Marshall Dillon and Terri Delgado
Logo: Kirk Benshoff

SPIRAL Vol. 3 © 2001 KYO SHIRODAIRA, EITA MIZUNO / SQUARE ENIX. All rights reserved. First published in Japan in 2001 by SQUARE ENIX, CO., LTD. English translation rights arranged with SQUARE ENIX CO., LTD., and Hachette Book Group USA through Tuttle-Mori Agency, Inc. Translation © 2008 by SQUARE ENIX CO., LTD.

Yen Press
Hachette Book Group USA
237 Park Avenue, New York, NY 10017

Visit our Web sites at www.HachetteBookGroupUSA.com and www.YenPress.com.

Yen Press is an imprint of Hachette Book Group USA, Inc. The Yen Press name and logo is a trademark of Hachette Book Group USA, Inc.

First Yen Press Edition: April 2008

ISBN-10: 0-7595-2637-0
ISBN-13: 978-0-7595-2637-2

10 9 8 7 6 5 4 3 2 1

BVG

Printed in the United States of America